2069.

**This book is to be returned on or before
the last date stamped below.**

To all those who have fought for the liberation of South Africa.

THE END OF A REGIME?

An Anthology
Scottish-South African Writing Against Apartheid

edited by
Brian Filling and *Susan Stuart*

Foreword by
Emeka Anyaoku
Commonwealth Secretary-General

ABERDEEN UNIVERSITY PRESS
Member of Maxwell Macmillan Pergamon Publishing Corporation

songwriter all over. Saw the end of empire in Uganda, Kenya and Aden - good riddance!

Govan Mbeki (named after William Govan,the first principal of the Lovedale Institution), a leading member of the South African Communist Party and the African National Congress, was born in the Transkei in 1910 and educated at Healdtown Secondary School and Fort Hare College. He was chief organiser of the Transkei Organised Bodies in the 1940s, took up a teaching post at Ladysmith in 1954 from which he was dismissed for his political activities, then becoming editor of *New Age*. In the early 1960s he was repeatedly arrested and detained. Much of his book, *The Peasants' Revolt*, was written while in solitary confinement. As it went to press in 1964 Mbeki sat in the dock and was sentenced to life imprisonment, together with Nelson Mandela , Walter Sisulu and other Rivonia trialists. He was released from prison in 1987.

Mzwakhe Mbuli is known as the 'Dub Poet of Soweto' and the 'Poet of the Struggle'. He has been detained several times and was held for six months in 1988 under Section 29 of the Internal Security Act and then released without charge. A recording of his poems 'Change is Pain' is banned in South Africa and he has repeatedly been refused a passport to allow him to perform at music festivals in Europe. He is a vice-president of the Congress of South African Writers.

James Leslie Mitchell (Lewis Grassic Gibbon) (1901-35) was born in rural Aberdeenshire. After working briefly as a journalist in Glasgow he joined the armed forces and spent some time in the Middle East. He is best known for the trilogy *A Scots Quair*, comprising the novels *Sunset Song, Cloud Howe* and *Grey Granite*.

Naomi Mitchison was born in Edinburgh in 1897. Throughout her long life she has combined radical and progressive politics with a prodigious literary output. She has had a long association with Southern Africa . Among her full-length novels are *The Corn King and the Spring Queen* (1930), *The Bull Calves* (1947) and *Solution Three* (1977). Some of her earlier short fiction is collected in *Beyond this Limit* (1986).

Benjamin Moloise, poet and political activist, was hanged in Pretoria by the apartheid régime in October 1985. He was 28 years old.

Edwin Morgan was born in Glasgow in 1920, and saw war service in the Middle East 1940-46. He retired as Titular Professor of English Literature at Glasgow University in 1980 and was Visiting Professor in English Studies at Strathclyde University 1987-90. He has worked as translator, editor, critic and writer of opera librettos. Most of his poetry is collected in *Poems of Thirty Years* (1982). *Graft/Takes* and *Master Peter Pathelin* (a version of the medieval French comedy) appeared in 1983 and *Sonnets from Scotland* in 1984. His most recent books are *Selected Poems* (1985), *From the Video Box* (1986) and *Themes on a Variation* (1988).

Sol T Plaatje (1876-1932) was born in the Orange Free State. A gifted linguist, he acted as interpreter to the Court of Summary Jurisdiction in his early days and translated Shakespeare into Setswana and Setswana folktales into English. His *Native Life in South Africa* was an attack on the Land Act of 1913; his novel *Mhudi* (1930) was the first novel in English by a black South African. The diary he kept during the Boer War was discovered some seventy years later and published in 1973. He made several extended trips to Britain (visiting Scotland on more than one occasion) and North America. Founder member of the South African Native National Congress (now the African National Congress).

Thomas Pringle (1789-1834), farmer and poet, was born in the Scottish borders and studied at Edinburgh University. He helped found the *Edinburgh Monthly Magazine* (1818), later *Blackwood's Review*. He emigrated to the Cape in 1820 with a view to resolving his family's financial problems. After establishing the settlement at Glen Lynden he returned to Cape Town but his liberal views were an obstacle to developing his journalistic and educational projects. He returned to England in 1826 where he became secretary to the Anti-Slavery Society. He published *Ephemerides* in 1828 and *South African Sketches* in 1834.

Alfred Temba Qabula, born at Flagstaff, Transkei, is known as a 'worker poet'. He works in the Dunlop factory in Durban, and was the initiator of a revival of traditional praise-poetry.

Dilys Rose was born in Glasgow in 1954. She has travelled widely and worked in a variety of jobs both at home and abroad. A collection of short stories, *Our Lady of the Pickpockets* (Secker & Warburg) and of poems, *Madame Doubtfire's Dilemma* (Chapman) were published in 1989. She lives in Edinburgh with her family.

Andrew C Ross has been Senior Lecturer in the History of Missions at the University of Edinburgh since 1966. Minister of the Church of Central Africa, Presbyterian, 1958-65. Founder member with Aleke Banda and Orton Chirwa of the Malawi Congress Party, like them later expelled. Taught at the Federal Technological Seminary, Mbali, Natal, 1976 and was Visiting Professor at the University of the

This volume, celebrating some two centuries of contact, tells as much about Scotland as South Africa and offers a glimpse of a long and complex relationship whose full story remains to be told.

We should like to thank the many people and organisations who helped in the preparation of this book: the writers themselves, Scottish and South African, who responded so generously to our invitation to contribute; Mongane Wally Serote, Junaid Ahmed and the Congress of South African Writers for advice and information; Bhekisani Mantoni for the front cover illustration; Marie Dillon, Gavin McGeoch and Isobel Tait who did most of the typing; Jim Dempster and John Nelson for technical assistance; Duncan MacLaren, Steve McGarry and other staff of the Scottish Catholic International Aid Fund, without whose immense practical and financial help this book would not have been possible; the staff at Glasgow's Mitchell library and Aberdeen City library; Strathclyde and Tayside Regional Councils for financial support; and Aberdeen University Press for their confidence that there would be a book.

Finally we are grateful for the forbearance and support of Mary Filling, John Filling, Paul Filling and Roddy Stuart who lived through this project with us.

Brian Filling, Susan Stuart
Glasgow, July 1990

PART I

Scotland, South Africa: History, Story, Poetry

until then a popular evangelical preacher in Aberdeen, was sent to the Colony of the Cape of Good Hope in 1819 along with another Scot, John Campbell, to examine and report on the state of the missions there for their fellow directors in London. Philip then stayed on as director in residence.

Philip took time to try to assess the situation, both within the colonial borders and among the peoples beyond the frontier where the Society had missionaries.

Meanwhile a major planned immigration of settlers from Great Britain was sent to the eastern boundaries of the colony where they were settled on land from which the Xhosa people had recently been driven by the British. This was the first major settlement of people of British stock in South Africa. Like many evangelicals of his day, Philip believed that the reform of society was an essential element in the work of the church as well as the conversion of individuals. Because of this conviction he became concerned about two things. The first was the social and political condition of 'the free people of colour'; the second was the crisis facing the new settlers whose crops failed in the first three successive years of their settlement. He was initially very popular with the latter in his attempts to get them government aid as well as charitable support to tide them over their bad times. However his concern for the 'Coloureds' soon brought him bitter condemnation from his erstwhile admirers among the British settlers. To them, so recently arrived, just as to the oldtimers, the frontier Boers, the so-called Coloured folk were simply a source of cheap labour. At this time in the Colony, there were slaves drawn from what are now Angola, Mozambique and Indonesia who worked in Cape Town and on the Afrikaner farms alongside the nominally free 'Coloured' labourers. Because Britain had already banned the slave-trade and was moving towards ending slavery itself, most British settlers did not employ slaves but they demanded all the more that the service of Coloured workers should be readily available and at a cheap rate. These people referred to by the name of Hottentot, were a mixture of people of pure Khoi descent with others who were of mixed Afrikaner/Khoi ancestry; all of them, by 1820, were speaking a language emerging from Dutch, which was to become Afrikaans later in the century. The Khoi were the small light-skinned people who were indigenous to the Cape Colony. When the slaves were freed by act of the British Parliament in 1834, the freed slaves joined with the 'Hottentots', to constitute the people usually called the 'Cape Coloureds', but who refer to themselves in their own language as *die Kaapse Volk*, the Cape People.

It was to these people that Philip dedicated much of his life's work. He encouraged the development of a series of mission stations upon which they were able to develop their technical, agricultural and commercial talents, he encouraged their setting up of autonomous Christian congregations, above all he committed himself to their gaining equal civil rights. He insisted that all His Majesty's subjects had to have the same legal rights, whether in the Cape Colony or in the United Kingdom. He insisted, unlike his predecessor van der Kemp, who had thought the problem was a matter of a number of unjust officials, that the very system with which Britain governed the Colony was at fault and had to be reformed. His appeals to the Anti-Slavery Society and other humanitarian pressure groups in the UK to try to influence the British government did bear fruit. He was able to get the Society on his side by pointing out that when they won their victory and slaves were freed (something they did in 1834) this would turn out to be a meaningless farce if the slaves were then treated as the supposedly 'free' Cape Folk were being treated.

The result of this pressure was Cape Ordinance 50 which, when built into a British Order-in-Council, meant in effect, that future Cape Legislation could not discriminate on the basis of colour. It was lobbying initiated by Philip and actively supported by the 'Coloured' congregations that, in 1834, made sure that the British Government did enforce this, overturning Cape Legislation that would have reversed the principle of equal civil rights. The decision in 1834 meant that the Cape Colony did become legally a non-racial society. The Kingdom of God had not come, and there were prejudiced social attitudes in plenty, but, the law was from then on until 1910, colour-blind!

Closely associated with Philip was his son-in-law James Fairbairn and his friend Thomas Pringle, both graduates of Edinburgh University and from the Borders. They can fairly be called the first white liberal politicians in South Africa. After a bitter fight with the British administration of the 1820s, they established the freedom of the press in the Cape Colony, a freedom which lasted reasonably well into the twentieth century. Pringle, an 1820 settler, was a minor poet, an acquaintance of Sir Walter Scott, who returned to Britain to become Secretary of the Anti-Slavery Society.

Fairbairn stayed on as editor of *The Cape Commercial Advertiser* a crusading progressive newspaper. He was unafraid to challenge the conventional views of the day. Indeed he went so far as to put the case for the rights of the Xhosa people even during colonial wars against them. Perhaps the greatest triumph of Fairbairn and his newspaper was the part they played in bringing about the low qualification, colour-blind franchise of 1853, when the Cape Colony received its first elected Assembly. This meant that from 1853 until 1910, 'Coloured' and Xhosa voters were on the same roll and in the same constituencies, qualifying by education or income exactly in the same way as whites.

Indeed it can be said that Philip and Fairbairn helped lay the foundations of the structure of the Cape Colony which was legally non-racial until, in 1910, it was forced by Britain into the new Union of South Africa. This achievement by a Liberal Government in Britain was a tragedy for South Africa. The Cape Colony, whose 'Coloured' and African citizens had equal rights before the law with whites, including the right to own freehold property in land anywhere within the Colony, was forced to unite with the three other territories whose legal, as well as social structures were thoroughly racist: Natal, the Orange Free State and the Transvaal. The new nation, not as formally racist as it was to become after the Afrikaner nationalist victory in 1948, was based on a fundamental presumption about white racial superiority in glaring contradistinction to the pre-1910 Cape Colony. The story of the old Cape Colony is something barely touched upon in too many history books, both South African and British.

Robert Moffat of Kuruman, in Scotland the most famous Scottish missionary, perhaps, after his son-in-law, David Livingstone, played a far less direct role in the history of South Africa. Indeed he constantly eschewed what he called 'politics'. However his linguistic work, his Bible translation and his extraordinary friendship with the great warrior king, Lobengula of the Matabele (amaNdebele) are not inconsiderable achievements. Almost more important, perhaps, is the sheer fact of his many many years of well-publicised service, which undoubtedly helped keep South Africa before the Scottish public, indeed the English and even American public to some extent.

His son-in-law, Livingstone gained his fame in the lands to the north of the Limpopo. What has been ignored by all his biographers was his radical attitude to the affairs of South Africa, where he worked for ten years. In so many ways, Livingstone's going north to find a dense population of Africans who were free from the pressures of land hungry Boer and British farmers and businessmen, was a deep loss to the cause of justice in South Africa. At the time of the bitter frontier war of 1851 with the Xhosa, Livingstone took up their cause and that of their leader Sandile. As the war was coming to an end, he wrote to a friend in September, 1852:

> By the same post I send a letter for my brother containing Sandillah's speech to Renton, to be printed in America. All we learn of the Caffre here is one-sided. We must hear both sides. It is well Sandillah speaks

out so nobly. Bringing out the converts to assist the English is infamous. We must either preach passive resistance or fighting for one's own countrymen.

Among his own Tswana people, Livingstone encouraged them to fight for their land against the encroachment of the Transvaalers. Indeed his stand was so notorious that a Commando burned his station, luckily for him, in his absence. Soon after this he wrote in September 1852:

> Everywhere there is a strong feeling of independence springing up...The destruction of my property is a fortunate thing for me. There is not a native in the country but knows now for certain whose side I am on.

Livingstone went north that year, never to return and his radicalism was lost to South Africa. What is interesting is the way his biographers have simply ignored this aspect of years in South Africa. This is understandable in the case of the late Victorian and Edwardian authors, but surprising in those who have written in the second half of the twentieth century. President Kenneth Kaunda knew better than they when he called him a freedom-fighter at the dedication of a new monument to Livingstone in Zambia in 1973! Livingstone, in his correspondence at that time, 1852, bitterly attacked another Scottish missionary Henry Calderwood for his pro-Government behaviour. Calderwood, along with his fellow Scot, John Brownlee, is seen, in South Africa, as an example of the true Scots missionary in contrast with John Philip. To be fair to them, they were willing to publicly take a stand against gross injustice meted out to Africans but, in any and every crisis where the interests of whites, particularly the British settlers, clashed with those of Africans, they always took the white side. Indeed they bitterly opposed Philip at every turn, and gained some support from Moffat in their criticism of what he saw as Philip's unnecessary antagonising of white South Africans. The straightforward assumption of human equality which van der Kemp, Philip, Fairbairn, Pringle and Livingstone shared was fundamentally alien to them.

Despite Calderwood, Brownlee and the others, Burns's marvellous poem with its climax insisting that one day 'man to man the whole world ower, shall brithers be for a' that' did represent an attitude among many Scots in the late eighteenth and early nineteenth centuries. However, Scots also played an important role in the development of scientific race theories which would come to completely dominate the British and American intellectual worlds by the seventies of the nineteenth century. This attitude, which posited a hierarchy of races with the blue-eyed, blond Nordic peoples held to be the final and perfect product of human evolution, lasted well into the twentieth century. It was powerful and insidious because it came to appear to be the truth 'proved' by science, something one had to live with even if one did not like it. A very clear example of the way it affected even decent human beings is the way that it shines through in the writings of John Buchan.

The first important scientist to insist that science 'proved' a permanent hierarchy of fundamentally genetically different races was Robert Knox, Professor of Anatomy at the University of Edinburgh, forever associated in most people's minds with Burke and Hare. Knox had served as a medical officer with the British army in the Cape Colony before he was appointed to Edinburgh. It was there that he wrote *The Races of Man*, which went through several editions in the 1840s and 1850s. What is interesting about his book and that of de Gobineau, the other writer who vies with him for the dubious honour of being the founder of modern scientific racism, is that they concentrate as much on proving the Celt an inferior species as they do Africans. Knox, like de Gobineau, portrays the Celtic peoples as a dangerously emotional and violent race, genetically different from and inferior to the Anglo-Saxon/Nordic race. Indeed Knox goes out of his way to show that neither religion nor education could do anything to alter this, pointing out that the Presbyterian and educated Celt was no less untrustworthy and dangerous than his Irish Catholic cousin! This was the beginning of an important movement in the British academic world that attempted to insist that the overwhelming majority of people on the main island of the British Isles were of Nordic/Germanic ancestry and that the indigenous Celts were a miniscule minority even in Scotland and Wales. The culmination of this movement can be seen in Scotland in the 1920s. It was then that a campaign against Irish Catholic immigration, led by very senior figures in the Church of Scotland, was defended from the accusation that it was anti-Catholic by the insistence that it opposed not Catholics but immigration by an 'alien race'! This is a reminder that the racial theories that have been used in South Africa are not simply a South African matter. Indeed the theories of scientific racism had to be imported into South Africa from Britain and the United States. These same theories had a profound effect on Britain and were taken up and revitalised by the Nazi theorists in the twentieth century.

Although it was the group of scientists, led by Professor T H Huxley who gave these theories their most sophisticated form as Social Darwinism, Robert Knox has to be seen as the most significant contributor to the foundations of this movement. From a Scottish perspective it is sad to have to add that he was ably assisted by that notable Scottish man of letters, Thomas Carlyle, whose 'On The Nigger Question' is one of the most bitter attacks on black people, missionaries and the anti-slavery movement penned during the nineteenth century in the United Kingdom.

Scots played a significant part in the creation of a non-racial tradition in South Africa, indeed they played a vital role in its being institutionalised in the constitution of the Cape Colony, which, tragically did not survive the creation of the Union of South Africa by a British Liberal administration. However Scots and the Scottish academic tradition also played a key role in the formulation of scientific racism with its appalling impact not only on South Africa but the world.

The combined Scottish missionary and academic tradition did however have one clear unambiguous success in its relations with South Africa. That success was in education. When, in 1841 William Govan of the Glasgow Missionary Society became the first Principal of the Lovedale Institution, it was the beginning of a tradition that the system of apartheid would attempt to suppress but which survives still. The educational tradition begun by Govan was that of absolute educational equality. If a subject was educationally worthwhile for whites then it must also be for blacks. It is interesting that when new progressive educationalists in the early twentieth century attacked this tradition of missionary education, they did so because they said that it did not suit African traditions or their way of life. These men and women were liberal sympathisers with Africans, but they were presuming that Africans had to stay in the 'African way of life' which meant that in a South Africa dominated by whites, economically and socially as well as politically, blacks had no place in the circles of power, only 'in their own culture'. It was no wonder that the apartheid theorists grabbed these 'liberal' ideas and on them based their hated 'Bantu Education'.

The Scots who founded and ran Lovedale were after something completely different. Govan and his immediate successor, James Stewart, created a vast educational institution in the Eastern Cape which, before it closed in the 1950s as a result of the Bantu Education Act, drew pupils from all over southern Africa. It had a primary school, a high school, a technical school, a teacher-training college, a theological school and finally, under Dr Neil MacVicar, the first hospital to train African women as nurses up to full SRN standard.

Lovedale was a non-racial institution as well as co-educational until the late 1890s when the certificate gained by whites at the teacher training college ceased to be recognised by the Cape Education authorities. The primary and high schools stayed non-racial, until after 1910 when the new Union of South Africa gradually made it impossible. Professor Monica Wilson, co-editor of *The Oxford History of South Africa*, was one of the last generation of white pupils of Lovedale.

However, the influence of Lovedale was such that nearly all the other missionary societies followed its ideals, not in having white pupils, but in creating a school system where the educational aims and requirements were the same as for whites. Education then came to presume, by its very curricular structure, equality even as South Africa, after 1910 went more and more the way of the racially stratified tradition of the Transvaal rather than the non-racial tradition of the Cape. When one also considers the use of English as medium of instruction in the whole mission system, which was the only channel of education for Africans, one can see a shaping influence on African society which held before it the image and ideal of equality and also created a common South Africanness. This was the case even when, in the thirties and forties of the twentieth century, some of the white teachers in the mission school system believed neither in racial equality nor in a common South African heritage. Their opinions had only marginal effect because the very structure of the educational system which they served conveyed these ideas. It was the influence of these ideas that built up a corps of black men and women who believed in racial equality and a common South African nationhood, the very core of the message of the African National Congress.

As early as 1928, J K Bokwe could ask in *The South African Outlook*, the national magazine of Christian opinion published by Lovedale, 'Why then educate me?' The point of his article was that the schools produced educated Africans in a Union of South Africa that reserved all jobs requiring education and technical skills to the whites. When Bantu Education was created by the South African Parliament, this was the very point seized on by the Nationalist government. It was the later Prime Minister, Hendrik Verwoerd, who was the minister responsible for getting the bill through Parliament. In his speech introducing the bill, he gave the tradition of missionary education its highest accolade. He said that mission and church education of Africans had to be taken over and reshaped, 'because it has raised the Bantu up to look over a wall into a meadow where he can never play'. William Govan and James Stewart devised a scheme of education which was based on the firm belief that the meadow was for all. Although the relationship of the Lovedale tradition to the African National Congress and the Freedom Charter is not a straightforward one, it is clearly there in 'One South Africa for all South Africans, Black, White and Brown'. So much so that in the minds of many

South Africans, Lovedale was Scotland's finest gift to South Africa.

The very technical skills that were taught at Lovedale are the focus of another Scottish-South African connection, not a happy one, however, but a bitter one.

From the creation of the Union in 1910, South Africa was an increasingly industrialised economy. Diamond, gold and coal mining were the backbone of this growing economy and Scottish miners and other craftsmen were a significant element in these industries. The white industrial workers who made up the skilled labour force at the beginning of the twentieth century had a high standard of living. The men were also well organised and their leadership was dominated by committed socialists associated with the Third International. On the eve of the First World War, the white gold miners on the Rand went on strike and despite the use of troops against them won a clear victory in 1913. There was to be no victimisation and their union was recognised and its position built into the laws controlling the industry. This was a union of the skilled white miners only. The movement spread to the white railwaymen who, in an era before effective motorised road transport, had a stranglehold on the economy. The white skilled workers in both industries came out in a general strike in January 1914.

Prime Minister General Smuts again used troops and the main leaders of the movement were deported. The strike petered out thereafter. However, the deportees were allowed back into the country and into the industry shortly after the outbreak of the war. The war meant that many whites in industrial jobs were called up into the army, as were many blacks, but there was still a need for skilled workers, and because of war conditions black workers were allowed to qualify for and to undertake skilled tasks in the mines and on the railways. At the end of the war the Miners' Union, still an entirely white organisation, wished to return to the pre-war status quo. This led to the massive strikes of 1922 when the white working-class suburbs of the Rand were shelled by the South African Defence Force in the violence that erupted. The movement for the privileges of white workers was bitterly anti-capitalist and among its leaders were Scots who had been members of the Independent Labour Party back in Scotland. However, the impact of Social Darwinism on the English-speaking world is nowhere more clearly shown than here. These dedicated socialists, men of genuine idealism and compassion, could not see their fellow black miners as fellow proletarians. The banners of the strikes of the Rand had slogans such as 'White Workers of the World Unite' and 'Workers of the World Unite for a White South Africa'. Although Smuts again broke the strike, the exclusivist Miners' Union won in the long run. In 1926 the Colour Bar Act was passed by Parliament which took it further than the mines and railways. The Colour Bar Act came to exclude Africans from a mass of skilled occupations in all industries throughout the Union. This legislation was brought in by the 'Pact' government of General Hertzog, the 'pact' being that between the Afrikaner Nationalist Party and the Labour Party. The Labour Party was the party of English-speaking skilled white workers. This alliance was to continue through many ups and downs till it helped bring about the Nationalist victory of 1948. Certainly this 'white' socialist movement cannot be blamed entirely on Scots, but Scottish radicals played a key role both in its organisation and its ideology.

Where Scots were the single most important influence in a major South African development was in the history of the Dutch Reformed Church. This church has been so much part of Afrikaner culture that in everyday speech it used to be referred to, in Afrikaans, as 'die Boere Kerk'. The British takeover of the Cape left it with very few ministers to cope with an enormous task. The solution was to recruit ministers for the Church in Scotland. This was done and for the rest of the century the Church, properly called *Die Nederduitse Gereformeerde Kerk van Suid Afrika*, was dominated by Scots ministers. Many of these ministers came from the new Free Kirk created at the Disruption of 1843 and from New College, Edinburgh, its seminary. The most prominent of them were Dr Andrew Murray and his two sons, Dr Andrew Murray junior and Professor John Murray. Indeed it was John Murray who was the key figure in the creation of the Divinity Faculty of the University of Stellenbosch, which, from the beginning of the twentieth century, has been the main source of the ministry of the DRC, and where the ideology of apartheid was created. The DRC, despite two secessions from it, obtained the devotion of the over-whelming majority of Afrikaners, and that was achieved in the middle decades of the nineteenth century under the inspired leader-ship of Andrew Murray senior. It was these Scots ministers, all of whom became loyal Afrikaners, who created what is now seen as traditional Afrikaner piety. For good and ill, and the reality is that some of it was good, the Afrikaner people are who they are, in part at least because of Scots. In ways that have not been explored by historians so far, the history of nineteenth century Scotland and of nineteenth century Afrikanerdom are deeply linked.

Looking over the Scottish-South African connection, 'Blessed be the tie that binds', really has to be a question and not a statement. Perhaps writing after the release of Nelson Mandela a mildly opti-mistic slant to the answer might be allowed.

In 1985, in the midst of the troubles that had broken out the year before, a new, young district surgeon was shocked by the wounds she saw on prisoners she visited, wounds that had clearly been inflicted AFTER arrest. Dr Wendy Orr, the daughter of a Scots minister of the Presbyterian Church of Southern Africa, obtained a legal injunction restraining the police in her area of the eastern Cape from beating prisoners in their custody. The story hit the headlines and as a friend has said elsewhere of the incident, 'all hell broke loose'. She lost her job and was decried as a communist sympathiser. At about the same time the great-granddaughter of John Philip went to jail with fellow leaders of student protest against the State of Emergency. Maybe their Scots heritage was not a part of what they did, but one hopes that it was.

THE BECHUANA TRIBES

SOL T PLAATJE

Two centuries ago the Bechuana tribes inhabited the extensive areas between Central Transvaal and the Kalahari Desert. Their entire world lay in the geography covered by the story in these pages.

In this domain they led their patriarchal life under their several Chiefs who owed no allegiance to any king or emperor. They raised their native corn which satisfied their simple wants, and, when not engaged in hunting or in pastoral duties, the peasants whiled away their days in tanning skins or sewing magnificent fur rugs. They also smelted iron and manufactured useful implements which today would be pronounced very crude by their semi-westernised descendants.

Cattle breeding was the rich man's calling, and hunting a national enterprise. Their cattle, which carried enormous horns, ran almost wild and multiplied as prolifically as the wild animals of the day. Work was of a perfunctory nature, for mother earth yielded her bounties and the maiden soil provided ample sustenance for man and beast.

But woman's work was never out of season. In the summer she cleared the cornfields of weeds and subsequently helped to winnow and garner the crops. In the winter she cut the grass and helped to renovate her dwelling. In addition to the inevitable cooking, basketmaking, and weaving, all the art-painting for mural decorations were done by women. Childless marriages were as rare as freaks, so, early and late in summer and winter, during years of drought and of plenty, every mother had to nourish her growing brood, besides fattening and beautifying her daughters for the competition of eligible swains.

Fulfilling these multifarious duties of the household was not regarded as a drudgery by any means, on the contrary, the women looked upon marriage as an art; the daughter of a well-to-do peasant, surrounded by all the luxuries of her mother's home, would be the object of commiseration if she were a long time finding a man. And the simple women of the tribes accepted wifehood and transacted their onerous duties with the same satisfaction and pride as an English artist would the job of conducting an orchestra.

Kunana, near the present boundary between Cape Colony and Western Transvaal was the capital city of the Barolong, the original stock of the several tribes, who also followed the humdrum yet interesting life of the other Bechuana Natives. They planted their stations in different directions over scores of miles; and it was often easier to kill wild animals nearer home than go to the cattle post for meat. Very often the big game ran *thalala-motse*** when there would be systematic slaughter of antelopes and orgies of wild-beef eating.

Barolong cattlemen at times attempted to create a new species of animal by cross-breeding between an eland and an ox. One cattle-owner, named Motonosi, not very far from Kunana, raised two dozen calves all sired by a buffalo. The result proved so disastrous that Barolong tradition stilll holds up his achievement as a master-piece of folly, and attempts at cross-breeding thereafter became taboo.

These peasants were content to live their monotonous lives, and thought nought of their overseas kinsmen who were making history on the plantations and harbours of Virginia and Mississippi at that time; nor did they know or care about the relations of the Hottentots and the Boers at Cape Town nearer home. The topography of the Cape Peninsula would have had no interest for them; and had anyone mentioned the beauty spots of the Cape and the glory of the silver trees on their own sub-continent they would have felt disappointed on hearing that they bore no edible fruit.

To them the limit of the world was Monomotapa* - a whiteman's country - which they had no ambition to see. Of monetary wealth they had none except their flocks and herds. A little bartering was done with neighbouring tribes in exchange for other commodities, and none could be so mean as to make a charge for supplying a fellow-tribesman with the necessaries of life. When the rainy season was good everyone had too much corn, and in years of drought the majority went short of porridge.

Strange to relate, these simple folk were perfectly happy without money and without silver watches. Abject poverty was practically unknown; they had no orphanages because there were no nameless babies. When a man had a couple of karosses to make he invited the neighbours to spend the day with him cutting, fitting in and sewing together the sixty grey jackal pelts into two rugs, and there would be intervals of feasting throughout the day. On such an occasion, someone would announce a field day at another place where there was a dwelling to thatch; here too the guests might receive an invitation from a peasant who had a stockade to erect at a third homestead on a subsequent day; and great would be the expectation of the fat bullock to be slaughtered by the goodman, to say nothing of the good things to be prepared by the kind hostess.Thus a month's job would be accomplished in a day.

But the anomaly of this community life was that, while the many seams in a rich man's kaross carried all kinds of knittings - good, bad and indifferent - the wife of a poor man, who could not afford such a feast, was often gowned in flawless furs. It being the skilled handiwork of her own husband, the nicety of its seams seldom failed to evoke the admiration of experts.

Upon these peaceful regions over one hundred years ago there descended one Mzilikazi, king of a ferocious tribe called the Matebele, a powerful usurper of determined character who by his sword proclaimed himself ruler over all the land.

Mzilikazi's tribe originally was a branch of the Zulu nation which Chaka once ruled with an iron rod. Irritated by the stern rule of that monarch, Mzilikazi led out his own people who thereupon broke away from Chaka's rule and turned their faces westward.

Sweeping through the northern areas of Port Natal, they advanced along both banks of the Vaal River, driving terror into man and beast with whom they came in contact. They continued their march very much like a swarm of locusts; scattering the Swazies, terrifying the Basuto and the Bapedi on their outposts, they drove them back to the mountains at the point of the assegai; and, trekking through the heart of the Transvaal, they eventually invaded Bechuanaland where they reduced the Natives to submission.

At length the Matebele established as their capital the city of Inzwinyani in Bahurutshe territory, the Bechuana inhabitants being permitted to remain on condition that their chiefs should pay tribute to Mzilikazi. Gradually enlarging their dominion, the Matebele enforced taxation first upon one and then another of the surrounding Bechuana clans, including the Barolong at Kunana, whose chief at the time was Tauana.

Perhaps the new administation might have worked well enough; but, unfortunately, the conquerers not only imported a fresh discipline but they also introduced manners that were extremely offensive even for these primitive people. For instance, the victorous soldiers were in the habit of walking about in their birthday garb thereby forcing the modest Bechuana women and children to retire on each appearance of Matebele men. This hide-and-seek life, which proved more inconvenient than accommodating, was ill calculated to inspire respect for the new authority. Needless to say, this outrage so shocking to local susceptibilities, was resented by the original population and became a perpetual source of discontent. Still, the new discipline was not stern; and as long as each chief paid taxes each spring time in acknowledgement of his fealty to Mzilikazi, the Bechuana were left in undisturbed possession of their old homes and haunts.

From the novel *Mhudi* (1930)

* *thalala-motse:* when wild animals continued their frolics straight through a native village
 * Monomotapa: Portuguese East Africa

PLACES OF STONE

Achmat Dangor

To Manuel this had always been a dark and sombre land. When he first arrived, many years ago, dark clouds spilled over the Mountain, and a storm was gathering in the bay. He was much younger then, a mere boy, and his body had felt numb to the touch of the chains which manacled his hands and feet.

Now he felt the chains more acutely. It was a dark day, full of gathering storms, even though they were on the other side of the Mountain, far away from the bay of storms. The clouds were a black and silent mass, unbroken by the Mountain which caused the clouds to cascade over its rim and into the bay and the city. It was the silent heaviness of the sky, here, that depressed him most of all.

Manuel's owner was being buried.

Lying bitch! How the dead can lie. How futile, impossible it is to try and bring them to account for their lies. You only frustrate yourself, drive yourself into a state of impotent fury. Better to control yourself, accept that she had no way of keeping her word now.

She had promised Manuel his freedom, upon her death. Now they were lowering her into the ground, and already his new master, the old woman's nephew, stood waiting to assume mastery over Manuel.

Johan Khul had inherited the old woman's property. He stood in a raincape, and wore the scuffed boots of a Freeburger, waiting to claim his property.

There was the house, with its gently sloping roof, built in the lee of the surrounding hills, so that the powerful wind passed harmlessly overhead. The farm 'Mijne Rust', which means 'my rest', the sheep, the two slow and unproductive cows; the young ewes and the ram recently bought because the old woman wanted, foolishly for this area, to keep goats as well. And, of course, the two slaves, Katie and Manuel.

Nowhere in her testament did it state that her two slaves were to be bequeathed their freedom upon her death. The old woman had not known much about such things, in any case she could not read nor write and a landdrost had written her last testament. What did he care about the rights of manumission that slaves had?

In order to shorten his journey, the dominee had read the document at Mijne Rust before the funeral proceeded to the hilltop where the sentimental old woman asked to be buried. Manuel of course, was not invited to attend the reading of his dead owner's last testament, but understood that he was not to be freed when Khul announced 'I am your new master'.

The dominee was saying the Lord's prayer in Dutch and it had started to rain softly. Manuel knew that it was the last, and late rain of the season and would not last for long.

But the other mourners were restless and anxious to get the ceremony done with. They helped Manuel to heap the earth back into the hole and close the grave. Then Manuel was chained and shackled again.

'He looks so sullen and angry,' Khul said in justification to the dominee and the family from the neighbouring farm.

But they did not bother themselves with such a trivial matter. The sky was dark, and they did not like the gloomy place between the hills where this strange old woman had established her home.

They greeted Khul and his family - 'ask if you need anything' and hastened on their way home.

Manuel struggled onto the back of the cart, hampered by his chains, while his new master waited patiently at the reins. Johan Khul's wife, a pale woman who narrowed her eyes shortsightedly whenever she looked closely at anything, sat beside Khul. And beside her, their two children who were about ten years of age and looked like twins.

The children had seen slaves before, disembarking from ships in the harbour, or at the Kompanje's garrison, but never this close. And this was the first time that they had owned a slave. The children stared at Manuel, and tried to touch him, as a child would fondle a new pet. But Manuel's cold, grave eyes preempted this, as did a curt click of their mother's tongue.

Khul flicked the reins inexpertly, causing the horses, and the cart, to jerk forward.

'Slowly now, Johan, you've never driven a thing like this before,' Khul's wife admonished him.

The horses settled down to a familiar rhythm of their own, leading Khul and his family to the house they now owned.

'Manuel. What a strange name for a Black man! Perhaps he's part Portuguese. Something *gebasterd* about him,' Manuel heard Khul's wife say to her husband.

Khul did not answer, concentrating instead on trying to direct the horses who led them, with jerks and jumps, along a worn, uneven path that the animals evidently knew well.

He would get Manuel to even out the path tomorrow.

Manuel knew that this was not his real name. He remembered vaguely that he came from a place less mountainous, a place with flat fields where rice grew and people waded knee-deep in water. There was a great river, slow and brown with mud, but heavy with water that poured with crashing grace into the sea. He had had another name then, but could not remember it now. He was registered in the Slave Register as 'Manuel of Bengal'.

Since the dim recollection of his arrival in the bay filled with storms and the darkness of clouds, Manuel's history had been anonymous. He was sold from master to master, until he was brought to Mijne Rust by the old woman who was already old then and who had lost her husband many years before.

Now there was this man with a carpenter's face who had never owned a slave and felt ill at ease with horses. May the son-of-a-bitch die as well!

Manuel was glad that the old woman had resisted the temptation to till the ground, which was uneven and stony. She was contented to farm with sheep, and to keep the two cows that moved slowly and flicked their tails as they grazed, as if aware that their mistress demanded no more than enough milk for her and her household.

She was happy to let Manuel roam about the farm and mend things and perform his chores without rigid patterns or plans. She took charge only when the time came to barter their wool or mutton in the city or with neighbouring farms for things that Mijne Rust did not produce. They rode in the cart, Manuel upfront, holding the reins, while she sat stiffly beside him, her wrinkled face shaded by the dignity of her broadbrimmed hat, so unlike the bonnets that most women wore.

Johan Khul preferred to manage things himself. His first act was to sell Katie. 'We do not need a house slave. There never was a need in the city, why should we need one now?' His wife accepted the burden her husband was imposing upon her with resignation.

'We mustn't allow this to soften us,' she reasoned silently.

Manuel was alone in the cowshed that he had shared with Katie. This did not bother him very much. They had long ago stopped sleeping with each other. Still, it had been pleasant at night to feel another presence beside the slow, imponderable cows that chewed endlessly. The place where Katie had kept her meagre belongings created a temporary void that Manuel had no time to ponder over, for Khul was changing things constantly.

Johan Khul wanted to grow things. 'What good is a farm where nothing is cultivated, where everything grows wild? A real boer creates an order around him, makes things grow, gives them a pattern.'

He made Manuel clear a patch of ground close to the house, in the same kind of lee that the house enjoyed.

'The first real rains will wash everything away. It comes off the hill fast, like a river,' Manuel said, making a gesture with his arms that indicated a flood.

Khul ignored him and turned away, leaving Manuel with the bitter task of doing something that he felt in his heart was going to be futile.

At first the small heads of cabbage, and other vegetables, gleamed in rows above the ground, nourished by the natural moisture in the earth. Khul was triumphant, but reserved. He would teach his slave not only how to farm, like a real boer, but some dignity as well. Working on farm for many years - as a slave - does not make you a farmer. There has to be some greater plan to it.

When the sheep crashed into the vegetable garden, and began to nibble the green, succulent heads of cabbage, Khul glared angrily at Manuel as if ready to strike him, but did not do so. Probably because he had never struck anyone, not even a slave, before. The cultivated area was fenced off, to keep the sheep and goats away. Khul also sold the two fat, languid cows, and combining the proceeds of their sale with profit he had made from selling Katie, purchased a real milk-cow from the market in the city.

Towards the end of summer, Mijne Rust had acquired an aura of well-being. The Khul family grew their own vegetables, produced their own milk and cheese. Manuel the slave was silent and obedient, having adjusted himself to the wilful ways of his new master. Khul felt the need to celebrate. Over Easter he invited his family from the city to visit.

They came, mostly the family of his wife, in a cart that shook and exhausted them, pulled along by a team of asses that had the curious habit of stopping when someone whistled. Manuel first heard them, the cries of one of the women echoing through the hills: 'Moenie fluit nie, moenie fluit nie. Don't whistle!'

The visiting party bathed and rested and, as it was Good Friday, held a service on the stoep of the house, all of them seated in rows upon the rough wooden chairs. Then the feast began. They roasted a whole sheep, one of Khul's elder relatives toiling before a huge fire that hissed from the drippings of fat. Manuel sat upon a rock and watched, joined by the dog which lay at his feet, his red tongue hanging from his mouth.

It was peaceful sitting in the shade of the huge old tree, observing people making merry according to their custom. Until Manuel was summoned to help in the kitchen. To wash things and clean after Khul's guests had eaten. His hands had grown used to working with rough things, with sheep and goats, and to using tools and moving rocks.

He broke things, not out of spite, but because of inexperience. He had never been a house-slave, and became sullen at the scoldings he received. The Khuls, and their guests, regarded the recalcitrant slave as 'part of the lot we have to bear'. Part of the need to bring Christianity and civilisation to this dark land. It became part of the prayers they said and the hymns they sang.

When at last, late into the darkness after Good Friday, the festivities ended, Manuel was able to go and sleep. In the cowshed Manuel found the elderly white man asleep upon the rough reed bed that Katie used to occupy, close to the nose of the new milk-cow, who regarded the intruder with large, indifferent eyes.

'Where's the *meid* that the old woman used to keep here?' he murmured to Manuel, then fell asleep again.

Manuel pretended to be asleep when the man, redfaced from the fire and the brandy that he had consumed, was fetched.

'*Oom, dis mos nie menslik om so hier te kom slaap nie. Tussen slawe en kooie!*, 'he heard Khul scold his uncle for sleeping amongst cows and slaves.

'*Ek't net n' stuk slaafbout kom soek. Jy't die vekeerde slaaf ve' koop,*' Khul's uncle replied in the bastard Dutch spoken by slaves and people of colour in the city. He had come to seek some 'slavecunt', the drunken old man admitted candidly.

'We do not tolerate such unchristian behaviour here,' Khul answered formally in Dutch.

Khul's voice was tired and irritable as he led his uncle back to the house.

A long while after the Easter period, with all his guests gone, Khul was still counting the costs in the number of sheep slaughtered and the depletion of the winter larder. Then it began to rain. Khul heard the sound of rain early in the morning, a soft, surging sound. The cleverly designed house did not take the full impact of the storm frontally.

This was the first significant rain that Khul had experienced since his arrival, it sounded soothing and rewarding as it washed off the roof. God had endowed them with something truly rich.

Khul dressed hastily, and was still fastening his raincape when he stepped out onto the fresh, wet earth. The hillside had been trans-formed into a torrent of muddy water poured into the fields around with such crushing grace that Khul stopped and stared in awe at its beauty.

The vegetable garden was washed away, as was the track that he had ordered Manuel to build up with sand and stone. Khul looked fearfully towards the kraals where the animals were kept, but they had been constructed on higher ground and were safe. Through the veil of rain he saw Manuel in the roofed kraal where the milk cow slept. The slave's face was calm and expressionless, but Khul saw in it a cold truimph.

Swine!

He felt a hatred for Manuel that would enable him to strike the slave mercilessly. But he went indoors, the cold rain too forbidding an obstacle for the moment, and sipped the coffee that his wife offered. It was too dark for her to see the tears streaming down her husband's face, mingling bitterly with the strong, unsweetened brew that he was drinking.

When the rain had stopped he found Manuel already at work, shoring up the areas around the kraals and the house with rocks and plaster made from cowdung and stone.

'What are you doing?'

'That storm was like the one we had so many years ago,' Manuel said, raising four fingers of his hand.

'So?'

'It rained a lot. The water rose and flooded the kraals. And the front stoep.'

Khul watched as Manuel resumed his work. It was the expression of sullen righteousness on the slave's face that bothered Khul, and the impertinence of his skill, and the authority it gave him over his master.

'You will do what I tell you.'

Manuel stopped working, and stood back from the half-built flood wall, his hands behind his back. Khul looked at the hillside, where the torrent had subsided into a steady stream, now clear and icily clean. Khul cursed the storm and the way it had betrayed him to this slave.

'Toe. Finish what you were doing,' Khul said curtly and walked back to the house.

It rained heavily that winter, so that at times even Manuel's floodwalls seemed threatened. Khul watched as Manuel sat in the kraal, seemingly indifferent to the danger, or was it that the slave's experience enabled him to calculate when the water would become a real threat?

Khul's anxiety grew when he discovered that they had been cut off from the city, and from the neighbouring farms. The ravines and paths that gave them access to the outside world, and escape from the fortress like valley where their house stood, had been flooded, transformed into strong, surging rivers.

Manuel continued to milk the cow and bring the pail of frothy white liquid to the house. Khul's wife baked milkbread in the stove, and they ate sparingly of the cured meat from the larder. But Khul knew that if the rain did not let up soon, they would soon not have enough to eat. Except the milk. And then they would have to begin slaughtering the sheep, or the goats, many of them just about ready to breed.

Khul cursed himself for the extravagant gesture he had made over Easter. As the rains continued, he reduced their rations even further. Manuel, and the dog, fared worst of all.

Khul saw the solemn anger in the slave's eyes as Khul's wife gave the slave his evening meal. He saw Manuel empty his plate, the food untouched, into the dog's bowl, and walk away into the rain. He heard the dog hungrily eat the food that Khul would gladly have given to his own family.

He became ashamed of the futility of his rage, at the way he snapped at his children, and because his wife recognised this futility. 'I will fix him in the morning!' Khul vowed.

In the morning Manuel brought no milk, nor was the box of wood fuel replenished with dry wood. Khul donned his boots and went out into the icy, driving rain, forgetting to put on his rain cape. His face was cold and pinched when he entered the dark and damp kraal, where he found Manuel seated by the cow, rubbing a sharp smelling substance onto the cow's teats.

'What the hell are you doing?'

'She has inflammation?'

'What from?'

'I don't know. Maybe all the damp hay she had to eat. Or we've been milking her too much.'

'How do I know you are not doing this deliberately? Poisoning her or something?'

Manuel looked up at Khul without answering. His dark eyes were saying that Khul did not know, one way or the other.

For the first time in his life, Khul raised his arm and struck the slave across the face.

'Get up. Let me see.'

Manuel rose and allowed Khul to seat himself. The effect of the blow, which caused Khul's hand to sting, did not show upon the slave's face. It was as if he had absorbed the pain into a hidden, inscrutable area of his being.

The cow's teats were red and swollen. Perhaps that is how a cow's teats are supposed to look.

'How long will she be this way?'

Manuel shrugged.

'A day, maybe two. Maybe a week.'

'What will we use for bread? It is all that is sustaining the children.'

'Take the milk from the goat.'

'The goat has milk? Why did you not tell me?'

'She feeds the kid.'

'If we take the milk?'

'The kid will die. Too young to eat anything else.'

Khul saw the tiny glint in Manuel's eye. He is making me choose between feeding the kid which we need to start the goat herd and feeding my children. The bastard is taunting me.

'Bring the goat's milk for the children. If the kid gets too weak we'll slaughter it for food.'

'Your choice.'

'Why did you not bring dry wood for the fire?'

'There is no dry wood. It has been raining for days on end.'

'You should have thought of that before the rainy season started.'

Again Manuel was silent, and Khul read in the man's eyes the question the man may have asked:

'You are the master, why didn't you think about it?'

The rain stopped and the cow got well, but it was too late to save the goat's kid which Khul slaughtered and offered the skin to his wife. She touched the moist inside, as if the kid still snuggled there, then said quietly:

'You'd better dry and cure the skin. It will smell before long.' He was about to tell her to instruct Manuel to do it, he knew how, then took the skin out of her limp hands. He would tell Manuel himself. Khul watched as Manuel went about his work, an unhurried, placid pace. The slave was nearing sixty, but his weariness was not physical. It was the solemn patience of the slave, the indifferent manner in which he obeyed the instructions given to him that bothered Khul.

And now Manuel waited for Khul to instruct him in all that he did. He no longer worked on his own, and would wait for Khul to direct him rather than take the initiative in things that he had taught Khul about. Johan Khul was no longer free to walk quietly amidst the green vegetation and observe the rows of plants, the simple pattern they formed, but that nevertheless demonstrated the presence of human will.

He had to pay attention to all the minute details on the farm that he had normally left to Manuel; ensure that the cow was led out to pasture, and returned at night to the kraal. Although Manuel did the work physically, Khul found it exhausting and exasperating, constantly to walk about the farm and ensure that all the chores were done.

What good was a slave if he did not free the master from the daily, mundane tasks that needed to be done? Khul had ambitious plans for Mijne Rust, but he needed time to think and develop his vision. Manuel was not helping him at all, and he resolved to rid himself of his slave.

Despite his wife's opposition, Khul sold Manuel, described in the market place as an 'experienced, well trained slave. Very adept at animal husbandry,' for fifty rix dollars. The purchaser was Jool Baartman, the owner of a farm neighbouring Mijne Rust. Baartman struck a hard bargain, refusing to pay more than one third of the market value of such a slave. No one sells a slave if he is all that useful, Baartman reasoned. The slave was probably a troublesome bastard.

Now Khul had to do all the chores himself. He rose early to milk the cow, feeling a strange peace within the cool darkness of the kraal. He paused in his work to watch the place slowly being lit up by the morning sun. Next, he drove the sheep out to pasture, using a cattle whip that cracked in the air, instead of the stick that Manuel had used. Khul also did not make the strange, ridiculous noises with his tongue like Manuel, he merely shouted at strays 'hier! hier! back! back!' to drive strays back on course.

The dog was useless at herding sheep, and merely followed Khul around, stooping to sniff around in the deeper grass, searching for little animals that took refuge in the foliage. It infuriated Khul that the dog, upon discovering a rabbit or squirrel, would yelp playfully at the animals, totally without any earnestness. The dog never gave chase to the 'quarry;' it was a dog without any of the natural instincts of its kind, and Khul detested it.

He chased the dog away, lunging at it with his boot, before entering the vegetable garden, to weed, and water the young heads of cabbage. He looked sorrowfully at the tender, dried up flesh of the tomatoes where the birds had pecked, and resolved to construct a scarecrow. The curious scepticism of his city mind told him that birds were not fooled by such still, inanimate imitations of humans, but he would build one anyway. What else was there that he could do?

Khul established a routine that was demanding, and that took its toll on his unpractised body, for although the garden had been moved to higher ground, and was now safe from flooding, weeds and wild grass sprouted more easily, and needed constant attention. His arms were strong, but his back ached from the constant bending and scraping he had to do.

By midday Khul felt hot and thirsty and drank water from the well, using only his cupped hands. The water tasted sweet and brackish, and was more refreshing than any water he had drunk. He sat down on the edge of the stoep and dusted his boots, surprised at how worn they were.

But Khul was happy, almost content.

He spoke Dutch to his wife, now that Manuel was no longer around. He had a great distaste, in any case, for this pidgin mixture of a language that people were beginning to use, especially here, in places far away from the city. We have to learn to preserve our culture, our language, he often preached in his young, strident way.

'I suppose that these boots were not made for farming.'

His wife's skin had turned a deep red, and was beginning to darken from the sun, so that her blonde hair hung in limp, glistening wisps on her forehead. She too had to share the burden of running the farm, caring for the chickens, cleaning their run.

'Johan, sometimes I think we two were not made for farming.'

'*Ag* nonsense. We'll manage. There's nothing a slave can do that we can't.'

'Fifty rix dollars was very little for a male slave. Especially like Manuel, he was well trained.'

'He was old, almost sixty.'

'We could have obtained more if we were not so hasty. Enough to buy a younger slave. Help around the house.'

Khul was silent. The tiredness in his body was like a void that had swallowed all the pressures he had felt before. The need to control Manuel, to give orders and make decisions, it was a terrible, unrelenting responsibility. He was happy inside of himself, and determined not to let his wife's uncertainty infect him.

He rose and said quietly:

'I have work to do.'

Khul began to learn about the hidden corners of the farm. The ravines stray sheep fell into and died. He learned how to salvage the flesh, if the carcass was discovered before it began to rot. In the beginning he had to throw half of the flesh away because it had not been properly cleaned before being salted.

It was a hard struggle, but gradually he began to accept the drudgery. At the end of the day there was a peacefulness in the dusk that enabled him to forget the things he had left undone. He sat on the stoep and sipped the dark brandy his visitors from the city had left behind. Small compensation for all that they had consumed. Soon he forgot about them as well, and thought less and less about the city.

There was silence all around him, apart from the gentle surge of the wind above the slope of the roof. The light from the lamps in the house lit up the surounding darkness, providing a man-made refuge from the wilderness that surrounded them. It was as if Khul was at the centre of the world, and the source of its light and life. He was filled with deep, and quiet pride.

Only his wife, tired from the many chores she had to perform, both in the house and on the farm, brought a weariness to the serene atmosphere. She did not complain, but her exhaustion and her resentment showed in her eyes. At night when he went to bed, she responded to his touch with a listless dutifulness.

The summer was coming to an end and Khul worked until late now, repairing the roof of the woodshed, where the dry wood was now stored. He would not make the same mistake again. It was dark and he could only see the shadows created by the shape of the kraal and the shed and the dark hulk of the hills.

There was a rider at the edge of the rims of hills. Both man and horse stood in absolute stillness. Not even the mane of the horse, which Khul imagined would have flowed in the air because of the wind, was seen stirring. Khul hurried home, but both rider and horse had disappeared before he had reached the refuge of his lamp-lit house.

From the elevation of the stoep Khul looked out into the darkness of the hills, shielding his eyes with his hands, as if from an extremely bright light.

'Did you see him too?' he asked his wife. 'Manuel. The slave, he was there, on horseback.'

His wife busied herself with the dinner, without answering. 'Johan, you have shut the door. Can you open it for a while? It is extremely hot in here.'

Khul went about the farm, filled with apprehension. His wife had told him that his obsession with this slave - that useless old man - was ungodly.

'Everything you do is on account of the slave. You work on the farm alone, killing yourself, and perhaps us, because you want to prove something to that slave. God, Johan, he is just another pathetic black that they caught in the jungle somewhere and brought here in chains!'

But Khul was certain the rider he had seen was Manuel. The patient stoop of his shoulders, and his head gravely bowed, like some wise elder. Yes, it was Manuel. The insolence of the slave was beyond belief. Khul searched the hills at dusk, slowly walking into the darkness, the old elephant gun loaded and cocked.

He saw the figure twice, and was on the second occasion able to get off a shot in the direction of the rider. The gun went off with a booming recoil, sending birds in frantic flight from the thickets. The echo of the explosion echoed for some moments in the hills, and Johan could see his family in the distance, watching anxiously from the stoep.

There was nothing in the spot where Khul thought he had seen the rider. The ball from the gun had shattered a tree, stripping the bark from the wood like skin ripped from human bone.

The next day Khul rode his horse, saddled and without the cart, to the neighbouring farm. Because of his inexperience with horses, he sat hunched in the saddle, his knees uncomfortably high. He allowed the horse to trudge along the landmarks that he had learned during previous journeys in the company of Manuel. He reached his neighbour's farm after a journey that took most of the day.

Khul stretched his cramped limbs and greeted his neighbour with the excessive gruffness caused by the nervousness he felt. He was uncertain of himself, and how his neighbour would react to his complaints about the slave that Khul himself had only recently sold to the man. Also, addressing another white man in this bastard language made him feel ill at ease, but he knew it was the language that Jool Baartman, strangely enough, preferred. He was in fact almost passionate about it.

The house was no different from Khul's house at Mijne Rust. Dark and angular, and cool in the stone-floored kitchen while the heat near the well of the grass roof was filled with the murmur of insects.

Baartman was much older than Khul, and had lived in this plateau beyond the Mountain for many years. He spoke in a sonorous tone, his language so inflected with words used mostly by slaves and Hottentots that he sounded to Khul astonishingly like one of them. But Baartman's voice had a cold authority that even Khul lacked and that allowed him to get to the heart of matters very quickly and brutally. Manuel had that ability.

A dog, half-blinded with age, his skin no longer able to glisten, lay on the cool floor of the kitchen where Baartman received his visitor. 'Out!' Baartman said curtly to the dog that raised itself stiffly and limped outdoors. 'He's old now. Was once a real good watchdog. Could smell them in the darkness, the Hotnots and slavethings.'

Baartman progressed without interruption from one topic to the next, about the locust plague the year before, and how it could happen again. 'The first sign of the pests up there in the hills and you warn us, hear?' He cautioned Khul about the inadvisability of keeping sheep in this area.

'They destroy the veld. Fuckall grows after they've been through the grass.' He had told Khul's aunt the same thing.

'Strange old crow that. You couldn't give her any advice!'

And without waiting for Khul to respond, he broached the reason for Khul's visit.

'But you didn't ride your arse off to come and speak to me about your aunt's madness - and befok she was, believe me - it's about this blerry slave Manuelthing, no?'

And so the subject of the slave Manuel was discussed. In the veld where he worked herding Baartman's cattle - on horseback - Manuel was unaware of the visit of his former owner. Manuel had had no experience with herding cattle, but had grown accustomed very quickly to their slow and tedious but deceptive habits.

Baartman had warned him not to be taken in by their docility. 'There's a madness in them like there is slaves. When that madness comes up and makes them run, then nothing will stop them. Especially not a slave that's asleep. So don't let me fukken catch you asleep here!'

The herd raised gentle clouds of dust as it grazed. The dust hung in the air, hot and still, so that Manuel had to concentrate and strain his eyes in his looking out for strays. He knew that it would soon be time for the herd to be driven into the kraal, before the sun was too low. It was hard to see straying cattle in the darkness, which came with bewildering suddenness here.

But Manuel would wait until Baartman came riding out from the house to give him instructions. Manuel had not changed his habit of refusing to do on his own the things that his master should instruct him to, and although he had not once since his arrival here disobeyed an instruction, his passivity was recognised by Baartman as a form of rebellion.

Baartman, unlike Khul, had many years of experience with slaves, and was ready to punish them at the slightest hint of rebelliousness. He had struck the slave Manuel with his whip many times since the slave's arrival, but although Manuel had winced, he seemed immune from the pain, absorbing the blows, and his master's heightened anger, behind the mask of his smooth, placid expression.

Baartman's wife in particular disliked this slave whose greying hair and silent eyes gave him an aura of solemn dignity. When he first arrived he stood back from the other slaves, many of whom gratuitously scrambled for the food Baartman's wife gave them. It was a cur-like fawning, intended to please and flatter the 'Missus,' in the hope that she would leave behind an extra ration.

She noticed that the slave preferred to go hungry. It was an apt punishment for his insolence. He would soon learn. However, it was the other slaves who changed their habits. They stood aside until Manuel had taken his share, scrupulously in accordance with what was available, and then quietly dished their own, their heads bowed in sheepish dignity when they passed her.

'He looks like he could have a lot of trouble in him,' she told her husband

Now out of the rapidly descending dusk, Manuel saw Baartman riding towards, a furious cloud of dust in his wake. Baartman was screaming at him even before the farmer had brought his horse to a halt, snorting and sweating from the hard ride.

'Get the blerry beasts back to the kraal, look how dark it is already. God! You dumb bastard. Do I have to tell you the same thing everyday?'

Manuel gathered the herd and began to guide them home. Despite the bad light, the slave had an astonishing expertise. He was clever and capable, but so damned stubborn. Baartman knew that if the slave stayed here, Baartman would have to crush that rebelliousness; very often such passive stubbornness would have to be killed along with the slave.

The district Landdrost set up a temporary court on Baartman's stoep, where in the languid coolness of an oleandar tree, he and his scribe listened to the evidence that Khul and Baartman gave. The slave, Manuel, manacled hand and foot, was made to squat in a corner of the stoep.

In accordance with Kompanje's rules and regulations, Baartman, legal owner of the slave, Manuel of Bengal, testified that the slave was not ill treated and had not been physically punished beyond the stipulated regulations. Manuel was asked if he concurred with this statement, but did not answer. He was silent, his face dull and blank.

Khul described in a petition how he had inherited the slave Manuel, who had become, without reason, sullen and insolent. Khul had been forced to sell him, at great loss, because of the disharmony that the slave had created on the farm Mijne Rust. He had also caused great losses, including the temporary barrenness of a valuable milk cow.

He described how he had seen Manuel observing the Khul household 'with great menace', even forcing Khul to shoot at the intruder on one occasion. The slave had illegally, without permission, used his new owner's horse to journey to Mijne Rust. It was a full day's journey there and back, it could only have been with the intention of intimidating and harassing his former owner and his family.

Khul was prepared to repay Jool Baartman one half of the amount that Baartmam had paid for the troublesome slave, and petitioned the Landdrost to have Manuel imprisoned 'in a secure place', so that the safety and well-being of the Khul family could be ensured.

Baartman was asked for his opinion.

'Lock the damn stubborn devil away!' Baarman answered curtly. Manuel listened to the exchange of words, to the scribe saying that he could not record such language. It would not be recognised and could jeopardise the whole case against the slave; there was the cry of birds in the thickets, and in the fields beyond the row of trees the cattle heaved in slow, bovine unison, dulled by the heat.

It would soon be time to take them to the water, which they tread into with ungracious haste, muddying the clear pools. It was always surprising to Manuel how quickly the river seemed to recover its flow, how quickly the pools regained their clarity. This place had an ability, beyond him - to restore itself.

The sea before the sun rose was calm, with the wind raising only small swells of water, with crests of silver, as far as his eyes could see. Manuel had never been this close to the sea before, and he found it beautiful, at first, to watch the sun rise as if out of the seabed.

Manuel's term of banishment to Robben Island - for 'being a threat to the lives of the Burghers, the property and peace of the colony' - still had three years to run. How bright the island had seemed, as the boat, manned by six oarsmen, sped through the water. Seated in the prow, Manuel had raised himself to peer over the edge of the boat, watching the sea calmly race towards them.

He found it difficult to manoeuvre his body because of the chains which bound his hands and feet. The rattling chains aroused the two guards from their early morning stupor, but neither paid much attention to what the slave was doing.

'It looks like that one wants to jump.'

'Let him. We'll see how he drowns.'

Their conversation was nonchalant, indifferent. They soon turned their attention to other matters.

'Look alive there!' they shouted to the oarsmen.

A storm was gathering in the Bay and the Mountain was hidden behind a cauldron of black surging clouds. Manuel did not jump. The dark, stormy mainland from which he was departing stirred uneasy memories within him, and he sat down within the deep recess of the boat, to contemplate the vague, dim memories that took him back to the point where this life had begun.

On Robben Island Manuel was put to work on the stone quarry

where prisoners cut and shaped stone to build the fortress, and to expand the prison. He learned to cut stone and raise it into walls of dull forbidding grey with remarkable ease. So quickly did he perfect his skill, in fact, that he was given more and more intricate work to do. He carved the innumerable crests and coats of arms that adorned each section of completed wall until the walls were decorated with chains of talismen.

He cut the grooves into which the windows and doors would be mounted, deep, straight and sinuous grooves that reminded him of the gorged out muscle sinew of gigantic men. He learned even how to fix manacles of chain into the walls of the punishment cells, where difficult and rebellious prisoners were held.

After one year - Manuel found it difficult to keep track of time since he disliked cutting meaningless notches into the stone of his cell - his hands had hardened, and his eyes seemed to grow dull from constantly staring at the rough and grey granite.

Time forgotten, no longer held any forlorn hope nor was its slow meaningless passing a source of anguish. He, like the stone with which he worked, had reconciled himself to the slow ravage that time wreaks. He would die one day or his term of banishment would be over and he would be returned to the mainland. The walls were invisible but no less hard and tangible.

He slept with the great ease of physical exhaustion and awoke in the slate blue hour before the sun was up, his thoughts ingrained like rough rock. He had succeeded in crushing the agony of his imprisonment into a stone prison of its own.

Manuel did not mix much with his fellow prisoners and did not even hunger after the news from the mainland, brought mostly by new prisoners and the rough sailors who manned the monthly supply ship. Even those who were doomed to life imprisonment on Robben Island, and those who would have no reason to be influenced by the slow unravelling of history on the mainland went to extraordinary lengths to obtain news from the city.

There was a small group, isolated from the others, who saved some of their rations to bribe guards for old copies of the *Koerant* that the prison governor received. What does it help them to know? Manuel thought. It did not even occur strange to him that this small group of slaves could actually read. Just an additional unnecessary burden.

To occupy himself, Manuel used the skill he had acquired to sculpt little objects from stone and discarded granite bricks. Figurines of soldiers that the Kommandant found attractive enough to display in his office. Manuel also had an eye for detail. He made mental note of the contours of the supply ship that called at the island each month and began to sculpt a replica.

Guards and prisoners alike were fascinated by the model that Manuel began to fashion. He sculptured one half of the boat, complete in minute detail before proceeding to the other half so that the sculpture resembled a strange animal that seemed to emerge from a womb within itself. When the sculpture was complete it had a mast and cannons that protruded from the side of the ship.

The ship gleamed with the white rawness of marble, the figure of a woman carved onto its bow. There flew a flag of rigid grey.

'A pity it will never sail,' the Kommandant remarked idly.

Indeed, all that the ship lacked was the inner dimension of air and buoyancy that would have allowed it to float. When Manuel had completed the carving of the ship of stone he abandoned it heavy and immobile, outside his cell. Soon the rain, and then the hot burning sun began to dull the raw marble until it was no different from the other stone edifices on the island; grey and sombre and lifeless.

For a long while Manuel did not carve anything. In his leisure hours he sat staring at the sea or lay on his mat in the darkness of his cell when the weather became hostile. He seemed to recede into the stone of his cell, indifferent even to the Kommandant who came to see 'what the slave was carving'.

He stood up obediently when the Kommandant entered his cell, but did not reply when asked '*Ag*! Why have you given up the work? You were quite good at it.'

The man before Manuel had long grey hair that fell to his shoulders leaving a powdery residue from his bad scalp upon the collar of the black uniform. And eyes like Khul's that do not look you straight in the face. What does he think of me as a man? The Kommandant's manner became cold and authoritative and Manuel dropped his eyes.

The polished boots are the symbol of the man's power. He could crush Manuel beneath them as if Manuel was 'some kind of vermin'. He remembered the old woman on Mijne Rust who used to pounce upon the lice that crawled upon her skin occasionally and the way she crushed frantic writhing shells beneath the soles of her boots. There was always a look of satisfaction upon her face.

Now the Kommandant was gone and Manuel was upon his knees searching for vermin he imagined infested the reed mat upon which he slept. He had heard the Kommandant say 'with regret that we have to place another prisoner with you. The cells are full. Anyway, he is a bad sort, perhaps your influence can change him'.

A man named Paulus was brought to Manuel's cell. He carried

his chains in his hands because they were too long and hampered him when he walked. His ear had recently been cut off to identify him as a dangerous slave for he had participated in a slave revolt. Manuel could see the conch of flesh where the surgeon had stemmed the bleeding and sealed the wound.

Paulus sat down with difficulty, dropping his burden of chains in a coiled and gleaming heap. He was asleep almost immediately but groaned with pain throughout the night. He slept bunched up, his knees drawn up to his chest like one used to sleeping in confined spaces. As a result he did not occupy much room within the cell but Manuel still felt uneasy at being so close to another human being.

In the plateau beyond the Mountain Manuel could choose where he wanted to sleep, in the warm hay, close to the warm smell of the animals. Of course there was a time he and Katie had slept together, soon after Katie first arrived. She was a house slave and slept in the kitchen so that she could easily respond to her mistress's needs. But their sleeping together was out of the mutual hunger of their bodies which ended with Manuel freeing himself from the warmth of her body, inevitably, long before dawn.

It was a solitary act of freedom to walk out into the darkness, aware of the sun slowly beginning to rise, with a raw incandescence, behind the hills. The taste of sleep in his mouth, and the first drink of sweet water from the well. Manuel remembered the dog muzzling his wet nose coolly against his leg as he washed.

During the lifetime of the Old Woman, Manuel had acquired a habit of solitariness that most slaves are incapable of and which prepared him badly for imprisonment.

Paulus stirred amidst his rattle of chains, and Manuel wrapped himself tightly in his blanket, determined to fall asleep.

He woke, unaccustomedly late, to the sounds of the guards unlocking the doors. Paulus was already awake, sitting with his knees drawn up under his chin. Manuel noticed that Paulus had a very dark complexion, a blackness caused by the sun and the elements. He was also very thin, and Manuel imagined that the man must once have been stocky and powerful.

Manuel left with the other prisoners, to wash and eat and perform his work for the day. He returned that night to find Paulus, his chains removed, kneeling in prayer in the Muslim manner.

When Paulus had finished his prayer he said to Manuel, 'My name is Ali not Paulus. That is my slave name, the one they gave me.' He indicated towards the guards who could still be heard outside their cell.

Manuel nodded and unrolled his mat. He was soon fast asleep;

not even Ali's presence in the cell could disrupt for very long the rhythm of life he had established in over two years on the island.

Ali had no particular skills, and was assigned to hard labour, splitting rocks and assisting artisans such as Manuel. From the beginning he refused to respond to the name Paulus, even at the risk of severe punishment, and soon compelled everyone to call him Ali. The guards called him 'Swart-Ali' or 'Black-Ali' because of his dark scorched skin.

He was also called 'Maargat-Ali' which meant thin-arsed Ali. Although the Kommandant had forbidden the guards from using the gruff, mixed language that the slaves used, the guards found it difficult to communicate with their wards in original Dutch. In any case it was a language that they took to easily for it described so precisely the things that they thought about in their minds.

Ali accepted the sharp graphic jibes that the guards used to describe him with great humour. He was a man who laughed easily, and this easy manner set everybody at ease in his presence. He was even able to turn the menace of his severed ear into an object of comedy listening with exaggerated attention to instructions by cupping his hands to the conch of the missing lobes.

But his eyes were alive, searching the sea and the horizon as if trying to decipher a secret pathway away from Robben Island. Manuel noticed this alertness in Ali, the tension beneath his jocular manner. Ali laughed and clowned while constantly taking meticulous note of the guard routine, the change of the watches, the tides and the wind.

Manuel saw in Ali the madness of an obsession. In the relative privacy of their cell there was not much conversation even though they were forced to spend many hours together. Ali prayed all the time, rising and prostrating himself, his prayers silent but nevertheless fierce, for his eyes were shut with the intensity of someone trying to expel the physical world around him. It was, Manuel thought, not only this stone cell he was escaping from, it was from all physical things, from physicality itself.

Manuel tried to shut out of his own mind the private intimate act that Ali performed, and which filled him with forboding.

Manuel very seldom prayed, even when he attended the compulsory church service held by the dominee from the mainland who came with the supply ship once each month. Manuel listened indifferently as the dominee, at the end of each service, ritually warned his captive congregation of the price of heathenism. Eternal damnation of their souls! Was there anyone present who deliberately wanted to shut himself out of the kingdom of heaven?

Upon the cross of stone, that Manuel had carved from raw granite upon the instruction of the Kommandant, a distorted agonised body of polished oak was affixed. The eyes of Christ were raised, in tortured hope, towards heaven. Would he damn Manuel's soul, that suffering man nailed like a slave onto stone, any more than Manuel's soul was already damned?

Ali had finished his prayer. The cell was silent and Manuel could hear the sound of the sea in the distance. A south-easterly was blowing, soon it would turn the calm sea into walls of raging water. And the rain will follow, icy squalls that clawed at the grey walls of the prison and the garrison.

Manuel wrapped himself in his blanket, welcoming the coarseness of its touch. He felt safe here, within the high rough walls of the prison. He wondered whether Khul, on Mijne Rust, was struggling against the wind, the rain cold and fierce in his face as he battled to secure the sheep in their pen?

'*Ek se ou*, how long do these storms last?' Ali asked in the peculiar sonorous voice that made him sound distant, unreal.

'A few hours. The wind carries it across the bay. It will strike the mainland in an hour or so, Manuel answered, struggling to maintain his slow subsidence into sleep.

'*Jurre, its mos goes amok ne*! Can you sail in this weather?'

'I'm not a sailor, but I think it would be stupid to try.'

'Has any *ou* ever 'scaped from this place?'

'I don't know. Not in this weather he won't, anyway.'

'Manuel, give me your ship'

'What?'

'That klipskip you carved. Give it to a *ou*.'

'It is made of stone. It can't go anywhere'.

'If you have faith. *As jy glo*, my broer, you can sail even in a stone ship. Faith moves stone, *vra vi' my*. But you must have faith, *imaan*!'

Manuel was almost asleep, the wind had carried the storm to Mijne Rust. Walls of water came crashing down upon the fields, the house. My mud walls won't hold all this water.

'Well, I have no use for it. Have it.' Manuel murmured and fell asleep, uneasy that the vengeance he was wreaking upon Khul, in this dream, was so violent, so final.

The next morning it appeared as if the storm had been fierce enough to wash away Manuel's ship of stone. He wandered about in the calm aftermath, past trees that had been uprooted, to the edge of the grey and placid sea. The storm was not strong enough to damage the fortress and the prison. Why had it chosen that dull, immobile vessel of rock?

Manuel was surprised at the apparent power of the storm, but soon dismissed the loss of his carving. He had learnt not to become attached to material objects. He remembered little of his conversation with Ali, his mind preoccupied by the vivid dream he had had about Mijne Rust. Khul had been sucked up into the vortex of the storms, his frail arms and legs flailing about like a huge, misshapen bird.

Three nights after the storm, Ali disappeared. The night was astonishingly clear for a winter's night, and the stars shone brightly against the blackness of the night sky. Ali did not return to the cell; for a while Manuel lay awake for he did not want to be disturbed once he had fallen asleep. Gulls flew overhead in noisy squadrons.

Manuel knew, at last, that Ali would not return. The man's madness - or faith - had taken him on a journey aboard a ship of stone, undoubtedly to his death in the deceptively calm sea. The next day the island was searched and the prisoners questioned. The investigation was routine and superficial. The foolish slave had probably drowned at sea, for the cross currents were strong and the water extremely cold.

Manuel returned to his solitary life, and habits. He cleared the cell of Ali's meagre belongings, not surprised that the runaway slave had taken nothing with him. The winter was nearing its end, and Manuel, uncharacteristically, had a feeling of contentment. He had only this summer to wait, before his term of banishment was over.

One morning, long before it was time to rise, Manuel was roused and roughly hauled to the Kommandant's office. There, he found the Kommandant in his night attire, a long flannel dress and a woollen cap on his head. He looked strangely shorn without the white wig of office. Manuel had never before seen a man in a nightdress, not even Khul who had brought to Mijne Rust many strange, city habits.

The Kommandant was weary, but obviously angered enough that he could not allow the business that forced him to bring Manuel before him to wait until daylight.

'Your cellmate Paulus - or Ali - as he proclaims himself has been reported to be on the mainland, preaching to the slaves. He preaches the particular heathenism which so many of you eastern people are afflicted with. The faith of Mohammed. As a mark of that faith - he is reported to be saying - he escaped from this island on a ship of stone.'

'Meester, no one can sail in a ship of stone.'

'I know that. You must have helped him. Another boat perhaps, or you know a way through the currents. You're a clever fellow.'

The inconsistent, and incredible interrogation of the cowed slave continued, until the Kommandant was weary and had seated himself on his throne-like chair beneath the window. The sun was rising, red like drenching blood, against the winter sky.

Manuel was sentenced to another ten years of imprisonment on Robben Island 'for complicity in helping a fellow prisoner to escape'. He was assigned to hard labour and the privilege of a single cell was removed. He was no longer allowed to keep his artisan's tools.

He was no longer able to fall asleep with the ease of peace and weariness. In the crowded cell into which he had been placed, men stirred and murmured, and made the unprecarious noises of slaves in a cell. They farted loudly, and those who shared blankets with each other out of the years of loneliness, did so with a stealth that was almost chaste.

Manuel remembered that he had not slept with a woman for many years, long before Katie was sold. And the Old Woman before Katie came. Does Khul know this secret? Ah, but why do I call her 'the Old Woman'? She was no older than me. It was loneliness and hunger. She used my body for sex, the same way she used it to clean the kraal, or herd the sheep. It was a measure of my slavery.

Yet, how much that old woman despised me when she found out that I also slept with Katie, in the kitchen.

Manuel did not hold anything against those men who slept with each other, it was one of the prices paid for being imprisoned here. It was the heat of that summer, and the suffocating closeness of human bodies that kept him away from his fellow prisoners, isolated in the little corner he secured for himself.

The summer was a meaningless season now, one of many seasons of heat and mist and the dull glare of the bluegreen sea. Manuel used half of his already diminished rations - for one whole month - to buy a stone chisel from one of the artisans. In the corner of the cell he had claimed - and protected - with the gleam of reckless madness that showed in his eyes, he began to carve miniatures of the supply ship. They were simple and hastily produced carvings, without the love and patience that his previous carvings showed. The guards laughed at the crudity of these stone replicas and ignored them.

But the story of Ali's escape had spread throughout the prison, fantastic tales of the slave aboard a ship of stone that cleaved through the heavy seas, driven by a wind that arose from the depths of the sky. Of Ali's faith that had conquered the walls of stone, and overcome the forbidding, sinister ocean that had been up to now Robben Island's most impenetrable wall.

There was much excitement, especially among the Muslim prisoners. The Kommandant, purely as a precaution, ordered the guards to confiscate the miniature ships, and to find Manuel's tools. The slave was to be put on punishment rations of bread and water. When this failed to stop the appearance of the small vessels, in all corners of the prison, and even on one occasion on the beach itself, he ordered Manuel to be isolated and placed in the solitary punishment cells.

Still the Kommandant's informants among the slaves reported continuous mutterings among prisoners, especially the Muslims from Batavia and Java. One even said that they were preparing for a mass escape on ships that Manuel had carved and hidden all over the island.

Then, to everyone's astonishment, a larger ship, very much like the one that Ali was said to have escaped on, was found among rocks close to the sea. Slaves and common prisoners alike were in a state of excitement. The workforce became sullen and surly.

It was time - the Kommandant knew - to act. Manuel was brought before him, manacled hand and foot, vainly trying to shield his eyes, which had grown accustomed to the darkness in the punishment cells, from the glare of the sunlight.

The heat inside of the stone walls of the Kommandant's office was unbearable to the guards and the Kommandant, who in defiance of the rigid dress-code demanded from someone of his station, had unbuttoned the top of his tunic completely. His chest was brawny, and tattooed with the figure of a gigantic, leaping fish. Probably a sailor once, or even a felon, who had redeemed himself through hard work, luck and bribery.

He raised his gleaming boots onto the desk, the bloodstains of innumerable vermin on the soles of the boots. Now the Kommandant was on his feet, fanning himself furiously.

'I could have you shot, for inciting the other prisoners. Or simply throw you into the sea. Who would know? No, do not speak,' he said to Manuel, who showed no intention of attempting to speak. 'I could brand you, cut your ear off to mark you as a dangerous animal and return you to the mainland. You would be hunted wherever you go. Ah, but why make a martyr of you?'

Manuel realised that the Kommandant was really addressing himself, debating aloud what the fate of this troublemaking slave should be. What did Manuel know of martyrdom, or even what the word meant? It was foreign to his vocabulary.

'Slaves do not become martyrs,' he heard the Kommandant say, 'they die or live because their masters decide that. You will not become the martyr of Robben Island. Fortunately for you. Your master Johan Khul died during a storm recently. His widow petitioned for your return - you are her rightful property - to the farm Mijne Rust.'

With a wave of his hand, the Kommandant dismissed Manuel.

Burdened again by the chains that bound him hand and foot, Manuel was escorted to the dock to await his turn to board the supply ship. He noticed that a storm was gathering in the bay.

Surely they would not set sail in such a storm? Suddenly Manuel became fearful of the journey ahead. Even if he survived the turbulent sea, what lay in store for him at Mijne Rust? Another 'old woman' bitter from being abandoned in a distant and inhospitable place where life offered nothing but continued struggle against the elements and against one's own loneliness?

He thought of Ali, the crazy logic of the man. 'Even chains can warm you, if you hug it to you like it was real sheepskin.' Manuel began to think of all the warm places on Mijne Rust, the kraal at night amidst the rustle of warm animals, the stone platform beside the well - heated by the midday sun it was like a cocoon of heat even in the heart of winter.

Manuel seated himself on the floor of the wooden jetty, his fears slowly subsiding in a flood of memories about Mijne Rust. A slave's life was like a ship of stone. You had to have faith in it.

SLAVERY

Oh Slavery! Thou art a bitter draught!
And twice accursèd is thy poisoned bowl,
Which taints with leprosy the White Man's soul,
Not less than his by whom its dregs are quaffed.
The Slave sinks down, o'ercome by cruel craft,
Like beast of burthen on the earth to roll.
The Master, though in luxury's lap he loll
Feels the foul venom , like a rankling shaft,
Strike through his reins. As if a demon laughed,
He, laughing, treads his victim in the dust -
The victim of his avarice, rage, or lust.
But the poor Captive's moan the whirlwinds waft
To Heaven - not unavenged: the Oppressor quakes
With secret dread, and shares the hell he makes!

THOMAS PRINGLE

NARRATIVE OF A RESIDENCE
IN SOUTH AFRICA

THOMAS PRINGLE

In April 1820 Thomas Pringle arrived at the Cape of Good Hope with a party of Scottish emigrants. The following extracts from his book Narrative of a Residence in South Africa *record his observations on the indigenous peoples and their treatment by white settlers, and the early frustration of his literary projects by an illiberal government.*

Caffer captive; Hottentot congregation

Shortly after disembarkation in Algoa Bay, Thomas Pringle calls on a missionary.

While tea was preparing, and before the twilight had yet closed in, my host was called out to speak to another stranger. This was a Caffer woman, accompanied by a little girl of eight or ten years of age, and having an infant strapped on her back, above her mantle of tanned bullock's hide. She had come from the *drostdy,* or district town, of Uitenhage, under the custody of a black constable, who stated that she was one of a number of Caffer females who had been made prisoners by order of the Commandant on the frontier for crossing the line of prescribed demarcation without permission, and that they were now to be given out in servitude among the white inhabitants of this district. The woman before us, he added, was to be forwarded by the missionary, under the charge of one of his people, to the residence of a certain colonist, about twenty miles to the westward. Such were the orders of the *landdrost,* or district magistrate.

While the constable was delivering his message, the Caffer woman looked at him and at us with keen and intelligent glances; and though she very imperfectly understood his language, she appeared fully to comprehend its import. When he had finished, she stepped forward, drew up her figure to its full height, extended her right arm, and commenced a speech in her native tongue - the Amakosa dialect. Though I did not understand a single word she uttered, I have seldom been more struck with surprise and admiration. The language, to which she appeared to give full and forcible intonation, was highly musical and sonorous; her gestures were natural, graceful, and impressive, and her large dark eyes, and handsome bronze countenance, were full of eloquent expression. Sometimes she pointed back towards her own country, and then to her children. Sometimes she raised her tones aloud, and shook her clenched hand, as if she denounced our injustice, and threatened us with the vengeance of her tribe. Then again, she would melt into tears, as if imploring clemency, and mourning for her helpless little ones. Some of the villagers who had gathered round, being whole or half Caffers, understood her speech, and interpreted its substance in Dutch to the missionary; but he could do nothing to alter her destination, and could only return kind words to console her. For my own part I was not a little struck by the scene, and could not help beginning to suspect that my European countrymen, who thus made captives of harmless women and children, were in reality greater barbarians than the savage natives of Caffraria.

After our interview with the Caffer woman, I attended the evening service of the missionary, in the rustic chapel of Bethelsdorp. The place was occupied by a very considerable number of the inhabitants of the village, a large proportion being females. The demeanour of the audience was attentive and devout, and their singing of the missionary hymns was singularly pleasing and harmonious. The effect of the music was no doubt greatly heightened by the reflections which the sight of this African congregation naturally suggested. I saw before me the remnant of an aboriginal race, to whom this remote region, now occupied by white colonists, had at no distant period belonged. As I sat and listened to the soft and touching melody of the female voices, or gazed on the earnest, upturned, swarthy countenances of the aged men, who had probably spent their early days in the wild freedom of nomadic life, and worn out their middle life in the service of the colonists, it was pleasing to think that *here*, and in a few other institutions such as this, the Christian humanity of Europe had done something to alleviate European oppression, by opening asylums where, at least, a *few* of the race were enabled to escape from personal thraldom, and to emerge from heathen darkness into the glorious light and liberty of the Gospel.

In subsequent conversations with the missionary, Mr Barker, who evinced great candour and openness, and in the course of a careful inspection of the village on the following day, I discovered that almost insurmountable disadvantages existed in the situation of the place; which was not chosen, as has sometimes been erroneously stated, by old Dr Vanderkemp, but forced upon his acceptance by the Colonial Government of the day. In the civil condition of the people also, and even in the system of management, there were, at the period of my first visit, impediments to be overcome, and defects to be remedied of no slight description. I shall content myself with observing that, even at this period, whatever there might be visible at Bethelsdorp of African wildness and want of the accessories of civilisation, there was little that could with propriety be called savage. There was, even amongst the rudest of the people, an aspect of civility and decent respect, of quietude and sober-mindedness, which evinced that they were habitually under the control of far other principles than those which regulate the movements of mere savage men. They appeared to be in general a respectable and religious native peasantry; as yet, indeed, but partially reclaimed from some of the indolent habits of nomadic life, but obviously progressing, and, in many instances, already farther advanced intellectually than externally.

From the account of his journey into the interior

It was not a little amusing after supper (as I sat in front of my wagon jotting down in my note-book the day's memoranda) to contemplate the characteristic groups which our rustic camp exhibited. The Dutch-African boors, most of them men of almost gigantic size, sat apart in their bushy *bield* in aristocratic exclusiveness, smoking their huge pipes with self-satisfied complacency. Some of the graver emigrants were seated on the trunk of a decayed tree, conversing in broad Scotch on subjects connected with our settlement, and on the comparative merits of long and short horned cattle (the horns of the native oxen, by the way, are enormous) and the livelier young men and servant lads were standing round the Hottentots, observing their merry pranks, or practising with them a lesson of mutual tuition in their respective dialects; while the awkward essays at pronounciation on either side supplied a fund of ceaseless entertainment. Conversation appeared to go on with alacrity, though neither party understood scarcely a syllable of the other's language; while a sly rogue of a Bushman sat behind, all the while mimicking, to the very life, each of us in succession. These groups, with all their variety of mien and attitude, character and complexion—now dimly discovered, now distinctly lightened up by the fitful blaze of the watch-fires; the exotic aspects of the clumps of aloes and euphorbias, peeping out amidst the surrounding jungle, in the wan light of the rising moon, seeming to the excited fancy like bands of Caffer warriors crested with plumes and bristling with assagais; together with the uncouth clucking gibberish of the Hottentots and Bushmen (for there were two or three of the latter tribe among our wagon leaders) and their loud burst of wild and *eldritch* laughter had altogether a very strange and striking effect, and made some of us feel, far more impressively than we had yet felt, that we were now indeed pilgrims in the wilds of savage Africa.

Hottentots ...

By degrees our situation became more comfortable. On the 25th of July, the ten Hottentots promised by our civil magistrates for a temporary guard, arrived; and we were thus relieved from the necessity of keeping up nightly sentinels of our own body, and from any apprehensions of being surprised by marauders from the waste country to the eastward. These Hottentots were all well-armed, and expert in the use of the musket. They were drafted for this particular duty from the service of the Dutch African colonists of the Tarka and Agter-Sneeuwberg, to whom all of them were under contract, and were supplied with provisions at the expense of the district. I appointed one of the oldest and shrewdest of them serjeant over the rest, and made him responsible to me for their good conduct. Nor had I ever cause to complain, except in a very few instances, of neglect of duty or misconduct of any sort in these men, although, during the eight months we were thus guarded, we had many changes of them, as they were usually relieved by other Hottentots once in three or four weeks. There was great diversity of character and of civilisation among them. Some were intelligent mulattoes (or, according to the colonial phrase, *Bastaards*), the sons of colonists by native women. Others were of true Bushman blood - *caught* young and *tamed* by the Boors. All of them however, were respectful, faithful, and honest. Although our stores, clothing, and other property of various kinds, were constantly within their reach, we never missed the smallest article.

... I ventured to assume the office of religious instructor to the poor ignorant natives placed under my temporary direction. Having, with the aid of a grammar and dictionary, made myself, since our arrival at Algoa Bay, so far acquainted with the Dutch language (now universally spoken by the colonial Hottentots) that I could converse in it on familiar topics, and read the Scriptures with tolerable fluency, I added, for the benefit of our Hottentot guard, a Sunday service in Dutch to our usual one in English. This service was of a very simple character, being confined to the reading and exposition of plain passages of Scripture, and of a short sermon or tract; some devotional portions of the liturgy used by the Dutch Reformed Church; and the singing of one or two hymns. Limited as were our ministrations in this way, they had a very pleasing effect. They were attended to with an earnestness which it was not less affecting than gratifying to witness. To two or three Hottentots (mulattoes) who could read a little, I presented Dutch New Testaments, which were received with the most lively feeling of thankfulness; and which they were afterwards observed to be often reading or spelling out, to their comrades. Several of them frequently came voluntarily to solicit further instruction; and one poor fellow, to whom my wife had given a New Testament, several months afterwards sent her, from his master's place, a hundred miles distant, the present of a milch-goat with twin kids, as a testimony of his gratitude. ...

... and Dutch-African neighbours

About this period, we were somewhat teased by Sunday visits from our Dutch-African neighbours of the lower part of the Glen-Lynden valley and the Tarka. Solicitous to keep upon friendly terms with these people, I always made it a point to receive them courteously and usually asked them to dine with me. But finding that they made a practice of visiting us on Sundays, either to gratify idle curiosity or with a view to commercial dealings, I fell upon a scheme which effectually relieved us from this annoyance. I took care to acquaint them that it was contrary to our principles to transact secular business on the Sunday; and when any of them came, I offered them a seat among my Hottentot audience, and invited them to read aloud the Sunday service. Few of them, I found, could read even the *New Testament* without much stammering and spelling; and they considered it, moreover, a shocking degradation to sit down amidst a group of Hottentots. We were therefore speedily relieved altogether from their Sunday visitations. In other respects, we found them generally, however uncultivated, by no means disagreeable neighbours. They were exceedingly shrewd at bargain-making, it is true, and too sharp sometimes even for cautious Scotch-men; but they were also generally civil and good-natured, and, according to the custom of the country, extremely hospitable. On the whole, their demeanour towards us, whom they might be supposed naturally to regard with exceeding jealousy, if not dislike, was far more friendly and obliging than could, under all circumstances, have been anticipated.

The case of the Hottentot, Booy

Some time in 1814, a Hottentot named Booy appeared at the magistrate's office at Cradock, and complained of the oppressive conduct of Frederick Bezuidenhout, a Dutch-African colonist, who resided at the place now called Cameron's Cleugh, on Bavian's River. Booy, it appeared, had been for several years in the service of this

Boor; but when the term of his contract had expired, Bezuidenhout peremptorily refused either to permit him to depart, or to remove what little property he had on the place. Captain Stockenstrom, who at that time filled the office of deputy-*landdrost* of the sub-district of Cradock, gave the complainant a letter to Opperman, the field-cornet of Bavian's River, directing that officer to inquire into the case, and in the event of the Hottentot's statement proving correct, to take care that his property was delivered to him, and that he was allowed to remove unmolested. The field-cornet having gone to Bezuidenhout's place with Booy, found the Hottentot's statement to be perfectly correct. The Boor at once admitted the facts; but instead of yielding obedience to the magistrate's order, he boldly declared that he considered this interference between him (a free burgher) and *his* Hottentot to be a presumptuous innovation upon his *rights* and an intolerable usurpation of tyrannical authority. He told the field-cornet that he set at defiance both himself and the magistrate who had sent him on his officious errand; and, to give farther emphasis to his words, he fell violently upon poor Booy, gave him a severe beating, and then bade him go and tell the civil authorities that he would treat them in the same manner if they should dare to come upon his grounds to claim the property of a Hottentot.

In elucidation of Bezuidenhout's conduct on this occasion, it is to be remarked that, up to a comparatively recent period, the Hottentot population within the limits of the colony had been universally subjected to a state of the most degrading thraldom under the African boors. They were, in fact, left entirely in the power of the white colonists: and in the remoter districts, their own limbs and lives, as well as the disposal of their children, were practically altogether at their master's mercy. In 1809, the Earl of Caledon, who at that time administered the government of the Cape, had made a benevolent attempt to rescue this class of men from their abject and unprotected condition, by issuing a proclamation, which, by one of its provisions, deprived the colonists of the power, so long exercised as a legal and unquestionable right, of retaining the children of the Hottentots in bondage, under the name of apprenticeship, until their twenty-fifth year, and the adults, under other pretexts, often for life. This proclamation contained several other clauses, framed unquestionably with an anxious desire to improve the condition and protect the persons and property of this people. Considering the state of public feeling, and the progress of just views on such subjects, perhaps Lord Caledon's proclamation was, *at that period,* an effort in the cause of justice and humanity nearly as great as the noble ordinance issued by General Bourke nineteen years afterwards. But, unhappily for the Hottentots and for the colony, many of the best provisions of Lord Caledon's enactment were neutralised by coercive clauses, admitted at the suggestion of certain provincial functionaries, to conciliate the feelings and serve the selfish views of the privileged classes, and which had a practical operation which his lordship most undoubtedly never intended to sanction. What was still more deplorable, Sir John Cradock, who succeeded Lord Caledon in the government, permitted himself to be so far influenced by the representations of the colonists, that he rescinded, by another proclamation in 1812, the most important clause of Lord Caledon's enactment - that, namely, which secured to the oppressed natives a right to their own children; and thus re-established the iniquitious claim of the colonists to force them into apprenticed servitude, and sealed for sixteen years longer the degradation of the race.

In this state of things, and with provincial functionaries in general deeply imbued with the feelings of the other colonists, the protection of the native race from oppression was out of the question. When the local magistrate happened to be, as in the present case, a man of enlightened views and determined character, a vigorous attempt might occasionally be made to interfere in defence of the natives, so far as the colonial law extended its feeble and faltering arm. But the indignant resentment with which such interference was repelled, clearly evinces how seldom it had hitherto been efficiently exerted. In regard to Bezuidenhout it is, moreover, to be recollected that, ever since the earlier days of colonial anarchy, which Mr Barrow has so forcibly depicted, when the Boors used to murder and mutilate the Hottentots at discretion, he and his comrades had resided on this wild and secluded part of the frontier, where colonial legislation in regard to the aborigines had reached them only by hearsay, and where such terms as the 'rights of the natives', were still treated with unqualified contempt. The angry defiance, therefore, with which this rude back-settler met the magistrate's intervention in behalf of Booy, and the warmth with which his resentful feelings, *as an insulted free burgher*, were sympathised with by a large portion of the neighbouring colonists, exhibits, in a light equally striking and instructive, the frightful perversion of moral sentiment in the dominant class by the uncontrolled exercise of arbitrary power, and the deplorable condition of the natives who lay prostrate under their feet.

Upon receiving the field-cornet's report of Bezuidenhout's outrageous conduct, the magistrate instituted legal proceedings against him before the local court. But the Boor treated the regular summonses that were delivered to him with the same audacious contempt with which he had repelled the monitory intervention of the field-cornet, even threatening with personal violence the judicial messengers. The case was thus brought regularly before the Judges of Circuit, at Graaf-Reinet, in 1815; when the defendant maintaining the same contumacy, and refusing to appear, he was sentenced to imprisonment for contempt of court.

On the condition of the Mulatto Hottentots

After the augmentation of our territory by the Colonial Government, I willingly availed myself of a convenient opportunity which offered for increasing the native population upon it, and thereby adding at once to our means of security and our profitable occupation of the land. It happened that several of the Mulatto Hottentots (*bastaards*) who had been stationed with us during the first six months, belonged to a small body of that class who had for many years resided at Zwagershoek, under the protection of an old German settler of the name of Stollz. A favourable report, it appears, had been carried to this man of the treatment the coloured caste had experienced at Glen-Lynden; for in August, 1821, old Stollz wrote me a letter, requesting me to receive hospitably (*herbergzaamlyk*) upon our grounds certain families of his Hottentot vassals; and some time afterward he sent over a messenger to entreat me urgently to visit him without delay, as he was about to die, and was anxious to confer with me respecting the future disposal and protection of his coloured dependants. I rode over accordingly with Mr G Rennie to see the old man; but when we reached Zwagershoek, we learned that Stollz had died two days before, and that we were only in time to attend his funeral. It took place the next day, and was curious and characteristic enough. The scene of the funeral dinner reminded me of some of Sir Walter Scott's graphic sketches. The only real mourners were the coloured people, who were not admitted to the feast, and only permitted to follow the funeral at a humble distance. The landed property left by the deceased fell into the hands of covetous strangers; and the Mulattoes, who had occupied a large part of it as tenants and cottagers, were speedily dispossessed. The most of these people flocked over to Glen-Lynden, where we engaged some of them as herdsmen and farm servants, and placed those who had cattle as tenants upon our unoccupied lands, upon condition, generally, of their rendering certain services in the cultivation of the soil. By this means we greatly strengthened our own hands, while we had at the same time the satisfaction of protecting and benefiting those oppressed and despised people. A dozen families or more thus found a temporary settlement in our valley, some of whom, under the sheltering patronage of old Stollz, had accumulated considerable property. ... Two brothers, Christian and Karal Groepe, who had previously become tenants to my father, had a stock of sheep, cattle, and horses, more numerous than any of the rest, and equal to many of the poorer Boors. These Groepes were the sons of an old German settler, who had once been field-cornet of Zwagershoek, but who (now in extreme old age) was considered to have *lost caste*, from his associating with his own children by a Hottentot woman.

When these people came to reside at Glen-Lynden, our immediate district magistrate, Captain Harding, had considerable doubts whether the colonial laws would sanction our receiving them on our grounds as *tenants* merely, without also indenturing them in every case as our *servants*. The almost universal usage throughout the colony was to consider all Hottentots, whether of pure or mixed blood, as under legal obligation to be placed under *contract of servitude*; and Captain Harding, though a humane man and an able and upright magistrate, had adopted the same prejudice. As I differed from him about the application of a coercive clause in Lord Caledon's proclamation of 1809 to such cases as the present, the matter was referred to the chief magistrate of the district, Captain Stockenstrom, who decided in favour of the more liberal interpretation, and thus the Mulattoes of Zwagershoek became our tenants.

As every adult male among them possessed at least a musket and a horse, and they looked to me as their immediate protector, I now found myself in the novel situation of a petty 'border chief'; being able to muster upwards of thirty armed horsemen (including our own party and the six Hottentot soldiers) at an hour's notice. We therefore considered our location perfectly secure from any serious attack of the wild natives in the vicinity.

These Mulattoes were an acute, active, and enterprising race of men; but their unhappy condition as a degraded caste, and the irregular sort of life they had led in some respects under old Stollz were not favourable to the formation of habits either of steady industry or strict morality. Stollz himself had exhibited the evil example of living in habitual concubinage; and, what was still more prejudicial, the sanctions of legal marriage were refused by the colonial church to their unions, except upon both parties exhibiting qualifications, which in nineteen cases out of twenty were quite unattainable in their existing circumstances. For instance, the clergyman of the district land refused to marry Christian Groepe, one of the most respectable and well-educated of these men, to the woman who had been his faithful partner for nearly a dozen years, and had borne him eight children, merely because the poor woman, after several attempts, could not accurately repeat the church catechism!

The fact is, there existed a strong prejudice among the white colonists against the full admission of the coloured class to ecclesiastical privileges, and the majority of the colonial clergy were so little alive to the apostolic duties of their sacred office as to lend their sanction, directly, or indirectly, to these unchristian prejudices, which were also countenanced by the colonial laws.

Notwithstanding, however, these and other disadvantageous circumstances, our Mulatto auxiliaries were, as a body, on the whole extremely well-behaved. Their marriage unions, though acknowledged neither by law nor the church, were, with occasional exceptions, permanently adhered to. Though too much addicted to hunting and other idle habits of semi-civilised men, they were not unwilling to labour, and to labour vigorously, when an opportunity was afforded them of thereby improving their circumstances. Occasional inebriety, when temptation assailed them in the shape of a brandy hawker's wagon (one of the worst nuisances of the colony), was perhaps their greatest vice. But some had virtue to resist even this besetting sin, when duly admonished of its enormity; and the worst of them did not surpass, in the indulgence of this vice, many both of the Dutch and English colonists. With few exceptions, they attended regularly and devoutly at our sabbath service; and, what was still more gratifying, they evinced great anxiety to learn to read, and to obtain copies of the Scriptures for the instruction of their children.

Attitudes of the Boers ... and the British settlers

I would not willingly give the impression, that Cornelius Vandernest is a mere savage ruffian. On the contrary, he is really one of the most respectable of these frontier boors; and, apart from his hereditary prejudices in regard to the natives, is generally, and I believe justly, considered as a decent, good-natured, and well-disposed person. The fact is that even the very best of these men (the frontier boors) have been trained from their childhood to regard Bushmen and Caffers with nearly the same feelings as they regard beasts of prey - only with far more rancorous animosity; so that they can scarcely be brought to view even the treacherous slaughter of them as a crime. But while this circumstance may be allowed to palliate the guilt of such untutored men, it casts a darker shade over the conduct of those in authority, who knowing well the habits and prejudices of those semi-barbarous back-settlers, yet entrust them with a perilous discretion towards the natives, which, from the very nature of things, cannot fail to be often grossly abused.

Nor would it be just to represent those feelings towards the natives as confined solely to the Dutch-African population. Some of the British settlers, I grieve and blush to say, and those not exclusively of the lower orders, appear to have imbibed, in their full extent, the same inhuman prejudices towards the natives of the soil, and have even had the hardihood to avow such sentiments in print. Some of the discharged soldiery who have settled on the eastern frontier have acquired a bad pre-eminence in this respect. One man of this class, who had married a sister of Vandernest's, had a prominent share in the slaughter of Makomo's envoys; and the following is another melancholy illustration of the prevalence of this spirit.

A month or two previous to this affair at the Plora, a party of five Caffers, armed as usual with assagais, but one of them wearing as a badge of peace a white linen shirt, came over to the residence of my father at Glen-Lynden. My father, who had never before been visited by any armed Caffers, felt rather apprehensive of their intentions; but he suppressed his suspicions, determined not to be the aggressor, and to treat them in a friendly manner, unless they gave him cause to act otherwise. One of them, who spoke Dutch, said that they were messengers sent out by the chief Makomo to the field-cornet Steenkamp on the Tarka; and that they only requested a little food, and permission to remain for the night. They were accordingly presented with a sheep and an empty hut to sleep in; and they soon kindled a fire, and sat down with the utmost good humour and confidence to dress their supper and smoke their pipes. While they were thus employed, and quietly conversing with the Hottentot servants, one Hozie, a disbanded serjeant of the 72nd regiment, who then occupied a farm on the location belonging to Mr Sydserff, came to the place in great haste with his gun. He informed my father that he had heard of the arrival of the strangers; and having been engaged in many commandoes, and consequently well acquainted with the 'nature' of the Caffers, (who, he said, 'were just the same as wolves, and very *treacherous*'); and as this party, he was sure, could only have come out for some wicked purpose, and might very probably murder all the family, and carry off the cattle in the night; he coolly proposed, as the best plan to prevent all this mischief, to surround the hut with their servants, while the Caffers were busy with their supper, *and shoot them all dead on the spot!* Happily not so 'experienced' as his martial countryman, my father rejected this proposal with horror and indignation! The poor Caffers were permitted to eat and sleep in peace; and next morning, before departing, they came and expressed, in affecting terms, their grateful acknowledgments for the hospitable treatment they had received. They parted in kindness. The Caffers proceeded on their journey, and returned by another way to their own country, without doing the slightest injury to any one whatever. One individual of this party (the man who spoke Dutch) was the same person who afterwards delivered his chief's message to Vandernest, and was the murdered by the boors, after escaping the projected treachery of the Scottish serjeant.

Thomas Pringle lived in Cape Town from September 1822 until February 1825

For some time after my first arrival in Cape Town things appeared to wear a very favourable aspect. The governor had declared himeself a friend to the mitigation of slavery, and had just issued a proclamation containing some beneficial and many plausible enactments; and for the first time in the history of the colony, a white man was capitally punished for the murder of a slave. Great anxiety was professed for the establishment of English schools, and the encouragement of the English language and literature in South Africa. The public library, now under my personal charge, appeared to be warmly patronised by the Governor, and by all the chief functionaries. There was some talk also of offering me the superintendence of the Government Gazette, and of rendering that journal subservient to the diffusion of useful information throughout the colony. This was an object quite to my liking, and in which I only wanted the countenance of government to engage my most devoted services ...

... Long before Mr Fairbairn [a friend whom Pringle had invited to come to South Africa] had joined me, however, I had acquired a more intimate acquaintance with the character of the colonial administration, and formed a truer estimate of their views. I soon saw that their professed anxiety to encourage education and the diffusion of knowledge, was a piece of political hypocrisy, assumed to cloak the real character of the government from the prying eyes of his Majesty's Commissioners of Inquiry, whose arrival in the colony was then daily expected ...

... In renouncing all idea of connection with the Government Gazette, however, I did not abandon my views of rendering the press subservient to the grand object of public instruction, but determined to establish, if possible, an independent periodical in Cape Town. I was encouraged to prosecute this purpose by the most enlightened inhabitants of the colony, both English and Dutch; and I soon found a zealous coadjutor in the Reverend Mr Faure, one of the Dutch clergymen of Cape Town, who entertained similar views for the instruction of his countrymen.

As we made no secret of our scheme, some rumour of it soon reached the ears of the Governor; and while we were engaged in preparing a prospectus for public circulation and a memorial to his

Excellency, soliciting permission to publish our projected journals (without which we knew we could not proceed a single step), I received a visit from a gentleman, previously unknown to me, a confidential retainer, at that time, of our Colonial Court. He strove earnestly to persuade me that the prosecution of the enterprise I had in view, would be detrimental to my personal interests in the colony; but finding me deaf to his representations on that score, he at length plainly told me that Lord Charles Somerset had expressed to him his opinion in regard to our projected undertaking - and that his Excellency's opinion was decidedly adverse to it.

Unmoved by this intimation, Mr Faure and I sent in our memorial to the Governor on the 3rd of February 1823. After waiting five weeks, we received a verbal reply through the lips of the Colonial Secretary, in the following words: ' His Excellency the Governor has not seen your application in a favourable light'.

From *Narrative of a Residence in South Africa (1834)*

THE CAFFER COMMANDO

Hark! - heard ye the signals of triumph afar?
'Tis our Caffer Commando returning from war:
The voice of their laughter comes loud on the wind,
Nor heed they the curses that follow behind.
For who cares for him, the poor Caffer, that wails
Where the smoke rises dim from yon desolate vales -
That wails for his little ones killed in the fray,
And his herds by the Colonist carried away?
Or who cares for him that once pastured this spot,
Where his tribe is extinct and their story forgot?
As many another, ere twenty years pass,
Will only be known by their bones in the grass!
And sons of the Keisi, the Kei, the Gareep,
With the Gunja and Ghona in silence shall sleep:
For England hath spoke in her tyrannous mood,
And the edict is written in African blood!

Dark Katta is howling: the eager jackal,
As the lengthening shadows more drearily fall
Shrieks forth his hymn to the hornèd moon;
And the lord of the desert will follow him soon:
And the tiger-wolf laughs in his bone-strewed brake,
As he calls on his mate and her cubs to awake;
And the panther and leopard come leaping along;
All hymning to Hecate a festival song:
For the tumult is over, the slaughter hath ceased -
And the vulture hath bidden them all to the feast.

THOMAS PRINGLE

GREAT HYMN

O thou Great Mantle which envelops us,
Creator of the light which is formed in the heavens,
Who framed and fashioned the heavens themselves,
Who hurled forth the ever-twinkling stars;
O thou Mighty God of Heaven,
Who whirlest round the stars - the Pleiades,
In thy dwelling place on thee we call,
To be a leader and a guide to us,
O thou who to the blind givest light.
Our great treasure, on thee we call;
For thou, O thou art the true rock;
Thou, O thou art the true shield;
Thou, O thou art the true covert.
On thee, O holy Lamb, we call,
Whose blood for us was sprinkled forth,
Whose hands for us were pierced;
O be thou a leader and a guide to us,
Creator of the light which is formed in the heavens,
Who framed and fashioned the heavens themselves.

NTSIKANA GABA
(c.1780-1821)

Translated from the Xhosa by Thomas Pringle (1827)

A MEETING WITH VILAKAZI,
THE GREAT ZULU POET

Sleep tried to split us apart
But the great dream created a new sun.
Through its towering rays two worlds emerged
And our twin planets opened to each other.
I saw you descending from a dazzling hill,
Your presence filled the whole world.
I heard the drums beat behind your footsteps
And the children of the south began to sing.
They walked on the ancient path of the goddess
    Nomkhubulwane
And the old dancing arena was filled with festival crowds.
Your great songs echoed to the accompaniment of the festival
    horn
It was the beginning of our ancient new year
Before the foreigners came, before they planted their own emblems.
I came to the arena and you held my hand.
Together we danced the boast-dance of our forefathers
We sang the great anthems of the uLundi mountains.

MAZISI KUNENE

Translated from the Zulu by the poet

ISANDHLWANA

BRIAN FILLING

On 22 January 1879 at Isandhlwana the British suffered the greatest single-engagement disaster in their military history when the Zulus in open combat killed all but 55 of 858 European personnel and 500 of their African auxiliaries. Benjamin Disraeli, British Prime Minister at the time, said, 'The terrible disaster has shaken me to the centre....' In the midsummer of 1879 when news reached Britain that the young Prince Louis Napoleon, exiled in England and who had volunteered for service with the British in South Africa, had been ambushed and killed by the Zulus while on reconnaissance, Disraeli exclaimed:

> A remarkable people these Zulus. They defeat our generals, they convert our Bishops and now they have settled the fate of a great European dynasty.

European settlement in South Africa dates back to 1652 when the Dutch established themselves at the Cape of Good Hope. The apartheid regime's version of history is that the black people crossed the Limpopo river from the north at exactly the same time as the Dutch arrived at the Cape and that the country had hitherto been a no-man's-land. This myth underpins 'official' history in the Republic of South Africa. In fact, the Khoi peoples had lived in Southern Africa since Stone Age times while the Sotho, the Xhosa, the Zulu and others had certainly established themselves by AD 400 in the territory which came to be known as the Transvaal. As Roland Oliver and J D Fage state in their *A Short History of Africa:*

> Most of our early information about South Africa comes, in fact, from shipwrecked Portuguese who trekked to safety across parts of the Transkei, Pondoland, Natal and Southern Mozambique. Their accounts show that at this time, contrary to the beliefs of most present-day white South Africans, South Africa was by no means empty of Bantu inhabitants.

Weaker tribes living nearest to the Cape were reduced to slavery by the early settlers but the Bantu-speaking peoples had evolved an iron-forging technology capable of making spears. The resistance to white encroachment was such that in the Cape alone there were nine wars of resistance over one hundred years. In 1779 the first large-scale military engagement between the indigenous people and white colonialists took place and is known in white history as the first 'Kaffir war'.

The arrival of the British military forces in South Africa at the beginning of the nineteenth century strengthened the forces of colonisation and repression. More British settlers arrived in 1820, and with the gradual establishment of a Cape Colony in which slavery was banned (following anti-slavery campaigns in Britain) the Dutch settlers there began moving north in 1836, a migration which entered Afrikaner mythology as the 'Great Trek'.

From this time onwards the history of South Africa became a three-sided affair. First, the Africans who resisted both Afrikaners and British, at times attempting to use the second against the first; second, the Boers or Afrikaners who founded the Republic of Natal in 1838 and, when that was annexed by the British in 1843, continued north-wards to found the republics of the Orange Free State and the Transvaal; third, the British of the Cape Colony who, for a variety of reasons including the desire to enclose the diamond and goldfields discovered in the 1870s and 1880s, pursued the Afrikaners attempting to dispossess them of their republics, out of which, eventually, there came the Anglo-Boer War of 1899-1901. The suppression of the Bambata Rebellion in 1906 brought to a close the first 250-year phase of resistance. Defeated militarily and totally disarmed, robbed of their land by foreign invaders, denied any say in the government of their country, the indigenous people of South Africa had to find new ways to continue the struggle. They adopted new methods of resistance: they fought without spear or gun, organising mass meetings, dem-onstrations, deputations, protests, passive resistance and strikes. The formation of the South African Native National Congress, precursor of the African National Congress, on 8 January 1912 was a logical culmination of the anti-colonial struggle.

A high point of the resistance to colonialism was the victory of the Zulus at Isandhlwana.

Dingiswayo, who became Chief of the Zulus in Northern Natal sometime after 1780, became convinced of the need to unify neighbour-ing chiefdoms into a single kingdom as a result of the so-called 'Kaffir wars'. Shaka of the Zulus, who succeeded Dingiswayo, revolutionised warfare in terms of weaponry, discipline and tactics. It was Shaka who developed the battle tactics which spelt disaster for the British at Isandhlwana. Instead of the traditional linear confrontation and assault, a strong central force launched the initial attack, while two wings or 'horns' of equal size wheeled rapidly right and left until their tips met behind enemy ranks. The enemy was thus completely encircled and, as no quarter was given, completely destroyed. By the middle of the 1820s

Shaka had built a powerful concentration of military and political power, the Zulu empire, and was unchallenged throughout almost all Natal and Zululand. Shaka was succeeded by Dingane and then Mpande. A dispute over the succession came to a head in 1856 between two of Mpande's sons, Cetshwayo and Mbulazi. Following his defeat of Mbulazi, Cetshwayo felt the need for an official adviser who might guide him in his relations with the British colonists and the Afrikaner settlers, both of whom flanked the kingdom he would rule in the future. Cetshwayo offered John Robert Dunn, 'a renegade Scot' (according to the *Oxford History of South Africa* but disputed elsewhere) this position along with the full rights of a chieftain and a large tract of country along the coast north of the Tugela. Within a decade Dunn was wealthy and ruled over kraals with a population of more than 10,000 Zulus. Known as 'Jantoni', Dunn had a number of Zulu wives and although a total was never established, at his death 49 wives and 116 children were mentioned in his will! Cetshwayo entered a period during which he exercised practical control of much of the kingdom and finally attained the throne on his father's death in 1872. In 1816 Shaka had begun to build the military strength of the Zulus; 57 years later his nephew, Cetshwayo was chief of this most powerful nation in all Africa.

No sooner had the ninth 'Kaffir war' been brought to a conclusion by General Thesiger (later Lord Chelmsford) than he was stating that

> It is still, however, more than probable that active steps will have to be taken to check the arrogance of Cetshwayo, Chief of the Zulus.

This statement concurred with the view of his political superior, Sir Bartle Frere, High Commissioner of Native Affairs for South Africa. In 1877 Britain had annexed the Transvaal on the pretext of Zulu incursions. For some time there had been disputed territories between the Zulus and the Boers. Cetshwayo had looked to the British for relief in the border dispute with the Boers of the Transvaal and had in fact applied for arbitration no less than eighteen times between 1861 and 1876. Nothing had ever come of these applications. A Boundary Commission was eventually established by the British and it met at Rorke's Drift in 1878 for five weeks, sifting every document and verbal claim produced by both sides, the Transvaal Boers and the Zulus. The Transvaal Afrikaner case melted away. One vital document turned out to be a forgery and others had been altered. The Commission concluded that there were two main questions: who had owned the land originally, and had any of it been properly ceded? Not even the Boers questioned the original Zulu ownership and it was found that no concession of territory had ever been made by the Zulus. The Boers at best had a few agreements to graze cattle on Zulu land.

2 CETSHWAYO, THE ZULU KING
This drawing of the Zulu King, who led the defeat of the British at
Isandhlwana in 1879, appeared in the *Illustrated London News*
of 22 February 1879

Before the findings of the report were published Frere had begun to discuss measures for enforcing on the Zulu nation what he assumed would be a verdict favourable to the Transvaal. When the report was received in July 1878 by Sir Bartle he was profoundly shocked. Nevertheless he had no intention of carrying out its recommendations. He gained some time by submitting the report to London since it would be several months before he would receive an answer. On 16 November Cetshwayo was informed that the boundary decision would be announced on 11 December. Even with Frere's modifications the report of the Boundary Commission largely upheld the Zulu claims, and Cetshwayo's delegation, which included John Dunn, accepted the decision with qualified satisfaction. Frere thought the decision unjust to the Transvaal and feared the Boers would rebel if he enforced it. Therefore he decided that the announcement of the award to the Zulus should be accompanied by an ultimatum to them.

The terms of the ultimatum included the disbandment of the Zulu army and the presence of a British diplomat in Zululand to enforce the various other provisions of the ultimatum. They were not so much a call for reform as an outline of the shape of the administration he intended to impose on the Zulus by force. It sounded the death knell of Zulu independence. A reply from Cetshwayo was sent to Frere via John Dunn which in effect accepted the first set of provisions of the ultimatum but asked for more time. Cetshwayo's reply was contemptuously dismissed and on 4 January 1879 Sir Bartle Frere issued the following statement:

> The British forces are coming into Zululand to exact from Cetshwayo reparation for violations of British territory... and to enforce compliance with the promises made by Cetshwayo at his coronation for the better government of his people ...

On 11 January 1879 British troops commanded by Lieutenant-General Lord Chelmsford advanced into Zululand. Chelmsford's plan of campaign was to advance with four columns converging from points on a two hundred mile front upon Cetshwayo's kraal at Ulundi. Of the four columns, one under Lieutenant-Colonel Durnford encamped at Rorke's Drift was to act in concert with the main column led by Chelmsford. Durnford crossed the Buffalo river at Rorke's Drift on 20 January and after a march of some ten miles, pitched camp on the southern face of a steep hill called Isandhlwana.

Isandhlwana is a lofty eminence, three sides of which are inaccessible. The northern side slopes gradually down to a range of hills. Chelmsford's camp beneath it was pitched with an open plain in front, a small kopje on the right flank and a long range of hills to the left and rear. No position more favourable for a surprise attack could have been chosen.

Despite warnings about the need for scouting and laagering of the wagons, the underestimation of the Zulus by the British was the basis of their forthcoming defeat. Early on the morning of the 22nd Chelmsford marched out with his main force in pursuit of an *impi* (Zulu regiment) which lured him further and further away. In his absence an immense body of Zulus issued from behind the neighbouring hills and completely surrounded the British camp. Within a few hours the camp was overrun. It was the greatest disaster in British military history since the Crimean War.

> The Zulu Kaffirs ... did what no European army can do. Armed only with pikes and spears and without firearms, they advanced, under a hail of bullets from the breech loaders, right up to the bayonets of the English infantry - acknowledged as the best in the world for fighting in close formation - throwing them into disorder and even beating them back more than once. ... Their capacity and endurance are best proved by the complaint of the English that a Kaffir can move faster and cover a longer distance in 24 hours than a horse. (Frederick Engels 1884)

The small defence force at Rorke's Drift was relieved by Chelmsford on January 23 and following the arrival of British reinforcements the war gradually drew to a conclusion with Ulundi, the royal kraal of Cetshwayo, going up in flames on July 18. The decisive factor ultimately was superior British fire-power.

The Zulus were subjected in a number of stages. First, the kingdom was conquered and its army broken up. Second, the country was split into thirteen separate units. (One of these units was given to John Dunn, who, unable to maintain his neutrality when the British moved against the Zulus, had gone over to the British.) Third, white magistrates supplanted the chiefs as the most powerful men in their districts. And fourth, the land was partitioned leaving only about a third of the former kingdom in Zulu hands.

Before the war Theophilus Shepstone (British Secretary for Native Affairs) had expressed the hope that Cetshwayo's warriors would be 'changed to labourers working for wages'. That process had now begun.

The battle of Isandhlwana stands out as a high point of African resistance to colonisation. Now the highest honour of the African National Congress, 'Isandhlwana' was bestowed on Chief Albert Luthuli (former Rector of Glasgow University), Dr Yusuf Dadoo (a student at Edinburgh University in the 1930s) and Father (now Archbishop) Trevor Huddleston at the Congress of the People on 25-26 June 1955 at Kliptown when the Freedom Charter was adopted.

THE BOERS: THEIR INFAMOUS TREATMENT OF NATIVES

DAVID LIVINGSTONE

One of the difficulties with which the mission had to contend was the vicinity of the Boers of the Cashan Mountains, otherwise named 'Magaliesberg'. The word Boer simply means 'farmer', and is not synonymous with our word boor. The Magaliesberg Boers are not to be confounded with the Cape colonists, who sometimes pass by the name, and who for the most part are sober, industrious, and hospitable. Those, however, who have fled from English law, and have been joined by every variety of bad character, are of a very different stamp. Many of them felt aggrieved by the emancipation of their Hottentot slaves, and determined to remove to distant localities where they could erect themselves into a republic, and pursue without molestation the 'proper treatment of the blacks'. This 'proper treatment' has always involved the essential element of slavery, compulsory unpaid labour.

One section of this class of persons penetrated the interior as far as the Cashan Mountains, whence a Zulu or Caffre chief, named Mosilikatze, had been expelled by the well-known Caffre Dingaan. They came with the prestige of white men and deliverers; but the Bechuanas, who had just escaped the hard sway of the tyrannical Caffres, soon found, as they expressed it, 'that Mosilikatze was cruel to his enemies, and kind to those he conquered; but that the Boers destroyed their enemies, and made slaves of their friends'. The tribes, while retaining the semblance of independence, are forced to perform gratuitously all the labour of the fields, and have at the same time to support themselves. I have myself seen Boers come to a village, and, according to their custom, demand twenty or thirty women to weed their gardens. These poor creatures accordingly proceeded to the scene of unrequited toil, carrying their own food on their heads, their children on their backs, and instruments of labour on their shoulders. 'We make the people work for us,' said the Boers, 'in consideration of allowing them to live in our country'. During the several journeys I made to the enslaved tribes I was invariably treated by the whites with respect; but it is most unfortunate that they should have been left uncared for by their own Church till they have become as degraded as the blacks, whom the stupid prejudice against colour leads them to detest.

This new and mean species of slavery which they have adopted serves to supply the lack of field-labour only. The demand for domestic servants must be met by forays on tribes which have good supplies of cattle. The individuals among the Boers who would not engage in the raid for the sake of capturing slaves can seldom resist the two-fold plea of an intended uprising of the doomed tribe, and the prospect of a handsome share of the pilfered herds. It is difficult to conceive that men possessing the common attributes of humanity (and these Boers are by no means destitute of the better feelings of our nature) should set out, after caressing their wives and children, and proceed to shoot down men and women whose affections are as warm as their own. It was long before I could give credit to the tales of bloodshed told by native witnesses; but when I heard the Boers either bewailing or boasting the bloody scenes in which they had themselves been actors, I was compelled to admit the validity of the testimony. They are all traditionally religious, and trace their descent from some of the best men (Huguenots and Dutch) the world ever saw. In their own estimation they are the chosen people of God, and all the coloured race are 'black property' or 'creatures' - heathen given to them for an inheritance. Living in the midst of a much more numerous native population and at fountains removed many miles from each other, the Boers feel themselves insecure; and when they receive reports against any tribe from some dissatisfied black, the direst vengeance appears to the most midly disposed among them a simple measure of self-defence. However bloody the massacre, no qualms of conscience ensue. Indeed the leader, the late Mr Hendrick Potgeiter, believed himself to be the great peacemaker of the country. There is not, however, a single instance of the Bechuanas attacking either the Boers or the English. They have defended themselves when assailed, but have never engaged in offensive war with Europeans. We have a different tale to tell of the Caffres, and the result has been that from the hour they obtained fire-arms not one Boer has attempted to settle in Caffreland, or even to face the enemy in the field. These magnanimous colonists have manifested a marked antipathy to anything but 'long-shot' warfare, and, sidling away in their emigrations towards the more effeminate Bechuanas, have left their quarrels with the Caffres to be fought out by the English, and the wars to be paid for by English gold.

The Bakwains at Kolobeng had the spectacle of various tribes enslaved before their eyes. The Bakatla, the Batlókua, the Bahúkeng, the Bamosetla, and two other tribes were all groaning under the oppression of unrequited labour. This would not have been felt as so great an evil, but that the young men, as the only means of rising to importance, were in the habit of sallying forth to procure work in the Cape Colony. After labouring there three or four years, in building stone dykes and dams for the Dutch farmers, they were content if they could return at the end of that time with as many cows. On presenting one to their chief they ranked ever afterwards as respectable men in the tribe. These volunteers were highly esteemed among the Dutch, under the name of Mantátees, and received a shilling a day and a large loaf of bread between six of them. The system was distasteful to the Boers of the Cashan or Magaliesberg country. 'If they want,' it was said, 'to work, let them work for us their masters,' though these masters boasted that they would not pay for the services rendered. A law was made, in consequence, to deprive these poor fellows of their hardly-earned cattle, and compel them to labour gratis at home. Fraud becames as natural to the slave-owner as 'paying one's way' is to the rest of mankind.

Wherever a missionary lives, traders are sure to come; they are mutually dependent, and each aids the other; but experience shows that the two employments cannot well be combined in the same person. Nothing would be more fair, and apostolical too, than that the man who devotes his time to the spiritual welfare of a people should derive temporal advantage from upright commerce; but the present system of missions renders it inexpedient. No missionary with whom I ever came in contact traded; and while the traders, whom we introduced into the country, waxed rich, the missionaries have invariably remained poor. The Jesuits in Africa were wiser in their generation. They were a large community, and went on the plan of devoting the abilities of every one to that pursuit in which he was most likely to excel. One studied natural history, another literature, and a third, skilful in barter, was sent in search of ivory and gold-dust, that while pushing forward the mission to distant tribes he might yet afford pecuniary aid to the brethren whom he had left at the central settlement. We Protestants provide missionaries with a bare subsistence, and are unsparing in our praise of them for not being wordly-minded when our niggardliness compels them to live as did the prodigal son. I do not need to speak for myself, and for that very reason I feel at liberty to interpose a word in behalf of others. It is quite possible to find men whose devotion to the work of spreading the Gospel will make them ready to submit to any sacrifice. What, however, can be thought of the justice of Christians who not only work their agents at the lowest terms, but regard what they give as charity!

English traders had sold the Bakwains what the Boers most

dread, arms and ammunition. When the guns amounted to five, so
much alarm was excited among our neighbours that an expedition of
several hundred whites was seriously planned to seize these weapons.
Knowing that their owners would have fled to the Kalahari Desert
rather than deliver them up, I proceeded to the commandant, Mr
Gert Krieger, and prevailed upon him to defer the attack. He wished
in return that I should act as a spy over the people. I explained the
impossibility of compliance, even if my principles had not stood in
the way, by referring to an instance in which Sechele had gone,
unknown to me, with his whole force, to punish a rebellious under-
chief. This happened when we had just come to live with the
Bakwains. Sechele consulted me, and I advised mild measures. The
messengers he despatched to the rebel were answered by a taunt: 'He
only pretends to wish to follow the advice of the teacher: Sechele is
a coward; let him come and fight if he dare.' On the next offence
Sechele told me he was going to hunt elephants; and asked the loan
of a black-metal pot to cook with. I knew nothing further until we saw
the Bakwains carrying home their wounded, and heard some of the
women uttering the loud wail of sorrow for the dead, while others
pealed forth the clear scream of victory. It was then clear that Sechele
had attacked and driven away the rebel.

Having made this statement to the commandant, I had soon an
example how quickly a story can grow among idle people. The five
guns were, within one month, multiplied into five hundred, and the
cooking-pot, now in a museum at Cape Town, was magnified into a
cannon; 'I had myself confessed to the loan.' Where the five hundred
guns came from it was easy to divine; for, as I used a sextant, my
connection with Government was a thing of course; and, as I must
know all Her Majesty's counsels, I was questioned on the indistinct
rumours which had reached them of Lord Rosse's telescope. 'What
right,' said they, 'has your government to set up that large glass at the
Cape to look after us behind the Cashan Mountains?' Many of the
Boers visited us afterwards at Kolobeng, some for medical advice,
and others to trade in those very muskets and powder which their
own laws and policy forbad them to sell to the natives. Many
attempts were made during these visits to elicit the truth respecting
the guns and cannon. Espionage, which is a proof of barbarism, is as
well developed among the savages as in Austria or Russia, and every
man in a tribe feels himself bound to tell the chief all that comes to his
knowledge. Sechele was therefore acquainted with every question
put to his people, and asked me how they ought to answer. My reply
was, 'Tell the truth.' Every one then declared that no cannon existed;
and our friends, judging of the denial by what they themselves

would have said in similar circumstances, were only confirmed in the opinion that the Bakwains possessed artillery. This was in some degree beneficial to us; the fear it inspired prevented any foray in our direction for eight years.

During the whole of that period no winter passed without some of the tribes in the East country being plundered of both cattle and children by the Boers. It is only in winter, when horses can be used without danger of dying from disease, that these expeditions can take place. One or two friendly tribes are forced to accompany a party of mounted Boers, and are ranged in front to form 'a shield'. The Boers then coolly fire over their heads till the devoted people flee and leave cattle, wives, and children to the captors. This was done in nine cases during my residence in the interior, and on no occasion was a drop of Boer blood shed. Letters were repeatedly sent by them to Sechele ordering him to surrender himself as their vassal, and stop English traders from proceeding into the country with firearms for sale. He replied, 'I was made an independent chief and placed here by God, and not by you. I was never conquered by Mosilikatze, as those tribes whom you rule over; and the English are my friends. I get everything I wish from them. I cannot hinder them from going where they like.'

I attempted to benefit the tribes among the Boers of Magaliesberg by placing native teachers at different points. 'You must teach the blacks,' said Mr Hendrick Potgeiter, the commandant in chief, 'that they are not equal to us.' Other Boers said, 'I might as well teach the baboons on the rocks as the Africans.' These sneerers declined my proposition to examine whether they or my native attendants could read best. When Sir George Cathcart proclaimed the independence of the Boers, a treaty was made with them by which they undertook to allow the English a free passage to the country beyond, and to abolish slavery. 'But what about the missionaries?' they inquired. *'You may do as you please with them,'* is said to have been the answer of the 'Commissioner'. This remark, if uttered at all, was probably made in joke. The general belief in its seriousness doubtless led to the destruction of three mission stations immediately after. The Boers, four hundred in number, were sent by the late Mr Pretorius to attack the Bakwains in 1852, and, besides slaughtering a considerable number of adults, carried off two hundred of our school-children into slavery. The people under Sechele defended themselves till the approach of night enabled them to flee to the mountains; and having killed a number of the enemy, the first ever slain by Bechuanas, I had the credit of having taught them to destroy Boers! My house was plundered in revenge. English gentlemen, who had come in the footsteps of Mr Cumming to hunt in the country beyond, and had left large quantities of stores in the keeping of the natives, were robbed of everything; and when they came back to Kolobeng found the skeletons of the guardians strewed about the place. The books of a good library - my solace in our solitude - were torn to pieces and scattered about. My stock of medicines was smashed; and all our furniture and clothing were carried off and sold by public auction to pay the expenses of the foray.

From *Missionary Travels and Researches in South Africa* (1899)

PROTEST ON BEHALF OF BOER INDEPENDENCE 1881

ROBERT LOUIS STEVENSON

I was a Jingo when Jingoism was in season, and I own I pall myself still of like passions with the Jingo. But, sir, it may be possible for you to understand that a man may be a Jingo and yet a man; that he may have been a Jingo from a sense, perhaps mistaken, of the obligations, the greatness and the danger of his native land, and not from any brutal greed of aggrandisement or cheap love of drums and regimental columns. A man may love these also, and be honest. But there often comes a time and the changes of circumstances, when a man is pleased to have held certain opinions in the past, that he may denounce them with the more authority in the present. I was not ashamed to be the countryman of Jingoes; but I am beginning to grow ashamed of being the kin of those who are now fighting - I should rather say, who are now sending brave men to fight - in this unmanly Transvaal war. It is neither easy nor needful to justify these changes of opinion. We all awake somewhat late to a sense of what is just; and it is ordinarily by something merely circumstantial that the sense is awakened. A man may have been right or wrong before, but it adds some weight to his intense conviction if his former thoughts were of a different and even contrary spirit. Now, sir, I am at the present hour - in company, I am sure, with all the most honourable and considerate of my countrymen - literally grilling in my own blood about this wicked business. It is no affair of ours if the Boers are capable of self-government or not; we have made it sufficiently plain to Europe of late days that we ourselves are not as a whole the most harmonious nation upon earth. That Colley and all his brave fellows are gone for ever, that we have been beaten and fairly beaten, by the stalwart little state are not, to my mind, arguments for any prolongation of the war, but for an instant, honourable submission. We are in the wrong, or all that we profess is false; blood has been shed, glory lost, and, I fear, honour also. But if any honour yet remains or any chivalry, that is certainly the only chivalrous or honourable course, for the strong to accept his buffet and do justice, already tardy, to the weak whom he has misused and who has so crushingly retorted. Another Majuba

D

Hill, with the result reversed, and we shall treat, I hear; but that may be long of coming; and in the meanwhile, many of our poor soldiers - many of them true patriots - must fall. There may come a time in the history of England - for that is not yet concluded - when she also shall come to be oppressed by some big neighbour; and if I may not say there is a God in heaven, I may say at least there is a justice in the chain of causes that shall make England drain a bucket of her best blood for every drop she now exacts from the Transvaal. As if, sir, there were any prestige like the prestige of being just; or any generosity like that of owning and repairing an injustice; as if in this troubled time, and with all our fair (?) and plucky history, there were any course left to this nation but to hold back the sword of vengeance and bare the head to that state, possibly enough misguided, whom we have tried ineffectually to brutalise!

From *Essays, Literary and Critical*

THE END OF THE BOER WAR

Trevor Royle

Britain gained little materially from the Boer War. The secure, British-dominated South Africa of Milner's dreams never material-ised and, by 1907, both the Transvaal and the Orange Free State were self-governing. Three years later the Union of South Africa was proclaimed and its first president was Louis Botha. For a military nation supposed to be capable of controlling and guarding its world empire, great defects had been exposed in the British Army, both in terms of its equipment and management and in its size and mobility: it was for those reasons that Brodrick asked Kitchener to be the new broom at the War Office. But however much Britain's stock had fallen in the eyes of the world, and however clear it had become to the politicians that 'splendid isolation' was no longer a feasible interna-tional policy, Kitchener's peace was not without its advantages. During the two world wars of the twentieth century South African troops fought on Britain's side, thereby justifying Kitchener's hopes, expressed at the victory banquet in Johannesburg on 17 June, that the Boers would be 'an asset of considerable importance to the British empire'. His handling of the Boers at Vereeniging, and his ability to acknowledge their sense of pride and patriotism, undoubtedly helped to bring about a lasting peace. If he failed to see that the treaty signed away the political rights of the native and coloured populations - one of Chamberlain's arguments for going to war in 1899 had been Britain's duty to rescue them from Boer serfdom - then he was no more or less blinkered than any other British politician or civil servant involved in the negotiations. To pay for white unity at the peace table, the black and coloured majority were sacrificed, and the legacy of the clause in the Treaty of Vereeniging lives on in South Africa today: the notorious Article 8 (no enfranchisement of the native population until *after* Boer self-government) has been used on several occasions by successive South African governments during this century as their principal constitutional justification for the gradual implementation of a colour bar.

Kitchener returned to Britain on 20 June 1902, travelling from Cape Town on the *Orotava* . On the day of his departure all the ships in the great harbour were dressed in bunting from bow to stern,

cheering crowds lined the quays, a military band played 'Auld Lang
Syne'...The enthusiastic scenes were repeated at Southampton on 11
July when the *Orotava* docked there at 8.50 am. Twenty-five minutes
later Kitchener, still wearing his South African service dress, came
down the gangplank with French and Hamilton to be met by a
military delegation and the Mayor of Southampton who later presented him with the freedom of his town - in thanking him Kitchener
was careful to request that the town's welcome to the returning
soldiers would take a 'non-alcoholic direction'. Then, having accepted
the Mayor's words of welcome, he pushed his way through the
crowds to inspect his guard of honour, a unit of Yeomanry and a
detachment of the Cameron Highlanders, his headquarters' guard in
South Africa and his favourite regiment in the Sudan. It was an
emotional moment: he had pulled every string to have the Camerons
accompany him on the *Orotava* but to no avail. They had been detailed to travel at a later date on the *Walmer Castle*. While pushing
through the western approaches, however, the faster Union Castle
vessel had overtaken the *Orotava* and Kitchener had immediately
ordered the captain to signal the passing liner that he expected the
presence of the Camerons on the quay at Southampton. Much to
Kitchener's chagrin there was no response to the signal but the
Camerons had seen it. Kitchener was mightily pleased to see them
and their presence put him in a high good humour. For the first time
in public he dropped his martial mask and beamed at everyone
around him - it was on this occasion that the famous 'laughing
cavalier' snapshot was taken, the only known photograph that
shows him smiling in public.

  After receiving the freedom of Southampton, and shortly before
eleven o'clock, he joined the special train that was waiting to take him
to London and further triumphal ceremonies. The carriages were
covered in bunting and the engine, a spanking new Drummond four-
wheeled couple-bogie express No.773, carried in front a huge 'K'
surrounded by laurel leaves. At Basingstoke it stopped briefly to
allow that borough also to make Kitchener a freeman and at 12.50 it
pulled into a beflagged and garlanded Paddington Station where
Kitchener was met by the Prince of Wales, the Dukes of Cambridge
and Connaught and by Lord Roberts, the Commander-in-Chief.
After a few brief words of welcome the party left in open carriages on
a triumphal procession from Paddington through Hyde Park and
Constitution Hill to St James's Palace where Kitchener was entertained
to lunch. The King's Coronation, which was supposed to have taken
place a fortnight earlier, had been postponed due to Edward VII's
illness and the grandstands erected along the processional route had

fortuitously been pressed into service for Kitchener's homecoming. It was a sensible move: thousands of Londoners had been waiting since dawn to catch a glimpse of Kitchener - the last time for many years that the capital city would be able to turn out in such numbers to welcome home a conquering hero.

In the afternoon the king presented Kitchener with the Grand Cross of St Michael and St George and made him a member of the newly founded Order of Merit. To those honours were added promotion to full general and he was also created a Viscount, taking the title Kitchener of Khartoum and of Vaal in the Colony of Transvaal and of Aspall in the County of Suffolk. Parliament thanked him and awarded him £50,000 which he was rumoured to have invested in the Rand goldfields. While it was true that, like other investors interested in post-war South Africa, Kitchener did put some money into Rand gold, he was by then too wily a bird to give his enemies any opportunity of casting financial doubts over his reputation. On 26 January 1902 he had refused to take out shares in the South Africa Cold Storage Company as it had been awarded an army contract and his honourable dealings in personal money matters continued until shortly before his death when he sold shares in a Canadian munitions firm after Lloyd George had contracted it to supply military weapons to the British Army. Not that Kitchener was indifferent to his own finances. Since the 1890s his financial adviser had been Sir Arthur Renshaw who remained a shrewd consultant and friend: in 1902 Kitchener became godfather to Renshaw's son, jocularly telling his friend that he had done 'his duty nobly on that score'. Renshaw performed other equally noble duties. Under his astute guidance Kitchener's bounty was placed in such growth areas as railway construction in Costa Rica, Mexico and the United States and in addition he looked after Kitchener's various family trust funds. While serving abroad in India and Egypt Kitchener had to meet fairly stiff expenses over and above his official allowances and that entailed considerable juggling of investments between Kitchener's bank accounts in Cairo, Calcutta and London.

In addition to his public rewards, Kitchener had also managed to bring back a good deal of loot from South Africa including the statues of the Boer leaders which he had removed from Pretoria and Bloemfontein and which he wanted to place in his own grounds once he had acquired a suitable country house. Until that happy time they were stored in the headquarters of the Royal Engineers at Chatham but in 1909, after discreet representations by the Colonial Office, they were quietly returned to South Africa.

The country, too, was anxious to pay its respects to Kitchener and

the summer of 1902 saw him accepting the freedoms of several
English towns as well as being much in demand as a speaker at public
occasions. Kitchener hated making public speeches and very rarely
departed from the texts which were prepared for him by his ADCs.
When confronted by the need to make an impromptu official utterance
his usual means of defence was to excuse himself by saying that his
audience probably knew more about the subject than he did. Only
once did a public speech of his give a revelation of the inner man. That
was in South Africa when he replied to Milner's eulogy at the victory
banquet in the Wanderers' Hall in Johannesburg. Choking with
emotion he touched briefly on the life of the soldier in the veldt, on
the early morning rides, the tang of woodsmoke and the sense of
shared comradeship. 'Though you may have to toil as before,' he told
his audience, largely made up of soldiers, 'you can never quite be the
same again. You have tasted the salt of life and its savour will never
leave you.' Even Milner's patrician Balliol mind was forced to admit
that it had been a good speech and that Kitchener had spoken well,
if perhaps over-briefly; but that sense of soldierly reserve only served
to add to the aura of martial glamour that surrounded Kitchener.
Wherever he went in the months after his homecoming large crowds
turned up to listen to him and to cheer him to the echo. And just as
he had done in the wake of the Omdurman celebrations, he let it be
known that instead of swords of honour he would prefer to be
presented with gifts of gold plate or furniture. Those requests were
eagerly granted and by the time Kitchener arrived in India he
possessed several sumptuous, though usually too garish to be called
tasteful, dinner sets which it gave him great pleasure to show off
when he entertained. It was a far cry from Suakin days and those
letters to Millie entreating her to send him out a set of plates for his
household in the governor's residence.

In the midst of the public adulation there were again those who
refused to be charmed by Kitchener's victory in South Africa and
who argued that his strategy had been brutal and uncaring. They
pointed to the bludgeon of the blockhouse system and the associated
sweeps and drives, to the wholesale burning of farms and above all
to the introduction of the concentration camps. Today the words
'concentration camp' are inextricably bound up with the policies of
the Nazi regime in Germany, and so emotive is their use that the
association of Kitchener's name with their introduction in South
Africa would be enough to damn him were it not for the facts. When
Goering pointed out to the British ambassador in Berlin that the
English introduced the term 'concentration camp' to the world, he
was merely employing sophistry to deflect British complaints about

the wholesale internment of Jews and other innocents. There is no connection between the purpose of the British internment camps in South Africa and the purpose of the Nazi death camps in Germany and eastern Europe; the former were introduced for the protection of the population, the latter for extermination. That said, the British camps in South Africa were far from being places of recreation.

As the conflict in South Africa gradually turned into a guerrilla war at the beginning of 1901 both sides realised that Boer women and children were bound to be caught up in the front line of the fighting. Farms were used by the Boers as bases and Kitchener's tactics of farm-burning meant that a large proportion of the population would be made homeless, hence the introduction of the protected laagers, or concentration camps, along the main railway routes. At the Middelburg peace talks Kitchener had told Botha that as long as the Boers continued to put pressure on their fellow countrymen to provide help for the commandos, he would be 'forced to take the very unpleasant and repugnant step of bringing in the women and children'. Between then and the war's end 120,000 Boers were herded into fifty camps; of that number 26,000, mainly women and children, were destined to die of disease.

The presence of the camps and a death rate of 21% amongst their inhabitants were difficult matters to keep from the public gaze, even though Kitchener did his utmost to divert attention from them by constantly offering bland answers to Brodrick's questions. That they did become a matter for public debate was due in no small measure to the resourcefulness and energy of a remarkable woman, Emily Hobhouse, the daughter of a Cornish rector. Kitchener called her a 'bloody woman' and on her second visit to South Africa in October 1901 he had her arrested as a security risk before she could leave her ship in Cape Town harbour. (On being repatriated she attempted to start legal proceedings against him, an action that appealed greatly to Kitchener's grim sense of humour.) By then, though, she had fulfilled the main points of a task that had begun that January - visiting the camps on behalf of the South African Women and Children's Defence Fund and making public her report. Those findings were not pleasing to the British conscience. 'If only the English people would try to exercise a little imagination and picture the whole miserable scene,' she reported back to her committee. Families had been herded, lock, stock and barrel, into the tented camps and forced to live on a meagre diet, medical facilities were primitive, water was frequently polluted, domestic arrangements squalid and no account had been made of the differing social and cultural backgrounds of the inmates. Many of the Boer families came from the remote areas of the Transvaal where they lived in basic conditions of isolation: their ideas of domestic hygiene tended to be very different from those held by Boers who lived nearer the towns. In those chaotic conditions disease became a daily companion - at the time of Miss Hobhouse's visit to the camps 30% of all the children were dead or dying of enteric fever, dysentery, typhoid, malaria, in addition to the illnesses commonly associated with childhood, such as measles, whooping cough and diphtheria. The spectre of so many children being put at risk smacked too much of the Black Death and Emily Hobhouse's findings caused an outcry of righteous anger in the liberal press.

Henry Campbell-Bannerman, the Liberal leader, was moved to call Kitchener's camps the 'methods of barbarism' and other politicians readily took up the cause. Keir Hardie and Lloyd George spoke vehemently on Emily Hobhouse's behalf and much to the discomfort of the Conservative administration, angry questions began to be asked in the House of Commons. In the European press Britain stood accused of waging a war of extermination and it is not an exaggeration to say that the war in South Africa in 1901 was as unpopular in the international community as the Vietnam war was in the 1960s. Brodrick pushed Kitchener hard on the subject but in the middle of 1901 Kitchener was too preoccupied with the problems thrown up by the fighting to concern himself with the camps which were controlled by two senior officers, John Maxwell and Hamilton Goold-Adams. For his part Kitchener preferred not to visit the camps and brushed off Brodrick's questions by telling him that he was told that the inhabitants were 'happy enough'. On the question of hygiene he also said, tongue-in-cheek, that he was considering prosecuting those mothers found neglecting their children. Kitchener looked on the camps as a means to an end and he found the details of administration boring. When political pressure began to build up he was equally happy to release those families who wanted to return to the Boer commandos. In December he wrote to De Wet informing him that 'all women and children at present in our camps who are willing to leave will be sent to your care, and I shall be happy to be informed where you desire that they should be handed over to you'. To Kitchener's satisfaction several families took advantage of the offer for he knew that they would be a burden on De Wet's commandos.

Emily Hobhouse's revelations did bring about some improvements. A Ladies Committee, headed by Mrs Millicent Fawcett, was despatched to South Africa and their recommendations led to an improvement in the conditions of the camps which by the end of the year were under the civilian control of Lord Milner. He was shocked by what he found.

It was not until six weeks or two months ago that it dawned on me personally (I cannot speak for others) that the enormous mortality was not incidental to the first formation of the camps and the sudden inrush of thousands of people already starving, but was going to continue. The fact that it continues is no doubt a condemnation of the camp system. The whole thing, I think now, has been a mistake.

Today in South Africa Kitchener is remembered not as the victor of Paardeberg, not even as the engineer of the peace of Vereeniging. It is for the concentration camps that his name lives on. Visitors to the museums devoted to the Boer war - which South Africans know as the *Tweede Vryheidsoorlog* (Second War of Independence) - are shown the powdered glass which Kitchener is supposed to have ordered to be sprinkled in the sugar given to the inmates of the camps, and there are stories of other outrages - such as poisoned food and fish-hooks deliberately inserted in the bully beef. There is no more evidence for believing that Kitchener would have been the agent of such atrocities than there is for believing the other *canard* of the Boer War, that he shipped out prostitutes from London to Pretoria in order to compromise his senior officers and to discover which of them should be sacked for military inefficiency. In both cases the facts are somewhat different. When the camps were first opened Kitchener ordered that there should be a basic ration scale made up of imported foodstuffs. Much of it was inferior in quality and caused violent stomach upsets which spread rapidly, leaving the Boer women to believe that they had been poisoned. There was also a blue substance in the sugar used as a whitening agent and its presence gave rise to the stories of powdered glass. As for the prostitutes, Kitchener had no need of them: when he purged his staff after taking command he simply marched into the leading hotels in Pretoria and sacked those officers whom he considered to be bar-room loafers.

As Milner admitted, the camps were a dreadful mistake and their existence a terrible blot in the pages of British history, but it would be unfair to make Kitchener shoulder the whole blame for the blunders that led to so many unnecessary deaths. 'War is war,' admitted Brodrick when questioned on the subject in the House of Commons and there was some truth in his idle cliché. In deciding to wage a guerrilla war the Boers knew that their families would inevitably be dragged into the conflict. In countering those tactics with his sweeps and drives and his farm-burning Kitchener created a situation which both sides agreed could only be salved by 'the repugnant step of bringing in the women and children'. That it led to tragedy was due less to a policy of indifference than to a lack of foresight. The British Army, busy fighting a war, could not provide the best facilities for the camps, some of which were better than others; the lack of hygiene and of a decent diet sealed the fate of thousands, while the absence of medical supplies and personnel accounted for many of the rest. Military expediency can never be an excuse for uncaring brutality but in 1901 the camps seemed to Kitchener to be the only sure means of protecting the families of those Boers who had surrendered and of providing shelter for those made homeless. Since he was also being pressed by the politicians to bring the war to a swift conclusion, the camps offered a convenient short-cut to bring that about.

As so often happens in the tragedy of war the real victims are the innocent civilians. South Africa was no exception.

From *The Kitchener Enigma* (1985)

RADICALS AND SOUTH AFRICA, 1899-1902; A CASE OF MISTAKEN IDENTITY?

JOHN HARGREAVES

> Some of us [in Senegal in 1900] were members of the musical society 'La Lyre de Saint Louis...' As I was never an outstanding instrumentalist, I am surprised to find that I still know the words and music of the Transvaal national anthem...We enjoyed listening to and playing this hymn, under the impression that it was the emancipation of the natives of South Africa that was at stake in the war between Britain and her former dependency. (Lamine Gueye, *Itinéraire africain*, 1966).

A Senegalese band saluting the forerunners of apartheid! This veteran nationalist could smile ironically at his youthful misunderstanding, but during the South African War of 1899-1902 most British radicals and socialists were equally ready to identify President Kruger, the epitome of Afrikaner nationalism, as the prime victim of British imperialism. Indeed, the anti-imperialist tradition of the British left largely developed out of its critiques of this war against the 'Boers'; J A Hobson's seminal work of 1902, *Imperialism: A Study*, was largely inspired by his experience in South Africa. Yet today Kruger's successors are universally seen as imperialists rather than as victims. It seems worth considering why such an identification was made, and how far radical contemporaries, in Scotland or elsewhere, were conscious that there were other sufferers in the South African conflict.

In the 'khaki' election of 1900 the justice of the war, and of the methods by which the Unionist government was conducting it, were central issues. Supporters of Joseph Chamberlain, the Birmingham radical turned colonial expansionist, made no secret of their faith in imperialism. Robert Williams, Unionist candidate for North Aberdeen, summarised their case: 'I believe in a strong and united Empire, as it is an instrument in the betterment of the world and the preservation of peace. It also leads to commercial development, giving more trade to the country and better wages to the workers.' But many Liberals either shared these beliefs or found it politically inexpedient to oppose them. Once the Transvaal had been pushed into declaring war, patriotism produced a sort of 'Falklands factor';

as the Liberal leader Campbell-Bannerman noted, 'The very difficulties of the war...help the Government in the country'. This was notably true in constituencies where many men were serving with Highland regiments; Sutherland and East Aberdeenshire were both lost to the Unionists. But the 'social imperialist' argument that colonial markets would provide jobs and keep up wages could also prove effective in industrial constituencies.

So the more critical Liberals found it difficult to respond coherently. Some concentrated their attack on the origins of the war, accusing Chamberlain of complicity with financiers concerned to obtain control of the Rand and its gold mines. One problem here was that the leading imperial entrepreneur, Cecil Rhodes, had closer links with Liberal than with Unionist politicians - as did Chamberlain's forceful pro-consul, Alfred Milner. Rather than pursuing the investigations begun after Jameson's raid of 1895, some found it safer to make vaguer allegations about other capitalists of cosmopolitan origin; anti-imperialism sometimes took on a racist and anti-Semitic flavour. Middle class Gladstonian Liberals were on surer moral ground in denouncing the attack on Afrikaner nationality; the young Lloyd George, increasingly conscious of his own Welsh identity, was particularly eloquent about the rights of small nations, and this theme was also heard in Scotland. Those who followed this line were in turn denounced as 'pro-Boers', a term of political abuse in Britain, but one which accurately described the consensus of world opinion. Kruger became a hero to enemies of British imperialism, in Europe and beyond.

In 1990 it seems curious that the Afrikaner ancestors of apartheid should be cast as the prime victims of imperialism. For the main losers by the war were of course the African majority. A recent book by Peter Warwick emphasises that, though both Boers and British were anxious that their conflict should remain a 'white man's war', both sides often had in practice to depend on collaboration with non-whites. Both armies made extensive use of African and Coloured non-combatants for transport, construction and especially for intelligence-gathering; and as the war went on the British increasingly issued such units with firearms - Kitchener admitted doing so in over 10,000 cases. Resistance to the Boers was also organised by irregular forces under African leadership - by Zulu, Pedi, Kgotla, among others - and locally raised black forces played a significant part in Baden-Powell's defence of Mafeking, where their plight was worse than the better publicised sufferings of the whites.

Non-white leaders in the British colonies mostly supported the war; they had some reason to hope that British victory would (to quote a resolution by the Natal Native Congress in June 1900):

> ... safeguard Native races from restrictive legislation in regard to (1) education (2) a certain amount of direct representation in the Legislatures of the different states (3) freedom of trade (4) acquisition of land.

Whereas the Boer Republics confined the franchise to white men, in Cape Colony 6633 Africans and 14,388 Coloureds made up 15% of the electorate (in 1909) (though in Natal the figures were only 50 and 6), and some Liberal Imperialists, like the Methodist minister Hugh Price Hughes, claimed that Britain was fighting for African interests. Much was made of Cecil Rhodes' slogan, 'Equal rights for all civilised men'. Even in Europe it was still acceptable that the degree of 'civilisation' qualifying for the franchise should be defined by education and property as well as gender; but whereas the general tendency was to lower or abolish such qualifications, in the Cape Rhodes himself had in 1892 put them up, to exclude any risk of an eventual non-white majority. Few however doubted that, whatever injustices might be sanctioned by British colonial law, the educational opportunities and political rights of Africans would be still less favoured under Afrikaner rule. There were no 'pro-Boers' among the black South African élite.

Whether their economic and social prospects would be improved by British victory was a different matter. The key issue in the war now seems to have been not so much the physical control of the gold-fields themselves (many capitalists had already struck satisfactory bargains with the Transvaal government) as their access to a large unskilled labour force, under legislative and fiscal conditions which would facilitate the profitable development of the mining industry. This aim was fully shared by Milner and the British Colonial administration, who looked to the mines to provide resources for a great new British dominion. Although there would be room for non-white enterprise at the lower levels of its society, fiscal and land policies were geared to turn African tribesmen towards labour in the mines, under conditions whose general nature was already clear. The industry needed a large supply of short-term male migrants, whose recruitment and residence would be closely regulated by Pass laws and other forms of state control, and whose employment would be subject to colour bars designed to restrict skilled occupations to whites. Although it was not immediately obvious, the economic foundations, if not the ideological refinements of apartheid, were already inherent in the British victory.

In the event, even the hopes for political freedom (which might have enabled African electors to mitigate the oppressive hardships

3. COMING EVENTS CAST THEIR SHADOWS BEFORE
Cartoon from the *BON ACCORD* of 27 September 1900

which awaited their people) were to be disappointed. In 1902 a war-weary British government agreed not to raise the question of 'granting the franchise to natives' in the Orange Free State and Transvaal until the Afrikaner population had recovered self-government; but once this happened, in 1906-07, votes for Africans were firmly excluded. The formation of the Union of South Africa in 1910, hailed as a triumph of Liberal imperialism, was based on a consensus among Europeans in the four colonies which, while preserving the restricted non-European franchise in Cape Province, left it at the mercy of a Union electorate which became progressively less liberal as the century went on. Dignified appeals and petitions to Westminster made little impression in face of Britain's dependence on collaboration with white South Africa; the South African Native National Congress, founded in 1912, had a long and unrewarding road to follow. The many non-Europeans who put faith in the British Empire had very little to show for it.

Ironically, British critics of imperialism, by identifying themselves as defenders of Afrikaner rights, actually weakened the position of non-whites. Liberal and Labour MPs elected in 1906 were ready to acclaim the grant of responsible government to the Boers as a triumph of generous statesmanship rather than an abdication of imperial trusteeship. By concentrating on the imperialist iniquities of Chamberlain, Rhodes, and their associates, the British Left seems to have mistaken the identity of the principal victims. The only question is: how completely? Is it true that the interests of non-whites were completely ignored in the 'khaki' election of 1900? For a preliminary impression it may be useful to look at the experience of a Scottish city later prominent in the Anti-Apartheid movement.

Since the Parliamentary reform of 1885 Aberdeen has been divided into two electoral constituencies, both of which returned Liberal candidates until 1918. Its political culture has always combined proud parochialism with some internationalism of outlook. Middle class commitment to the anti-slavery movement was by the end of the century turning into support for colonial expansion, rationalised as necessary to save Africans from the new slavery supposedly represented by Portuguese or Arab rule. Towards such Africans as, rather rarely, visited the town, press and people displayed a rather patronising goodwill. Shortly before the election crowds lined the streets to cheer a detachment of the West African Force on its way to Balmoral; the *Free Press* not only praised the beaming smiles of the barefoot Yorubas, but noted how at Castlehill Barracks they 'overshadowed the majority of the [Scottish] recruits in appearance'. But such benevolent interest was not matched by awareness of the real problems of Africans in a country to which Aberdeen was beginning to send a growing number of emigrants.

Yet three of the city's four Parliamentary candidates in 1900 could claim some South African experience. Captain D V Pirie, MP for Aberdeen North since 1896, was actually on staff service in South Africa during 1900 - which did not prevent him from being attacked as a 'pro-Boer' on the strength of votes critical of government policy. James Bryce, MP for South Aberdeen since 1885 and a former Liberal minister, was a more weighty figure. A distinguished academic lawyer with a somewhat oracular style, Bryce was criticised for holding aloof from the domestic concerns of his constituency, which he visited twice a year. In 1895 he had published a substantial volume recording his *Impressions of South Africa* which was frequently cited in contemporary debates. A chapter dealing with the non-white population was, if allowance is made for prevailing racialist vocabulary and assumptions, not unperceptive. Bryce recognised that 'the strong feeling of dislike and contempt - one might almost say of hostility' between white and black was strongest among Afrikaners, but recognised that the British shared such attitudes. Economic development would increase the number of 'semi-civilised' Africans qualified to vote; meanwhile legislation should aim 'to safeguard the private rights of the native and to secure for him his due share of the land'. But this was a minor theme; Bryce concentrated his attacks, both in Parliament and in his election speeches, on the failings of British policy towards the Boers.

Robert Williams, Liberal Unionist candidate for North Aberdeen, had left the city as a young engineer of twenty-one, and made a fortune by working with Cecil Rhodes, in the Kimberley diamond-fields and then in the Rand gold mines. He shared Rhodes' ambitions to push the financial and political frontiers of the British empire northwards, and had recently founded the Tanganyika Concessions Company, which would play important roles in the twentieth century histories of the Belgian Congo and Portuguese Angola. This capitalist entrepreneur nevertheless made a serious bid for working-class votes. The Aberdeen labour movement had for some years been questioning its historic alliance with the Liberal Party. Social tensions (exemplified by Liberal councillors' reluctance to fix evening meetings, which working colleagues could attend without loss of wages) were increasingly reinforced by socialist critiques from the growing Social Democratic Federation and Independent Labour Party. Unionists perceived that only labour voters could break the Liberal hold on North Aberdeen; in a by-election of 1896 they gave a clear run to the Socialist Tom Mann, who came within 500 votes of unseating

Pirie. And in 1900 Williams attempted to secure endorsement by the Trades Council, emphasising his support for such causes as old age pensions, workmen's compensation, slum clearance and promising an open mind on the eight-hour day. On such issues (which, in Aberdeen as elsewhere, were the most important ones for many electors) some trade unionists preferred Williams' positions to those of the Liberals. But the Trades Council had already registered its opposition to 'a war ... in the interests of Jewish and British speculators' and for this reason resolved to support Bryce and Pirie. Nevertheless Williams with 35% of the poll achieved the best Unionist result of the period in North Aberdeen, and his social imperialism clearly attracted many working-class supporters.

There were a few references in election meetings to non-Europeans, chiefly by Unionists who sought Church support by arguing that they would have a better future in a British South Africa than under the Boers. Professor John Dove Wilson, a Unionist lawyer who had appeared on SDF platforms, recalled that Scottish missionaries 'from Livingstone down to Stewart (he might have added the Aberdonian John Philip) had told them how infamous the conduct of the Boers had been ... the native in Africa, Black though he be, should be treated as a human being and with every manner of justice'. The Reverend C C Macdonald, minister of St Clements since 1879, who had preached at the inaugural Congress of the Scottish TUC and supported Tom Mann in 1896, took a prominent part in Williams' campaign. Two clergymen from Johannesburg, Brown and Phillips, also appeared on Unionist platforms, the latter claiming that British victory would 'break the shackles of the natives'. But the clearest statement on this issue came from W C Smith, the second Unionist candidate, on 22 September:

> ... the Boer constitution not only failed to recognize any rights in the blacks in that country but it expressly said that neither then nor at any future time would any Black in South Africa enjoy any civil or other rights. They treated the blacks - the Kaffirs - as men beneath their feet, as dumb and driven cattle. He asked them not to imagine that these Kaffirs were savages roaming about the plains of South Africa. They were intelligent men, entering business, getting on in life, many of them extremely prosperous.

Few labour voters however were primarily interested in Africans' political rights. James Leatham, an eloquent and attractive disciple of William Morris, argued in his pamphlet *What is the Good of Empire?* that 'imperialism has proved a curse to the inferior races'; but, resigning himself to the possibility that such races might go down before the 'Caucasians', he concentrated on the damage which imperialism did at home. But many trade unionists, nationally and locally, were suspicious of the labour policies of South African capitalists, becoming 'pro-Boers' because of their mistrust of Rhodes. William Diack, a socialist stonemason, wrote a pamphlet on *Boer and Briton in South Africa* in which, after comparing Afrikaner patriots to Bruce and Wallace, he claimed that they had 'placed the Kaffirs on an equality with the white man before the law'. Quoting a description by a British mine-worker of living conditions in the Rand compounds, he cited predictions by associates of Rhodes that British government in the Transvaal would reduce labour costs by 20% - by importing Chinese coolies and by fiscal pressure on Africans to enter the labour market. Diack did not dwell on the suggestion that this would also drive down wages of skilled white workers; but in some constituencies fears of 'cheap Black labour' competing with skilled British emigrants were used to counter Unionist claims that the demand to enfranchise the 'Uitlanders' reflected their concern for British artisans.

Diack was well aware of the social and legal disabilities of blacks in the British colonies, and heckled Smith on the subject at his meeting of 25 September. But in general it seems to have been the Gladstonian principle of respect for the rights of small nations, sharpened in the Scottish context, which determined Aberdonian attitudes to the war. J H Elric, President of the Trades Council, summed this up at Bryce's eve-of-poll meeting:

> The Trades Council had for two years recognised that there was a conservative force in the Transvaal and that there was a progressive force fighting against the Transvaal government. But they also recognised the time-honoured old maxim of loving their neighbours as themselves and recognising that other nationalities could be just as patriotic as ours and should be respected when they were prepared to stand by their opinions and sacrifice their lives for their liberties.

But some of his colleagues opposed the war out of distrust of South African capitalists and fears about the future of labour in a British Transvaal, rather than respect for Afrikaner nationalism.

In Aberdeen this distrust was focused on the person of Rhodes' colleague Robert Williams. Although the daily press was wholly Unionist, the *Bon Accord*, an illustrated weekly journal of local news and gossip which was edited by the socialist W N Cameron, gave space to radical critics. Early in the war a correspondent compared a recent disfranchisement of Indians in Natal with official concern about votes for Uitlanders; and an atrocious parody of Kipling declared that:

> The enemies of Boer and Briton are
> The capitalists and all their 'devil's fry'.

On 20 September 1900 Cameron urged electors to press Williams on labour policy, suggesting that his friend Rhodes was hoping 'to extend still further his compound slave system - and introduce Asiatic labour as well - and the more he succeeds the higher will be his ill-gotten dividend and the worse the lot of white labour'. Only a few questions on the subject appear in press reports of election meetings; but a week later the *Bon Accord* printed a cartoon of a workman entitled 'North Aberdeen' applying the brake to a rickshaw in which Rhodes and Williams were being drawn by one African and one Chinese coolie.

The association with Rhodes may have been unfair to Williams, whose later enterprises in Katanga and Angola practised what for the time were progressive labour policies, based on the permanent residence of African families; but Cameron had seized a point about the rights of African workers. Two years later the *Bon Accord* was more cynical than its contemporaries about the lavish entertainment which Williams offered on Deeside to the Lozi king Lewanika: 'If he falls into the hands of the South African financier he and his Kingdom will be engineered to some purpose'. And in 1904 Aberdeen's civic hospitality to the Alake of Abeokuta was compared with the lot of:

> The slaving, sweating jigger
> You keep as your gold digger.

It would be unhistorical to expect the Aberdeen public of 1900 to have shown deep understanding of the issues at stake for non-Europeans in South Africa, but some electors at least had glimpsed the issues which would later inspire the city's Anti-Apartheid Movement.

THE CRY OF SOUTH AFRICA

Give back my dead!
They who by kop and fountain
First saw the light upon my rocky breast!
Give back my dead
The sons who played upon me
When childhood's dews still rested on their heads.
Give back my dead
Whom thou hast riven from me
By arms of men loud called from earth's farthest bound
To wet my bosom with my children's blood!
Give back my dead,
The dead who grew up on me!

(Wagenaar's Kraal, Three Sisters, 9 May 1900)

OLIVE SCHREINER

MR SOL PLAATJE ON SLAVERY IN SOUTH AFRICA

Forward[*], *20 December 1919*

Many people were under the impression that the interests and rights of the natives would secure some recognition when Home Rule was granted to South Africa, but the recent incident at Southampton, when four members of the African National Delegation were not allowed to return home on the *Edinburgh Castle* because African officers and soldiers threatened to throw them overboard if the ship authorities allowed them to travel, shows that the colour bar is just as strong today as it ever was.

In proof of this, Mr Sol T Plaatje, author, lecturer and journalist, had a moving story to tell to a *Forward* representative. Mr Plaatje, who is editor of the *People's Friend* (Kimberley) is Chairman of the Native Delegation to Britain and is on tour of this country, lecturing under ILP and UDC auspices. He is probably the first black lecturer to appear on the Socialist platform in this country. Mr Plaatje said it was a crime to employ a native at skilled work. They are allowed only to do menial labour, for which they receive 1/6 per day, and they require a special pass to enable them to work. In addition, they must have a pass to leave by the front door, and another to leave by the back, so that if a native got a pass to visit his brother, say, at a certain street in Kelvinside, and on going there found that the brother was two or three streets distant, he would require another pass. If he exceeds the limits of the pass, he would be fined £2, or the alternative of a month's imprisonment. If a native is employed at a farm, at say, £1 per month, he is not allowed to take a job with another farmer at, say, £3, per month, unless he gets the written permisssion of his employer. In some States a married woman is not permitted to live with her husband unless she gets a pass from the town clerk for which she must pay 1/- per month. Girls are not allowed to live with their parents unless they are working for Europeans and have secured a similar pass. These girls employed by Europeans are paid from 8/- to 12/- per month. In some districts the native women banded themselves together and refused to buy passes, with the result that they were put into prison, and in Johannesburg last April, a procession of native women was charged by mounted police, who rode down half-a-dozen to death and injured many others. Natives are compelled to pay the same taxes as white people and, in addition, they have to pay special native taxes. With the proceeds of these special taxes the Government builds and maintains schools for the education of white children, but from which the children of black taxpayers are rigidly excluded. All these severe discriminations were keenly felt by the natives, but nothing tried them so much as the law of 1913, which makes it a criminal offence for a native to buy or hire fixed property from white people. They may only purchase or hire from other natives who have no land or property to sell or lease. This law is making it extremely difficult for a native to live in the Union except as a serf, and many who formerly earned a decent livelihood as farm-tenants have been absolutely deprived of their livelihood. Many have cleared out of the Union altogether and gone to the Protectorates or Portuguese East Africa. ...

. 'What is the attitude of the trade unions to the natives?'

'They do nothing. No coloured man can become a member of a trade union, because that would entitle him to do skilled work, which is the prerogative of the white man.'

'Is there no Socialist Movement to help you?'

'There is the International Socialist League with which Mr Andrews and Mr Bunting are connected, and which is not in sympathy with the exclusive character of the Labour Party. Mr Andrews was unseated at the last general election because of his tolerant attitude to the coloured people.'

'Has the League been able to do anything at all for the natives?'

'No; they are a hopeless minority.'

'What about the Church?'

'British missionaries have protested against the treatment of the natives for the past nine years, until they got sick and tired of protesting. The Dutch Reformed Church got a law through Parliament in 1911 under which no coloured person can claim rights in that Church outside of the Cape Colony.'

* *Forward* was the journal of the Scottish Independent Labour Party

JOHN BUCHAN AND SOUTH AFRICA

OWEN DUDLEY EDWARDS

John Buchan's writings with reference to South Africa must have won a wider circulation than those of any other Scot. Their individual sales certainly varied greatly. Born in Perth in 1875 and raised in Pathhead, Fife (1876-88), and Glasgow (1888-95) whither his father had received successive callings as Minister in the Free Church of Scotland, the Oxford graduate and *Spectator* staffer came to South Africa in 1901, serving for two years under Lord Milner during the conclusion of the Boer War and its post-war Reconstruction. His *The African Colony: Studies in the Reconstruction* (1903) published on his return had a sale of 500 copies in two years.

His *A Lodge in the Wilderness* (1906), a multi-character symposium casting enthusiastic discussion of varieties of friendly attitudes to imperialism into fictional form set in an eloquently-depicted luxurious 'lodge' in equatorial Africa, went into two editions in a few months, (the first only being anonymous), and a cheap hardback issued in 1916 was followed by at least five reprints up to 1950: while its debate was couched in general terms, Southern African issues predominate explicitly and even more implicitly. A short story, 'The Kings of Orion', was published anonymously in *Blackwood's* (January 1906) and later in a volume of Buchan's short stories *The Moon Endureth* 1912) with a fictional East African setting and Southern Africa in mind, as it avowedly is for 'The Grove of Ashtaroth' in the same volume, originally appearing in *Blackwood's* (July 1910): sales of *The Moon Endureth* were not spectacular, at least until 1936 when it benefited by being brought out by its Edinburgh publisher Blackwood in an omnibus volume with *The Thirty-Nine Steps, The Power-House* and a collection of five stories *The Watcher by the Threshold* under the absurd title *Four Tales*. Both short stories were included by David Daniell in his somewhat questionably entitled *The Best Short Stories of John Buchan* (2 volumes, 1980, 1982 now paperback). A third short story, 'The Green Wildebeeste', made its first appearance in the *Pall Mall Magazine* for September 1927 to start his series of fictional reminiscences from protagonists in concert, later collected (with additions) as *The Runagates Club* (the volume selling 85,000), but this story was evidently in the making for many years - an allusion is made to an early version of it in *Mr Standfast* (1919, chapter 12). The novel *Prester John* (1910) had reached a quarter-million in British paperback sales by 1964: its total sales are unknown but they may well be in the region of a million.

Buchan also created two fictional characters not seen in Southern Africa (save in 'The Green Wildebeeste' for one of them and in chapter 4 of *The Island of Sheep* (1936, four years before his death) for both), but each is South African. One of them, Peter Pienaar, is Boer, although described as having supported the British in the Boer war: he appears in *Greenmantle* (1916) and *Mr Standfast*, as well as in the reminiscent chapter interrupting the contemporary narrative of *The Island of Sheep*. The other, Scots-born Richard Hannay, is the narrator of 'The Green Wildebeeste', as well as of *Greenmantle, Mr Standfast, The Three Hostages* (1924), the Prologue to *The Courts of the Morning* (1929),*The Island of Sheep* and the predecessor of them all, Buchan's most famous book, *The Thirty-Nine Steps* (1915), selling well over two million, three times filmed, and the classic archetypal thriller of the twentieth century. Hannay must be the best-known South African in fiction.

Buchan was a Scottish Tory who died in 1940 as Governor-General of Canada, and he may seem a natural victim to be jettisoned into a Tory pantheon, eliciting unthinking platitudes from votaries and equally unthinking execrations from those outside. He would not have thanked us for it. He admired Edmund Burke, in part (though only in part) for Tory reasons, but he refused to classify Burke among Tory ideologues in the way that such intellectualism as attends the Thatcher administration attempts to do today. His introduction to his selection *Burke's Political Writings* (1911), states of Burke:

> All his life he stood a little apart from his contemporaries, and his detachment gave him a curious distinction. He was never quite Whig and never quite Tory, but a kind of impersonal magazine of universal truths...while believing in party, he was not partisan, and in time his works became the Bible of both Whigs and Tories. ... Long ago Burke lost all party character. Even before his death he was regarded as an armoury from which both sides could draw their shafts.

Buchan could not say the same of himself, but he writes as though he wished posterity could grant him some claim to the spirit of this thesis.

If Buchan is placed in the Thatcherite pantheon, he begins to resemble the ancient British god in his 'The Wind on the Portico' (*The Runagates Club*) who engulfs his worshipper in flames. Here is his John S Blenkiron, in context an American mouthpiece for himself speaking in *Mr Standfast* (chapter 14) wholly extraneously to the formal plot:

> You English have gotten business on the brain, and think a fellow's a dandy at handling your Government if he happens to have made a pile by some flat-catching ramp on your Stock Exchange. It makes me tired. You're about the best business nation on earth, but for God's sake don't begin to talk about it or you'll lose your power. And don't go confusing real business with the ordinary gift of raking in the dollars....Your nation's getting to worship Mammon, Dick. Cut it out. There's just the one difference in humanity - sense or no sense, and most likely you won't find any more sense in the man that makes a billion selling bonds than in his brother Tim that lives in a shack and sells corn-cobs....

Similarly, if opponents of apartheid accept Buchan crudely at their adversaries' evaluation and reject him out of hand, they may be in danger of losing much that is valuable for them. Buchan's thrillers are the subject of a fairly astute if somewhat nostalgic study in Richard Usborne's *Clubland Heroes* where they are grouped with the best-known works of 'Sapper' and Dornford Yates. Usborne actually does much to differentiate them, but he was popularly taken as having established them all as a genre, and readers revolted by the ethics of Bulldog Drummond or another Yates (who found his final chosen domicile in white Rhodesia, dying in 1960) are sometimes inclined to dismiss Buchan as a more devious 'Sapper'. So we may begin with the question of racial prejudice in Buchan.

Should we conclude that Buchan is racialist, even offensively so, this still does not constitute a reason for dismissing him, however much it is one for despising him. To ignore works that traduced ethnic groups is to deafen and blind ourselves to the psychological sufferings of those same ethnic groups in the past. If A traduces B, does C do B any service by saying 'I sympathise with your wrongs so much that I refuse to discover what they were?' We will eliminate prejudice only by investigating it, exposing it, and distinguishing its varieties.

Buchan has in some respects been badly served by defenders as well as by opponents. Apart from the unlovely but largely non-literary coterie who celebrate racialist writers for their racialism (and Richard Usborne is certainly not one of them), Buchan has obtained confused apologetics in, for instance, Janet Adam Smith's largely excellent biography, (*John Buchan*, 1965, 1985) and David Daniell's useful but hyper-defensive critical study (*The Interpreter's House*, 1975). It is probably best, therefore, to begin with one ethnic group everyone seems to agree Buchan really did dislike: my own, the Irish Catholic.

His daughter Alice (*A Scrap Screen*, 1979) records (p.149):

> Pornography and the Irish were regarded by him with equal distaste (the poetry of Yeats and A E excepted). So, fighting for emancipation, I smuggled in *Ulysses*; it lived in a dust jacket of *The Pilgrim's Progress*, not unapt...*Ulysses* being *Irish pornography* the combination would have been altogether too much for him!

It gives one a thriller chill to imagine Papa, on a visit to his daughter's bedroom, wanting to check a quotation from his beloved Bunyan or read her an improving passage. Alice Buchan's apparent insensitivity to Irish religious differentiation prevents her seeing that Yeats and A E would naturally have been exempt, as Protestants, and they were not alone.

Buchan ecstatically reviewed Lady Gregory's version of Irish heroic legend, *Gods and Fighting Men* (1904) and was so anxious to repeat his praises that he reprinted the notice, misleadingly, in his *Some Eighteenth Century Byways* (1906). But Joyce qualified, ethnically and obsessionally, as Irish Catholic. In any case, Buchan and he were indeed best kept apart. One could imagine where thirty-nine of Joyce's steps would have led.

In literary terms, Catholic Ireland is a target in *Mr Standfast*, chapter 4, when Andrew Amos denounces its emigrants to Glasgow for opposing World War I and picking up jobs left vacant by native volunteers or conscripts. The diatribe is irrelevant to the story, but actually quite valuable as social comment, and supplies a rationale for popular anti-Catholic sentiment from returned soldiers after the war's end. This is even more instructive for Belfast, where in 1919 the Protestant workers drove Catholics out of the shipyards allegedly with red-hot rivets. That episode lingers yet in the murderous folklore of Northern Ireland, and if Buchan makes it easier to understand, though not to condone, he has done a service. *The Three Hostages* is shot through with abusive references to Ireland, including an Irish super-fiend, but the novel is set during the Anglo-Irish war when such allusions might be expected, and their more demoniacal fictional deployment is instructive as to the psychologically shattering effects of Collins and de Valera on Tory political imagination. But here, as in *Mr Standfast*, Buchan is anxious to assign the greatest expressions of prejudice (however much he agrees with them) to appropriate characters:

> '...Look at the Irish! They are the cleverest propagandists extant, and managed to persuade most people that they were a brave, generous, humorous, talented, warm-hearted race, cruelly yoked to a dull mercantile England, when, God knows, they were exactly the opposite.'

Macgillivray, I may remark, is an Ulsterman, and has his prejudices.

The passage is actually, if probably involuntarily, quite funny, once you apply logic to it. (To be 'exactly the opposite' the Irish must be a dull, mercantile race, kindly yoked to a brave, generous, humorous, talented, warm-hearted England.) Buchan might subscribe to all the adjectives for England - sometimes - but one doubts if he saw the dull mercantilism of the Irish as their most obvious feature. It certainly existed.

But as a boy I did *not* think it funny.

This is the ugly reality on the question of anti-black prejudices articulated in Buchan's fictional writing. They are likely to hurt young people, of an age, if not of a race, for whom the stories were intended. The most wounding are the casual references. Thus Hannay, in *The Three Hostages*, speaking of the Irish super-villain Medina testing an (actually unsuccessful) attempt at hypnosis (chapter 8):

> Then he spat in my face.
> That, I admit, tried me pretty high. It was such a filthy Kaffir trick that I had some trouble in taking it resignedly. But I managed it. I kept my eyes on the ground, and didn't even get out my handkerchief to wipe my cheek till he had turned away.

The same thing happens in *Greenmantle* although here the context is less hostile, in that the spitter is Peter Pienaar, being otherwise joyously introduced in person to the reader (chapter 3):

> I first asked him what he had been up to since the war began. He spat, in the Kaffir way he had, and said he had been having hell's time.

We are to assume his expectoration, however Kaffir, was not intended in Hannay's direction, and that his aim was good.

It is nasty, but it is a useful piece of evidence. Hannay is of course not saying that Kaffirs who had the honour of his acquaintance were in the habit of spitting in his face. It is an unspoken assumption that white rule in South Africa did not encourage such forms of address. Nor is it assumed Kaffirs would be spitting at one another in his presence. Imperialism made it clear that at such points it would intervene. What is clear is that the tension involved in having to play a deferential role induced an excess of saliva from which the sufferers sought to rid themselves by spitting. Irish Catholic peasants used to spit surreptitiously in court-rooms, clearly for the same reason. Neither Hannay, nor, one suspects, Buchan, understood why, but the observation is noteworthy.

There is a little spitting in the pre-Hannay *Prester John*, where the half-breed Portuguese Henriques is annoyed by the nineteen-year-old prisoner David Crawfurd's abusive rejection of his offer of conspiracy (chapter 12):

> 'Stew in your own juice,' he said, and spat in my face.

A little earlier Henriques has sought Crawfurd's support in the words:

> 'I am a white man, Mr Storekeeper, and I play the white man's game. Why do you think I am here? Simply because I was the only man in Africa who had the pluck to get to the heart of this business. I am here to dish Laputa, and by God I am going to do it.'

Later on Crawfurd, again a prisoner, seeks to warn the Reverend John Laputa against Henriques.

The black leader replies (chapter 17):

> 'You misunderstand again, Mr Storekeeper. The Portuguese is what you call a "mean white". His only safety is among us. I am campaigner enough to know that an enemy, who has a burning grievance against my other enemies, is a good ally. You are too hard on Henriques. You and your friends have treated him as a Kaffir, and a Kaffir he is in everything but Kaffir virtues...'

Laputa proves wrong in trusting Henriques, who mortally wounds him and whom he kills, but he is never answered, and apparently Buchan intends him not to be answered, on his argument that white society had made Henriques the ugly thing he had become. Henriques may be presumed to owe some parentage to Mark Twain's horrific Injun Joe, in *The Adventures of Tom Sawyer*, but Buchan can claim to have gone deeper than Twain in being ready to look, however briefly, for objective explanations for half-breed blood-lust, treachery and degradation. Injun Joe himself offers such an explanation, but the quiet voice of the black man giving his judgement on white and half-breed is far more compelling than Joe's preliminary plea in justification of the murder he then commits. Injun Joe's excuses are forgotten as he becomes the nightmare terror of Tom Sawyer; John Laputa's argument is not so easily forgotten, nor does it seem intended to be.

Buchan had the popular writer's trick of linking his fictional works together by casual reference as well as by series around specific characters: it would be pleasing to his constant readers and send new ones back to his earlier works. Hannay in *Greenmantle* (chapter 4), posing as a pro-German Boer, seeks to impress the awesome von Stumm:

> 'I have been for years up and down in Africa - Uganda and the Congo and the Upper Nile. I know the ways of the Kaffir as no Englishman does. We Afrikanders see into the black man's heart, and though he may hate us he does our will. You Germans are like the English; you

are too big folk to understand plain men. 'Civilise', you cry. 'Educate', say the English. The black man obeys and puts away his gods, but he worships them all the time in his soul. We must get his gods on our side, and then he will move mountains. We must do as John Laputa did with Sheba's necklace.'

The reader is intended to have read *Prester John*. Hence Hannay's strictures on the blacks, whether in his own person or in his assumed identity, are made to acquire their irony. In fiction and in fact, Buchan constantly noted Boer claims of 'understanding' the blacks as the British could not do, and of the brutality for which this was the excuse. 'The Green Wildebeeste' is a bitter little ghost story in which what Hannay, for all of his anti-Kaffir remarks, regards as sacrilege, a Boer's assault on an old, blind ascetic black priest ('I dare say Andrew used his sjambok, for a backveld Dutchman can never keep his hands off a Kaffir') is punished by the assailant's enchantment, in which he murders, is tried and is hanged. The Boer courageously accepts his fate as a just atonement. Hannay infers that if the anti-black Boers have any claim to understand black minds, it is because of some racial intermingling. 'The Du Preez family had lived for generations close to the Kaffir borders, and somewhere had got a dash of the tar-brush.' In the end the inter-racial telepathy proves under black, not white, control presumably assisted by these genealogical complications. It looks as though Buchan may have known Eugene O'Neill's *The Emperor Jones* (1920), his prejudices against Irish Catholics from the 1916 Rising onward not extending to Irish-Americans. The sophisticated figure is repossessed by the primitive gods from whom he foolishly imagines himself immune.

The plea in Buchan's defence, that it is not he talking racial prejudice but his characters, needs to be handled with care. He did not need to have Scudder in *The Thirty-Nine Steps* talk about conspiracies being master-minded by 'a little white-faced Jew in a bath-chair with an eye like a rattlesnake', especially when this proves to have no bearing on the actual case. Scudder is made a sympathetic figure by being murdered with Hannay becoming heir to his cause. Sir Walter Bullivant (chapter 7) says Scudder had 'odd biases': 'Jews, for example, made him see red'. So Scudder's anti-Semitism is not a blind, though it may be lunatic. Bullivant says Scudder is in any case wrong on aspects of his thesis and that the threatened Greek premier Karolides (declared by Scudder to be doomed) is safe, and then receives news which makes him 'apologise to the shade of Scudder', to wit that Karolides has been murdered. The last word, then, might seem to lend some weight to all of Scudder's obsessions, including the irrelevant anti-Jewish.

What is this doing here? Buchan if anything was unimpressed by the pro-Boer arguments which attacked Jewish financiers as having master-minded the South African war for gain. He introduced a nice Jew as one of the disputants in *A Lodge in the Wilderness*. So why the outbreak in *The Thirty-Nine Steps* ? It may be that Buchan had been infected by the Tory reaction to the Marconi scandal of 1911-15 in which the Jewish Attorney-General Sir Rufus Isaacs had been implicated, after which he was made Lord Chief Justice by the Liberal Government. Kipling's resultant poem *Genazi* directly on the matter is fairly poisonous in its use of Jewish imagery. Buchan dropped such sentiments later, although initially not very felicitously: Hannay's remarks about one Jew, about whom he wishes to be complimentary, is fairly choice. 'Blenkiron, who didn't like his race, had once described him to me as 'the whitest Jew since the Apostle Paul' *(The Three Hostages*, chapter 2). Buchan himself described E Phillips Oppenheim as 'the greatest Jewish writer since Isaiah', a remark too Philistine to be told in Gath (he had read Spinoza). But in 1933, as soon as Hitler came into power, Buchan went out of his way to have a Jewish subsidiary hero in an anti-Nazi story, 'A Prince of the Captivity'. There had been other favourable Jewish portraits in the interval, but this was clearly a manifesto. So it is necessary to consider Buchan in relation to the pressure of outside events and varying times.

Hannay changed. He is widely credited with having been based on the future Field Marshall Lord Ironside, whom Buchan had known in South Africa, but Janet Adam Smith raises gentle questions about this family tradition and it seems probable that Ironside only became a significant model when Hannay was depicted as professional secret service man (*Greenmantle*) and General *(Mr Standfast)*. The lone figure of *The Thirty-Nine Steps* is much more South African than Ironside (Hannay having supposedly reached the country at age six), and much more uneasy with officialdom. In 'The Green Wildebeeste' and in *The Island of Sheep* Hannay is again strongly South African, and much more of a private person. But his South African identity is frequently asserted in the other books, usually by proximity to Peter Pienaar, and nowhere more so than by what seems a more offensive habit than his allusions to Kaffir spitting, his frequent allusion to being a white man as a virtuous condition. Blenkiron's comparable allusion to the whiteness of Jews plays to an almost pathologically sympathetic audience on that designation. In the first chapter of *Mr Standfast* Hannay complains of what certainly seems a peculiarly lunatic assignment from Bullivant : 'There are some things that no one has a right to ask of any white man'. Later on Peter Pienaar (chapter 15) telling of the nice German air ace who has shot him down and visited him in hospital, affirms him to be 'a white man, that one'. It is repeated elsewhere, to the point of absurdity. Captain Zorn, in *Greenmantle* (chapter 4), slings out a round of bullying chauvinism to his two supposed new recruits from Boerdom:

'You seem the right kind of fellows,' he said. 'But remember' - and he bent his brows on us - 'we do not understand slimness in this land. If you are honest you will be rewarded, but if you dare to play a double game you will be shot like dogs. Your race has produced over too many traitors for my taste.'

'I ask no reward', I said gruffly. 'We are not Germans, or Germany's slaves. But so long as she fights against England we will fight for her.'

'Bold words', he said, 'but you must bow your stiff necks to discipline first. Discipline has been the weak point of you Boers, and you have suffered for it. You are no more a nation. In Germany we put discipline first and last, and therefore we will conquer the world. Off with you now. Your train starts in three minutes. We will see what von Stumm will make of you.'

That fellow gave me the best 'feel' of any German I had yet met. He was a white man and I could have worked with him. I liked his stiff chin and steady blue eyes.

When Buchan wrote this the war was on, the greatest propaganda war the world had yet known. The book is a highly sophisticated exercise in propaganda: much more subtle than other British fictionists turning a chauvinist penny, Buchan distinguished himself by a positively gentle portrait of the Kaiser, but did his work all the better by extending this sympathy to what was presented as a haunted, guilt-ridden, neurotically defensive figure. There is a beautiful scene with a German family at Christmastide, Buchan deliberately exploiting any readers' war-hatred to strengthen war sentiment, by showing the innocent sufferers from 'Germany's madness'. Buchan is given little credit for skill in character-drawing, but he knew his business as a propagandist and could play skilfully with his audience's emotions. Nor is Zorn the product of inability to depict a likeable German *Greenmantle* produces one in the engineer Gaudian, unquestionably 'a good fellow' if also of necessity 'a white man': Buchan used Gaudian in *The Three Hostages* again to assert ideas of post-war reconciliation, which he had greatly stressed with respect to the aftermath of the Boer War in his *Spectator* journalism before going to South Africa, and thereafter. The Zorn episode seems intended to convey to the reader the limitations of Hannay, indicating that his nature and experience led him to confuse regimental bullying with boy-scout ethics. His identification of white men, consciously or unconsciously, becomes a slightly dotty signature-tune by repetition. P G Wodehouse was to build brilliant satire on von Stumm's taste for domestic violence and lingerie, transposed in *The Code of the Woosters* (1938) to the Fascist bully Spode who designs ladies underclothing. And Wodehouse dealt effectively with the white man in *The Girl on the Boat* (1922) when Mrs Horace Hignett, wishing to know how what she regards as her country-house has been let to Mr Rufus Bennett, is unable to acquire the information because of his reconciliation with Mr Mortimer:

> 'There's nobody's word I'd take before Henry Mortimer's.'
> 'When Rufus Bennett makes an assertion', said Mr Mortimer, highly flattered by those kind words, 'you can bank on it. Rufus Bennett's word is his bond. Rufus Bennett is a white man!'
> The two old friends, reconciled once more, clasped hands with a good deal of feeling.
> 'I am not disputing Mr Bennett's claim to belong to the Caucasian race', said Mrs Hignett testily.

Did Buchan realise he was setting himself up for this? Or did he deliberately invite such a reaction? Hannay is his hero, although inclined to make much more of other heroes, but he is quite definitely a Philistine. The Hannay-narrated Prologue to *The Courts of the Morning* gives one instance:

> 'You're like Ulysses,' I told him. 'The fellow in Tennyson's poem, you know. Well, there's a widish world before you, and a pretty unsettled one. Ships sail every day to some part of it.'

Even Bertie Wooster would have difficulty improving on that. At moments of crisis Hannay can become inarticulate even in recollection, witness his comment on the discovery that the Germans are intending to use anthrax against the British Army (*Mr Standfast*, chapter 13):

> '...I was fairly well used to Boche filthiness, but this seemed too grim a piece of the utterly damnable...'

Buchan was a stylist of deliberation. And in Richard Hannay he drew a crude colonial. Conscious of metropolitan sneers at colonials (and Scots) he was careful not to load his hero with ridicule. But his very first introduction of Hannay, beginning *The Thirty-Nine Steps*, should be read with a South African accent to get the full force of the British Southern Africans' resentment, disillusion and inferiority complex in relation to the supposedly revered capital of Empire.

> I returned from the City about three o'clock on that May afternooon pretty well disgusted with life. I had been three months in the Old Country, and was fed up with it. If any one had told me a year ago that I would have been feeling like that I should have laughed at him; out there was the fact. The weather made me liverish, the talk of the ordinary Englishman made me sick. I couldn't get enough exercise,

and the amusements of London seemed as flat as soda-water that has been standing in the sun. 'Richard Hannay,' I kept telling myself, 'You have got into the wrong ditch, my friend, and you had better climb out.'

London throughout history has looked down on its peripheries, whether 'the provinces' or 'the colonies', and the very marks on which white Protestant Anglophones prided themselves - Irish Protestants that they were not Catholic, Scots Lowlanders that they were not Highland, colonial Americans that they were not Amerindian - were all too frequently denied them in the derisive metropolis. Colonial or Revolutionary America was habitually portrayed in feathers, brandishing tomahawk. Hence the wretched Hannay's obsession with the virtues of whiteness, ready himself to deny it to others or confer it as some sort of honorary degree, unspoken in his fear that it might be denied to him. He even insists that 'like all South Africans I have a horror of dirt' (*Mr Standfast* , chapter 4), despite having admitted that Peter Pienaar (*Greenmantle*, chapter 4) 'was not of the washing persuasion' (a neat little turn on the popular adage of the day 'cleanliness is next to Godliness': perhaps Joyce and Buchan had something in common after all). Hannay monotonously repeated his Caucasian credentials because it was what Buchan took white South Africans to do, not because he associated himself with such obsessiveness. It becomes a fairly naked joke by *The Island of Sheep* where Hannay, having married into English gentility and bought himself a country house and estate, explains that he 'usually' felt it was 'the only life for a white man'. It is like some pious ritual whose relevance has vanished and whose repetition is now nonsensical. He knows - it is one of the underlying themes of that story - what his old (white) mates in South Africa would make of him and his country house, which they would hardly accept as an invalidation of their own white lives.

Stephen Leacock, an English settler in Canada from infancy, replied definitively to the cleanliness school of which Hannay was so repetitious a representative (*Literary Lapses* , 1910): 'How to Live to be 200'):

...drop all that cold-bath business. You never did it when you were a boy. Don't be a fool now. If you must take a bath (you don't really need to), take it warm. The pleasure of getting out of a cold bed and creeping into a hot bath beats a cold plunge to death. In any case, stop gassing about your tub and your 'shower', as if you were the only man who ever washed.

Buchan had enough colonial defensiveness within his Scot-in-the-power-house self-consciousness to prevent his taking satirical elements in his Hannay portraiture to these lengths. There is much of him in Hannay, especially in Hannay's initial unease with England, and much in Hannay that he liked: and if he mocked colonial Philistinism he did not wish to encourage London contempt for colonials. But even in his high imperialist tract *A Lodge in the Wilderness* he could not shake off his mockery for colonial intellectual and artistic limitations. As he put it very politely in a review of South African poets ('Recent Verse', *Spectator*, 10 March 1906), 'Their work, like all verse from a new colony, is a little marred by irrelevant English echoes. The true *genius loci* has scarcely yet granted the inspiration.' *The Lodge* (chapter 4) goes into ruthless parody:

> Rests not the wild-deer in the park,
>   The wild-fowl in the pen,
> Nor nests the heaven-aspiring lark
>   Where throng the prints of men.
> He who the King's Path once hath trod
>   Stays not in slumbrous isle,
> But seeks where blow the winds of God
>   His lordly domicile.
>
> Where 'neath the red-rimmed Arctic sun
>   The ice-bound whaler frets,
> Where in the morn the salmon run
>   Far-shining to the nets;
> Where young republics pitch their tents
>   Beside the Western wave,
> And set their transient Presidents
>   As targets for the brave;
>
> Where through th' illimitable plains
>   Nigerian currents flow,
> And many a wily savage brains
>   His unsuspecting foe;
> Where gleam the lights of shrine and joss,
>   From some far isle of blue,
> Where screams beneath the Southern Cross
>   The lonely cockatoo;
> Where in the starlit Eastern night
>   The dusky dervish sleeps,
> Where the lone lama waits the light
>   On Kangchenjunga's steeps;
> Where Indian rajahs quaff their pegs
>   And chase the listless flies,
> Where mazed amid a pile of kegs
>   Th' inebriate trader lies;

> There, o'er the broad and godly earth,
>   Go seek th' imperial soul.
> Broken the barriers of his birth,
>   Th' eternal heavens his goal.
> In wind or wet, in drink or debt,
>   Steeled heart no fate can stir,
> He is the Render of the Net,
>   Th' Immortal Wanderer.

'It is long,' said Lady Flora when she had finished, 'but, like the White Knight's poem, it is very, very beautiful. Charlotte said it had the true ring of colonial poetry. ...'

(Oddly enough, Oscar Wilde, also reviewing South African verse, compared it to 'The Hunting of the Snark'.)

Buchan has been very cunning in his choice of an irrelevant English echo: the structure and rhyme-scheme are based on the highly (Roman) imperial last verses in Macaulay's 'The Prophecy of Capys'. But if we have to grant an underlying mockery in his picture of the white colonial bard, it could return to him in imagery he intended as sublime. 'The King's Path' and the targetted American Presidents (alluding to the assassinations of Lincoln, Garfield and McKinley) ultimately inspired his *The Path of the King* (1920) culminating in the death of Lincoln. Panegyric and parody formed a fascinating *pas de deux* in his writing. But apart from Peter Pienaar's very belated enthusiasm for *The Pilgrim's Progress* (unsullied by Joycean substitutions), there is only one exception to South African Philistinism. He appears as such in *Prester John* (chapter 17):

> The wooded bluff about Machudi's glen showed far in front. He told me the story of the Machudi war, which I knew already, but he told it as a saga. There had been a stratagem by which one of the Boer leaders - a Grobelaar, I think - got some of his men into the enemy's camp by hiding them in a captured forage wagon.
> 'Like the Trojan horse,' I said involuntarily.
> 'Yes,' said my companion, 'the same old device,' and to my amazement he quoted some lines of Virgil.
> 'Do you understand Latin?' he asked.
> I told him that I had some slight knowledge of the tongue, acquired at the University of Edinburgh. Laputa nodded. He mentioned the name of a professor there, and commented on his scholarship.

Now, whatever Buchan's respect for worthy men of brawn and strategy, his whole life had been given to book-worship. It gained him his social and financial rise, and Burke was but one of many authors for whom he sought a mass audience when he became a

partner in Nelson's and pioneered their sixpenny classics. It's probably untrue to say that Buchan was a snob - his dedications to persons
of title and consequence are more like big-game trophies than social
claims - but if he was, his snobbery was intellectual. (His undervalu-
ing of Shaw and Chesterton seems to have arisen from their not
having been at university, although when he liked he could appropriate a little Shavian logic or Chestertonian paradox.) So on this
most powerful of all Buchan's grounds of appraisal, the Reverend
John Laputa comfortably beats Richard Hannay, Peter Pienaar,
Andrew the anti-clerical biracial Boer; and David Crawfurd as
humbly acknowledged here. This is perhaps the turning-point for
Crawfurd. Anti-black sentiments in *Prester John* from Crawfurd and
his friends and associates are made to look as mean as Henriques by
this passage, and henceforward Laputa is not simply Crawfurd's
respected enemy, but positively revered. At the end when both men
realise that Crawfurd has been the principal agent of Laputa's defeat,
they also realise it is the smaller man in all senses who has won.

Buchan built on many writers and produced variations on distinguished themes. The great adversary of order and civilisation pre-
cipitates himself into a torrent far below in the fall of Professor
Moriarty in Arthur Conan Doyle's 'The Final Problem' (whence
Buchan presumably borrowed the waterfall: Crawfurd's climb to
safety after Laputa's death follows naturally from Holmes's climb
and flight told in the sequel, 'The Empty House'), in the death leap
of the Bushman leader from the Boer commandos reported in George
W Stow's *The Native Races of South Africa* (reviewed by Buchan in the
Spectator on 12 August 1905), and in Thomas Gray's poem 'The Bard'
whose title-figure throws himself in the Conway after spectacular
and all too accurate curses on the posterity of Edward I. But in each
case the suicide dies in hatred against his adversary. Crawfurd
attends Laputa's last moments like a devoted squire, as Laputa
recognises in his quotation of Shakespeare's Antony, 'Unarm, Eros'.
Arguably, Crawfurd is not Eros but Augustus to Laputa's Antony,
the younger, undervalued man triumphing in the cause of imperial
order against the challenge of African revolt, and Augustus was a
great hero of Buchan: but it is not as Augustus that Crawfurd runs to
'aid with all my strength' the dying Laputa to rise for the last time.

Laputa is the highest point of cultured humanity presented by
Buchan in a fictional Southern African context (even if the ladies and
gentlemen of *A Lodge in the Wilderness* could compete with him,
which they can't, none are African whites in any real meaning of that
term - they, much more than Laputa, inhabit a flying island, a true
Laputa, above the African protagonists). Yet Buchan advocated

personally and in parable at the end of *Prester John*, an education for African blacks of the kind being preached and practised in the United States by Booker T Washington's Tuskegee Institute. They are to be given useful skills, including mechanical and agricultural, but not to be trained as missionaries or teachers. W E B du Bois complained that Washington's methods excluded the 'talented tenth', the intellectuals: Laputa himself is the foremost of any 'talented tenth', and his statue (inscribed 'Prester John') inspires the workers in the college founded with the wealth Crawfurd obtained because of Laputa's death, but he must have no potential imitators even as pure intellectuals without his Messianism. In one way the reason is told in the continuation of that conversation with Crawfurd where the latter replies to his critique of Edinburgh University scholarship:

> 'O man!' I cried, 'what in God's name are you doing in this business? You that are educated and have seen the world, what makes you try to put the clock back? You want to wipe out the civilisation of a thousand years, and turn us all into savages. It's the more shame to you when you know better.'
> 'You misunderstand me,' he said quietly. 'It is because I have sucked civilisation dry that I know the bitterness of the fruit. I want a simpler and better world, and I want that world for my own people. I am a Christian, and will you tell me that your civilisation pays much attention to Christ? You call yourself a patriot? Will you not give me leave to be a patriot in my turn?'
> 'If you are a Christian, what sort of Christianity is it to deluge the land with blood?'
> 'The best,' he said. 'The house must be swept and garnished before the man of the house can dwell in it. You have read history. Such a purging has descended on the Church at many times, and the world has awakened to a new hope. It is the same in all religions. The temples grow tawdry and foul and must be cleansed, and, let me remind you, the cleanser has always come out of the desert.'
> I had no answer, being too weak and forlorn to think. But I fastened on his patriotic plea.
> 'Where are the patriots in your following? They are all red Kaffirs crying for blood and plunder. Supposing you were Oliver Cromwell you could make nothing out of such a crew.'
> 'They are my people', he said simply.

The plunder ultimately goes to Crawfurd and the Crown, and the Crown will have blood too, before the thing is finished, although much less because of Crawfurd's use of Laputa's name.

Buchan is not, I think, under his own full emotional control here. He was conscious within him of forces questioning his own theses: he amused himself in 1909-10 with the short story 'A Lucid Interval' (later included in The *Moon Endureth*) where disguised but identifiable Liberal ministers such as Lord Advocate Alexander Ure (much hated by Tories for virtually calling Balfour a liar) are drugged with effects releasing their suppressed Toryism. But much of his own stature derives from releases, not always necessarily intended, of his own ideological repressions. Laputa should be a simple, terrifying proof of the dangers of educated leadership in some fanatical quest: but he has become by his existence a splendid protest against the injustice of stunting and denying black intellectual potential. In his journalism one can see pull and counter-pull in Buchan on the point. Writing in the *Spectator* on 9 September 1905 on 'The Basuto Question' he began enthusiastically by pointing out Basutoland was 'created less than a century ago by the adroit diplomacy of Moshesh', only to add hastily 'the only statesman ever produced by the Bantu races'. But other than its self-protection in A P Herbert's later formula ('By statesmen I mean the members of my party; by politicians I mean the members of yours.' *(Uncommon Law))*, the reservation is nonsense. Buchan could not possibly lay down such a judgement with any scholarly authority: who could answer for unknown statesmen in countless centuries of unwritten Bantu history? The device is of importance chiefly in showing Buchan's uneasy awareness of the implications of saluting Bantu intellectual achievement. Dr Juanita Kruse puts it crisply in her J*ohn Buchan (1875-1940) and the Idea of Empire: Popular Literature and Political Ideology* (1989):

> When the interests of races conflicted, Buchan instinctively sought the welfare of the white man. Only in the last ten years of his life did his vision become more humane.' (p.51)

She is absolutely right for Buchan in the 1930s, culminating in the grand humanity of his dying and greatest book, *Sick Heart River* (1941), where the new sense of identification with non-whites is shown towards Amerindians. In *The Island of Sheep*, in the reminiscence of pre-1914 Southern Africa, the heroes are saved from death by the blacks, and Hannay, against all his previous bibliographical history, rejoices in their militancy against villainous whites:

> I was pretty dazed and wild, and I decided that it was all up now, when suddenly the whole business took a new turn. Above the crackle and the roar of the flames I heard a sound which I had not heard since the Matabele Rising [of 1893], the deep throaty howl of Kaffirs on the warpath. It rose to heaven like a great wind, and I clutched at my wits and realised what had happened. Mafudi's men were up. They had been like driven cattle all day, but this outrage on their sacred place had awakened their manhood. Once they had been a famous fighting clan and the old fury had revived. They were swarming like bees round the

acherm, and making short work of our assailants. The Kaffir sees better in the dark than a white man, and a knobkerrie or an axe is a better weapon in a blind scrap than a gun. Also there were scores of them, the better part of a hundred lusty savages, mad with fury at the violation of their shrine.

It must be the first moment when Hannay admits to gratitude for allies whom in context he finds preferable to the white man. And it is on this occasion no involuntary expression of inter-racial fellow-ship.

In *The African Colony* and elsewhere Buchan after the Boer war distinguished between Boer degradation of the blacks and his own British insistence on black rights linked to a lower form of citizen-ship. The short-lived Natal Rising of 1906, one of the origins of *Prester John*, elicited an article in the *Spectator* from the returned Milnerite administrator entitled with what seems intentional double entendre 'The Native Peril in South Africa' (17 February 1906):

> In the long run, the only safeguard is to give him [the native] a share in a higher civilisation. By this we do not mean the political franchise, or any such expedient. White must rule over black for the present, and the sooner this is frankly recognised the better. But we can give him an interest in the prosperity of the country by fitting him to take his place in our social fabric. ...we must protect him against exploitation by doubtful [i.e. dubious] fanatics whether under the guise of 'Ethiopianism' or any such creed. The decaying tribes will not be united by a military famine, but they may come together for a dangerous moment under the influence of some crazy faith. It is our duty to prepare the uncivilised against the danger of their status, and meanwhile to do all in our power to raise it.

This is obvious white self-interest, but he was very clear that any attempt to reduce blacks to servitude was unacceptable. His Burkeanism recognised that the whites' disruption of black society was fundamental to the situation. As he wrote in the *The African Colony* (p.308):

> There are three forces already at work which, if judiciously fostered, will achieve the experiment which South Africa is bound to make, and either raise the Kaffir to some form of decent citizenship, or prove to all time that he is incapable of true progress. Since we are destroying the old life, with its moral and social codes and its checks upon economic disaster, we are bound to provide an honest substitute.
> The forces referred to are those of a modified self-government, of labour, and of an enlightened education. The first is an experiment which must be undertaken very carefully, unless our case is to be prejudiced from the outset. I have given reasons for the view that a political franchise for the native is logically unjustifiable; but on

district councils and within municipal areas the native, wherever he is living under conditions of tolerable decency and comfort, might well play a part in his own control. It may be doomed to failure, or it may be the beginning of political education, but it is an experiment we can scarcely fail to make. In labour, short of a crude compulsion, every means must be used to bring the Kaffir within the industrial circle. We shall be assisted in our task by many secret forces, but it should be our business to frame our future native legislation as to place a bonus on labour outside the Kraal. ...

All this was grounded on the thesis that

the native is psychologically a child, and must be treated as such; that is, he is in need of a stricter discipline and a more paternal government than the white man. He is as incapable of complete liberty as he is undeserving of an unintelligent censure.

As Laputa pointed out, the native had had the liberty. Crawfurd condemns the proposal to restore it as putting the clock back. Ironically, it was Buchan and his hopes which were quickly swept into oblivion as far as South African policy was concerned. To his bitter regret, the blacks were placed under control of the Boer majority as 'the price of magnanimity' (as Professor Nicholas Mansergh has termed the British Liberal abandonment of obligations to the blacks in the search for reconciliation with the defeated Boers). Buchan had hoped, vainly, for a British control until British immigration won the battle of numbers among the whites (the blacks were the winners in that battle, however much losers everywhere else), but the Government which had swept away his Tories in 1906 were indifferent to the imperialist dreams of young enthusiasts now out of office or influence. Buchan was left as early as 7 April 1906 (*Spectator*) to complain of undue clemency in Privy Council reversals of death sentences on Natal insurgent leaders while the Government turned over all South African blacks to Boer servitude. *A Lodge in the Wilderness*, conceived as a dream of imperial future, became a nostalgic storehouse of forgotten hopes of the past. Perhaps this lent additional ironic force to Laputa's triumph in the moral debate in *Prester John* while losing in the material conflict. The great power of the novel, as Professor George Shepperson has shown in his study of the John Chilembwe Rising in Nyasaland in 1915, *Independent African* (1958), seems the stronger in that, however accidentally, Chilembwe's rising followed it so quickly as to make some contemporary observers wonder at the apparent prophecy. Janet Adam Smith notes that Jomo Kenyatta is said to have read *Prester John* in prison.

Yet this prophetic quality did not come from much knowledge of black Africans of any kind on Buchan's part. He was alert to ill-treatment of blacks by Boers or Belgians; yet he seemed to ask few questions of milder inhumanities from the British. Perhaps Recessive Buchan insisted on noticing them while Propagandistic Buchan could not afford to denounce them. Thus Crawfurd in an early talk with Laputa pretends to be drunk:

> First I made him sit on a chair opposite me, a thing no white man in the country would have done. Then I told him affectionately that I liked natives, that they were fine fellows and better men than the dirty whites round about. I explained that I was fresh from England, and believed in equal rights for all men, white or coloured. God forgive me, but I think I said I hoped to see the day when Africa would belong once more to its rightful masters.

It is surely not intended to be ironic, but Crawfurd's prized white rule is hardly displayed to best advantage in universal rejection of the human civility of offering a chair to an interlocutor. Buchan was impressed, rather after the manner of incompetent teachers, by the supposed effects of a show of patronising authority. 'The Kings of Orion' turns on a justly enraged African man being overawed when a Governor dresses up in panoply having worked out with some difficulty which continent he is in. As a young journalist, Buchan's anonymous reviews were sometimes written with a high pomposity to express their authoritative character, more especially when the book under review was on a matter rather beyond his expertise. In one such case, the posthumous memoirs of the Reverend W Barbrooke Grubb on his life among Paraguayan Indians, Buchan noted (*Spectator*, 8 April 1911):

> On the first expedition Mr Grubb assumed the manner of a *grand seigneur* with admirable results. The surprised Indians could only believe that such high-handedness meant the possession of an occult power... Mr Grubb was, indeed, a remarkable type of pioneer, for while he never allowed his authority to weaken, he entered fully into Indian life as one of themselves, and even donned a feather head-dress and shared in their festivities, being one of the committee to organise such functions. Few white men in any part of the world can have penetrated so far into savage life without losing caste. ...He read his childish flock like a book, and knew when to be firm and when to be tolerant.

Buchan might have added that Grubb took the precaution not only of reading his flock like a book, but of writing the book himself. He seems to have been typical of most imperialist journalists in assuming that a few ancedotes from plausible white travellers placed their readers in complete mastery of 'the native mind'. At the end of his own life, Buchan as Governor-General of Canada did don an Amerindian head-dress, which suited him very well. He was absolutely delighted by being given the name 'Teller of Tales': his Amerindian hosts evidently realised that the Governor-General was psychologically a child.

The 'child' thesis in relation to the South African 'native' showed a want of imagination: Buchan simply had not thought his way through to seeing the defensive apparatus with which vulnerable blacks composed themselves under white scrutiny, although he had made Crawfurd go through such a charade when under Laputa's black scrutiny. Perhaps this once more was Recessive Buchan under-standing more than Propagandistic Buchan would admit. But in another way it seems that Buchan's sense of black African child status arose from a view of history. 'We stand at the end of a long line of development and the native is at the beginning', he declared, reviewing Archibald Colquhoun's recent volume on South Africa in the *Spectator* (10 April 1906), quoting Colquhoun 'we murdered our prophets, burnt our reformers and generally ill-treated all of our race who were ahead of their time'. It is hardly surprising that Recessive Buchan should suffer to make Laputa indict this exemplary agenda. What it meant for Buchan was that he regarded the Africans as Scots in an earlier period of history. It was this which led him to see some fetish or symbol as potentially lethal in rousing the black Africans to revolt: he was thinking of the fiery cross rousing Covenanter senti-ment (or Campbell supporters) in seventeenth-century Scotland. It is the basis for so much turning on Laputa's possession of Prester John's necklace (which the black leader identifies with the fabled Emperor but the whites - both Crawfurd and Hannay - constantly refer to in the more exotic and much more historically questionable association with the Queen of Sheba); it also accounts for the plot of *Greenmantle*. (*Greenmantle* itself is directly from Scottish literary antecedents, in the girl known as 'Greenmantle' in Scott's *Redgauntlet* and that, as Buchan may or may not have known, derives from Scottish fairy lore.) This made Buchan in some ways unusual among white writers on South Africa: Dr Andrew Roberts in his 'The Imperial Mind' (*Cambridge History of Africa*, vol. 7 (1986), p.40) finds Buchan exceptional in his readiness to accept Randall MacIvor's archaeological finding that the stone monument at Great Zimbabwe 'was built by natives'. White colonists disliked acknowledging black achievements of so remarkable a kind. Buchan simply thought of prehistorical remains in Britain and Ireland.

The Scottish identification is picked up ably by David Daniell in *The Interpreter's House* with reference to the Laputa rising, noticing the Covenanter (well, anyway, Presbyterian) allusions in the first chapter, and then (p.112):

Laputa, one suddenly realises, is a black Montrose - his military skill, high charisma, and religious vision also gone 'black', in the sense that they are superb but aberrant ... he differs not one jot from the Covenanting ministers who pursued Montrose.

This may spread its butter on both sides of the bread, and it would not be hard to make mountains of difference from Daniell's non-jot, but the Covenanting parallel and inspiration are certainly strong in Laputa's mission to scour the land from contaminating metropolitan influences. It is also to stress Buchan's essentially literary ideas on the Scottish past, both as biographer of Montrose and as reader of Scott's *A Legend of Montrose* and *Old Mortality*. The Covenanting analogy is one Buchan also applied, with rather more basis in observation, to the Boers. In his autobiography *Memory Hold-the-Door* (1940), Buchan saw the Boer farmer as endowed with 'many of the traits of my Lowland Scots, keen at a bargain and [prepared] to imperil his immortal soul for a three-penny bit, but ready to squander pounds in hospitality' (p. 114). He drew Peter Pienaar, it would seem, rather more deeply from Scottish than from Boer antecedents, and indeed in *Mr Standfast* it seems as though Peter has become something close to Buchan's father. (There was an original Pieter Pienaar in late eighteenth-century South Africa: he was a pioneer explorer who sustained incredible privations and discovered the mouth of the Orange River, which was no doubt inspirational for Buchan, and was ultimately murdered by a black who said that Pienaar as an employer had most brutally ill-treated him - and that no doubt was not inspirational, although Buchan's Peter does not have much closer relations with blacks than sedulous imitation of their methods of exploration, hunting and intelligence-gathering, until *The Island of Sheep* when he states very firmly 'I have always been good friends with Mafudi's folk'.)

Buchan's constant use of religion as the key force in rousing native populations to revolt may also have owed something to his father's enthusiasm for the revivalists Moody and Sankey, whom he had supported in their Scottish tour the year before Buchan's birth. In the cases of both Boers and blacks, it seems to have made him fearful: for all of his cheerfulness in *Memory Hold-the-Door* he assigned Boer intransigence towards blacks to a very dark and grim Calvinist predestinarianism. David Crawfurd is made to share some of this, and even to be preserved by it: he tells Laputa at the end when the dying man threatens to kill him 'I am in God's keeping and cannot die before my time'. Crawfurd's Scottishness, and his offensively anti-black racialist schoolmate, deepen the identification of boy and Boer, although Buchan found Crawfurd's fatalism depressing in the extreme when he encountered it among the Boers themselves.

However Covenanter Laputa and his followers might seem, Buchan's real analogy for the blacks would seem to be Highland (the Argyll fiery cross blends those categories). It would be natural for the Scottish Buchan to see Boer hostility to the blacks as Lowland sentiment towards the Highlanders. He noted, in the *Spectator* (23 January 1904) how Boers would shoot 'in cold blood' blacks conscripted for espionage by the British in the Boer War, once they had been taken prisoner. He also was touched by reports of a black woman weeping with joy at the relief of Ladysmith, presumably realising that her delight was less from love of the British as from fear of the Boers.

This plays a significant part in the making of *Prester John*. Buchan was a highly derivative writer, although not necessarily from the sources usually ascribed to him. Rider Haggard's *King Solomon's Mines* is only superficially relevant, the disguised Zulu king being quite unlike Laputa, and the story itself seems chiefly intellectual in its terrain. Kipling's *Kim* is important, at least in establishing the triangle of boy / intelligence officer / holy man, and the growing admiration of Crawford for Laputa's spiritual significance probably owes something to that. Scott's *Redgauntlet* probably helped supply the idea of a grim votary whose commitment in 1759 to Stuart restoration meant undoing decades of Scottish history and who takes a boy hero prisoner as part of his whole-hearted intransigent resolution. Scott's *Waverley* has the clear exemplar of a multi-faceted Highland leader in Feargus Mac-Ivor Vich Iain Mhor, now cattle-rustler and ransom-extortionist, now regal highland host, now devious and questionable intriguer, now Stoical martyr:

> I had seen Laputa as the Christian minister, as the priest and king in the cave, as the leader of an army at Dupree's Drift, and at the kraal we had left as the savage with all self-control flung to the winds. ....he now became a friendly and rational companion. (chapter 17)

> He had ceased to be the Kaffir king, or the Christian minister, or indeed any one of his former parts. Death was stripping him to his elements, and the man Laputa stood out beyond and above the characters he had played, something strange, and great, and moving, and terrible. (chapter 20)

Feargus's death symbolises the death of Jacobite Gaelic Scotland. Laputa tells Crawfurd:

> No one will come after me. My race is doomed, and in a little while they will have forgotten my name. I alone could have saved them. Now they will go the way of the rest, and the warriors of John become drudges and slaves.

Laputa's intended genocidal war against the whites recalls Conan Doyle's 'J Habbakuk Jephson's Statement' where the black leader dreams of emancipating his people and carries out a murderous private war against whites: unlike Laputa he hates the white narrator but is in a sense linked in understanding with him in their final association. The growing human mutual recognition between Crawfurd and Laputa may owe a little to Huck and Jim on their raft in Twain's *Huckleberry Finn*.. But the pre-eminent influence is Robert Louis Stevenson.

Janet Adam Smith and others have pointed to the virtual invocation of *Treasure Island* from the beginning of *Prester John*, and Buchan opens on Crawfurd's first sight of Laputa virtually in the words with which Jim Hawkins recalls his first sight of Billy Bones. Laputa's pursuit of Crawfurd and his friends when he finds them spying on him derives initially from Blind Pew's much more homicidal search for Jim and his mother. Then Laputa moves into the role of Silver, without Silver's treachery, while Henriques obviously echoes Israel Hands. Crawfurd's declaration to Laputa that he is the author of his misfortunes follows Jim Hawkins's comparable declaration to Silver and his remaining pirates. The anger of the intelligence leader, Captain Arcoll, at Crawfurd's folly in leaving him to venture alone in pursuit of Laputa recalls Captain Smollett's cold greeting to Jim on his return after his secret journey to the *Hispaniola*. Buchan could claim to have resolved Crawfurd's relationship to Laputa in Laputa's last moments in the way that Silver's surreptitious theft of a little treasure and clandestine flight leaves his ambiguous links with Jim Hawkins unresolved. But Stevenson's *Kidnapped*, while less directly analogous in point of detail, is probably more important in certain of its implications.

Treasure Island is set in Cornwall before the heroes go to Bristol and the sea, but the traditional Lowland image of the Highlanders as thieves could make it easy for Stevenson to transpose such an attitude into the forces of law and order against the pirates. *Kidnapped* is clearly Lowland versus Highland, but here the boy hero is not merely thrown into the pirate world against his will, he becomes the supporter of the Highland Jacobite outlaw Allan Breck against all his own previous training. Crawfurd does not do that, but his growth of admiration and reverence for Laputa, subject to variations caused by specific events, has no parallel in Jim's view of Silver which is always sanctimonious and sometimes horrified; David Crawfurd finds in Laputa a kind of Allan Breck to respect against his own background and former attitudes, and while Laputa's enemy he comes to look up to him far more than David Balfour does to Allan. (Buchan on his arrival in South Africa compared himself to David Balfour, and called his pony 'Allan Breck'.) Curiously enough, it is Allan Breck whom David Balfour decides is a child; David Crawfurd never takes that view of Laputa. Captain Arcoll does, a little, with his old-Africa-hand stuff about black inability to take the long view, but this plays relatively little part in Crawfurd's impression of Laputa.

Thus Buchan's idea of the black as a child probably derived from the Balfour conclusions on Allan Breck, extended to Highlanders generally, and existed in all probability before he arrived in South Africa at all. (The fact that he was carried about by a being he called Allan Breck may also suggest to the psychobiographically-inclined that he saw blacks as intended to bear his weight and respond to his direction where he sought to go.)

Looked at like this, Buchan produced a highly imaginary South Africa, but one in which the source of his imagination was the historical divisions and suspicions of his own country. The speed with which Milner imperialism turned into a lost dream probably assisted the imaginative identification. Buchan remained uneasy at bottom about the world the whites had destroyed in the name of improvement, as Stevenson and even Scott occasionally reflected unease about the fate of the Highlands. Buchan's impotence in face of the Liberal solution of handing the blacks over to the Boers may have recalled David Balfour's impotence in his attempts in *Catriona* to save James Stewart of Appin from the Campbell judge and jury. But even beyond all this, Buchan's interest in black achievements in prehistoric times as revealed by archaeology, and his enthusiasm for the Bushmen as possibly having shown a remarkable character of humanity, echo some of his fictions about Pictish survival and Celtic inheritance. His story 'The Grove of Ashtaroth' captures his unease about the unknown black past and its destruction by white incursion. He uses the symbol of an Assyrian cult in Africa and its demolition in the interest of white sanity much as the forces of improvement in eighteenth-century Scotland had reduced the Highlands to civilisation at considerable cost to the inhabitants. It ends:

> I knew that I had done well for my friend, and that he would come to his senses and be grateful. My mind was at ease on that score, and in something like comfort I faced the future. But as the car reached the ridge I looked back to the vale I had outraged. The moon was rising and silvering the smoke, and through the gaps I could see the tongues of fire. Somehow, I knew not why, the lake, the stream, the garden-coverts, even the green slopes of hill, wore an air of loneliness and desecration.
>
> And then my heartache returned, and I knew that I had driven something lovely and adorable from its last refuge on the earth.

THE PEDIGREE OF THE SCOTTISH GOD

R F Mackenzie

I'd like to tell the young about the weird story of how some tribes, nearer our own day, interpreted the Bible story in a manner congenial to themselves and appropriated its ideas to support their own policies. The Children of Israel were a small tribe fighting for survival against more powerful neighbours, the Philistines (Arabs). The Scots, the New England colonists and the South African Boers were small tribes fighting against strong, sometimes overwhelming, enemies, the English, the North American Indians, and the Xhosas and Zulus. These small, threatened groups identified with the Children of Israel and made the Jewish holy book their own.

For us Scots, suckled on the Jewish Bible like the New England colonist and the Boers, like them seeing our national destiny as a pilgrimage through the wilderness, a battle with the heathen, which would lead to occupation of the Promised Land (for us Scots none the less potent for being metaphorical, the New Jerusalem) to read their story is like folllowing the career of your own twin who has emigrated. It's like looking at a mirror image, recognisable but in part distorted. In the Dutch Reformed Kerk at Laingsburg in the Cape I felt at home. We also put on our best clothes which we called always our 'Sunday clothes' to go to the kerk, which was pronounced in the same way as they do. The Laingsburg Kerk has beautiful pews of imported oak. It is a decent, dignified building, spotlessly clean, sunny, simple after the style of opulent Quakers. The Predicant is head of the local community, he has a free house, free hens and vegetables, sits on committees, exacts tithes and controls the neigbourhood. It is a community of god-fearing people like the Aberdeenshire of my early days. I was steeped in the same culture, its usages and beliefs. I would have felt far more at home in a Dutch Reformed Church in the Cape than in an Episcopalian church in Aberdeenshire whose Anglican rituals were alien to us. The idiom of the Old Testament was intimately intertwined in their daily speech as in ours. Like theirs, our perception of reality was that which was filtered down to them through the medium of the Bible. A century ago David Livingstone felt at home in a community of Boer farmers in the North Transvaal, or nearly at home. In the Boer War, fighting at Aliwal North in the Cape,

Dingwall crofter's son, Major-General Sir Hector Macdonald, said what a pity it was that they should take up arms against such a godly people.

Outside the Laingsburg Kerk a foundation stone is inscribed 'JEHOVAH-Nissi Exodus 17, 15b. JEHOVA-Nissi means the Lord my banner. The Exodus context is a battle in which 'Joshua discomfited Amalek and his people with the edge of the sword'. The verse referred to on the foundation stone and the following verse say:

> And Moses built an altar, and called the name of it
> JEHOVA-Nissi
> For he said, Because the Lord hath sworn that the LORD
> will have war with Amalek from generation to
> generation

Scottish national poet Robert Burns was as familiar with the story as the Boer farmers were. In *A Cotter's Saturday Night* the big family-Bible is taken out and:

> The priest-like father reads the sacred page,
> How Abram was the friend of God on high.
> Or Moses bade eternal warfare wage
> With Amalek's ungracious progeny.

The twinship ties had been closer than I expected.

The Voortrekkers, fleeing oppression in the Cape, used the Bible as a manual for their pilgrimage, a King's Regulations for their campaign. Few religious tribes in the history of the world can have obeyed holy books which so closely reproduced their own experience. The English in the Cape were like Egyptians, rich, arrogant, irreligious oppressors. The native Kaffirs were hostile like Amalek; the journey was through the wilderness. The Voortrekkers, a Chosen People like the Children of Israel, shared the troubles recounted in the Book of Exodus - shortages of food and water, skirmishes and pitched battles against the local inhabitants, loss of heart, murmurings and signs of revolt against the expedition's leaders. The Voortrekkers would not have found it extraordinary that the desert that the Israelites' pilgrimage took them through bore the name, 'The Wilderness of Sin'. The mirror reflection of their daily experience confirmed and reinforced in them the faith that they walked with destiny, the Lord's Elect, like the Scottish Covenanters and the Pilgrim Fathers.

Like the area of Rephidim near Mount Sinai where the battle with Amalek took place, the area round Laingsburg was fought over. The descendants of the Voortrekkers who made the exodus from bondage to seek a Promised Land were vividly aware how closely their history followed the history of the Jews making the exodus from Egypt. I found myself in tune with the Boers' Voortrekker Memorial outside Pretoria. It's like a laager, the main building protected by a circle of outspanned ox-waggons. Inside are murals of the Great Trek. A circle in the roof lets the midday sun shine on a sarcophagus below the floor. At midday on 16 December, the date of the Battle of Blood river in 1838, the ray of light strikes on an inscription. In the lower half of the building a perpetual flame burns to symbolise the light of civilisation, white civilisation. The nearby museum fortifies the imaginative impression and the intended political indoctrination with details of life in a canvas-covered ox-waggon.

Each waggon contained a Bible, a baby's bottle of narrow, cylindrical glass, saddles, thongs, tools to make the felloes of waggon wheels, cooking pots, home-made clothes and home-made shoes, the basket that swung below the waggon. There are pictures of parting scenes, of the use of a raft to float a waggon across the Orange River, a letter from a young man urging his parents to join the trek. Like the Americans in their covered waggons, they developed confidence in their skills to defend themselves and to improvise, and, I expect, in their skill in creating a self-governing community. And their descendants who built a memorial were, I am sure, aware of the injunction of Moses in that Exodus passage, 'Write this for a memorial in a book, and rehearse it ...'

They were re-living Biblical history. Like the Jews in the Sinai Desert, they made hard bargains with their god, which they called covenants. The Scottish Covenanters, searching the Scriptures, were sustained by the same metaphor of life. When the Voortrekkers came to a place in the Orange Free State where they got supplies of wheat, they called it Bethlehem, knowing that Bethlehem means 'the place of bread'. The same detailed Biblical knowledge is found to this day in Aberdeenshire. A favourite name for a fishing boat is *The Fruitful Bough.* ... The reference is to Genesis 49,22. Joseph was a fruitful bough because his roots were in the water.

Down the hill from the Memorial, in Pretoria, Paul Kruger's house, now a museum also, has evidence showing how close he, a Bible fundamentalist, was to the spirit of *A Cotter's Saturday Night.* The statues of the members of Kruger's cabinet in the station square in Pretoria have the bearded, patriarchal, righteous, god-fearing appearance of an Aberdeenshire school board at the beginning of the century. Their clothes are the same. The elders that we were schooled to look up to were dour, forbidding, reproving, tholing, Sabbatarian, shunning sex. Boer speech sounded guttural like farm speech in Buchan and some of the words, like breeks for trousers, were the same. The metropolitan Dutch regarded their speech as uncouth, just as the English regarded ours. The Boers and we Scots disliked the posh speech and fine manners of the English upper class. Like the Children of Israel, the Covenanters and Pilgrim Fathers and Boers were oppressed minorities and therefore they responded to the promise that the Old Testament god made to his Chosen People, 'I have broken the bands of your yoke, and made you go upright'. The promise helped them to cling to their faith and cultural identity and stand out against the compromisers whom St John and the Scottish Convenanters exercrated as 'the Laodiceans'. I can visualize a Boer farm-kitchen reading from the Revelation of St John the Divine as clearly as I can visualize the same reading in an Ayrshire cotter house or the ante-room of an Aberdeenshire village hall. The members of the church in Laodicea, one of the seven primitive Christian churches in Asia, were back-sliders and St John was commanded to write to them:

> I know thy works, that thou are neither cold nor hot: I
> would thou wert cold or hot.
> So then because thou art lukewarm, and neither cold nor
> hot, I will spue thee out of my mouth.
> I counsel thee to ... anoint thine eyes with eye-salve
> that thou mayest see ...
> To him that overcometh will I grant to sit with me in my
> throne, even as I also overcame, and am set down with
> my Father in his throne.
> He that hath an ear, let him hear what the Spirit saith
> unto the churches.

The nearest we can get at the end of the twentieth century to entering into the spirit of those heady words is to hear them thundered with total conviction from a Belfast pulpit by the Reverend Ian Paisley. In Northern Ireland they reverberate with their ancient force. In a Transvaal farm-kitchen these words would be followed by a prayer and a benediction, and the Boer family would go to bed sustained in their resolution to stand firm for their faith, its message and its idiom incorporated into their being, a gospel for the conduct of life. But a century later the children of the Voortrekkers are losing their attachment to the gospel. No laager can exclude foreign signals flashing from television aerials seductively presenting the case for Economic Man. Mammon lured many Boers into the affluence and influence of the boardrooms of Johannesburg. The landscape round the Voortrekker Memorial was desecrated by orange manganese smoke belched into the air from their own ISCOR chimney. Having overcome the anglicising elements in their country, the Boers were relishing industrial power, but still trying to reconcile the practices of multinational capital with the precepts of the Old Testament.

An account of how the Scots were thinking this century can be illuminated by taking note of how our twins, the Boers, were thinking. But only up to a point. After that the paths diverge. We go our separate ways and it is no longer helpful, it no longer sheds light, to compare the stories. It was more difficult for the Scots to escape from anglicising influences. Ulster respected longer the traditions followed by the Boers, but Scotland, influenced not only by English economics but, ironically, by the freer-thinking English culture, followed a different course. The questions we asked were different. When I went to South Africa I saw life differently from the way a Boer farmer saw it. In the veldt, black labourers were poorly housed at a hygienic distance from the white baas's stoep; in the Aberdeenshire of my childhood the cotter houses, 'potato-pits of houses', were similarly sited. Black 'locations' were like slums in Glasgow and Edinburgh. Black pupils were segregated from white pupils as in Scotland 'non-academic' from 'academic' pupils. 'They are so stupid, man,' exploded the rulers of South Africa when speaking of the blacks; the Scottish rulers spoke of 'the limited pool of ability'. The history of Scotland that Scottish pupils were taught, star-billing a succession of acquisitive chiefs, was no more the history of Scotland than the adventures of European-born expropriators was the history of Xhosas and Zulus. Both ruling minorities talked about *scroungers* amongst the majority.

I talked to a senior class in an English public school about the disadvantages encountered by working-class schools in Scotland. In Fife we had had to sell pupil-made canoes in order to buy a tyre for the school bus. I asked them if they thought it was fair. 'Yes,' answered all of them except one; 'Britain depends on its future rulers and it is important that we should have educational advantages so that we can be educated to be good rulers.' They were in the tradition of the seventeenth century Earl of Clarendon who said that 'It is the privilege of the common people of England to be represented by the greatest and learnedest and wealthiest and wisest persons that can be chosen out of the nation.' He said that people in 'great towns and corporations' had a 'natural malignity'. 'The common people in all places' showed 'barbarity and rage against the nobility and gentry'. The MPs opposed to the Royalists, the Parliamentarians, were 'dirty people of no name'. He said that in the long run the economic power of 'the natural rules' would prevail. But these were the tones in which Robert Burns had spoken of the Philistines, the Palestinians, whom the Children of Israel had dispossessed. 'Amalek's ungracious progeny'. Two centuries after Burns, we Scots were asking questions different from those he asked. Unlike him, we weren't accepting the Bible's opinion on Amalek.

The best text I know for bringing home to pupils of a Scottish school the lesson on Amalek comes from a school in Soweto. Eight years ago in Johannesburg a Soweto headmaster told me the story. A black teacher was teaching a lesson on citizenship, and a white inspector was sitting at the back of the classroom. A black pupil asked, 'Sir, am I a citizen of this country?' The black teacher answered with care. 'You have heard what was said about the rights of citizenship and the duties of citizenship. I must leave it to you to decide the answer to your question'.

Before then, most black parents in Soweto, like ambitious working-class parents in Scotland, were eager that their children should 'better themselves' and do the lessons and pass the examinations. It's different now. They've lost faith in the schools. They have discovered that the master race uses the schools to discipline its work force without conferring on them the dignity of citizenship.

The same idea is beginning to dawn on the minds of some Scottish pupils. Apartheid is clear in South Africa because it is a matter of black and white. In Scotland it is masked, white and white; but it is apartheid just the same, the privileged rulers and the majority who work for them. After all those years in Scottish education, it is only now that I have become aware that the schools are not on our side. They are the agencies of the rulers. They bring us up to do what we are told, and not to speak back, to learn our lessons and pass the examinations. Above all not to ask questions. Another surmise like a new planet swims into our ken. Is that our appointed role in history, playing the part of Amalek?

From *A Search for Scotland* (1989)

AFTER READING THE SPEECH BY THE REV ANGUS SMITH, PARTS OF WHICH WERE REPORTED IN THE *WEST HIGHLAND FREE PRESS*

At the General Assembly of the Free Church of Scotland in May 1986 the Moderator, the Reverend Angus Smith, attacked the World Council of Churches and the Roman Catholic Church:

Last year 37 organisations and activist groups shared 396,000 US dollars in grants from the WCC special fund to combat racism. Most of the money was aimed against South Africa and apartheid. If South Africa happened to be ruled by a Roman Catholic cabinet would they be so keen to help bring about her political destruction? We wot not.

Can it possibly be that South Africa's real crime is that she is Calvinistic, with praying members in her cabinet? Marxist liberation movements bent on violence seem to be the main beneficiaries of the fund.

Reported in the *West Highland Free Press* of 23 May 1986

Lord God, go with them so long as they have the Bible in their
   hands.

Let them, in their flat unyielding tones, order the bullets to be
   fired, the faces of the blacks to be broken, the children to be
   cut off in free flight. This is the work of the Lord.

Let them laugh when the women wail outside their jails, when the
   aggressors dive out of windows, the curved rainbows of Thy
   Grace.

O Lord, hound the homeless blacks, to their deaths, for after all
   they are Marxists, and it is possible they may be Catholics as
   well in their rich whorish dresses.

Let the pages of the Bible open like the wings of vultures.
In northern Ireland, in South Africa, there is not enough killing: in
   Glasgow there is as yet only shadow-boxing.

Lord God, who demanded the sacrifice of Isaac, we have to offer
  you more.

Paisley is the instrument of your providence, against the rich
  Catholic traitors of the North,
who sway governments, who are the Cabinet of the Demon.

In the flattened graveyards of Soweto let the Lord God crow like a
  cockerel, let the rich blacks be crucified.
Out of the Western Isles there comes a voice of the true God, out
  of Ulster, out of South Africa.

Let them sing to him in the gravelly accents of violence.

The flares shall blaze out in the light of Damascus,
over the shaven heads of the peasants,
in the interrogation rooms of Durban.

O the perfect triumph as the mother cradles her dead child like
  the traitorous picture of the Mother and the Saviour created by
  these Catholic painters.

In the green avenues of the righteous, may the jewelled blue-rinsed
  ones flourish,
for out of the Western Isles there comes a voice,
let us listen to him, the saviour of the righteous,
for he bears a sword, a Bible in his hand.

Out of the safe landscape of the West he speaks,
out of the calm Sundays of the Millennium.
See, he fights the Devil in Lewis, and the Marxist blacks of Skye
  he abominates,
and the Catholics with their safes packed with treasure.

Out of the desert places, out of the besieged periphery he comes
  with a crown of thorns on his head,
he who testifies against love, he who is clothed with the blood of
  the innocent.

I see him preparing his sermon in the military theatre of his study.
The children run past his window with their broken heads, but he
  doesn't see them.

But my dear friend, he is studying statistics.
My dear dear friend, can you not see the blacks crossing the
    Minch bearing their Marxism?

The Ulster Catholics are clad in the blaze of riches and influence,
    and so are the blacks, pagan, dispensable.

How should they not accept their position as the anvil of the Lord?
The Lord God is against them, who shall be for them?

In the heat of the battle, against the Devil, the Bible opens its cool
    leaves.

IAIN CRICHTON SMITH

IN THE BOTANIC GARDENS

Zoë Wicomb

There were several accounts of his last movements. But she remembered only two. And the first only dimly, so that she imagined that it had been whispered by one of the other South African students, a girl called Tsiki, who held her hand and puffed continuous smoke into a small narrow room: he had been brought home by a friend who saw him to his room at eleven thirty pm. Then he disappeared.

The other was delivered by the man from the British Council, Mr MacPherson. Dorothy Brink did not quite catch his name but decided that Sir would be an appropriate form of address. The man was in national dress; he wore a green tartan kilt, a short tweed jacket and tassels on his socks. He spoke very fast so that it was difficult to follow him, but perhaps she would not have understood anyway. This English was very smart, she supposed, quite different even from the English of the SABC newsreader; he might as well have been speaking a special language understood only by those in national costume.

She tried to concentrate but could not get rid of the funny feeling that these sounds did not add up to functional words that would tell her anything about her son. For she could summon up no image of Arthur whose blue aerogrammes lay in a ribbon-tied bundle in her bag. Like a lover's letters. She knew them by heart; she had read them all night long. This soft, clipped voice claiming to follow footsteps now, twelve days later when not an echo remained, prevented her from imagining a young man called Arthur. She wanted to ask what shoes he wore, but here in Glasgow her English would squeak like crickets in a thornbush; besides, the man did not expect her to say anything. He had introduced her to himself: 'Eh, Mrs Breenk' and replied to his own enquiry after her welfare, 'How are you? As well as can be expected, eh.' Not that Dorothy was not grateful, for she seemed to have no control over the thickening of her tongue, but if she could hear something like 'black brogues', perhaps then she could understand that he was indeed speaking of Arthur, a young man who stood with her only three months ago in Bata's in Kerkstraat and explained, 'Mamma, they're back in fashion.' But these kilted words were about inaudible footsteps; in a strange city where she had as yet not seen a single person in black brogues.

They sat in a room that reminded her of the in-flight film which she saw through an insistent reel of still images. Of Arthur as a toddler, in his school uniform, with the first traces of a stubble, at the airport with a scholarship to Glasgow University. An elegant room, Michael Caine said from the corner of his mouth as he strode about, idly - and rudely if you asked her, she had certainly taught her children manners right from the start - picking up an ornament before sitting down in a chintz arm-chair. Then Arthur as a young man, never ashamed of helping her with the housework. She had waited by the door while her host emerged from behind his desk to shake her hand. They sat in a cluster of chintz chairs and coffee table at the far end of the room and like Michael Caine she looked at the high ceiling while the man in the kilt poured coffee from a glass pot with a plunger. At the cornice, elaborately moulded, and the ornate ceiling-rose, an intricate pattern of spiky leaves, and she recognised the paintbrush heads of flowering thistle. A room of muted colours in which to speak about a death. The walls were a pale grey, the woodwork a shade deeper, the lush carpet another bluish grey and looking out through the tall windows, sets of panes imposed a grid on the vast canvas of uniform grey representing a sky that spoke nothing of the weather. For by weather she understood either rain or the clear sky of Namaqualand.

She started at his movement. He placed his right leg across the other, his left hand clutching the right ankle. His eyes wandered, then came to settle just below Dorothy's left ear lobe. She dropped her eyes on to the large knee, a brutally scrubbed plain of cartilage, and resolved to concentrate. He was still speaking of the Botanic Gardens where a guard saw a young man at eleven pm who answered to the description of Arthur and whom he recognised as someone who frequented the Kibble Palace. But why was he telling her about the huge hot-house; he had said that she should go and see the place for herself and she had nodded dutifully. But he went on:

'... a lovely structure, our Kibble Palace - very old - built a long time ago on Loch Long, where it was privately owned, and then the entire glass structure was floated down the river Clyde on a raft. Brought to the Botanic Gardens in the nineteenth century. But it's unbearably hot, of course. Tropical conditions you understand for these marvellous plants from all over the world: Australia, South Africa, New Zealand, India and, of course, America. Absolutely marvellous, like travelling ...'

Arthur wanted to travel - right round the world. Wanted to be first an engine driver, then a pilot or a ship's captain, nothing special, just dream-boasted like the other children, like Jim and even little

Evvie. A slight boy in short trousers and scarred knees, darker than the rest of his skin, almost black, who stuck his hands in his pockets and with the remarkable combination of lisping and rolling his r's which she knew would take him far, managed to say, 'Sthee-e, sthee-e, when I come back with bagth full of money I'll marry Mamma and we'll have sweeth everry day.'

She shut her eyes momentarily to wrench her mind from the image of the boy and concentrated on the man's words. But he too had slipped up, had allowed his mind to wander, so that he carried on like any tourist guide, '... also the People's Palace is well worth visiting. Another glass structure, smaller, but devilishly hot too - eh, for the plants, of course. Lovely tropical things. The rest of the building is a museum - the history of the working people of Glasgow. You'll find that interesting, coming from South Africa. Very important to have these records. Of the struggle ... you'll understand how here in Scotland ... but remembering the people of the city, eh, that's what being human is all about. Aye, well worth a wee visit and not a bad place, of course to have a bite of lunch either eh ...'

He faltered as Dorothy leaned forward, frowning. How could Arthur be the subject of this talk? What was the man saying? Who was this man in the kilt? She had surely come to the right place; he had expected her, welcomed her himself. Or was he speaking in code? Arthur had once said to her after a strange telephone conversation, Don't worry, you can't speak plainly anymore; you can't be safe without a code. *Ag*, then she let it ride; she didn't want to be bothered with such things and now, now knowing nothing of politics, she was failing Arthur. A bird flapped its dark wings in her chest. Panic widened her eyes.

Mr MacPherson whose words had strayed so wantonly, bit into a syllable then shot out a hand that hovered in the horizontal to steady her. He had seen television images of South Africans at gatherings, black women ululating and stamping their feet and really he would not know what to do about such behaviour in the office; he would steady her with practical advice.

'Mrs Breenk, you'll need distraction of this kind. This is a difficult business eh coming to terms with Arthur's eh ... but above all it is important to keep calm. The People's Palace is outwith this area but trying to find your way is, of course, good for occupying the mind. Keep going and you'll keep in control.'

As if she would lose control here amongst strange white people. Oh, she did not understand this talk that had nothing to do with her and it was all her fault, no good finding out about a code now when it was all too late. She, a woman without learning, who had not managed to keep Arthur from politics, could only sit quietly and obey the hand stretched out like dominee's with blue veins and liverish patches, commanding her to remain seated. Only when the hand dropped to his side and the knees moved and the body folded out into the vertical did she read his movements as a sign for her to rise. Her movements followed his; the navy-blue handbag, held with both hands before her, faced his sporran apologetically.

'So, Mrs Breenk, as you can see, we're doing our best. But,' and he paused to look at her gravely, 'one must be realistic. It would be foolish to hold out too much hope.'

She did not care about her words squeaking. In a high voice that ran like mice along the curlicues of the cornice, she said, 'Yes sir. No hope. I have no hope at all. But it's the body. It's please, the body sir. I am his mother; I must see Arthur's body.'

He pressed his hands together in pointed compassion. And lowered his voice.

'Mrs Breenk. I understand. I understand your concern but we are doing our best. We shall have to be patient but I can assure you that the police are doing their best.'

'Sir, I would like to speak to one of the other children from home. There was a girl, Tsiki; I saw her yesterday ...'

'I'm afraid Mrs Breenk that that won't be possible. These young people - and not only the students from South Africa - have a heavy programme. An unfortunate time really. You see they're taking exams and we here at the British Council are concerned that the unfortunate disappearance of Arthur should not cause any further upset amongst our students. It's a difficult business being a student in a foreign country where you're not only contending with new ideas but also a foreign language, of course. I think you'll agree Mrs Breenk, that further contact with the other students would be inadvisable. Young people and especially the young women are so vulnerable, so easily upset.'

Mr MacPherson prised apart his hands for the greeting. She fumbled with the bag and transferred a scented handkerchief to her left hand in order that her right could be vigorously shaken by him.

A taxi waited to take her back to the hotel and she had to say that she was well looked after. That at least she could take back to Vlaklaagte· that the British Council provided taxi-drivers who said Yes Ma'am and drove her to a comfortable, if old-fashioned, hotel. Also, a nice young woman from the British Council had taken her to the hotel last night even if she did go on rather foolishly about the light switches: On and Off as if she were God trying out the sun on the first day. On. See. Pointing to the lampshade suspended from a high as heaven ceiling and Off, with a voice inflected for darkness. Quite ridiculous and funny how it made her think of the oil lamps of the early days. Arthur was the one who could not bear a smudge of smoke on the lamp glass. He kept it sparkling; always particular her Arthur who loved his Mamma, she promised herself, loved his Mamma, but the girl asked if she wanted to try for herself - On. Off. She shook her head. Whatever would these people say next? Still it had been easy enough to understand the girl who said, as if she could read her thoughts, 'If you prefer to eat alone here in your room, just telephone down and order something and don't worry about money. The British Council will see to everything.' She wished she had asked Arthur what this British Council business was; she had hoped to ask one of the other students.

Dorothy eased herself on to the bed still holding the handbag, its base pressed against her bosom. Her cousin Celie's bag, for she had decided that she would not wear black, would not believe the worst. Navy-blue crimplene was smart and she sighed, a good compromise and she wanted everything to match, to ensure that Arthur would not feel ashamed of her. So particular he was - Always look your best Mamma - with that fastidious flattening of lips against his teeth as he checked her clothes for the prize-giving at high school. Her boy who did not want to know about his father, about the fathers of Jim and Evvie - men whom she remembered only as eerie, elongated shadows that fell now and again, accidentally, across the frowning or smiling faces of her children. She had barely begun her story, choked with shame, when he interrupted, 'Mamma, it's just you and us and let's not talk about it, let's not talk about anyone else. You've done everything by yourself. From nothing you started the shop and look now everything's OK. That's all I want to know.' Or something like that, something that promised to wash away the shame of twenty years and from Arthur, her youngest, who was so particular. Too particular? That's what Celie thought, she knew what Celie-them thought, but no one would dare say anything to her.

From the start, from the very moment of his conception, there had been a weight in her womb which told of the specialness she was carrying so that she hardly registered the disappearance of the man. Or perhaps she had just come to expect it. But this time she didn't care. The foetus absorbed what little shock there was. She loved the child who lurched about wildly in her belly, a child who wanted to be born. No ambiguous flutterings in the womb; he moved purposefully and three weeks before he was due, manoeuvred into position and fought his way out, a strong, healthy baby. If surprisingly slight. No ordinary boy he; she knew that he would be a bank manager or a president or something else even bigger although she warned him against messing about with politics. Always particular he was, her Arthur. How, and Dorothy's fists beat at the pillows, how could they tell her that there was no trace of him, that he had just disappeared? Just a name? A missing person? An absence? A nothing? Oh, she felt the emptiness, the lightness that would make her body rise to that heaven high ceiling and cackle at the nothingness that had been her soul snuffling against a handbag.

She grabbed the handbag, slipped on her shoes and coat and rushed out. She would not cry here in this barbarous place where no one cared to find his body. That was what the girl, Tsiki, had said. That they had done nothing: a tired police constable had arrived two days later to ask obscure questions and did not come back. That it was a conspiracy, but she did not know what that could mean. She would find her child and she boldly hailed a taxi, one that stood right outside the door as if it were waiting for her, to take her to the Botanic Gardens. The man did not say Ma'am; he asked for money and shrugged and shook his head and just held out his hand when she said British Council. He joked about her twenty pound note - Lots of money eh - and gave her as change a ten pound note with a picture of what seemed to be smiling Africans. Something was written across the image in blue ball-point pen. This taxi driver was not to be trusted. To hell with blooming mysteries and secret codes. Politics was one thing, but joke currency quite another. For ten years she had been running her own village shop successfully; a business woman was not to be fooled in this way.

'Listen man, here in England the notes say Bank of England,' she said, and in response to his frown, added, 'No good sitting there with a mouthful of teeth; if you've got someting to tell me why don't you speak? I'm a shopkeeper; I trade groceries for cash; don't think you can cheat me with signs and codes,' and checking the other side of the note, 'and false money from some Clydesdale Bank.'

The man engaged a gear as he hissed, 'Just fuck off Missus. Bank of England! Where do you think you are? This isn't fucking England,' and drove off.

But surely Scotland was part of England ... *Ag*, she couldn't understand these people; she would have to speak to the official man in the kilt and if there were any problem with the money perhaps he would sort it out.

* * *

The Kibble Palace was a fairy-tale house of glass and wrought iron painted silver. In the first, smaller dome the distant crown of a palm-tree brushed against the glass top. There at the top each row of panes grew narrower, tapering until the tiny rectangles of glass turned into sharp triangles which would, had there been sunlight, sparkle like diamonds. Fat, orange fish floated in the pond at the base of the tree. It was warm. She sat on a wooden bench, one she was sure Arthur would have sat on. It was no doubt the heat that had brought him here so often. But she would not give in to grief, would not allow her heart to howl with pain. She would get to the bottom of this; she owed it to Arthur who never, never would have killed himself.

She took out the ten pound note. On the front, where a picture of a man labelled David Livingstone was trapped amongst palm leaves, it claimed to be issued by Clydesdale Bank PLC. On the back - and she flushed with shame - a naked woman was flanked on either side by naked men, captives or slaves, squatting serenely in their leg-irons under palm trees. An overdressed Arab on a camel occupied the middle-ground whilst in the distance a sailing boat drifted on the water. Across the picture and across the plain white strip at the edge marked simply with the £10 figure, someone, the taxi-man perhaps, had written in blue pen: If dat bastard Geldof don't git 'ere soon I goes eat dat camel.

Dorothy smoothed the note and put it into her wallet, carefully, in order not to crease it. What was she to make of this message? And who would write such bad English on what she now had to believe was a perfectly good note? A visiting dominee had once explained about the Bible, how the stories meant something other than the actual words said. Then the story about the leper which he explicated turned out to mean exactly what she had always thought it to mean and she checked with Mrs Willemse who said the same. So, if one thing did stand for another she was perfectly capable of working it out. But which figure was she to attribute the words to? Livingstone, an explorer, she remembered, but could he really be showing off his slaves? And who was Geldof? Should she substitute Arthur for Geldof which was surely a Boer name? And geld meaning money? She flushed with shame, or was it rage, at the 'bastard' which suggested that someone knew all about Arthur. But if Arthur were the victim, to be ... oh, she would not think the monstrous thing through. The British Council man was right. She had to keep going, keep moving. The horror thickened in the heat but she steadied herself and carried on.

In the approach to the main dome, on either side of the glass corridor, a discreet notice announced that this was South Africa. Not that she recognised many of the plants. A raggedy tree labelled Greyia seemed familiar but the Erica tree, sprinkled with icing-sugar, she had certainly never seen before. It was blossom: a million miniature white chalices with the slenderest of brown stamens. Camellia japonica flowered a deep pink that Arthur loved. He would have come in from the biting cold into this brilliance of heat and pink. And recognised, perhaps from his books, the lilies, nerine, strelitzia, agapanthus and of course hen and chickens posing under a posh name. She said the names of the flowers aloud in Arthur's measured tone. And she heard his new black shoes on the floor of bricks packed into neat chevrons as he followed the lure of the heat into the dome.

Palm trees squashed together in the inner circle and from the wrought iron beams, drops of condensation plopped into the dome of silence. Dorothy unbuttoned her coat. She turned right into the outer circle through Australia, New Zealand, a South American jungle, the undergrowth of temperate Asia, the Canaries and the Mediterranean. How quickly it took to tread the entire world for in no time she was back at the icing-sugared Erica, entering South Africa once again.

It was in his fourth letter that Arthur spoke of lithops, of the hot stony beds where they kept prickly pears and other succulents. She found the room and smiled at the Namaqua vygies, made up, like platteland girls in Town, sitting pertly behind glass if you please.

But she knew nothing of the reed and timber but that beckoned from another room. Its walls were lined with boards displaying texts and photographs of the Trades House of the Glasgow Expedition to Papua New Guinea. There were pictures of bearded white men with rucksacks walking through forests or bending over indistinguishable plants. Then Dorothy gasped, for there before her very eyes was Arthur poring over a table of uprooted plants. His spread right hand was held out as if in blessing over the collection. The caption called him the High Commissioner for Papua New Guinea. Dorothy held on to the wooden post. Oh, she could have sworn it was Arthur, her own boy, tall and slender, but she supposed the man was somewhat older. Why was this photograph of a black man mounted here to break her heart? She would not look again at this High Commissioner and she felt a chill creep up from her feet and spread through her entire body. But she carried on, now stiff with cold. As the man from the British Council said, there was nothing to do but carry on. She read out the text on the next board, loudly, like a child learning to read:

> ... to seek out orchids, begonias and ferns for display at the Glasgow Garden Festival and, thereafter, to become part of the permanent collection maintained at the Glasgow Botanic Gardens, part of the cultural heritage of the City.

Dorothy sank to the earth floor of the Papua New Guinea hut, leaned her head against a wooden post and spread out her legs comfortably. A young child came upon her and skipped to and fro between those legs and shouted, 'Mu-um, look a Papoo person', but his mother whispered 'Shush' and dragged him away. It was ten minutes later that a guard took her by the arm and lifted her to her feet. She did not brush the dust from her navy-blue coat. What did it matter. She knew that Arthur had been swallowed by this city, that he would never again pick a thread from her lapel - Always look your best Mama. Always look your best. Still she held her head high. But she could not answer the uniformed man's questions. He spoke softly, kindly, and she handed over her handbag to him. So he called a taxi which took her back to the hotel.

Months later, leaning over the shop counter and peering into the heart of a cloud shaped like a camel, Dorothy could have sworn that the man had spoken to her in Afrikaans, '*Alles sal regkom Mevrou,*' but she could of course not be sure.

PART II

Apartheid South Africa

4 SOUTH AFRICA, THE IMPRISONED SOCIETY
A drawing by Matthew Krouse

SOUTH AFRICAN ELEGY

Bodies broken beneath a blood-red sun,
Casting shrivelled shadows on the soil.
Everlasting life dissolving in the dark,
Twisting fingers searching for the soul.

An agony ago, a pallid promise:
A squalid offer of an old exchange.
Forgotten children with expectant eyes
Hear mournful murmurs of revenge.

An echo of an ancient agony,
A body broken, bleeding on a cross;
A scream of pain across a continent,
Each single death a separate sacrifice.

A multitude of martyrs pierced with pain,
A deep wound turning in the side.
A passion piled upon the dead,
The carcass of a country crucified.

See the figures on forsaken ground,
The features of that ancient agony.
The hand that opens on that promised land
Extends the last touch of its elegy.

ALAN BOLD

VERWOERD

Harold Macmillan

The important business of the tour began only on 2 February when I reached Cape Town. We stayed in a delightful house called Groote Schuur where we were the Prime Minister's guests. I had long discussions with Dr Verwoerd, at most of which Mr Louw, as well as Norman Brook and John Maud, were present. These were most illuminating, and it was only during these days that I began to realise to the full extent the degree of obstinacy, amounting really to fanaticism, which Dr Verwoerd brought to the consideration of his policies. Apartheid to him was more than a political philosophy, it was a religion; a religion based on the Old Testament rather than on the New, and recalling in its expression some of the attitudes and even the phrases which had become famous in the Scottish history of the seventeenth century. If Dr Verwoerd spoke in that strange but attractive lilting voice which is characteristic of Dutch South Africans speaking English, he had all the force of argument of some of the great Calvinist leaders of our Scottish kirk. He was certainly as convinced as John Knox himself that he alone could be right, and that there was no question of argument but merely a statement of his will. He would have made a good impression on the Synod of Dort. Even in small matters he had pressed apartheid to its extreme. In a country where there is at least the advantage of being able to enlist the services of an African staff, he refused to have a single African in his house. An old and rather incompetent Dutch butler looked after us. The house, which might have been so gay, was strangely grim. Yet I have seldom met a couple with greater charm than Dr Verwoerd and his wife. She was particularly attractive in her quiet and friendly attitude and looked after my wife with a genuine warmth which could not be mistaken for mere convention. The Prime Minister, with his quiet voice, would expound his views without any gesture or emotion. At first I almost mistook this calm and measured tone for a willingness to enter into sincere discussion and at least to try to understand the position which I was upholding. All through I had the strange feeling that, although on the South African side there was an almost pathetic desire to be understood, there was no comprehension of how the fixed policies of her Government were regarded by the outside world.There was a plaintive, almost naïve sense of grievance. They believed that their unpopularity, whether external or internal, arose not from their own policies but from the cold attitude shown to them both by the United Kingdom and the United States. The Foreign Minister seemed to be convinced that South Africa might form an effective bridge between the Western Powers and the uncommitted African states if we would only show more sympathy with South Africa's objectives.

From Pointing the Way, *Volume V of Harold Macmillan's memoirs (1972)*

VERWOERD'S SOUTH AFRICA: THREE YEARS AGO THERE WAS STILL A CHANCE

JAMES CAMERON   *News Chronicle, 7 July 1959*

My friend, who was driving, swung through the suburbs into the country and said: 'The great thing is to keep going.' Johannesburg lay behind, all carnival with lights; the dark farmland ahead. 'Don't pull up for anything. Never mind if it's a car overturned or someone's injured or a baby in the ditch; carry straight on; that's the way to stay out of trouble.'

The road stretched through the fields, full of shadows. 'Try not to hit a cow. Don't worry about dogs. If it's a native, keep going; he's hard to see and he has no right on the road anyway.'

We came to the place of a farmer I know. It seemed he had missed one of his boys - that is to say, one of his Africans had not showed up for a while and (since not all South African farmers are tyrants) he had gone to the police. Sure enough, the boy was inside - a pass-law charge; the risk every African takes every day of the year. Taking advantage of the law, the farmer bought him back from the prison; a farmer can have a convict for ninepence a day.

So now he had bought him back for ninepence a day, instead of the four shillings he had been paying him. The prisoner doesn't get the ninepence, the Government does, but my friend paid him the four bob anyhow. That was indeed the luckiest African in the Union.

'And what would you do if you saw him in the garden right now?' I asked, after dinner.

'Why, shoot him', said my friend. 'After dark, you shoot them.'

It would have been a paradox anywhere else.

Suddenly my friend said: 'I'm retired. I love this place. I put everything I've got in this place. I hate the country, I hate the Government, I hate the filthy laws, but I love my place; why shouldn't I?'

'I don't want to shoot anyone, but I'd sooner do that than get shot. Where can I go? How do I *know* the time's come to go? I detest what goes on in this damned country, but what can I *do* ?'

Three years ago he would not have said that.

A business man took me into the Rand Club. I remember when

the Rand Club made the Carlton look like the Universities and Left Review coffee bar.

They used to hem me in corners and harry me like beagles as an intruder, a red-neck liberal. They always knew best - about money, about gold, about kaffirs, about morality.

Now the businesss man said: 'It's got to the point of no return. I never gave a damn about race laws if they were going to keep the white man in business; the native isn't a person to me.

'But this Government has gone stone crazy, man, and they're here for good. What do I *do* ?'

Three years ago he would not have said that.

But I couldn't tell him what to do. I didn't know what to do myself. What I did was go to Cape Town.

The city of Cape Town, where are made the ugliest laws ever framed by modern bigotry and intolerance, has perhaps the loveliest situation of any capital in all the world. It sits among the mountains and vineyards of a land more enchanting than Provence.

It is the seat of Parliament, and its principal products are wine and fruit, hatred and despair. Turnover in the first has been average this year, but productivity in the last is the greatest of the century.

The Parliamentary session has just ended in a blaze of acrimony almost frightening in its desperation - all debate crushed by the Government guillotine, every measure another bar in the cage of apartheid, every speech a declaration that the die is cast, there is no more going back.

The last act was the elimination of Fort Hare University. Fort Hare, in Grahamstown, was the one remaining African institution of higher learning, created by itself, sustained for 40 years alone.

It conflicted in no way with the Government's apartheid policy, since it was wholly Bantu.

It offered no threat to anyone, and it has been destroyed and replaced by a mock 'tribal college' resembling nothing, leaving no African seat of higher learning at all.

The Nationalists are honest. 'If there is one thing the white man must guard against' said Mr D J Mostert, MP for Witbank, 'it is African indoctrination through the medium of education.'

All over the Union thousands of minds - white minds- recoiled at the ultimate cynicism.

They had flinched at the slave-farms, the convict labour, they had winced when Minister of Justice Swart publicly sanctioned the police patronising the brothels they prosecuted; they shrank intellectually if prudently, from the ruthless extension of racial legislation.

'But nothing,' said the *Johannesburg Sunday Times* last week, 'will disgust the world as much as this'.

Three years ago it would not have said that.

By making *no* concessions to the smallest urges of conscience, by grinding *all* argument into the dust, by making 'liberal' a dirtier word than Communist, by gerrymandering itself into an impregnable position, Dr Verwoerd's Government has solidified almost all English-speaking South African opinion against it for the first time.

Nor is it only English speaking. There are the three now-famous professors of the ultra-Afrikaans University of Potchefstroom - Coetzee, Du Plessis and Kruger - who 'solemnly protested' at the Verwoerd policy of disaster.

Furious, the Nationalists disciplined them, but the revolt of Afrikaner intellectuals had begun.

There were stirrings even in the monolith of the Dutch Reformed Church, which theologically believes Africans are sons of Ham, without human rights.

Several Predikants denounced the worst of apartheid as 'against the teachings of Christ'.

Three years ago they would not have said that.

For the works of the Nationalist Government of South Africa, which have sickened all decent people outside the Union for years, have now begun to alarm - perhaps even disgust - many inside who have held their peace so long.

For the blows against freedom and decency need no longer be struck by Dr Verwoerd carefully and quietly, but can be hammered out openly and crudely and proudly, in the sure knowledge that by now the machinery of law and Constitution has been distorted into his own shield.

Dr Verwoerd knows that he is doomed, and his arms are already around the pillars of the temple.

Three years ago I would not have said that.

STARRYVELDT

Starryveldt
  slave
southvenus
  serve
SHARPEVILLE
  shove
shriekvolley
  swerve
shootvillage
  save
spoorvengeance
  stave
spadevoice
  starve
strikevault
  strive
subvert
  starve
smashverwoerd
  strive
scattervoortrekker
  starve
spadevow
  strive
sunvast
  starve
survive
  strive
SO:VAEVICTIS

EDWIN MORGAN

REMINISCENCE

Angus Calder

The closest I've ever been to the Republic of South Africa is Malawi in 1978, for a memorable month as Visiting Lecturer at the University - 'teaching' mostly creative writing. It is a very beautiful country, with highland views to rival Scotland. By its huge lake, I prudently (as I thought) wore a dressing gown while sitting outside a friend's holiday cottage. I forgot that shins and feet burn as easily as one's face and that sun does not spare wearers of dressing gowns who leave them partly open. I carry burn marks on my stomach to this day and my legs have never fully recovered from an incineration which in an hour or two was sufficient to make them swell rawly and painfully. Nevertheless, I remember the wonderful sight of that lake with a pang of nostalgia. Exiles have convinced me that parts of South Africa have the same heart-breaking beauty.

Malawi, alas, imitated the Republic's repression, and still does. President Kamuzu Banda, almost uniquely among Black African leaders, had friendly links with Pretoria. Friends on campus offered South African wine and brandy as a matter of course: it was what you could get in Zomba's supermarket. Censorship imitated South Africa's, and was as much absurd as evil, slashing essential narrative out of films on grounds of politics, race, or mere prudery, and prohibiting works by Tolstoy and Solzhenitsyn which referred approvingly to the dedication of Jehovah's Witnesses in Russian prison camps, since Banda persecuted witnesses himself. While white lecturers risked being 'PId' - declared prohibited immigrants - if they talked indiscreetly, black intellectuals courted far worse danger. When I talked in Zomba's OK Night Club with Jack Mapanje, Malawi's leading poet (as I write, he has been detained without trial since 1987) he communicated his views about Malawi by hints, innuendoes, making it clear to me that the place was crawling with informers who might hear us over the incessantly repeated strains of a scratched record of 'Rivers of Babylon' played for dancers on a tiny gramophone. Historians could not work safely on twentieth century Malawian history, in case their view of events during Banda's very long lifetime did not concur with his.

Nevertheless, I could use an evening with historians as evidence that even Banda's grim little dictatorship provided a measure of freedom, of the utmost significance, denied to people in the Republic.

I had developed from several years in Nairobi a distaste for the type of ex-colonial club where expatriates drank or played squash with a a few rich members of the African élite. I spent my evenings mostly with African colleagues. This commended me to Bertin Webster, Professor of History, who had the same prejudice, sufficiently for him to invite me to a barbecue at his home. Bertin, a Canadian, had a straightforward liking for the Africans whose past he studied, pioneering techniques in oral history. As we sat in his garden that night with African colleagues he spoke movingly about the occasion when his mother had come to visit him in Malawi. Such is the respect for age in this, as in other African countries, that guests arriving at a party of his all swept past him at once to pay her homage: she was clearly the most significant person present. Nevertheless, that night I was at his barbecue he had the broad humanity to entertain very graciously a young Afrikaner women, a 'yarp' up from the South.

Her reasons for visiting Malawi might seem discreditable enough. She had just graduated from a teacher training college in Johannesburg. Before the prison house of career with marriage and life in an all white suburb closed gates on her, she was buying a special kind of 'freedom', such as, I understand, male Afrikaners have sought in Swaziland and Sun City. Across the border, one could sleep with black people. A charming young African historian had picked her up, or been picked up, and had brought her along to Bertin's. But she found more freedom than she had bargained for: the freedom to hear the truth about her own country's history. Her sincere amazement, her dawning delight, are what dominates my memory of that evening: a big, handsome, fair haired, freckled woman sitting in half-light, overwhelmed by what she heard.

She had learnt a Boer view of history. She knew the story of the Great Trek of the 1830s and the supposed savagery of the Zulus defeated at Blood River. She did not know that the human geography of the interior into which Boers escaping, as they saw it, from British oppression, had been disrupted by Shaka's Zulu armies in the *Mfecane*, 'the grinding of peoples' beginning some twenty years earlier. She had not grasped that other peoples in South Africa had thrown up leaders at least as impressive as Piet Retief; she had not heard of the vast treks which took refugees from Shaka's rule north, Mzilikazi's Ndebele into what is now Zimbabwe, Nwangendaba's Ngoni as far as Lake Malawi. She had not heard of the subtle and wise Moshoeshoe who rallied the Sotho people in the mountains of what is now Lesotho and was ultimately responsible for that country's independence, though it is landlocked by the Republic of South Africa, or of Sobhuza, the founder of Swaziland, or of Adam Kok, leader of the mixed-race Griquas. To her the name of Dr John Philip, who left Aberdeen in 1820 when already middle-aged to supervise the London Missionary Society's work at the Cape, would have reeked of evil: that of the man whose fulminations against slavery and influence at Westminster largely contributed to the decision by Afrikaner farmers to trek north under such tough leaders as Retief and Pretorius.

The history of South Africa in the early and mid-nineteenth century has an epic grandeur, conveyed by the earliest black South African to publish a significant novel in English, Sol T Plaatje in his *Mhudi* (1930). It is no more a narrative merely of massacre and attempted massacre than that of Napoleonic Europe. It reveals a certain dignity in the Boer trekkers - pious frontier farmers - not evident in the wealthy, cynical whites who have governed South Africa in this century. Interaction and alliance between cattle herders of several ethnic groups, including the white Afrikaners, were not impossible.

Was the amazement of that Afrikaner woman at Bertin's that night just the effect of his generous hospitality? Did she go back South in the end sealing her mind again, preparing herself to teach incomplete and perverted history to her pupils? I don't know. I like to think that the shine in her eyes had to do with a realisation that her pride in her country - even her pride in Afrikaner heritage - had been enhanced by what she had heard.

I've thought of fictionalising this episode. A short story could have conveyed, perhaps, the strong sexual overtones to that gathering. But how could I have reproduced the erudition of gifted colleagues which bowled her over? Perhaps they wouldn't have talked so well if she hadn't been young and attractive - perhaps, for that matter, I wouldn't remember the meeting at all. But I knew just enough myself to realise that what she was getting was truthful and intricate history, such as can help to free minds from prejudice. I like to think that intellectual liberation has meant more in the long run to that friendly woman than whatever sexual pleasure she obtained in the 'Warm Heart of Africa', Banda's police state.

SOWETO PHOTOGRAPHS

i

Entering Soweto, we pull up to photograph
the contrasted sides of the street: huts
of corroded metal, opposite shacks even older,
squatting in their own detritus. Half
naked children play among rubber tyres.
A dog grapples with a hoop of wire.

A car draws in: a plainclothes patrolman
in shirt and slacks, gun-butt showing.
He asks the driver's occupation.
'Minister of religon...my friend
from abroad is keen to see round'.
He gestures dismissively. We drive on.

ii

Outside the United Congregational
pre-school nursery, twenty children
by means of a plastic mickey-mouse
are taught the words for different colours
in a language not their own. When they get over
the novelty of my presence, I take my pictures

then saunter self-consciously to the street.
There screeches up a van, from which dangle
men in balaclavas: they leap off, empty
dust-bins, are on again and away.
A coalman reins up, wets his eyebrows
and poses as if to say *Take me, Take me...*

iii

'Down there, all that remains
of Sophiatown...remember Huddleston,
the bulldozing?' Smoke obscures the sun.
Next, Tutu's house: the brave one.

And on, and on. Soon we approach
Orlando stadium for which,

in '76, the children were heading.
My guide saw the bodies lying,
bullets in their backs. For the anniversary
next month, police will congregate
on this open ground, truncheons
and canisters of tear-gas at the ready.

iv

The faces of the elderly,
runnelled as by long drought;
children caught between one moment
and what the next may bring;
hard to believe these photos
are of the Soweto I saw;

squalid browns, even the brick latrines
picturesque in a way that lessens
their power to horrify - defusing
the rage that should augment
pity. What, I ask my companion,
does one do? *The little one can.*

v

Last, a child in a blue tee-shirt,
the lower part of his body bare.
In this light the side of his head
seems cropped. He stares
gravely as I peer
at him, get him in focus...

Now he is on my study wall,
where I tilt at meaningless
windmills, far from his hell.
Huge-eyed, he touches the heart.
Meanwhile, in another murderous
dawn, the world prises itself apart.

STEWART CONN

MOTHER IN EXILE   (For Lorna)

My twins are fourteen now
the last time I saw them
they were five
by the time they're twenty
they'll probably hate me
if they don't already.

The sea slaps. I want to watch
Moses walk across to her twins.
The sea slaps. How could she?
Even the blacks who live there
Are exiles -

PASS PASS PASS

The waves froth at the mouth of themselves
There are no words

Coming here you told me about the man
Who walked into the sea singing an Azanian freedom song.
Now I hear him - his voice swells the waves
He sings in such a deep bass the very fishes leap

Everyone watched him
till the sea came higher and higher
he looked so happy

On the beach half-skeleton fishes lie
Surreal as a war scene

My husband? He didn't approve
of my political activities
you know what he said to me?
You can have everything you want
Mercedes and servants, can you imagine?

PASS PASS PASS

At first he told the twins
your mother is a hippy
then he told them
your mother is a commie
now he tells them
your mother is dead.

Last night I dreamt
about the twins again
they were dolls shrinking
I woke soaking
it comes like this
the loss in tides

The waves froth at the mouth of themselves
There are no words

The man at the bottom of the sea
Is singing for all his might
His body is decomposing
The fishes are feasting

You know I phone all the way from London to Cape Town
his present wife tells me they're sleeping
I write letters and send presents
he writes back saying
I don't know why you bother
they never receive them
so now I don't, I don't bother

Your mother-tongue is Afrikaans
His is Urdu; you used to speak in English

I wonder whether I'll even like my sons
when they come to find me
they'll be like their father
Doctors with wallets and wives, Mercedes and servants
you know he's the Head of the Dept of Psychiatry
all these blacks he diagnoses paranoic
can you believe that?

PASS PASS PASS

The night before last
I lay in bed trying to imagine
my twins now
the photo I have is nine years out of date
each year on their birthday
I add some flesh, some height
but they keep reducing down to five

How can you be a mother
When your country and your husband won't let you?

The first time I had the nightmare
my twins were only an inch long
I was playing with them on the sand
one minute, the next they were gone
I dug and dug until I found them
two tiny worms
their mouths and eyes drowned in sand

The waves froth at the mouth of themselves
There are no words

We walk in silence
Your eyes have the sea in them
Your back is stiff
There is no comfort I can offer

The waves roar
I can see him wading the water
The sea coming higher and higher

We walk in silence
listening to the tide coming in

JACKIE KAY

JUSTICE WEARS A CLOTH
TO CATCH THE TEARS

Mourn Sizwe Bansi.
An identity rubbed out
to permit life.

Mourn a milk money thief
Blasted so that white people's cats
may grow fat.

Mourn Biko.
A red flame snuffed.

Mourn the Sharpeville children
And the Soweto children.
Expelled from life
To teach their fellows
A lesson.

Mourn the lost souls
Of the perpetrators.
In the sad mad delusion
Of white rightness,
Of black red bogiemen,
They insult Christ
With their allegiance
And insult intelligence
With their assertion
That a patch of desert
Is a home.

Mourn the blood
Past, present and future,
And share the blame
For this
our world.

EWAN R McVICAR

FLYING VISIT

The great ship shifted through space,
Approaching the speed of light
As it moved through the gyroscopic galaxy
With its plan and purpose
To see if the third planet
From a certain star
Supported sentient species.
Was there, its builders asked,
Intelligence on Earth?
Plunging unseen
Through the atmosphere
Of the blue planet
It surveyed the scene
And decided to land
In the land
Earthers call South Africa,
Covering its tracks
As it settled
In a secret sun-struck place.
It opened its lower doors
And its team of observers
Emerged, each of them black
In their search for intelligent life
They sought a city
And there, being black, they were
Brutalised, beaten and broken
By a race of white faces
Perpetually enraged.
When the observers returned,
Their tongues torn out
And their black skins scarred,
And their brains befuddled,
The great ship shifted again,
Leaving the blue sphere behind,
Caressing the blackness of space,
Knowing the answer to its question
Was negative.

                                    ALAN BOLD

THOUSAND FORCED TO FLEE DISPUTED REGION

I have read the paper too I know
The story of the thousand forced to flee
Their disputed region though no doubt
The thousand called it something else
Such as home for example here
No it did not say what forced them
Nor whether they were forced to go
Together towards the same unknown
Or to scatter as insects do
When their stone is lifted I imagine
They had time to round up the kids
Take their old if not infirm maybe
A cherished horse a particular goat
The dogs would no doubt follow
After all they were the thousand
And would pack what food they could
A bag of apples tipped from a bowl
A live chicken or two a t.v. dinner
What about the t.v. what about the radio
Leave them what have they ever done
For us take that amulet this ribbon
Those plates cups spoons a good knife
Whatever could be crammed into the pram
On the roofrack in the wheelbarrow
It could not have been much not much
Given that their time was short
Their warning brief I imagine
They themselves did not know where
And the question how to get there
Would have to be answered on the way
No it did not say what forced them
Nor whether they are fleeing still
I imagine they are they will be
Until the day we open our doors
And see the thousand there and say
You must be the thousand come in

We have read about you take a seat
Stay here make yourselves at home
Until you get your disputed region back
That doesn't happen though does it
You have read the paper too you know

BRIAN McCABE

RESETTLEMENT

These people say we have no right to live here where we've lived
so long
They have a piece of paper they say it says we must move on
We who've lived here all our lives must pull our little houses
down
Carry them for forty miles, then build another shanty town
Their orders say
We must obey

These people say we have no right to live here where we live
They have a piece of paper that a judge said they must give us
We who live in no man's land, we put no trust in uniforms
We wonder what the price is if that piece of paper should get torn
Their orders say
We must obey

These people say we have no right to live here
They have a piece of paper that will make it clear
We who live upon the road must kill our fire and lift our load
Trudge to find another place to lie between the earth and sky
Their orders say
We must obey

These people say we have no right to live
They have a piece of paper
We who live upon our knees
Must die for those who live at ease
Die because we have no voice
Die because we have no choice
Die for what the papers say
Die because we're in the way
Their orders say
We must obey

These people have
We live
Here.

Ewan R McVicar

STOP-OVER IN BOTSWANA

(i)

A deluge at Mafeking - first rain
for two years. Each intersection
a mud ravine. Food-stalls open,
the museum closed for Saturday afternoon.
I bolt a portion of chicken, move on.

No longer the limitless grainlands
of Western Transvaal; rich farms like bulwarks;
filling-stations a dependable distance between.
Scrub. Vans laden with soaked workmen.
Bophuthatswana. Terrain of orange and green.

A black boy I give a lift to
beckons to be set down. The next
points at the sky. 'More to come'.
The rainbow's end, in a shanty
suburb, ever more illusory.

Soon, the outskirts of Gaborone.
The rainbow double now, and full.
Darkness falling I phone,
from the disdainful President Hotel,
the friend of a friend with whom

I am to stop over. Allocated 'the room',
I wake before dawn. Above my head,
squashed shapes. Mosquitos,
I assume. Till one is hard to the touch.
The light on: gobbets of chewing-gum.

(ii)

Next day in the township of Oodi,
Seated on roasting rock, I wait
for the weavers' co-operative to open.
A maze of mud huts, roofed
with corrugated iron. Beauty in desolation.

A tinkle of goat-bells obscured
by a passing congregation. Cries of joy.
The leaders in white; the others
a merging in the clear distance
of, it seems, all the colours of the rainbow.

Wall-hangings bought, I say goodbye
and drive to the compound gate
only to find it locked. The weavers have gone.
No-one in sight, I sense eyes everywhere;
was never so conscious of being white.

I retrace my steps, explain. No problem;
just a matter of keeping the goats out ...
But the feeling lingers, that night
at a Kalihari concert, the din
insuperable, Masekela on flugelhorn

amplified to an extent that makes it
impossible, seated in an alcove
with two poets I briefly meet,
to yell other than, 'Talk later!'
The rainbow's arc is hammered into sound.

(iii)

Early morning, in Gaborone. Familiar
sounds assume a resonance of their own.
Distant dogs howl. Cocks crow,
presaging a dawn it is hard,
in such darkness, to believe will come.

Then leaving, by way of Lobatsi,
and east. At the border a man
cracks a hide whip at an imaginary
victim; and the Toyota in front of me.
hitting a mirage-patch, rides on air.

Beyond Ustenburg I book in
(having let attractive Swartruggens slip by)
to an unsavoury hotel where instantly
I become another brand of alien:
an Engelsman at the heart of Afrikanerdom.

So Botswana recedes in the memory
while comprising part of what supplants it,
itself to be supplanted in turn
by the evolving pattern of the whole.
In a morgue-like hotel bedroom

I shrink at the pounding roar
from a shunting-yard; not the din
but the brute force it manifests -
and an awareness, the cocks still crowing,
of the imminence of that savage dawn.

STEWART CONN

EARLY DAYS: RIVONIA

My room overlooks an oval pool, lit from below.
Between one and the other, trelliswork of vine. For two
Years, no rain. So that the perimeter is a dust-track.
Lemon and pomegranate trees. On the verandah
Azure-necked peacocks strut and squawk.

On my first day I am taken to Melrose House,
Site of the signing of the Treaty of 1902.
These Kitchener's quarters. I imagine
His rigid frame and incongruous behind him, a ring
Of pretty officers with butterfly-nets cavorting on the lawn.

The jacarandas have no bloom, being out of season.
On the return journey, the car picking up speed,
We pass brightly clad Blacks in the backs of vans
Or at bus-stops, lying in what shade there is,
Otherwise they only occasionally impinge - as when

Going to the theatre in Johannesburg,
We swerve to avoid a black youth, another
Prancing round him with a knife.
In the wing mirror, I see them rock together
As though caught in an irresistible slipstream.

Meanwhile the parasols on the verandah
Fade in the sun to a uniform pastel.
Distant barking of dogs: a reminder
That the world still spins. Was this once jungle?
I turn, half fearing to find some creature savaged in the pool.

STEWART CONN

NOBODY LIKES A REFUGEE

Naomi Mitchison

Nobody likes a refugee. They are a nuisance. They cause trouble. They are frightened and unwashed. They do not speak our language, at least not the way it should be spoken. They smell of over there.

All the same I think we have to help them, though it is good when they can be passed on. I remember very well that time in Lobatsi. Yes. I was much younger then and more afraid of what might happen to my future. It was not so long after Independence and I was still excited about that, as many of us were. I had passed my Cambridge and I had qualified for work in the Ministry of Education. Yes, I was a real Government Service man and it was at last truly our own government, even if there were still many whites in it, one of them my boss. But I had won my interview.

Well, I went over to see my aunt. We are from the Barolong and my aunt was a proud woman. Once she and my uncle, who had died a few years before, had land, a good farm across the border in the Republic. Yes, it had water and they had built a brick house with three rooms, as well as sheds and places for the plow oxen and the hens. She had a garden. How often she spoke of it! But it became a black spot in a white land, so the Boers took it, paying very little for the fields my uncle had cleared and fenced and nothing for the house, since they said that no white would live in it. Yet my aunt had kept it so clean you could lay a blanket down anywhere, and it was well thatched.

People spoke for my uncle, mostly other farmers, even Boers, for my uncle was well known and liked by all. But it was no use except that they let him stay until after the harvest. Then he must harness the oxen to the great waggon with all their things from the house and my aunt threw dust on the last fire she had lit and perhaps she cried and she and her children got themselves onto the waggon and they turned their backs on what was no more their home.

They crossed into Botswana which was then Bechuanaland and they made a farm, although much of it needed to be de-bushed before the next ploughing. The Barolong are good farmers and there were cousins who helped, among them my father. So it was not too bad. But my aunt was always grieving for the old house and the fruit trees she had planted, which had to be left and would be bearing fruit for others. There was less water in the new place, though the grazing was good enough. I used to visit them and meet my cousins. Then my uncle died and my elder cousin who should have done Junior Certificate failed, perhaps because he had been too sorry about his father. Moswetsi, that was his name, and his mother managed the farm well enough, but when I went to visit he sometimes became angry and sad because I had stayed on with education, and he had missed.

My aunt cooked nice food although she always complained that her kitchen was not like the old one. This time I brought her gummy sweets and half a bottle of whisky which I had shared with a friend. Myself, I do not like the taste of whisky, but it is the most expensive, so I liked to put down my own earned money and ask for it, more especially if there were white men at the bar who could see me pay proudly. This whisky I had bought out of only my third pay cheque. My aunt liked the whisky; it made her able to laugh a little and tell stories. I remember she told me about Plaatje; he had been some kind of a relation, I think. In all her stories the bad people had been the Boer men. This I could believe and I was very glad that new Botswana had shaken them off. Or almost.

Well, the next day was Sunday and we went to the church. I like to sing a few strong hymns, but I do not think they mean much, not to ourselves. My cousin Moswetsi, who was with us, slipped out after the second verse and I could see through the window that he was speaking with someone. His mother also seemed to see this and I could tell that it made her not happy. But that was all for the time. Later in the day Moswetsi and I took a lift into Lobatsi. In those days it was not so grand as it is now, the abattoir did not look the fine way it looks today and the shops were smaller. But it was more than that. We in Gaborone were lighthearted because of Independence and all our plans and the big Government buildings and the Mall and this feeling we had that everything must go well now and we had all voted, so that now we were a democracy and as good as the big countries. But in Lobatsi people went dodgingly, not looking at one another, nor greeting loudly and with laughter. Not everyone, but enough to make me uneasy. I found myself thinking that this was because it was so near the border with the Republic. I tried to speak of this with Moswetsi, but he shook his head. It seemed to me that, although he barely greeted one or two persons, yet he exchanged looks with a few. I waited for him to speak.

He said no, no. Yet I knew inside myself that he was not yet speaking from the heart and perhaps I had made him anxious, so I said we should have a drink and we should go to the Cumberland Hotel. As you know, that is the big place and indeed I thought to myself that perhaps I had been too bold and after all and in spite of Independence we could be treated coldly or even thrown out. But then I thought no. I am a citizen of the new Botswana and I myself am part of the Government, though as yet only a small part.

So we went in to the bar and several white men gave us hard looks and two of them whispered and laughed and I hated them. So I wondered if I should ask for whisky so that I could show that we Batswana could ask for anything and were as good as them. But then I thought that was a show-off and they could laugh at me secretly, so I asked for beers and when we got them another white man looked in a nice way and raised his glass to us. So for a while we sat in a corner and watched.

Then Moswetsi began to seem uneasy and said 'Let us go' and we walked along the road a little way out from Lobatsi and we spoke about the whites and so long as they were not the Boers it was all right.

In a while we saw a white man with a camera and he seemed to be taking photographs, as the tourists from everywhere are always doing, even of the most common things, so this was nothing new. The man walked slowly under the trees with the camera slung over his shoulder. He was wearing a jacket buttoned tight and suddenly it seemed to me that there was no shirt under it. Moswetsi said: 'Come, we will see' and he walked following the white man.

I said 'He is taking many photographs' and Moswetsi said 'Yes, but is there film in his camera?' And I was surprised, but I said to myself that white people sometimes do mad things.

And now we had come a little way out from Lobatsi and I thought we should begin to look for a lift. But Moswetsi was walking quickly and soon he was beside the white man and seemed to speak with him. They moved off the road to where there were some bushes and I asked myself what could my cousin be doing and whether we should stand and sign for a lift, since it had begun to be late and nobody could take photographs even if what Moswetsi had said was just a joke against the whites.

My cousin came and stood beside me. He said: 'The Boers took my mother's farm. The same Boers would take this man's life.'

'Why?' I said and then I began to understand, so now I whispered 'They are chasing him? The police?'

'We must get him to Francistown' Moswetsi said. 'That will take two days. You must keep him in your room in Gaborone.'

This made me angry. 'No!' I said, 'A big no. I am a Government servant. I am not interested in politics.'

'You will do this for my mother who is your aunt' said Moswetsi, and I did not answer. I wanted to go back to where we were before. I said 'It is time we got our lift.'

'Yes, yes,' said Moswetsi, 'but it is a certain safe lift, not any one. And I shall leave you when we get to my place and you will take him on to Gaborone.'

So we waited and I very much did not want this thing to have happened. Before, I had seen myself on a straight road that might lead to great advantages. And now I would perhaps be breaking some law, for I did not know why the Boers hated this man and he might have murdered one of them and he might have a gun as well as an empty camera. But my cousin said: 'It is good that our Botswana is now an independent country, and we can choose what way to go.'

So I began to think that after all this was so and we could decide who were our true friends. But still I would be going into trouble. Yet my cousin was so certain that I would do what he asked that I began to accept that the thing must be done. And soon there came a certain truck and Moswetsi stepped into the road and made a sign and it stopped. Then came the man out from the bushes and when the truck started he was sitting between the driver and me. We dropped Moswetsi off and he and the white man shook hands and passed certain words together and then we took the long road to Gaborone. Most of it was a dust road in those days, though it is a fine highway now.

I did not like the man's smell; perhaps he had not washed for too long; and sometimes he made swallowing noises. I talked across him with the driver, who was not from the Barolong but from Mahalapye, up north. He was an educated man but we did not speak in English since we were speaking about the one who sat between us and stared at the road rushing backwards under our lights and now and then there was a small animal or a bird that flashed across.

This driver told me that the South African police were after this man to be a witness in a big trial, saying what they wanted. A white man could be police-hurt just as well as a black and he had been much threatened. We all know well what is done in South African prisons. Now it is the same for the whites, the driver said. Yes, said the driver, all that unless he agrees to witness. And he will not do that.

'Yet he seems not to be a strong man' I said, for he had sagged back, and I saw he had not been able to shave.

'No', said the driver, 'he is not strong. But God might give him strength.'

'He will need that' I said, and I began to pity the man and wondered what was to be done.

The driver said he was taking the man as far as Gaborone. Later, he said, there will be a safe lift to Francistown.

I asked could not the man go by train, but the answer was that many of the train people were still from the Republic and not to be trusted even if now they were our citizens. That is not so today, but in those days the railway was not properly ours. So it seemed I must keep him safe until the next lift came. 'Do not let him go out of your house' he said. 'I will come back perhaps tomorrow. He must not be seen.'

'Must I feed him? ' I asked, and the driver said yes.

So it came that I took this man into my room, which was in one of the old houses, and I gave him a blanket and he slept and was still sleeping when I left for the office. It was a difficult day for me. I had many figures to copy and add up or perhaps subtract. In those days we must do all that by hand; now the small computers make it easy. But not then. I went over and over my figures and my boss became impatient. I made a small mistake. Oh, I cursed this refugee man who had made me so anxious.

He slept most of the day and after work I brought sandwiches and made tea. In the dark I took him out to shit. Late that night came a knock on the door. The man was most frightened. But I went and it was my cousin Moswetsi and someone with him whom I did not know, but he had a truck. So this white man whose name I never knew was put onto the truck and we all wished him well, but I was most glad not to see him again. No, he never told me his name and I did not ask.

'That' said my cousin, 'is your share of payment for the farm.' And I knew how he and his mother and even his younger sister had talked for many evenings about their farm and wept for the beautiful days there.

But my boss had found that small mistake in one of my sums and he was very angry and said hard things about my education. And I washed the blanket because it smelled of this man. All he had with him was the empty camera which he could use in pretending to be a tourist, and a little soap and a pair of socks. Even, he had no cigarettes. I never asked him his name. I did not ask, had he a wife, a home, what he did. Better not to know. But he had ink stains on his hands.

Later my cousin told me that this man had got safely to Francistown and the plane that took the refugees away. There was a powerful white man there who saw to it and protected them. But it was many days before my mistake over the adding was forgotten. I am not happy to remember it, even if it is now long ago.

Today I am a married man with an office that is wholly mine and my aunt is no more. Also the refugees who came from South Africa at the time of the terrible trials come no more. We have other kinds of refugees today, from further north, not white. Some are good people, but have lost their homes. They are at Dukwe now. But some among them are not good and are sent from the Boer Republic to make harm.

That is most difficult, for how can we tell which are the true refugees whom we should help, although we hope very much that they can be passed back to their old homes near Bulawayo. Yes, it is hard to know what to do. But it is a most sad thing to be a true refugee with no home, and always, always we must help them since we ourselves now have our own home and our own country. Which is Botswana.

ALEX LA GUMA (1925-1985)

James Kelman

(Said Chinaboy):

'I'd like to sit down in a smart caffy one day and eat my way right out of a load of turkey, roast potatoes, beet-salad and angel's food trifle. With port and cigars at the end.'

'Hell,' said Whitey, 'it's all a matter of taste. Some people like chicken and others eat sheep's head and beans!'

'A matter of taste,' Chinaboy scowled. 'Bull, it's a matter of money, pal. I worked six months in that caffy and I never heard nobody order sheep's head and beans!

'You heard of the fellow who went into one of these big caffies?' Whitey asked, whirling the last of his coffee around in the tin cup. 'He sits down at a table and takes out a packet of sandwiches and puts it down. Then he calls the waiter and orders a glass of water. When the waiter brings the water, this fellow says: "Why ain't the band playing?"'

We chuckled over that and Chinaboy almost choked. He coughed and spluttered a little and then said,'Another John goes into a caffy and orders sausage and mash. When the waiter brings him the stuff he take a look and say: "My dear man, you've brought me a cracked plate." "Hell," says the waiter. "That's no crack. That's the sausage".'

- an extract from a short story of Alex La Guma, a South African writer who died of a heart attack in October 1985; he was sixty years of age and living in Havana, the ANC's representative in Cuba. I first came upon his work a few years ago, the early collection entitled *A Walk in the Night*. One story in particular really stuck with me, 'A Matter of Taste', from which the above is taken. It is a marvellous bit of writing, telling of three men who meet over a pot of coffee in the middle of nowhere. They have a meandering conversation centred on food, then the two help the third hop a freight train heading for Cape Town wherein lies the possibility of working a passage to the USA. In the racial parlance of white South African authority the two are coloured and the third is white. La Guma himself was coloured. If the reader forgets such distinctions it won't be for long, for it is always there, the backdrop to his work, inextricably bound in with the culture he worked from within. Even in that brief extract above the divisions are evident, where Whitey sees choice and Chinaboy knows differently.

G

The title story of the collection is a novella, 'A Walk in the Night', a very fine piece of writing which I did not appreciate at the first time of reading. There was something missing for me which I see now as structural. In 'A Matter of Taste' that element existed and in consequence my appreciation of the story was much more immediate. 'A Walk in the Night' is a bleak tale, set in the coloured District 6 which used to be one of the worst slums in Cape Town until it was done away with altogether, to create space for white building development. A young man by the name of Michael Adonis gets the sack after a verbal disagreement with a white man. For the rest of the evening he wanders about in a semi-daze, going for a meal, periodically meeting with acquaintances, would-be gangsters. Eventually, in a moment of stupidity he vents his anger on an elderly white Irish alcoholic who lives in the same rooming house. The old man dies. Then the white policemen arrive and one of Michael's acquaintances winds up being mistaken for him, i.e. the killer. It is a memorable story, like most of the others in the collection. The structural element I spoke of as missing for me in my initial reading is to do with empathy; I found it very difficult to be with Michael Adonis, the world he moved in, it was alien to me. It was less alien on the second reading. The last time I read the story I knew the world he moved in even better.

Speaking purely as a writer it is good to feel anything and everything is possible in experiential terms. The existence of apartheid makes such a thing less easy to assume. In a good *Cencrastus* interview by Ian Fullerton and Glen Murray the South African writer Nadine Gordimer - who regards La Guma as 'the most talented black (sic) novelist since Peter Abrahams' - believes it is not possible for a white writer, like herself, in South Africa to write from within 'particular areas of black experience' and because of this

> cannot create black characters. The same thing applies the other way about. But there is that vast area of our lives where we have so many areas of life where we know each other only too well, and there I see no reason why a black writer can't create a white character or a white a black.

There is a fine point being attempted here although at first sight it might appear contradictory. In fact she doesn't quite bring it off and a question later seems to me to back away, saying there 'is something beyond the imaginative leap'. It has to be remembered that Gordimer was replying in an interview and to the best of my knowledge did not have the benefit of being able to work out her comments on the page. I think that if she had, to risk being presumptious, she may have brought in the use of basic structural techniques like the first and third party narratives, and developed her argument from there. In a straightforward manner, third party narrative allows the writer to create characters from the outside, where 'skins rubs against each other', but allows the writer to draw back from certain areas of experience, the sort which are to the fore psychologically and seem to demand the creation of character from the inside, more commonly wrought by the writer through first party narrative, although other methods are always possible.

Alex La Guma has written at least four novels; they have been published in Heinemann's African Writers Series, just about the most exciting list of English-language writing available anywhere, but difficult to get a hold of and at the time of writing not a solitary thing by La Guma is available in Europe's largest reference libary, Glasgow's Mitchell. I managed to read two of the novels; on which basis I have to agree with Lewis Nkosi, in his *Tasks and Masks* that La Guma is only 'a competent novelist who after the flashing promise of that first collection of stories seems to have settled for nothing more than honourable, if dull, proficiency'. *The Stone Country* is an extended version of the short story 'Tattoo Marks and Nails'; it is written in the third party and is based on the writer's personal experience of prison. There are many good things about the novel and too there are its defects, including a bit of a rushed, fairly predictable ending. But Yusef the Turk is a fine character and the Casbah Kid also, though occasionally La Guma glamourises a little too much. And the converse of that is the deadened Butcherboy, a creation that only manages to get beyond the stereotype of 'hulking bully'. The central character is George Adams, in prison for belonging to an illegal organisation which in the case of La Guma could simply have been the Communist Party since it has been banned for some forty years in that country. The novel is certainly 'competent' and La Guma's dialogue and working of the relationships between the prisoners often rises to the standard of the early stories. He uses the third party narrative in a restricted fashion, only rarely attempting to get within characters other than George Adams; thus we are seeing how folk act rather than how they think - which lies at the root of Gordimer's point as far as I understand it. This also provides a structural base for the reader unfamiliar with prison life in South Africa. I mean that to some extent we can *be* with George Adams in his dealings with an environment alien to him.

La Guma's last published novel seems to have been *Time of the Butcherbird* which appeared in 1979; this ended a silent period of seven years. According to the publisher's blurb the author gives 'a rounded picture of all the people in a small community inexorably moving towards tragedy.' I think that is what La Guma intended but

I also think he fails and that he fails in a predictable way. He uses the third party narrative voice but does not restrict it. Instead he sets out to give the psychological workings of assorted individuals, blacks, whites and coloureds, but falls into the trap of stereotyping: the poor white woman, Maisie Stopes, and the militant black woman, Mma-Tau, are both obvious examples of this, the former being a sleazy semi-slut while Mma-Tau is a vast 'Mother Earth'. It has to be said that the writing is hurried, often clumsy, and requires a straight-forward editing. The person for this would have been La Guma himself. Failing that maybe someone at the publisher's office should have performed the job properly. I'm not sure what Heinemann's policy is. Given the great literary merit of the African Writers Series the productions themselves are inferior, the actual paper cheap, the proofing generally substandard - and did La Guma censor himself in *The Stone Country*, or was it done by another hand?

La Guma's very fine skill lay in his dealings with day-to-day existence, his precise and 'concrete observation which is the correct starting point for all materialists' (Nkosi in *Tasks and Masks*). The highpoint in *Time of the Butcherbird* is the introduction of Shilling Murile from the time that he is 'sitting in the ditch' straight through until the end of the period he spends with the shepherd Madonele, some four thousand words later, as they move off together 'through the crumbling dunes, smelling the smoke'. It is a brilliant piece of writing. It shows the true mark of the artist. Perhaps it shows also why La Guma could have felt capable of trying a novel as ambitious as this. It was a risk and he failed. In that short story 'A Matter of Taste' the risk was an easy sentimentality but he succeeded. The best artists always take risks.

Realism is the term used to describe the 'detailing of day-to-day existence' and most writers who advocate social change are realists. Incidentally, one of the areas of exclusion under the South African censorship Act is the 'advocation of social change'; and, of course, the writings of La Guma have always been banned there. Nothing is more crucial nor as potentially subversive as a genuine appreciation of how the lives of ordinary people are lived from moment to moment.

Ordinary people. In the African Horn the children of ordinary people are eating insects to stay alive. It is a fact of existence so alien to other ordinary people that it cannot be admitted; there is an element lacking, a sort of structural base that does not allow us to *be* with folk for whom starvation is death and not simply a concept. To face such a fact in literary terms seems to be possible only in the work of a writer prepared to encounter the minutiae of day-to-day existence. And as far as I can see, any formal advances in prose have occurred directly because of that struggle; formal advances and 'imaginative leaps' may not be the same thing but they cannot easily be prised apart.

As long as art exists there are no areas of experience that have to remain inaccessible. In my own opinion those who think otherwise are labouring under a misapprehension which will lead to a belief that it is not possible to comprehend someone else's suffering, that we cannot know when someone else is in pain, that whenever I close my eyes the world disappears. It is an old problem. It has been kicking about in philosophy for several centuries. Just when it seems to have gone it reappears under a different guise and leads to the sorts of confusion we get in discussions to do with art and realism - naturalism - relativism - modernism - existentialism - and so on. One good example of this concerns the work of Franz Kafka. He is probably the greatest realist in literary art of the twentieth century. His work is a continual struggle with the daily facts of existence for ordinary people. Kafka's stories concern the deprivation suffered by ordinary people, ordinary people whose daily existence is so horrific other ordinary people simply will not admit it as fact, as something real, as something verifiable if they want to go and look. He seems to bend our lines of vision so that we see round corners and perceive different realities. A few other artists also do this or attempt to; they work in the minutiae of existence, trying to gain access to and make manifest the dark areas of human experience, and suffering.

Most artists from oppressed or suppressed groups are under pressure of one kind or another. Time becomes the greatest luxury. Without time the work just cannot be done properly. To read *Time of the Butcherbird* is to see a writer of enormous potential labouring to perform a workaday chore. But to criticise the lack of development in La Guma's prose is to assume certain general points concerning the role of the artist in society. In his *Twelve African Writers* Gerald Moore says differently. He believes La Guma's short stories are inferior to his novels which I find extraordinary. La Guma would not be divorced from his society, no matter how hard the white South African racist authority tried to achieve it. His whole background was one of radical commitment. His father was James La Guma, a former president of the Coloured People's Congress. Both he and Alex were members of the Communist Party throughout their lives and in 1955 they were involved in the formation of the Congress Alliance. This comprised the Indian Congress, the African National Congress, the Coloured People's Congress and the white Congress of Democrats. When the treason trials took place in 1955-61 Alex was one of the 156 leaders of the Alliance to be charged by the state. Then began the series of imprisonments and house-arrests which only ended with his departure from South Africa in 1966. He lived in London from then until 1979, although the literary people in control down there seem never to have noticed. For several years he was secretary of the Afro-Asian Writers Organisation (in 1969 he had won their Lotus Prize for literature).

Exactly one week after La Guma's death the poet Benjamin Moloise was murdered on the gallows by South Africa's white racist authority. Only a few years before that another good young poet, Arthur Nortje, committed suicide in Oxford while awaiting deportation 'home'.

In Roque Dalton's 'Declaration of Principles' (see *Edinburgh Review* No. 69) the poet can only be, as far as the bourgeoisie is concerned, a clown, a servant or an enemy. In South African society at present there is no alternative role available, whether for ordinary people or ordinary poets.

As a personal footnote; one of my treasures is a telegram I received from the man in early 1983. I had sent him an invitation to come and give a reading of his work at the Paisley Writers Weekend. Unaware of his whereabouts I sent it c/o the ANC in London; eventually came his reply:

THANK YOU FOR INVITATION FORWARDED ME FROM LONDON STOP
REGRET THAT AS AM RESIDENT IN CUBA WILL FIND IT DIFFICULT TO JOIN YOU   HAVE A GOOD WEEKEND STOP.

ALEX LA GUMA

Available works by Alex La Guma: *In the Fog of the Season's End, Time of the Butcherbird* and *A Walk in the Night and Other Stories* (Heinemann African Writers Series). An anthology, *Apartheid,* and an account of his travels in the USSR, *A Soviet Journey,* do not seem to be available as far as I know though both are mentioned by his publisher.

This obituary first appeared in *Edinburgh Review* No. 73 1986

A MATTER OF TASTE

Alex La Guma

The sun hung well towards the west now so that the thin clouds above the ragged horizon were rimmed with bright yellow like the spilt yolk of an egg. Chinaboy stood up from having blown the fire under the round tin and said, 'She ought to boil now'. The tin stood precariously balanced on two half-bricks and a smooth stone. We had built the fire carefully in order to brew some coffee and now watched the water in the tin with the interest of women at a child-birth.

'There she is,' Chinaboy said as the surface broke into bubbles. He waited for the water to boil up and then drew a small crushed packet from the side pocket of his shredded wind-breaker, untwisted its mouth and carefully tapped raw coffee into the tin.

He was a short man with grey-flecked kinky hair, and a wide, quiet, heavy face that had a look of patience about it, as if he had grown accustomed to doing things slowly and carefully and correctly. But his eyes were dark oriental ovals, restless as a pair of cockroaches.

'We'll let her draw a while,' he advised. He put the packet away and produced an old rag from another pocket, wrapped it around a hand and gingerly lifted the tin from the fire, placing it carefully in the sand near the bricks.

We had just finished a job for the railways and were camped out a few yards from the embankment and some distance from the ruins of a onetime siding. The corrugated iron of the office still stood, gaping in places and covered with rust and cobwebs. Passers had fouled the roofless interior and the platform was crumbled in places and overgrown with weeds. The cement curbing still stood, but cracked and covered with the disintegration like a welcome notice to a ghost town. Chinaboy got out the scoured condensed-milk tins we used for cups and set them up. I sat on an old sleeper and waited for the ceremony of pouring the coffee to commence.

It didn't start right then because Chinaboy was crouching with his rag-wrapped hand poised over the can, about to pick it up, but he wasn't making a move. Just sitting like that and watching something beyond us.

The portjackson bush and wattle crackled and rustled behind me and the long shadow of a man fell across the small clearing. I looked back and up. He had come out of the plantation and was thin and short and had a pale white face covered with a fine golden stubble. Dirt lay in dark lines in the creases around his mouth and under his eyes and in his neck, and his hair was ragged and thick and uncut, falling back to his neck and around his temples. He wore an old pair of jeans, faded and dirty and turned up at the bottoms, and a torn leather coat.

He stood on the edge of the clearing, waiting hesitantly, glancing from me to Chinaboy, and then back at me. He ran the back of a grimy hand across his mouth.

Then he said hesitantly: 'I smelled the coffee. Hope you don' min'.' 'Well,' Chinaboy said with that quiet careful smile of his. 'Seeing you's here, I reckon I don' min' either.' He smiled at me. 'You think we can take in a table boarder pal?'

'Reckon we can spare some of the turkey and green peas.'

Chinaboy nodded at the stranger. 'Sit pally. We were just going to have supper.'

The white boy grinned a little embarrassedly and came around the sleeper and shoved a rock over with a scarred boot and straddled it. He didn't say anything, but watched Chinaboy set out another scoured milk-tin and lift the can from the fire and pour the coffee into the cups.

'Help yourself, man. Isn't exactly the mayor's garden party.' The boy took his cup carefully and blew at the steam. Chinaboy sipped noisily and said, 'Should've had some bake bread. Nothing like a piece of bake bread with cawfee.'

'Hot dogs,' the white boy said.

'Huh.'

'Hot dogs. Hot dogs go with coffee.'

'Ooh ja. I heard,' Chinaboy grinned. Then asked: 'You going somewhere, Whitey?'

'Cape Town. Maybe get a job on a ship an' make the States.'

'Lots of people want to reach the States,' I said.

Whitey drank some coffee and said: 'Yes, I heard there's plenty of money and plenty to eat.'

'Talking about eating.' Chinaboy said: 'I see a picture in a book, one time. 'Merican book. This picture was about food over there. A whole mess of fried chicken, mealies - what they call corn - with mushrooms an' gravy, chips and new green peas. All done up in colours, too.

'Pass me the roast lamb,' I said sarcastically.

'Man,' Whitey said warming up to the discussion 'Just let me get something like that and I'll eat till I burst wide open.'

Chinaboy swallowed some coffee: 'Worked as a waiter one time when I was a youngster. In one of that big caffies. You should've seen what all them bastards ate. Just sitting there shovelling it down. Some French stuff too, patty grass or something like that.'

I said: 'Remember the time we went for drunk and got ten days? We ate mealies and beans till it came out of our ears!'

Chinaboy said, whimsically: 'I'd like to sit down in a smart caffy one day and eat my way right out of a load of turkey, roast potatoes, beet-salad and angel's food trifle. With port and cigars at the end.

'Hell,' said Whitey, 'it's all a matter of taste. Some people like chicken and others eat sheep's heads and beans!'

'A matter of taste,' Chinaboy scowled. 'Bull, it's a matter of money, pal. I worked six months in that caffy and I never heard nobody order sheep's head and beans!'

'You heard of the fellow who went into one of these big caffies?' Whitey asked, whirling the last of his coffee around in the tin cup. 'He sits down at a table and takes out a packet of sandwiches and puts it down. Then he calls the waiter and orders a glass of water. When the waiter brings the water, this fellow says: "Why ain't the band playing?" '

We chuckled over that and Chinaboy almost choked. He coughed and spluttered a little and then said, 'Another John goes into a caffy and orders sausages and mash. When the waiter bring him the stuff he take a look and say: "My dear man you've brought me a cracked plate." "Hell," says the waiter. "That's no crack. That's the sausage".'

After we had laughed over that one Chinaboy looked westward at the sky. The sun was almost down and the clouds hung like bloodstained rags along the horizon. There was a breeze stirring the wattle and portjackson, and far beyond the railway line.

A dog barked with high yapping sounds.

Chinaboy said: 'There's a empty goods going through here around seven. We'll help Whitey, here, onto it so's he can get to Cape Town.   Reckon there's still time for some more pork chops and onions.' He grinned at Whitey.' Soon's we've had dessert we'll walk down the line a little. There's a bend where it's the best place to jump a train. We'll show you.'

He waved elaborately towards me: 'Serve the duck, John.'

I poured the last of the coffee into the tin cups. The fire had died to a small heap of embers. Whitey dug in the pocket of his leather coat and found a crumpled pack of cigarettes. There were just three left and he passed them round. We each took one and Chinaboy lifted the twig from the fire and we lighted up.

'Good cigar, this,' he said, examining the glowing tip of the cigarette.

When the coffee and cigarettes were finished, the sun had gone down altogether, and all over the land was swept with dark shadows of a purple hue. The silhouetted tops of the wattle and portjackson looked like massed dragons.

We walked along the embankment in the evening, past the ruined siding, the shell of the station-house like a huge desecrated tombstone against the sky. Far off we heard the whistle of a train.

'This is the place,' Chinaboy said to Whitey. 'It's a long goods and when she takes the turn the engine driver won't see you, and neither the rooker in the guard's van. You got to jump when the engine's out of sight. She'll take the hill slow likely, so you'll have a good chance. Jus' you wait till I say when. Hell, that sound like pouring a drink!' His teeth flashed in the gloom as he grinned. Then Whitey stuck out a hand and Chinaboy shook it, and then I shook it.

'Thanks for supper, boys,' Whitey said.

'Come again, anytime,' I said, 'we'll see we have a tablecloth.' We waited in the portjackson growth at the side of the embankment while the goods train wheezed and puffed up the grade, its headlamp cutting a big yellow hole in the dark. We ducked back out of sight as the locomotive went by, hissing and rumbling. The tender followed, then a couple of box-cars, then some coal-cars and a flat-car, another box-car. The locomotive was out of sight.

'Here it is,' Chinaboy said pushing the boy ahead. We stood near the train, hearing it click-clack past. 'Take this coal box coming up,' Chinaboy instructed. 'She's low and empty. Don't miss the grip, now. She's slow. And good luck, pal!'

The coal-car came up and Whitey moved out, watching the iron grip on the far end of it. Then as it drew slowly level with him, he reached out, grabbed and hung on, then got a foothold, moving away from us slowly.

We watched him hanging there, reaching for the edge of the car and hauling himself up. Watching the train clicking away, we saw him straddling the edge of the truck, his hand raised in a salute. We raised our hands too.

'Why ain't the band playing? Hell!' Chinaboy said.

DO NOT PUSH US TOO FAR

The National Party came to power in 1948,
They introduced Apartheid policies,
Since they came to power,
They began the pushing,
Created a forum for white South Africa,
And this was done in the presence of the deprived landowners.

The pushing continued,
And this pushing never stopped,
From Smuts-Malan-Verwoerd-Voster's era to the current incumbent,
Yesterday the pushing intensified,
But today the pushing is no more easy.

Years have gone past,
Decades of turmoil and toiling,
Years of negotiations and pleas,
Decades of detentions, killings and forced removals,
Years of patience and hope,
Years gone by to this bitter end of bondage.

'Do not push us too far', so goes the saying,
Suppressing freedom in the name of Law and Order,
The voiceless silenced without a parliament,
Reform implemented by coercion,
Like inferior education received at gunpoint,
If this is slavery - where is true democracy?

Nats do not push us too far,
And later protest that you have been pushed too far,
Stop and think, who initiated the pushing?
My people have been pushed into overcrowded graveyards in South Africa.

Human beings created by God,
Pushed into a bitter corner,
Are bound to strike back,
Inevitable and courageously,
Like a sting of a dragon,
The people's patience is not endless,
Yes, victory is certain.

Mzwakhe Mbuli

I Will Wait

I have tasted, ever so often,
Hunger like sand on my tongue,
And tears like flames have licked my eye-lids
Blurring that which I want to see,
I want to know.
But Oh! Often, now and then, everywhere where I have been,
Joy, as real as paths,
Has spread within me like pleasant scenery,
Has run beneath my flesh like rivers glitteringly silver;
And now I know;
Having been so flooded and so dry,
I wait.

MONGANE WALLY SEROTE

5 I WILL WAIT

An excerpt from the score by William Sweeney which is a setting of the
poem by Mongane Wally Serote. It was first performed at the opening of the
Sechaba International Conference and Festival in Glasgow on 23 September
1990 by the Scottish Chamber Orchestra, the Scottish Philharmonic Singers,
the choir of the Association of South African Students and soloist
Tommy Smith.

Part III

The Struggle

PIXLEY ISAKA KA SEME

LALAGE BOWN

Dr Pixley Isaka ka Seme was born in the 1880s and went first to Columbia University, then to Jesus College, Oxford, where he studied jurisprudence. While still at Columbia he forged his own brand of fiery eloquence and entered in 1905 for the university's oratory contest. He took up the theme of the African personality and the need to revive the African past; and he created a sensation by winning the gold medal. His style has some of the blemishes of youth, but his message comes across with passion and has appealed to and inspired later generations of African nationalists, particularly those educated in the United States. In 1962, at the first International Congress of Africanists, Dr Kwame Nkrumah, who as he himself remarked, was not given to using the words of others, quoted Seme's whole oration and was obviously still moved by it.

Called to the Bar at the Middle Temple, Seme was one of the first Africans from South Africa to qualify as a lawyer. He practised in Johannesburg and was appalled at the humiliation of Africans in the Transvaal. With three other African lawyers, he called the conference of chiefs and leaders in 1912 which resulted in the formation of the South African Native National Congress (forerunner of the African National Congress), aiming at the extension of democratic rights to Africans. He was its first treasurer-general and founded and edited as its organ the first national African paper *Abantu-Batho* (The People), which was published in English and three African languages. He became legal adviser to the Swazi Royal House and was given a doctorate by the University of Columbia. From 1930-40 he was secretary-general of the African National Congress, and active in the struggle against the Natives Land Act and pass laws for women.

Seme died in 1951.

A ZULU STUDENT'S PRIZE SPEECH

PIXLEY ISAKA KA SEME

I have chosen to speak to you on this occasion upon *The Regeneration of Africa*. I am an African, and I set my pride in my race over against a hostile public opinion. Men have tried to compare races on the basis of some equality. In all the works of nature, equality, if by it we mean identity, is an impossible dream! Search the universe! You will find no two units alike. The scientists tell us there are no two cells, no two atoms, identical. Nature has bestowed upon each a peculiar individuality, an exclusive patent - from the great giants of the forest to the tenderest blade. Catch in your hand, if you please, the gentle flakes of snow. Each is a perfect gem, a new creation; it shines in its own glory - a work of art different from all of its aerial companions. Man, the crowning achievement of nature, defies analysis. He is a mystery through all ages and for all time. The races of mankind are composed of free and unique individuals. An attempt to compare them on the basis of equality can never be finally satisfactory. Each is self. My thesis stands on this truth; time has proved it. In all races genius is like a spark, which, concealed in the bosom of a flint, bursts forth at the summoning stroke. It may arise anywhere and in any race.

I would ask you not to compare Africa to Europe or to any other continent. I make this request not from any fear that such comparison might bring humiliation upon Africa. The reason I have stated - a common standard is impossible! Come with me to the ancient capital of Egypt, Thebes, the city of one hundred gates. The grandeur of its venerable ruins and the gigantic proportions of its architecture reduce to insignificance the boasted monuments of other nations. The pyramids of Egypt are structures to which the world presents nothing comparable. The mighty monuments seem to look with disdain on every other work of human art and to vie with nature herself. All the glory of Egypt belongs to Africa and her people. These monuments are the indestructible memories of their great and original genius. It is not through Egypt alone that Africa claims such unrivalled historic achievements. I could have spoken of the pyramids of Ethiopia, which though inferior in size to those of Egypt, far surpass them in architectural beauty; their sepulchres which evince the highest purity of taste; and of many prehistoric ruins in other parts of Africa. In such ruins Africa is like the golden sun, that, having sunk beneath the western horizon, still plays upon the world which he sustained and enlightened in his career.

> Justly the world now demands:
> Whither is fled the visionary gleam,
> Where is it now, the glory and the dream?

Oh, for that historian who, with the open pen of truth, will bring to Africa's claim the strength of written proof. He will tell of a race whose onward tide was often swelled with tears, but in whose heart bondage has not quenched the fire of former years. He will write that in these later days when Earth's noble ones are named, she has a roll of honour too, of whom she is not ashamed. The giant is awakening! From the four corners of the earth Africa's sons, who have been proved through fire and sword, are marching to the future's golden door bearing the records of deeds of valour done.

Mr Calhoun, I believe, was the most philosophical of all the slaveholders. He said once that if he could find a black man who could understand the Greek syntax, he would then consider their race human, and his attitude towards enslaving them would therefore change. What might have been the sensation kindled by the Greek syntax in the mind of the famous Southerner, I have so far been unable to discover; but oh, I envy the moment that was lost! And woe to the tongues that refused to tell the truth! If any such were among the now living, I could show him among black men of pure African blood those who could repeat the Koran from memory, skilled in Latin, Greek and Hebrew - Arabic and Chaldaic - men great in wisdom and profound knowledge - one professor of philosophy in a celebrated German university; one corresponding member of the French Academy of Sciences, who regularly transmitted to that society meteorological observations, and hydrographical journals and papers on botany and geology; another whom many ages call 'The Wise', to whose authority Mahomet himself frequently appealed in the Koran in support of his own opinion - men of wealth and active benevolence, those whose distinguished talents and reputation have made them famous in the cabinet and in the field, officers of artillery in the great armies of Europe, generals and lieutenants-general in the armies of Peter the Great in Russia, and Napoleon in France, presidents of free republics; kings of independent nations which have burst their way to liberty by their own vigour. There are many other Africans who have shown marks of genius and high character sufficient to redeem their race from the charges which I am now considering.

Ladies and gentlemen, the day of great exploring expeditions in Africa is over! Man knows his home now in a sense never known before. Many great and holy men have evinced a passion for the day you are now witnessing - their prophetic vision shot through many unborn centuries to this very hour. 'Men shall run to and fro,' said Daniel, 'and knowledge shall increase upon the earth'. Oh, how true! See the triumph of human genius today! Science has searched out the deep things of nature, surprised the secrets of the most distant stars, disentombed the memorials of everlasting hills, taught the lightning to speak, the vapours to toil and the winds to worship - spanned the sweeping rivers, tunnelled the longest mountain range - made the world a vast whispering gallery, and has brought foreign nations into one civilised family. This all-powerful contact says even to the most backward race, you cannot remain where you are, you cannot fall back, you must advance! A great century has come upon us. No race possessing the inherent capacity to survive can resist and remain unaffected by this influence of contact and intercourse, the backward with the advanced. This influence constitutes the very essence of efficient progress and of civilisation.

From these heights of the twentieth century I again ask you to cast your eyes south of the Desert of Sahara. If you could go with me to the oppressed Congos and ask, What does it mean, that now, for liberty, they fight like men and die like martyrs; if you would go with me to Bechuanaland, face their council of headmen and ask what motives caused them recently to decree so emphatically that alcoholic drinks shall not enter their country - visit their king, Khama, ask for what cause he leaves the gold and ivory palace of his ancestors, its mountain strongholds and all its august ceremony, to wander daily from village to village through all his kingdom, without a guard or any decoration of his rank - a preacher of industry and education, and an apostle of the new order of things; if you would ask Menelik what means this that Abyssinia is now looking across the ocean - oh, if you could read the letters that come to us from Zululand - you too would be convinced that the elevation of the African race is evidently a part of the new order of things that belong to this new and powerful period.

The African already recognises his anomalous position and desires a change. The brighter day is rising upon Africa. Already I seem to see her chains dissolved, her desert plains red with harvest, her Abyssinia and her Zululand the seats of science and religion, reflecting the glory of the rising sun from the spires of their churches and universities. Her Congo and her Gambia whitened with commerce, her crowded cities sending forth the hum of business and all her sons employed in advancing the victories of peace - greater and more abiding than the spoils of war.

Yes, the regeneration of Africa belongs to this new and powerful period! By this term regeneration I wish to be understood to mean the entrance into a new life, embracing the diverse phases of a higher, complex existence. The basic factor which assures their regeneration resides in the awakened race-consciousness. This gives them a clear perception of their elemental needs and of their undeveloped powers. It therefore must lead them to the attainment of that higher and advanced standard of life.

The African people, although not a strictly homogeneous race, possess a common fundamental sentiment which is everywhere manifest, crystallising itself into one common controlling idea. Conflicts and strife are rapidly disappearing before the fusing force of this enlightened perception of the true intertribal relation, which relation should subsist among a people with a common destiny. Agencies of a social, economic and religious advance tell of a new spirit which, acting as a leavening ferment, shall raise the anxious and aspiring mass to the level of their ancient glory. The ancestral greatness, the unimpaired genius, and the recuperative power of the race, its irrepressibility, which assures its permanence, constitute the African's greatest source of inspiration. He has refused to camp for ever on the borders of the industrial world; having learned that knowledge is power, he is educating his children. You find them in Edinburgh, in Cambridge and in the great schools of Germany. These return to their country like arrows, to drive darkness from the land. I hold that his industrial and educational initiative, and his untiring devotion to these activites, must be regarded as positive evidences of this process of his regeneration.

The regeneration of Africa means that a new and unique civilisation is soon to be added to the world. The African is not a proletarian in the world of science and art. He has precious creations of his own, of ivory, of copper and of gold, fine plaited willow-ware and weapons of superior workmanship. Civilisation resembles an organic being in its development - it is born, it perishes, and it can propagate itself. More particularly, it resembles a plant, it takes root in the teeming earth, and when the seeds fall in other soils new varieties sprout up. The most essential departure of this new civilisation is that it shall be thoroughly spiritual and humanistic - indeed a regeneration moral and eternal!

Curtis Medal oration, Columbia University by Pixley Isaka ka Seme, 1905, published as *The Regeneration of Africa*, New York, Columbia University Press, 1906.

ON SOUTH AFRICAN POETRY

Hugh MacDiarmid

If I had known nothing about the development of the protest literature sampled in this collection,* and nothing about the South African
liberation movement it represents, I could have hardly begun to read
through it without recognising that it powerfully emphasised the
sense of that superb specimen of contemporary graffiti which runs:
' "Mr Gandhi, what do you think of western civilisation?" - "I think
it would be a good idea" ', and alongside it, to account for the
acquiescence of so-called, or self-esteemed, civilised people in the
appalling iniquities of the system, might well be put this other one,
which reads: 'God *is* alive - He just doesn't want to get involved.'
     There can be no greater mistake than to criticise these poems for
not answering to the requirements of what reactionary academics
regard as 'high poetry'. I am sure my friend, that great linguist, the
late Professor W J Entwhistle, who, when he wrote his great book,
European Balladry , describing the interaction over the centuries of the
ballad literatures of the European countries, replied to the criticism
of the bulk of ballad verse that it was deficient in aesthetic value by
saying:

> If we are to measure by an absolute poetic standard, no doubt - and if,
> perchance, such a standard exists. The classic and the critic demand
> the application of such standards; but the search for a poetry that shall
> be pure dissolves even the greatest works of art into unrecognisable
> fragments. ...The poetry of the commonalty we neither produce nor
> admire. Those who seek to express what many men feel we the more
> likely esteem for their art; while, on the other hand, the tribe of those
> who refine and polish and sublimate their art is left to prophesy to the
> void. It is not so that much of the world's greatest poetry has been
> composed, and it is not the way of the ballad. The greatest poets have
> written neither to extrovert their personalities nor to comply with the
> demands of taste, but to voice the common thought of masses of men.
> ...There have been great poems which can be assessed as 'pure poetry',
> such as the *Orlando Furioso*; but to the men of the sixteenth century
> Ariosto's masterpiece seemed wanting in substance or seriousness.
> We cannot be sure that it expressed something clamouring for utterance:

Glory and generous shame,
The unconquerable mind, and Freedom's holy flame.

But these are the themes of a 'God-gifted organ-voice', and these, rather than absolute perfections, assure survival in literature. And common, fundamental, moving themes of this kind inspire the best of the ballads. ... It has been worth while to recreate them time and again throughout the centuries, since on each single occasion they have signified something to their unlettered bearers, and have moved them more than a trumpet. It is a glory not often achieved by the great artistic poets, and, when achieved, it is through some partial endowment of the generous ballad simplicity.'

Bourgeois writers and readers may decry 'commitment' in poetry, but they have not been subjected to the intolerable pressures which render it unavoidable and invaluable. It is still too widely believed that great literature is a prerogative of the Big Five, but 'the race is not to the swift nor the battle to the strong', and all over the world today millions of people, feeling they have been cut away from their real roots, are striving to re-root themselves in their native languages (even where these have long been obsolete or obsolescent, and never previously media of any written literature; and are seeking to create new indigenous literatures on the basis of their native traditions). The contemporary Scottish Gaelic poet, George Campbell Hay, in a brilliant essay on 'Gaelic and Literary Form' put the whole matter into a nutshell when he said:

The slash at the 'general stream of European literature' as understood by people like Quiller-Couch (whom I choose as a particularly horrible example) and as embodied in tomes with that title, a selected list of countries and a selected list of names from each of these countries, starting of course with the Greeks, well-bowdlerised into 'Christian gentlemen' is a ramp that no longer impresses - like 'Western Europe'. I am all for the 'minor literatures' and the 'backward races', whose literatures have not been 'etherealised' out of life. Our contacts might as well be with the Islaendings or with those great rascals the Serbs as with Bloomsbury or the Seine. The big countries share a common foreign-ness and repulsiveness to me, and like Wilfrid Scawen Blunt I sometimes wish they would destroy one another.

This collection heartwarmingly demonstrates the great ground for hope expressed recently by a reviewer of 'the flowering of Russian poetry' when he wrote: 'What always seems so contradictory and yet so reassuring is that in no matter what country, Communist or Capitalist' [and this book shows throughout Africa too] 'a poet is the same, the same breed continues to love beauty and hate oppression, to believe in spiritual values and the mind's affinities, to recognise and appreciate each other in 'this terrible age' (Akhmatova), 'the age rocking with the waves of man's anguish', when 'above the black river the transparent spring has been shattered and the wax of immortality is melting.' '

I express my solidarity with, and send my fraternal greetings to, all the contributors to this volume. We shall overcome!

From* *Poets to the People*, ed Barry Feinberg, (1974)

THE NOBLE CHARTER

Let me remember a day of the vow in Africa,
A vow that shook foundations of plunder,
A heroic vow that broke chains of slavery,
And blurred them beyond recognition.

I remember Kliptown 1955,
It was like a day of freedom,
Hearts and hands joined together,
The spirit of peace and friendship prevailed,
And dynamically the people's document was drawn.

Before that year of the doctrine,
The deprived people bribed survival with streams of blood,
Dehumanised majority bought life with rivers of sweat,
Terror and felony reigned,
And blood flowed like a river in flood.

The people's march began in 1912,
A march in quest for freedom,
The march that ushered humanity enthusiasm,
And the people's invincibility ignored state intimidation,
For legislation without representation is tyranny.

When the charter was drawn,
A vision of a true society was drawn,
It was like a dark cloud giving way to the blue sky,
And the freedom wagon moved with direction,
Yes, the people's agenda was adopted.

Africa's tarnished children did not know,
That pillars of fascism were shaken,
Like knocking together in despair,
Pixley ka Seme's people did not know,
That black and white coalition meant fear,
State fear, insecurity and oppression.

Chief Bhambatha's colonised people did not know,
That tyranny and death awaited them,
From time immemorial.

The entire continent is soaked with blood,
The blood of gallant heroes of the soil,
Apartheid the obstacle to peace and security,
Shall come to an end,
The colonised society shall crush and grind colonial power,
And humankind shall double assaults against evil,
Ultimately there shall be peace and friendship,
And the people shall govern.

MZWAKHE MBULI

LISTEN MANDELA!

Listen Mandela!
To black feet pounding
and black throats sounding
the knell of white rule.
Hear the sound of your brothers' feet
stamping now in unison, on the march
to FREEDOM!
Feel Africa tremble
to the stamping, raging feet
that will no longer be shackled
by the white man's chains

Listen, Mandela!
to the chanting of your sisters' voices
as they dance rhythmically, relentlessly
upon the writhing, thrashing body
of the mortally wounded white snake.

Join in the dance, Mandela!
While your jailers are resting.
Pound your feet and beat your breast
in time with the throbbing heart of Africa
whose black innocence will no longer be defiled
by the white exploiters.

And when they come running, Mandela!
roused by your exultation.
Cease your rejoicing and sit upon your cot.
Compose your features
and gaze steadily, serenely
at the Judas hole,
at the piercing blue eye,
violent with puzzlement and terror.

Now, Mandela!
Now our time has come.
The spark of your words has caught
in the tinder of the townships
and the homelands.

The blaze has begun that will not stop
until the white fungus has been seared
from the living trunk
of the African ebony.
The day of wrath is now, Mandela!
And after the inferno
when the blood has ceased to flow
and the black Phoenix rises
our children will remember your name
will utter the shibboleth
Mandela! Mandela!
And in honouring your name.
          will prove their own honour.

JOHN McINNES

COLD

the clammy cement
sucks our naked feet

a rheumy yellow bulb
lights a damp grey wall

the stubbled grass
wet with three o'clock dew
is black with glittery edges;

we sit on the concrete,
stuff with our fingers
the sugarless pap
into our mouths

then labour erect;

form lines;

steel ourselves into fortitude
or accept an image of ourselves
numb with resigned acceptance;

the grizzled senior warder comments:
'Things like these
I have no time for;
they are worse than rats;
you can only shoot them.'

Overhead
the large frosty glitter of the stars
the Southern Cross flowering low;

the chains on our ankles
and wrists
that pair us together

jangle

glitter.

We begin to move
  awkwardly.

(Colesberg)

DENNIS BRUTUS

THE DAITH O SIMON TUBAKWE

Fir three voices

FIRST VOICE

Even yit ye'll mind
o thon 'deep' boy that wis here - Simon Tubakwe;
Even yit ye'll mind
Hou birkie he wis, yit caum; yin fir a blether,   birkie: lively, spirited

But ye had ti get him stertit. Even yit
Ye'll mind hou unbekent he cam amang us,
An sleed awa withoot a cheip.   sleed awa: slipped away
                        Here's news.
Dinna speir hou A got it, but gin fir the maist pairt
He wis sic a quait-like lawdie - A'll tell ye this, neib,   neib: neighbour
The word is that oor Simon's quait fir aye,
An the word is that he's left some stishie ahent him.   stishie: fuss

SECONT VOICE

Simon Tubakwe - born at the slauchter o Sherpeville:
Simon Tubakwe - growin on histie grun: histie grun: dry infertile ground
Simon Tubakwe - his bairnspeil passed in a blink: bairnspeil: children's play
Simon Tubakwe - skrimp wis the buik-leir they gied him.
                                                       skrimp: scanty
                                        buik-leir: education (book learning)
A core o halflins kickin a baw roun the tounship
                                        core o halflins: group of adolescents
Then kickin ilk ither, forby, an ony puir sowl
that's passin their wey - shair, Simon wad jyne in
Sae's no ti be thocht a jessie. Aince he ettled   jessie: cissy ettled: attempted
Ti brak up a gullie-fecht, but he'd nae chance,   gullie-fecht: knife fight
An wis gey near steikit hissel. 'Simple Simon' they cried him.
                                                          steikit: stabbed

Simon Tubakwe - aince backart an blate wi the lassies
                                        backart: backward blate: diffident
Syne fand whaur there's nae precaution, there's consequence:
                                                          fand: found

Simon Tubakwe - husband, an faither o fower,
that's twa still leevin, an skartin fir whit they can get.   skartin: scratching

His Beth wis nanny ti a pair o white bairns,   bairns: children
Wha'd coorie up close ti her, while there wis time.   coorie: snuggle

FIRST VOICE

Even yit ye'll mind, neib,
Hou we'd sit aroun playin at cairds, or, feelin forfochen,
                                                    forfochen: exhausted
An no juist fain fir ti crack, licht up an gruntle.
Simon, though,
Wad lean oot frae's bunk,
An his speik wad drift uncanny throu the seelence:
                                                    seelence: silence

THIRD VOICE

'Here we are, stowed inti raws o stany pallets,
Fir a pickle oors o sloom, an oor weemenfowk pickle oors sloom: few hours sleep
Alane theirsels - or sae we howp - nicht efter nicht.
Nicht? It's aa nicht fir us - sae mirk, sae snell,   mirk: dark snell: biting cold
We quak an stivven richt throu yokin time   quak: quake stivven: go numb
Until - dounby - we're fasht the contrair gate,
                                        fasht: troubled   contrair gate: other way
As we sweit an birstle i the hettest hell   birstle: scorch
Yont onythin Auld Hornie cuid devise.
That's us, aye nabbed at flistin o extremes,   flistin: exploding
As the walth we howk doun there   walth: wealth howk: dig
Raxes the bosses' pouer, thirls us the mair,   raxes: increases thirls: binds
An we canna kep t'oorsels some twa-three grains
Ti adorn oor wives, or ti amuse oor weans.'   weans: children

FIRST VOICE

Efter this
We were mair in wi Simon, an him wi us.
Ye'll mind thon nicht at the bevvie   bevvie: boozing
Whan he teuk a hantle mair nor the lave o's;   hantle: lot lave: rest
Then back wi's doun the brae, he keckled sae glorious
                                        keckled: cackled glorious: inebriated
That his teeth daunced in his mou; he stauchered awa frae's,
                                                    mou: mouth

That we had ti haud him in, fir fear o the caurs

stauchered: staggered   haud: hold

An the polis forby...thon nicht, he wis fair gaun his dinger.

gaun his dinger: behaving with gusto

Ye'll mind o this, nou an the days ti be
Whan the fecht is dune, an the kintra's fowk are free.   kintra: country

SECONT VOICE

Simon Tubakwe's vainisht, wha kens whaur,
Frae's wife, his bairns, his mates, vainisht fir aye;
Simon Tubakwe's spreit canna lay by   spreit: spirit
An wauners aa-roads nou.   aa-roads: everywhere
                    The legends hae   caucht: caught
That he caucht the tow as yaishal on that day,   tow: cage yaishal: usual
Gaed ben the road ti's stint, fair gone in thocht.   stint: place of work
Some say an unco haar thickened aroun him,   unco: strange haar: mist
As gin he saw sic things he suidna see,
As throu the gaitherin driffle he wad peer   driffle: drizzle
At sleekit chiels in buirdrooms, aye concludin   sleekit: smooth, sly, bland
The weirds o fowk like him; at the posh shops   concludin: deciding
o London an New York, whaur blinterin jewels   blinterin: glittering
Proclaim the fancie freedoms o the Wast.   Wast: West
Aiblins in deepest vaults he saw thir ingots   aiblins: perhaps
That coff the whups, guns, bombs, that threit his kin...   coff: buy

He wis happit bi the reik, an seen nae mair.   happit: surrounded reik: vapour
Yit some tell o a rummlin o the yird   yird: earth
As gin his forefowk had been summoned there,   forefowk: ancestors
in drumlie raws, ti caa him ti tak tent.   drumlie: troubled raws: rows
His faither, runchit whan a rance gied wey,   tak tent: pay attention
An's faither's faither, the hale o thaim gaun back

runchit: crushed rance: pit prop

Lang or the shank wis sunk...They glowered at Simon,   shank: shaft

But spak nae word.
                    There wis an awesome bouff,

bouff: loud dull sound heard when a mine roof cracks

An inklin that the ruif wad faa, an yit
It cam frae faur ablow: a crack, a cleavin,
An a blae-like vapour gurgit ti the face,   blae-like: bluish gurgit: surge
Swurled, an dissolved
Ti kythe the Forehand Mither, wyce an braw,   kythe: reveal wyce: wise

Wha is the verra wame an grave o's aa.   braw: impressive wame: womb

She pyntit lang at Simon. Then he fand
His future set, ti haud wi her command.

FIRST VOICE

Simon Tubakwe - ay, A've thocht masel
That he teuk some saicret cundie, an got oot,   cundie: tunnel
Syne jouked up North.   jouked: escaped
          Forby, A'll tell ye this, neib,
Simon Tubakwe'll gang doun nae mair
I the pit, or at the wuddie,   wuddie: gallows
Ti faa bi's craig an shoogle i the air,   craig: neck shoogle: shake, sway
Or breenged bi the polis frae their heichest flair...
          breenged: pushed flair: floor
An we'll mind o him, an aa that had ti dee,
Whan oor fecht is dune, an oor kintras fowk are free.

TOM HUBBARD

H

NOZIZWE*

You were to be the centre of our dream
To give life to all that is abandoned.
You were to heal the wound
To restore the bones that were broken.
But you betrayed us!
You chose a lover from the enemy
You paraded him before us like a sin.
You dared embrace the killer of your father
You led your clans to the gallows.
You mocked the gods of our Forefathers.
You shouted our secrets before the little strangers
You mocked the sacred heads of our elders
You cast down their grey hair before the children
Their lips that hold the ancient truths were sealed.
By their sunken eyes your body was cursed.
The moving river shall swallow it!

MAZISI KUNENE

Translated from the Zulu by the poet
* Nozizwe: a traitor who served the South African police

from WALKING ON AIR

White and 52
so they treated him nice.
They only made him stand

on two bricks
for three days
and three nights and

When he asked to go to the lavatory
they said:
Shit in your pants.

But the state needed witnesses
So they changed their tune.
Tried sweet-talking him round.
Think of your career
(that didn't work)
Think of the shame of going to jail
(That thought only
filled him with pride)
You really want kaffirs to rule?
(like you said)
Think of your wife
(Dulcie. Dulcie
7 kids. Dulcie
She's not political at all.)

And there they had him
On that score he was worried, it's true
And they promised him freedom.
And they pressed him for weeks on end
until finally he said:

Okay, agreed.

- But first I must speak with my wife.

Barely an hour it took them to find
and rush Dulcie Matthews
out to Pretoria Jail.

Then looking nice, because they let him
shave,
let him comb his hair, looking nice then,
chaperoned by smiling, matrimonial
policemen, shaven and combed, John
Matthews
got led out to his wife, and holding her
hand, they let him hold her hand, he said

- Do you know why they've brought
you?
- I do.
And he said
- Dulcie, I will never betray my
comrades.
And with a frog in her throat she replied
- I'm behind you. One hundred per cent.

So back they hauled John Matthews then
and there,

Back to the cells,
that was that, then, but
all the way down the passage
toe-heel, heel-toe, diddle-diddle
ONE HUNDRED PER CENT
I mean, he was high
off the ground, man.

He was walking on air.

                                    JEREMY CRONIN

BENJAMIN'S SANG
(Benjamin Moloise)

Blythness wis his fiddle   blythness: joyfulness
freedom his jiggin pipe;   lilt: rhythm

syne thrabbed a lilt tae brak a shank tae,   brak a shank: break a leg (dance)
fankilt wi the wunds o life.   fankilt: tangled

But Cape Toun's lugs are thirled   thirled: bound
tae anither sang (that's no a sang ava,
but a skirl, a skelloch, an a greit,   skelloch: scream
sklentin aff prison waas).   sklentin: glancing

So they stappit his mou wi quaitness: stappit: stuffed
an threidit anither thrum   thrum: thread
intae the flag that'll flee owre
the heapit knowe o their ain dooncome.   knowe: hill

Blythness wis his fiddle,
freedom his jiggin pipe.
Monie's the nicht I hear his sang,
fankilt wi the wunds o Fife.

JOHN MCDONALD

POEM WRITTEN ON DEATH ROW

All the armies that ever marched,
All the parliaments that ever sat,
Have not affected the life
Of man on earth as that one
Solitary life.
I am proud to be what I am,
The storm of oppression will be followed
By the rain of my blood.
I am proud to give my life,
My one solitary life.

BENJAMIN MOLOISE

TELLIN

tellin: warning

There's a weir-daunce i the nicht
stoundin   stoundin   stoundin
(the spreit's ill tae sowse in sic a tid)
soondin   soondin   soondin
as they steik doun ilk kist lid.

weir-daunce: war-dance
stoundin: throbbing
spreit: spirit   tid: mood
sowse: extinguish
steik: stitch   kist: chest

Africa's hert gaes
stoundin   stoundin   stoundin
(the chyce is freedom wi a fleggit face)
soondin   soondin   soondin
as dayset bleeds owre Kilimanjaro; an hyenas screich.

fleggit: frightened
dayset: nightfall

screich: shriek

JOHN McDONALD

CHILD OF SOUTH AFRICA

I have a heart as large as oceans
And eyes as bright as the sunshine.
I have friends as many as stars
I carry their love in my little heart.
When a star falls by a blind hand
There are still many stars to replace:
For our hearts are full of love
And our sky is full of stars.
The clouds that have surrounded us
The prison walls that are built around us
Are the only power that our enemy possess.
Our sun is rising behind clouds
The voice of freedom is heard behind prison walls,
And the doors of prisons are forced open.
Our prison guards are forced to leave their camps
We are firm in our aim.
And clear in our vision
Our strength is in our unity
And our liberty is at reach.

GHOLAM-REZA SABRI-TABRIZI

MIGRANT'S LAMENT: A SONG

If I have wronged you Lord forgive me
All my cattle were dead
My goats and sheep were dead
And
I did not know what to do
O Creator forgive me
If I had done wrong to you
My children: out of school
Out of uniforms and books
My wife and I were naked - naked ...
Short of clothing

If I have wronged you Lord forgive me
I went to WENELA
To get recruited for the mines
I went to SILO
To work at sugarcane
O Creator forgive me
If I had done wrong to you
But they chased me away
They needed those with experience
With long service tickets and no one more

If I have wronged you Lord
Forgive me
I left my wife and children
To look for work alone
I had to find a job
O Creator forgive me
If I had done wrong to you
I was despairing in Egoli
After months searching for this job
And when I found one
I lost it
For I didn't have a 'Special'

If I have wronged you Lord
Forgive me
I found a casual job
I felt that my children would be happy
With my earnings
Oh how happy I was!
O Creator forgive me
If I had done wrong to you
Yes, as my children were happy
And as I was working
The blackjacks arrived to arrest me
So again I lost my job

If I have wronged you Lord
Forgive me
When out of jail I searched again -
Another casual job, happy again
The boss was happy too
And he gave me a letter
To fetch a permit from back home
O Creator forgive me
If I had done wrong to you
But the clerk said: 'I can't see the paper'
And added, 'You must go in peace my man'
So I had to buy him beer, meat and brandy
For him to 'learn' to read my piece of paper

If I have wronged you Lord
Forgive me
I was working again
But I realised so far for nothing
O Creator forgive me
If I had done wrong to you
So I joined the union to fight my boss
For I realised: there was no other way Lord
But to fight with the employer
There was no other way
Now go trouble maker go.

(*MAWU AGM, Curries Fountain Stadium, 1984*)

ALFRED TEMBA QABULA

CHANGE IS PAIN

I have been to the mountain top,
And I have seen a glimpse of Africa to come,
I have seen a political cyclone emerging,
Radically to halt the sting of evil,
And emancipate captive human race from shackles.

I have been to the mines,
And I have seen gruesome scenes of agony,
I have seen Amagoduka * buried alive,
Natives losing their limbs and organs for life time,
Sacred soul geared to permanent disability.

I have been to Winterveld slums,
And I have seen victims of deliberate policies,
Man and beast dying of hunger alike,
Falling apart under the dove of peace,
All in the name of christianity.

I have been to Sisa Dukashe Stadium,
The square of torture and murder in Ciskei,
I have been to Oshakati and Ovamboland,
Pains and tears was their story,
Nevertheless modern socialism shall blunt the blade of evil.

I have been to Ethiopia,
And I have seen a display of countless human corpses,
I have seen a natural episode,
Conducted by nature itself,
Upon defenceless and foodless human population.

I have been to a convention,
And I have seen your leaders and mine,
Your leaders are shrewd and cunning,
My leaders are human and democratic,
Leaders are not born but produced by experience.

Change is unknown in my ghetto,
Change is an endless bucket system in Alexandra,
Change is pain in Africa,
Change is throttled by misdirected surrogates of the world,
Change to a free non-racial society is certain,
 Revolutionary change shall set man free from bondage,
And the ruins of autocracy shall fall.

MZWAKHE MBULI

* Amagoduka: migrants

THE CHANGE

For all its banks bursting with bullion,
   the land of injustice will not prosper.

The skyscrapers shine as if they could never
   smell black smoke or shake to thunder.

Tanks, whips, dogs, laws - the panoply
   cracks steadily, being built over a fault.

Of course there are battleships, communications,
   planes; but the sophisticated do not have it.

The spirit has it, the spirit of the people has it,
   townships, shantytowns, jails, funerals

have it. It is no use digging in,
   rulers, unless you dig a pit to be

tipped into. Ruling has gone on too long,
   will not be saved by armbands or the laager.

The unjust know this very well.
   They lay ears to the ground, hear hooves.

Beasts, one time; an express, one time;
   men, one time; history, one time.

Straighten up and pat your holsters.
   Self-righteousness and a ramrod back

will not help. The sun goes down with you,
   other fruits ripen for other lips.

EDWIN MORGAN

THE BREEZING DAWN OF THE NEW DAY

Many things have come and gone
come with the night of silent footsteps which stole some children
who went and left us with empty spaces which are full of noises
noises which ring and ring
yet some day has gone and left some children here
who ask and ask and so teach us how to talk and fix an eye on
  any other eye
so things go -
sometimes as if a wink of an eye
at times as if thick darts of tear droplets
time -
that movement of people
the dark and the daylight, we do what we do with them -
so with trees
or the sky
and the earth
it could have been so with our lives
it is not
since we have sense thought and memory
also
since we have hands and legs
also
since we have come to know what we want
since we know that the mind and nature are god
and that indeed we are our god
we keep the record:

isandhlwana. bulhoek. sharpeville. are milestones of
which the latest is soweto; as most travellers know,
people who walk the road do now and then come to
junctions. if they know the road, they walk on without
stop, if they don't they wait around and ask around until
they find their way or the night comes or the daylight
goes, which is to say, ah, how much do you know about
yourself and where you are and where you are going to:
blood river. cato manor. or another type of soweto ?

we keep the record here
and give the report straight
since
so many people have gone
so many things have gone
the heat
the fire
swept all that was then
some saw the smoke and some saw the smotherings
some even -
left their footprints on the cold cold ashes
and day by day one by one we come still
and the new paths are begun
when those of us, whose falling was like a pebble in the pond,
hit the bottom of the grave
or by night jump fences feeling footsteps rearing them
of some of us in jails whose cells howl like empty graves
we keep in our hands, as if a fresh hot coal from the fire
our memory
this is when we keep choosing the weapons
and like a storm
keeping calm before it emerges
we gather force
we *are* here
betrayed by everything else but ourselves
and our best ally is our clarity about who we are
where we come from
who our enemy is
where we want to go to
and these begin to define our natural allies
as we gather force
as we create the storm
since here, we are
talking about a land of many colours and sounds
we sing here, for we can sing still, about a national life
which will be chiselled by the long long gone time
by the long gone lives of some of us
and by what we do now,
what we do now
is that we say we cannot work and be exploited
we refuse too to be oppressed
some don't like to hear this, but we say it, not only that,
we are fighting now

did you hear
how some people, god's children, talk
about us
all we can say or sing now
is that
many things have come and gone
come with footsteps which have no sound
gone with some of our children -
we keep the record:

nothing stays forever, even our oppression or our oppressor. and
we know that it is us who must make this true. since we were
once conquered, we have lost too many things, that is, we have
had to do with nothing at times. now we look into that, and find
that we need our country, also, that our country needs us to fight;
and then we find out that we are ready, all this time, of having
nothing, has prepared us. which is to pitch the price of our country at the height of our life - nothing less.

who, who we ask, does not know our story
the story of our country
if you lift your hands and say you know it
listen,
we sing here, for we can sing still, about our national life
a life
which must grow now,
like a child
a child looked after and taught well
that is our future,
we keep the record:

africa needs south africa. not america or europe because these two
have no manners, know nothing about being guests; we give
them the full fury of our wrath, they will leave our land. and
those inside the country, black or white, who own the south
african army and money, or who want to defend these, at the
expense of the lot of the people, we count down on them.

and day by day one by one we will come
and the new paths will be started
and the old will turn to chaos
the house of law will turn mute
the house of reigns will turn limp

and their security will go blind
something terrible for them will be around, without sound
  stalking every thing
the old days dying
and some child somewhere in the mist of this death will know
the breezing dawn of the new day -
they will put brick on brick
and build, a new country.

MONGANE WALLY SEROTE

CULTURE IN THE STRUGGLE FOR A NEW SOUTH AFRICA

GOVAN MBEKI

Distinguished guests, comrades and friends,

I bring you warm greetings: from comrades Oliver Tambo, president of the ANC, deputy president, Nelson Mandela - their special concern with issues touching both national and international culture is well known - from the leadership of the ANC and the South African Communist Party, the mass democratic and trade union movements and, of course, from the thousands of cultural workers in South Africa - musicians, poets, painters, craftsmen and women - who are each and all making their contribution to the struggle to end the scourge of apartheid, to purge both South African society and the world community of its poisonous dogmas, so that the new world of national unity and international peace and fraternity may become a reality.

I am particularly pleased and honoured to be in Glasgow as I consider myself an honorary Scotsman. Ever since I learnt that I was named after William Govan of the Glasgow Missionary Society I have had a burning desire to visit the country of this wonderful human being and educationalist. The Scottish Missionary Society and a number of Scottish religious figures and educationalists have played a significant role in helping to train and educate generations of Africans including myself.

William Govan was the first principal of the Lovedale Institution. He firmly believed that Africans had the same right to a full and proper education as whites. He and his successors such as Neil MacVicar, Dr Stewart, Alexander Keir and the Reverend Shepherd never accepted the prevailing racist's attitudes that Africans were not suited to receiving an education equal to that of whites. Govan and his immediate successor, Dr Neil MacVicar, turned Lovedale into a powerful and immensely influential educational institution. It was the pride and joy of African people in many parts of Southern Africa.

Scottish educationalists such as Dr Stewart and religious figures also played a vital role in setting up and developing the University of Fort Hare. From this University have graduated many of the foremost academics and political figures of our people including Comrades Oliver Tambo and Nelson Mandela.

I retain many vivid memories of Lovedale and Fort Hare. I always treasure a sermon given by the Reverend Shepherd whom we called Shepherd of Lovedale, in which he said in 1934:

> About twenty years ago a pistol shot was shot in Central Europe summoning all the nations together, am I my brother's keeper?

The racist regime compelled institutions such as Lovedale to close down. In the new political situation we are going to re-establish Lovedale, Healdtown and other similar institutions of learning. To do that requires finance and resources.

We call upon Scottish religious figures, political formations, trade unions and educationalists to help us re-establish Lovedale as an educational institution of excellence.

Culture is a form of resistance to apartheid. But how we might transform the various facets of our cultural life into weapons for the destruction of racism and tools for the creation and protection of the non-racial and democratic way of life we aim to establish is no easy labour - indeed, there are some who think that, in the current perilous economic and political climate, it is an inappropriate labour.

The pessimists point to the seemingly endemic violence which threatens the peace process and the efforts to achieve a negotiated settlement to which the ANC and its allies are committed. They remind us that the state of emergency remains in force in Natal and in the Transvaal; that rightist terrorists continue to threaten such peace as remains to us and that the economic plight of the vast majority of our people continues unremittingly, bringing disease, malnutrition and even starvation in its wake.

In such circumstances, they ask, is it not more apt to apply our minds to the problems of crisis management, public administration, industry and commerce rather than devoting our attention to questions of culture?

This is an understandable attitude, but it is incorrect. Culture in all its manifestations has always played an absolutely fundamental role in the South African liberation struggle, particularly in its most recent phases.

Cultural manifestations may carry obvious and self-conscious political messages, like the chants, freedom songs and political poems which sustained our people through many a battle in the townships and kept up the morale of our soldiers through the long years in the bush.

But also - perhaps chiefly - there are those unsung heroes and heroines who kept alive the essence of our country's many cultures by living it themselves and teaching it to others. Parents and teachers, in the darkest days of poverty, passed on to our youth the customs, folklore, belief-systems and values of our particular indigenous cultures. School and university teachers, often working in the most appalling conditions, strove to share with their students what was best and most beautiful in that universal culture - literary, musical, and scientific - which is the common heritage of all humankind.

Without their efforts the struggle for a non-racial democracy would never have advanced to its present stage, and without further and more intensive efforts of the same kind the goal of the Freedom Charter to open the doors of learning and culture to all South Africans will not be realised.

Without a deepening of our cultural life, there can be no real deepening of our political life and therefore only a superficial intensification of the revolutionary dynamic.

No revolutionary movement - least of all a national democratic one such as ours - can sustain itself unless it draws on all the cultural resources available to it, for without national cultures there is no nation - only the semblance of nationhood. A nation which has lost contact with its moral and spiritual roots, no matter how economically sound or militarily powerful it may appear to be, has lost touch with those things which make it a nation.

But there is a more particular reason why South African revolutionaries dare not forget the importance of culture, both in its particular and its universal aspects. It is this: apologists for apartheid - especially since the era of Verwoerd - have used cultural differences to erect a racist ideology which, in its most virulent form, lives on today in the hearts and minds of many white South Africans. Verwoerd and his successors erected a political and economic system which deliberately suppressed the languages and cultures of the colonised South African masses and ensured the hegemony of the culture and languages of the colonisers. Thus two 'official' languages - English and Afrikaans - were imposed in schools, courts of law and Parliament. African languages were neglected and despised, our ancient customs and religions scorned as 'backward'.

Peoples and their cultures were isolated from each other behind walls of legislation and sheer superstitious prejudice. Further, in their eagerness to preserve the 'purity' of their Eurocentric vision, the supporters of apartheid began to cut themselves and the rest of South Africa off from contemporary world culture. Books were banned, ideas suppressed, a meshwork of censorship interposed itself between ordinary South Africans and the rest of the world, giving them a distorted picture of that world and their place in it.

Predictably, the process turned inwards: these 'guardians and saviours of Afrikaans culture' began to turn on their own most creative writers and artists whenever their creations failed to meet the criteria imposed by apartheid dogma. The cultural laager, designed to protect Afrikaner culture, became a prison and a vice which threatened to strangle it.

Against this isolationism, the ANC, SACP and their allies offered another vision: a nation with a multiplicity of thriving cultures, each and every one of which would one day become the common possession and pride of all South Africans. We aspired to build a country in which the poetry of Louw, the praise songs of the Zulu and Xhosa peoples, the novels of Schreiner and Gordimer, the genius of our black jazz musicians would interfuse to produce a unity which had lost none of its diversity - a cultural richness which would be the envy of all the world.

We saw too that South Africa, if she was truly to be called a nation, could not isolate herself from the tradition of 'universal culture', from mankind's common wellspring of learning and creativity. For if we continue to cut ourselves off from that tradition we could never hope for a respected place in the community of nations.

While the Verwoerdian ideologists saw the European culture as something pure and unchanging which ought not to be sullied by indigenous cultures, the ANC and its allies have tended to treat all South African cultures as indigenous forms which would only be strengthened in the long run by dynamic interaction with one another. Thus two completely antagonistic perspectives took hold.

It was not possible for them to co-exist, for the apartheid blueprint with respect to culture - like its economic and constitutional facets - could not be implemented except by recourse to injustice on a vast scale. Apartheid cultural policy meant inferior education for the masses, with the government spending seven times as much on the education of white children as was spent to educate blacks. The 1976 student's revolt began when our youth fought back against the attempt to force them to learn science in Afrikaans. The township revolt represented the clearest possible indication to date that cultural policy had become a site of struggle and that a developing revolutionary culture was confronting the cultural outlooks of the oppressor.

Now terms like 'revolutionary culture' and 'culture of resistance' are often used rather loosely and it is important to get clear what we mean by them. In fact, the notion of 'culture' itself is a pretty elusive concept - and a very general one at that. We use it to denote the artistic and literary productions of a people, their customs, rituals and mythology. But we also use it to describe the tools they use, the way they dress, cook their food and in general go about the day-to-day business of living.

The best way, it seems to me, of explaining this concept is to say that the culture of any given social formation is the shape or form of its life together, which stamps it distinctively as being their life. So, for example, the various dance forms and traditions of African peoples are expressions of the form of their life. They tell us something of how those peoples relate to the world about them, to other peoples and to each other. To participate in these forms is to enter the life-world of those to whom they belong: it is, as it were, to find one's feet with them. The varieties of human language too are inseparable from human cultures - as we can see if we try to imagine a language without imagining the form of life in which it is embedded.

Furthermore, these cultural forms are not uniform and static but fluid and dynamic. Once a culture ossifies into a rigid form, we know that we are dealing with a dead or dying culture. When a culture is alive it evolves - often in surprising ways - and interacts and even merges with other cultures. Afrikaner culture is a prime example of this: it originated from Dutch parentage, but developed and gained potency by assimilating elements from Malay, French and even Portuguese ways of life and modes of expression. This, incidentally, is why a culture cannot be preserved by legislative formulae alone, and still less by legislation which seeks to segregate one culture from another. If cultures are living processes, then they are subject to the same laws of evolution, transmutation and extinction as are other life-forms.

We can and should try to preserve and deepen our cultures, but we cannot hope to preserve them indefinitely by some legalistic life-support mechanism, any more than we can keep an individual person in a state of eternal youth and immortality through medical science. Cultures constitute the natural history of humankind and they are subject to the natural processes.

If culture must be viewed as a distinctively human form of life, then a culture of resistance will give form to the living process of struggle against oppression - in our case the struggle against racist and colonial oppression. Obviously such a culture will to some extent be political and self-conscious. But there is a need to be cautious in our formulations here: just as a culture cannot be kept alive by legal artifice alone, so a revolutionary culture cannot be founded on simplistic political doctrines or sustained by dogmatic preconceptions as to what is and what is not 'progressive' or 'revolutionary'.

Genuine cultures do not function in that way. What may appear 'irrelevant' or even 'reactionary' at one conjuncture or perspective can turn out to be highly pertinent and progressive at other times and from other points of view. There are glaring examples of failed attempts to contain human creativity within the confines of political doctrine, and we in the national liberation movement have seen enough of the distortions and deformities imposed by apartheid's censors and ideologues to be fully aware of the dangers of attempts to imprison our people's talents within the confines of narrowly conceived policies.

This is not to say that there is no place for committed literature, painting, sculpture and music in the South African culture of resistance: such a culture would be unthinkable without such commitment. I am saying only that political commitment, in and of itself, cannot substitute for but can only supplement such virtues as learning, imagination and sheer artistic talent.

Mbuli's passionate poetry, Cronin's prison poetry, Serote's vivid imagery, Sol Plaatje's and Gordimer's novels are all examples of committed literature which matches these other criteria. By the same token, it does not follow that cultural productions which purvey reactionary ideas have no artistic merit - that T.S. Eliot's *The Wasteland* has racist overtones does not prevent him from being a great poet.

The culture of resistance must also be strong enough to be a culture of tolerance which has no need of police-state censorship. Just now, I made a distinction between what I called particular or indigenous cultures and universal or world culture. I should like to develop that point: by particular cultures, I mean those cultural products and forms which either originated in or have taken root in and become distinctive of South Africa. Serote's writings and our ancient musical and craft traditions are all creations of our particular culture.

By universal culture I mean those artifacts and traditions which - regardless of origin - have now become the property of all humankind. Bach's fugues, Rodin's sculptures, Dostoevsky's novels and Shakespeare's plays are all very obvious examples.

Of course, not all cases fit neatly into this classification, but, difficult cases aside, the distinction is a crucial one: it brings out the crucial political truth that a culture of resistance - which seeks to create a distinctively national form of life - has always to co-exist in a dialectical relationship with the productions of universal culture. South African music and literature, for example, must expect to be influenced by - and hope to exert an influence on - European and Asiatic music and literature.

We must hope that what passes from each to each will be what is best and most noble in both. But of course there can be no absolute guarantee of this, and we cannot and ought not to rely on the offices of government censors and bureaucrats to ensure it. The project of building a national culture of resistance involves a clear-sighted appreciation that we belong to a world community and a world culture with all the risks and challenges that that entails.

What are the strategic implications of this for a non-racial and democratic South Africa? This much seems clear: the ANC and its allies - both in the prelude to their assumption of power and as a government - must work to ensure that, on the one hand, universal culture becomes the common possession of all South Africa's cultural groups, while on the other hand promoting the free development of all our particular cultures so that the finest fruits they can bear become part of the universal treasury of mankind. If these interrelated goals are pursued, then I believe we may see a recognisably South African culture, the evolution of which will not threaten those from which it derives.

These are very high ideals. It may even be said that they are unreachably high: that, given the stark socio-economic realities attending the birth of the new South Africa, we can ill afford to set ourselves such lofty goals. The only possible response is, I think, that we cannot afford not to, because only through this effort will the rich cultural diversity of our country - about which the spokesmen for apartheid have talked so much and done so little - be preserved and enhanced.

Only by this road can we sustain that unity in diversity which must be the source of true South African nationhood. Only in this way can all our citizens - Xhosas and Zulus, Venda and Tswana, English-speakers and Afrikaners, Hindus, Muslims and Christians - both retain what is uniquely theirs and draw sustenance from what is the common birthright of all. Only by these means can the lacerations of apartheid be ended and the spiritual scars that are its legacy be permanently healed. Only through this strategy can hatred, fear and suspicion be allayed and peace, trust and brotherhood become the order of the day.

Constitutional measures to entrench language rights and protect cultures, important as these may be, will not in themselves be sufficient to nurture cultural life and defend heritages. Still less will this be achieved by coercion, force or violence. The victory can be won and secured only by the South African masses themselves struggling on the terrain of culture

This strategy needs to be implemented at three levels. Firstly, at the organisational level, the ANC, SACP and the mass democratic movement must build on and enhance foundations which are already laid down. We must develop structures to facilitate cultural activity and, where necessary, erect others. A cautionary word is in order here: our aim is to provide facilities, not to exercise control. If we allow command tactics to creep in to this work, we will succeed only in stifling what ought to flourish in accordance with its own nature.

Secondly, there is the role of cultural workers: not only musicians, actors, writers and so on, but importantly too, schoolteachers and academics. Their task will be to nurture and spread both South Africa's own particular culture and the universal world-culture. To this task they will bring all their creativity, learning, patience and skill. They will best know how to do this: we politicians may assist them, if and where we can, but we must not interfere with them. We must not get in the way.

Finally, and most important of all, is the role of the masses. Without their creativity, energy and faith nothing will be possible. Everything depends on them, for it is their culture, their traditions, their life-world we are proposing to assert against the claims of apartheid. But they have carried us on their shoulders in every other phase of the struggle. They will not let us down.

Obviously what I am proposing will not be accomplished overnight. It is a labour for a whole generation. Equally, it has implications for educational and economic policy which I cannot deal with here. To achieve the cultural world we wish to see in the new South Africa implies the allocation of a major part of the nation's resources - both human and financial - into education. This implies an economic policy which refuses to put profits before people: an attitude on the part of legislators, industrialists and business people which declines to judge everything in purely utilitarian terms. It asks all South Africans to recognise that there are some things which are of value in themselves: precious just because they are ours.

My own faith - and the faith of the ANC and the South African Communist Party - is that, together with all our compatriots, we can build this culture of resistance to racialism and hatred and, as time moves on, transform it into the culture of a nation.

As that immortal and great Scottish poet Robert Burns wrote:

Then let us pray that come it may
As come it will for a' that
That sense and worth, o'er a' the earth
Shall bear the gree, an a' that
For a' that, and a' that
It's comin yet for a' that
That man to man, the warld o'er
Shall brithers be for a' that.

Address to the Sechaba Conference, Glasgow, 23 September 1990

Part IV

The International Dimension

6 OLIVER TAMBO LAUNCHES THE MANDELA FREEDOM MARCH
On 12 June 1988 Oliver Tambo (President of the African National Congress), Archbishop Trevor Huddleston, Andimba Toiro ja Toiro (Secretary-General of the South West African People's Organisation), the Reverend Dr Allan Boesak and Susan Baird, Lord Provost of Glasgow launched the Nelson Mandela 'Freedom at 70' march to London. The 25 marchers left that day and arrived in London for a rally on 18 July, Nelson Mandela's birthday.

7 MANDELA FREEDOM RALLY
A view of the crowd at Glasgow Green on 12 June 1988.

APARTHEID'S ENGINE WORKS IN EUROPE

Neal Ascherson   *The Observer, 28 July 1985*

As South Africa burns, the world stands peering into the smoke and chanting abuse against apartheid. The very use of that Afrikaans word suggests something unique to South Africa, a localised disease. But the mechanism underlying apartheid is, in fact, world-wide.

Most outrage boils down to several statements. South Africa is a police state, where the forces of order kill , torture and arrest at will. South Africa maintains grotesque inequality based on skin colour. It is an undemocratic place in which a white minority holds a monopoly of political power. It segregates the races, who must live, play, travel and - until recently - love apart.

Although true, these statements suggest that apartheid is a stagnant condition, something like slavery in the Roman Empire. Americans often imagine South Africa as rather like the old South before the Civil Rights movement, a plantation where pouchy old men with shotguns invigilate black chain-gangs. All that's needed, they may conclude, is to give blacks equal rights and a vote.

But apartheid, at its core, is not so much a condition as an engine. Beneath the race laws lies a huge economic machine which, far more than whites-only bathing beaches, preserves white domination and prosperity and minimises their political cost. This engine, designed by Hendrik Verwoerd a generation ago, is a labour pump. It sucks in cheap black labour, pours it through the wheels of industry and agriculture, and then expels it to distant pools of unemployment until required again.

Its name is 'influx control'. First, blacks in the white regions of South Africa were declared to be 'migrants'. Even those resident for generations in white areas were redefined as citizens of black 'Homelands' and denied rights of settlement or citizenship in their place of work. Labour was to be recruited on limited contracts from the Homelands (arid tribal areas established by the British as 'native reserves'), pumped in to work and then, if and when it is no longer required, pumped out again to be 'dumped' in one of the Homelands.

Migrant labour was nothing new in South Africa. But the horrible brilliance of the apartheid system was to see how the idea of the nation-state could be perverted to serve it.

In any capitalist economy subject to slumps and booms, workers become costly and dangerous when they are unemployed. Deporting the unemployed back to their villages still leaves the Government responsible for them. But what if the workers can be transformed into foreigners?

So there was born the idea of constructing around 'white' South Africa a periphery of 'independent' black states. Many miners, especially, already came on contract from abroad, from Mozambique or Lesotho. Dr Verwoerd and his successors now began to convert the Homeland reserves into 'Bantustans', statelets like Bophuthatswana or Transkei whose independence was basically fraudulent but which took over responsibility for their so-called 'citizens'.

The influx-control engine pumped away, recruiting labour as it was needed and deporting hundreds of thousands of unwanted men and women back to the Bantustans. What became of them there no longer concerned the Pretoria Government or their white employers. South Africa seemed to have discovered the philosopher's stone of economic management: how to export unemployment.

Human beings have paid a grim price for this discovery. The price includes incessant police raids for illegal migrants and blacks with no pass. It includes the brutal bulldozing of Crossroads and the other vast squatter camps near Cape Town. It includes the misery of those dumped in camps in Homelands they had often never seen, and the shocking rise of hunger, disease and overcrowding there.

These are South African realities. But the South African system of influx control is not isolated. There are other places where nation-states have been used as the foundations of a machine to exploit migrant labour.

One of these engines has been pumping away on our doorstep for many years. The European Economic Community, especially the old EEC of the Six, had a structural resemblance to South Africa. The overt violence of the European machine was far less, but the mechanism was the same.

Northern Europe, especially West Germany, came to rely on migrant labour as its own internal labour reserves were absorbed or became too expensive. In the boom years of the 1960s and early 1970s, millions of short-term contract workers were recruited from Spain and Portugal, then from Greece and Yugoslavia, finally from Turkey. Sweden, Austria and Switzerland, though not EEC members, recruited too.

Here was another industrial heartland - the Witwatersrand of Northern Europe - served by a periphery of small states which were politically independent but economically dependent. The heart's diastole drew in trainloads of dark, bewildered little men clutching cardboard suitcases, guitars, parcels of mother's cake. The heart's systole pumped them back again, richer by a Grundig stereo or a second-hand Volkswagen, to dying hill villages in Croatia or Anatolia. And West Germany's unemployment figures remained negligible. It was all exported.

Much the same goes on in the United States. Anyone who saw 'El Norte', the marvellous film by Greg and Anna Thomas about migrant workers in California, was watching yet another influx-control pump drawing in cheap labour from Mexico and Central America and sluicing it out again when it was no longer required. Along the Rio Grande frontier, helicopters and jeeps hunt down the 'wetback' illegal immigrants. The inlet valve must not open too widely.

But when migrants are allowed to settle in the heartland, the pump can't work. Britain, in its casual, good-natured way, brought in West Indians to correct the labour shortage of the 1950s without any plan to export them again: it was supposed that unemployment was as extinct as smallpox. Before Algerian independence, Algerians flocked freely to France and settled in dismal *bidonvilles* around the cities. By the time that Britain passed immigration acts and France limited labour movement from independent Algeria, it was too late to dislodge these 'new Europeans'.

Even in Germany, the pump is breaking down. Recession means that the demand for immigrant labour is slack, but over a million Turks have managed to settle and acquire residence. And now Portugal, Spain and Greece have entered the EEC, which means that their citizens have freedom of movement within the Community.

Foreign contract labour is an ugly thing. It is about cheerless barrack-hostels, about men without women bawled at by foremen of a 'superior' race. It is about homesickness for villages with no young men to break the earth , about the hostility of rich 'host' nations too mean to share their freedoms. It would be good to feel that its day is over, even in South Africa, where employers now want their workers to settle permanently and learn skills and become consumers.

But it is not yet over. As long as there are rich nations, poor nations and trade cycles, it will go on. The world is growing small; whole continents are bursting to discharge their surplus peasants into the international labour market. The rich want them as miners and houseboys, not as neighbours or fellow-citizens on the dole. The poor used to be always with us. Now they can only visit us if they have a return ticket.

THE NEW WORLD

Alasdair Gray

Millions of people lived in rooms joined by windowless corridors. The work which kept their world going (or seemed to, because they were taught that it did, and nobody can teach the exact truth) their work was done on machines in the rooms where they lived, and the machines rewarded them by telling them how much they earned. Big earners could borrow money which got them better rooms. The machines, the moneylending and most of the rooms belonged to three or four organisations. There was also a government and a method of choosing it which allowed everyone, every five years, to press a button marked STAY or CHANGE. This kept or altered the faces of their politicians. The politicians paid themselves for governing, and also drew incomes from the organisations which owned everything, but governing and owning were regarded as separate activities, so the personal links between them were dismissed as coincidences or accepted as inevitable. Yet many folk - even big earners in comfortable rooms - felt enclosed without knowing exactly what enclosed them. When the government announced that it now governed a wholly new world many people were greatly excited, because their history associated new worlds with freedom and wide spaces.

I imagine a man, not young or especially talented, but intelligent and hopeful, who pays for the privilege of emigrating to the new world. This costs nearly all he has, but on the new world he can win back four times as much in a few years if he works extra hard. He goes to a room full of people like himself. Eventually a door slides open and they filter down a passage to the interior of their transport. It resembles a small cinema. The émigrés sit watching a screen on which appears deep blackness spotted with little lights, the universe they are told they are travelling through. One of the lights grows so big that it is recognisable as a blue and white cloud-swept globe whose surface is mainly sun-reflecting ocean, then all lights are extinguished and, without alarm, our man falls asleep. He has been told that a spell of unconsciousness will ease his arrival in the new world.

He wakens on his feet, facing a clerk across a counter. The clerk hands him a numbered disc, points to a corridor, and tells him to walk down it and wait outside a door with the same number. These instructions are easy to follow. Our man is so stupefied by his recent sleep that he walks a long way before remembering he is supposed to be in a new world. It may be a different world, for the corridor is narrower than the corridors he is used to, and coloured matt brown instead of shiny green, but it has the same lack of windows. The only new thing he notices is a strong smell of fresh paint.

He walks very far before finding the door. A man of his own sort sits on a bench in front of it staring morosely at the floor between his shoes. He does not look up when our man sits beside him. A long time passes. Our man grows impatient. The corridor is so narrow that his knees are not much more than a foot from the door he faces. There is nothing to look at but brown paintwork. At length he murmurs sarcastically, 'So this is our new world.' His neighbour glances at him briefly with quick little shake of the head. An equally long time passes before our man says, almost explosively, 'They promised me more room! Where is it? Where is it?' The door opens, an empty metal trolley is pushed obliquely through and smashes hard into our man's legs. With a scream he staggers to his feet and hobbles backward away from the trolley, which is pushed by someone in a khaki dustcoat who is so big that his shoulders brush the walls on each side and also the ceiling: the low ceiling makes the trolley-pusher bend his head so far forward that our man, retreating sideways now and stammering words of pain and entreaty, stares up not at a face but at a bloated bald scalp. He cannot see if his pursuer is brutally herding him or merely pushing a trolley. In sheer panic our man is about to yell for help when a voice says, 'What's happening here? Leave the man alone, Henry!' and his hand is seized in a comforting grip. The pain in his legs vanishes at once, or is forgotten.

His hand is held by another man of his own type, but a sympathetic and competent one who is leading him away from the trolley man. Our man, not yet recovered from a brutal assault of a kind he has only experienced in childhood, is childishly grateful for the pressure of the friendly hand. 'I'm sure you were doing nothing wrong,' says the stranger, 'You were probably just complaining. Henry gets cross when he hears one of our sort complain. Class prejudice is the root of it. What were you complaining about? Lack of space, perhaps?'

Our man looks into the friendly, guileless face beside him and, after a moment, nods: which may be the worst mistake of his life, but for a while he does not notice this. The comforting handclasp, the increasing distance from Henry who falls further behind with each

J

brisk step they take, is accompanied by a feeling that the corridors are becoming spacious, the walls further apart, the ceiling higher. His companion also seems larger and for a while this too is a comfort, a return to the safety of childhood when he was protected by bigger people who liked him. But he is shrinking, and the smaller he gets the more desperately he clutches the hand which is reducing his human stature. At last, when his arm is dragged so straight above his head that in another moment it will swing him clear of the floor, his companion releases him, smiles down at him, wags a kindly forefinger and says, 'Now you have all the space you need. But remember, God is trapped in you! He will not let you rest until you amount to more than this.'

The stranger goes through a door, closing it carefully after him. Our man stares up at the knob on it which is now and forever out of his reach.

EAST IS WEST

J Leslie Mitchell (Lewis Grassic Gibbon)

I

See to the dip and play of them above Heliopolis! They are like birds, despite the good Mogara. . . .--The fighting machines, I think.

Incongruous over Cairo - those aeroplanes? They outrage the atmosphere Eastern? But why? Was not Daedalus of the East - of Crete and the Crete prehellenic at that? Was it into La Manche so-admired that the first of the aeronaut martyrs fell? ... Yours the geography unreliable, my friend. The Icarian Sea lies not in Western Europe!

East is East and West is West - it is the heresy pitiful, the concept pre-Copernician. Those the fighting-birds of steel: they were made in your England - and are numbered with symbols evolved in the East two thousand years ago; your aeronauts - they bear on their tunics the winged crests of ancient Egypt!

For East is West and West is East; they merge and flow and are the compass-points of a dream. And the little jingo men who walk the world, lifting here the banner Nordic and there the flag Mongolian - in the white hands that raise the banner is the blood of cannibals pre-Aryan, the banner itself is a-flutter with symbols obscene first painted in the jungle-towns of Cambodia; the little Jap is a White, a mongrel Ainu, and salutes on his flag the design first graved on the ancient stones of Cuzco! . . .

Then of race or culture-barriers I would recognise none? God mine, I can recognise nothing else! Like Simon Mogara, like all of us, my life is fenced about with tribe-taboos, my ears deafened with the whining rhymes of cultures troglodyte! Like Simon -

II

But I will tell you of Mogara the while we sit and watch the aeroplanes. And the tourists haughty who pass us by this dusty Abbassieh roadway will think us tramps or the Europeans gone native!

Mogara. It is almost four years ago since I first met him, the one

evening in January. I had gone to live in Heliopolis that I might be
near my clients of the hotels, and that day had spent the many and
wearying hours indoors, in the Cairo Museum, explaining to a party
indifferent and irreverent the unauthentic history of King Oonas.
Returned at sunset, I set out to walk across the sands towards
Helmieh, so that I might meet the evening wind.

I remember that evening very well. There was a thin ghost-play of
lightning on the horizon and presently a little wind stirring to
whorling puffs the tops of the sand-hillocks. I had stopped to light
the pipe in a miniature nullah and from that climbed out, and so came
abruptly on Mogara, the silhouette.

'Good-evening,' I said in the uncertainty.

He also spoke in the accent un-English. 'Good-evening.' He
wheeled slowly on his heels till almost he faced me. Then: 'Would
you mind stepping aside - or falling flat? The wind's just coming
behind you and I'm going to launch her.'

I stepped aside in the hurriedness and some bewilderment. A little
film of mist-powder came drifting over the tundra. Mogara raised his
arms and flung a glittering bird into the air.

For a moment it swayed perilously, as if about to fall. Then came
a little click and sputter, and with the flapping of great wings the fowl
amazing soared upwards. So, for perhaps the hundred yards, it
soared, in the long curve towards Cairo. Then, unaccountably - for
the wings beat quickly as ever - it began to fall, but backwards, and
towards us, like a boomerang. Mogara ran forward and I followed
him. The bird slipped down into his arms the moment I came to his
side.

'This bird,' I said, 'it is - '

He turned on me the face deep-scowling in thought, and with the
little start I realised that he was no European. It was a face of the
heavy and even bronze, with thin nose, straight brows and lips, and
with the startling disfigurement of two long-healed scars stamped
darkly from right eye to ear. For the little we looked at each other, and
then he smiled slowly.

'It is, God willing, an ornithopter.'

III

I grew to know him well and made the occasional visits to his hut in
Zeitoun. It was little more than the hut, being an American bungalow
set in a little garden. The one half of it he used as workshop and study,
the other he slept in and therein cooked the much of eggs, and rice,
being inexpert in the preparation of foods more ambitious.

'Flying? There has been no flying yet. Aeroplanes are not flying-machines. They're structures of cambered planes juggling with artificially-created currents of air. The aeroplane is a mistake - no true forerunner of the flying-machine. Like the pterodactyl, it's only a tentative air-experiment, destined to die childless. . . .'

'And this,' I would say, pointing to the bird-winged model, with its little petrol engine and gleam of aluminium, boat-shaped body, 'this the ornithopter - presently it will fly?'

He would scowl and laugh at that, then jump to his feet and stride to the window and watch a flight of desert-making birds. 'Damn it, colonel, it flies already. You've seen it. Only - ' he would peer upwards unfriendlily at the dots that were birds - 'it doesn't keep flying. There's something - '

There was something, some law of the flight insoluble, which brought his models to ground after every first hundred yards or so, albeit the wings still beat. Model after model he had tried out. In itself the tremendous achievement, he had solved the initial difficulty of the ornithopter - the building of wings strong, yet flexible, capable of the under-sweep and the poising blow, capable of lifting the machine into air. But in the air it refused to stay.

He would expound these things to me, the child in matters aeronautic, with the great logic and clarity, and in the swing of exposition would a strange thing occur. His voice would lose its mechanic staccato and acquire an alien lilt and rhythm. Once, in the midst of such converse, he pulled himself up and laughed.

'Did you notice that - the half-caste sing-song? Funny. And quite ineradicable.'

He had the genuine, impersonal amusement in these traits betrayed by his own personality. But it was the same half-sardonic, half-impatient amusement which personalities always stirred in him. He had none of the half-breed's resentments or enthusiastic championings - 'perhaps because I'm a quarter-breed. The snarling of the bleached and the coloured go over my head. People don't count. Aeronautics is my job.'

He was of the lesser breeds intermingled enough. His grandfather, a Goanese half-caste, had settled down in Jaffa after wanderings dim and inexplicable. There, as the orange-merchant, he had flourished, acquired a Cretan wife, and, in the course of time and nature, a son. This son, exported to France for education, married, and returned to Jaffa after the several years with a Parisian lady who took life as a jest and the circles orange-growing by storm. . . . Such Mogara family-history and social advancement till the appearance of the little Simon.

His appearance seemed to his father the event retrogressive. The Parisian lady, true to character, found him the oddity amusing. They had expected the child who would show no trace of the Goanese grandfather. Instead, they found themselves parents to an atavistic little infant who might have been a Hindu undiluted. As soon as he was old enough his father, in the some disgust, exiled him to school and university in Lyons, where colour is little bar and they of the skins dark-pigmented accounted amongst God's creatures.

He was twenty-nine years of age that evening I encountered him on the Helmieh sands. In that interval from the Jaffa days he had become the French citizen, had during the War served in a French air regiment and acquired the high Legion decoration, had succeeded to and sold the business orange-exporting on the death of his father and mother, had travelled to America -

Of those the American days I heard only in disjointed, sardonic outline. Early after the War, dissatisfied with aeroplanes, he had set about experimenting with helicopter-models, and, abandoning that second stage, with flexible gliders and winged kites. He might have remained in France to this day but for the lack of readily-procurable apparatus in that country immediately after its exhausting triumph. The experimenter's needs drove him to America to work and study.

There he found himself, to his own amusement, treated as servant and inferior. Even from other experimenters and aeronauts was the occasional jibe at the 'nigger birdman'. Settled in a new town built on the aircraft trade, he went out one night and found the streets in the excitement and turmoil. The usual story had spread of the negro and white woman. Presently was the negro, as usual dragged out of jail by the crowd and lynched. Ensued a kind of anti-colour pogrom.
. . .

Mogara brought out of that turmoil the scarred face and a week in hospital. A citizen of France, apologies were made through stiff consular representations and an indemnity offered. . . . I can see the light of amusement flicker on that brooding brown face as he lay in hospital and heard of the indemnity.

For he was as completely indifferent to revenge as to reconciliation. Mankind I think he envisaged largely as the straying packs of parti-coloured puppies, baying unaccountably at the moon and indulging in the dog-squabbles equally unaccountable. Amidst all this canine pride and uproar his the 'job' to find a corner obscure and pacific where he could build an ornithopter that flew. . . .

I remember making the interjection.

'But for whom, then, do you work - for whom add to the sum of knowledge? If such is humanity, why seek to build this flying machine?'

'For my own private pride, I suppose. . . . To visit the moon and see what all the howling's about.' He shrugged. 'How should I know? . . . Anyhow, I decided against returning even to France, and came to Egypt instead, where there are other browny men in charge. Being the shade they are I calculated they'd probably neither hinder nor mutilate me, nor look askance at my feet.'

'Your feet?'

He grinned, the scars creasing in dark serrations on his cheek. 'Yes. You see, I have the half-caste's passion for yellow boots.'

So, with such jest indifferent, to switch to other matters. I remember he told me these things at his garden-entrance on the Zeitoun road one evening, the while we smoked a parting pipe. When he had ceased speaking there was the little clatter and cloud of white dust far up the road towards Cairo, and I watched it idly.

They were the man and girl on horseback, and as they cantered near I drew a breath of admiration. The man young, of the thirty-forties, with the soldier's shoulders, the cold, narrow face with clean-cut features, the cold stare of blue eyes. But the girl - like her companion of the English, like him result of that fineness of breeding and the much nursery-scrubbing that has made the English aristo-crat. And the something - as so often in the feminine of that type, and so seldom in the masculine - it had brought to flower in her: the beauty indefinable as the grace of a lily. Very young, bare-headed with the shock of the tidily-untidy hair, slim and upright and with easy hands she rode, head a little thrown back. As she went by her eyes passed over us in the momentary scrutiny, distant, indifferent, impersonal - and bored.

So they passed into the evening, and I, who love types and so seldom find them, had the sting of gratification. These the English, the Aryans ultra-bred, dominant, blood-proud, apart. How apart from all the lesser breeds, they of the pigmentation, 'without the Law'!

I glanced at Mogara in the little shame for my own thoughts. And then I saw that he had scarcely noted the passing of the riders. He was staring up into the sky at the inevitable flight of sunset-winging birds.

IV

All next day he worked on a new modification of the keel of his model, and about five of the afternoon went out across the ranges beyond Helmieh to test it anew. For a little, near the original mound where I had found him, perhaps, he stood awaiting the coming of the wind. Deep in thought and the calculation of mathematical minutiae he saw the sand-heaps at length begin to puff, and, setting a dial, launched the bird-machine into the air. It beat upwards with stiffer motion than formerly. A clatter of stones behind him drew his scowling attention. He glanced over his shoulder.

Not a dozen feet away a bare-headed girl sat on horseback, her eyes fixed on the flight of the ornithopter. So only for the moment he noted, then his attention also went back to the model. It flew perhaps two yards further than usual, then commenced its usual boomerang descent.

He swore, ran forward and caught it, and heard behind him the amazed intake of breath. The girl had dismounted, and as he turned with the bird-machine in his arms her eyes were very bright with excitement.

'Oh . . . sorry if I'm spying. But that was wonderful!'

'It was rotten,' he said, neither graciously nor ungraciously, but with complete indifference to either her apologies or applause. Undiscouraged, she came nearer, her horse following with down-bent, snuffling head.

'But why? It's an ornithopter, and it flew. Real flying, not just aeroplane gliding. . . . And my brother argues we'll never have ornithopters - never anything more than a lop-sided helicopter or so. Wish he could have seen that! It wasn't a secret test, was it?'

He had been aware of a slight surprise at meeting someone who knew the difference between an ornithopter and a helicopter. Now, still with the absent-minded scowl, but half-heeding her presence, he answered the question.

'No. Why should it be?'

'I thought all experimenters did these things secretly and then pestered Governments.' This with the flippancy, but then a return to excitement. 'I say! Most thrilling thing I've seen in this boring country - most thrilling thing I've ever seen, I think. . . . Do you know the old Frost ornithopter in the London Science? Is yours on the same principle?'

'If you've seen the Frost -' He was launched the more successfully than ever had been his model. He set the bird-machine on the ground, demonstrating its build and principal departures from the Frost model. He brought out the pencil and scrap of paper and dashed off lines of the calculations dizzying and algebraic.

The girl remained undizzied. Still holding the bridle she knelt down in the interest, and the horse extended over her shoulder the inquisitive head. . . . They must have made the amusing grouping there on the sands.

She had flown many times in aeroplanes, had the English Aero Club's pilot certificate, had, like himself, an obsession that the aeroplane was traitor to aviation and that Romance which had lured men to the conquest of the skies since the days of Cretan Daedalus.

'It wasn't for the sake of a world of super-engined kites that Icarus and Egremont and Lilienthal died. But real flying. . . . And you won't sell your model to any Government, or make it a war machine?'

'Good Lord, no.'

'Good man!'

He saw a hand stretched out towards him, and stared at it. His thoughts came hurtling down from rarefied heights like an aeroplane disabled. He found himself kneeling side by side not with a pleasant voice and a disembodied enthusiasm, but an English girl. . . .

That stare and silence of his drew her eyes. So, for a little, they looked at each other in the mutual wonder: the girl, white and gold, radiant and aloof even in excitement; Mogara, lithe and slight, with the slightness un-European, the dark, scarred face, the scowl of thin-pencilled brows. . . . He saw the girl's eyes widen, and at that, with a sardonic little laugh, he was on his feet.

'Yes, I'm a native. But you're quite safe.'

And then, dimly, indifferently, he realised that he had made a mistake. The girl's eyes looked through him as she too rose to her feet.

He had ceased to exist.

V

At nine o'clock that evening, passing down the Sharia Kamil, my eyes fell on the small car unmistakable. It was the yellow runabout, the property of my friend the Dr. Adrian, and it stood in front of a little open-air café with many tables. At one of those tables, deep in the usual self-game with dominoes, sat Adrian himself.

This is to him relief and narcotic in one, this game played with the great seriousness. To me recurred the wonder whimsical: Is he ever victor - and over whom? ... He looked up and saw me and swept aside the pieces.

'Hello, colonel. Haven't seen you for ages. Sit down and gossip. How's Heliopolis?'

'It is the place dry,' I said, and at that he ordered me the wine. Then:

'Seen anything of the Melforts there? Cousins of mine - air-people, newly come from Malta?'

'I did not know you possessed the cousins,' I said. He grinned and yawned, having passed the toilsome day.

'Knowledge that was never kept from me, unfortunately. I was forced to punch the aristocratic Melfort nose quite early in my career.' He was reminiscent. 'And was getting as good as I gave till Joyce, in a pinafore and a white wrath, separated us with a shower of stones and pelted us impartially...Murderous little pacifist.'

He expounded the brief and irreverent family history the while I drank the wine. These Melforts were the remote cousins only: the grandmother of Adrian had been sister of the grandfather of Reginald and Joyce Melfort.

'But we come from the same county town, you see, and there's been a kind of family friendship - patronising on both sides - kept going for three generations. The Adrians have been the medical and improverished branch; they've assisted new Melforts into the world and signed their certificates of departure for the next during the last seventy years or so. Know more of Melfort history than the Melforts themselves, who've only passed on the highlights to their descendants.' He chuckled as at some secret jest. 'Grandfather Melfort went out to Jamaica, raised rum and a great deal of money, and returned to perpetuate a military and gentlemanly stock. Put his son into the army, and grandson Reginald followed in his father's footsteps...It was he whose nose I punched.

'Not a bad chap really, I suppose. Only - he never had a chance. Born in India and reared on the usual pap. A Nordic snub-man with highly-scrubbed virtues and a disposition to pronounce what as hwaw. Transferred to the Air Force during the War and is a squadron leader or something now. Has taken the latest wonder of science and made of it a means for forming fours in the air and inspecting engines to see if they're properly shaved...That kind'.

He broke off, as in conversation he so often did, to refute his own exaggerations. 'No. That's damned unfair. A very good airman, I believe. Straight as a die, efficient, proud of the Service, an excellent example of the breeding of an aristocrat in three generations...Let's be unfair. Impartiality's too much of a strain. He has less imagination than a wombat, and the colour, caste and class prejudices of a tabu-ridden Brahmin. In his secret soul he believes the Anglo-Saxon saheb evolved from a special type of ape which always cleaned its teeth in the morning and even in the early Miocene wore badges of rank on its fur...I've been invited to dinner in ten days' time, and if Reginald and I don't quarrel and bandy authorities and sneers, it'll be the first occasion since the nose-punching episode. Joyce had better stand by with an armful of stones.'

'She is the sister?'

'Occasionally. When she remembers. Keeps house nominally for Reginald: keeps him on tenterhooks actually. Modern and un-modern.

A romantic's idealisation of English womanhood in appearance - she'd delight your eyes, Saloney - and in mind a quattrocento adventurer, mystic and mountain-storming. Flies aeroplanes and innumerable outrageous opinions, waxes hot over all kinds of unexpected things and cold over everything which her appearance warrants...By the seven goats of Egypt - Hi!'

He leapt from his chair with the beaming face and the startling shout, and seized the arm of a passer-by - the man bareheaded, absorbed, chest-clasping the large and ungainly parcel. Thus assaulted, the stranger dropped the parcel - which split, grocery-disgorging - and turned scowlingly upon Adrian. Almost immediately vanished the scowl.

'God, the doctor of Chaumont!'

'Air-ambulance 30Q!'

They fell to the hand-shaking, the enquiries innumerable, the laughter of men who had shared the war-episode unforgettable. Adrian turned to make the introduction, but I forestalled him.

'I am acquainted,'I said, 'with M. Mogara.'

VI

For four days after his meeting with the unknown girl on the sands, and with the little Adrian and myself in the Sharia Kamil, Mogara kept to his workshop, fitting the new keel to his ornithopter. On the fourth evening he tramped out beyond Helmieh again to put his modification to test. As usual, he walked in the study brown, and so almost dashed his head against horse and rider - both of which had been regarding his approach for over a mile.

It was the girl, and she surveyed him insolently. 'What is your name, Mr - Native?'

He was in a good humour, expecting better results from his model. He twinkled at her sardonically. 'Mogara - memsaheb. ...And my grandfather was a Goanese'.

She flushed angrily. 'He may have been a Chinese albino for all I care. You are very much concerned with your family history, M. Mogara. Hasn't it ever struck you that it may be boring to others? Or your role of the dark and dangerous male the other evening - wasn't it rather cowardly?'

He was sardonically undisturbed. 'No doubt I'm both a bore and a coward. Meantime my job's not psycho-analysis but amateur aeronautics.'

'Of course it is! And since the tests aren't secret why mayn't I come and watch them? Why have you kept away from the trial-ground these last three evenings? Can't you see that I want to learn, that it's your ornithopter I'm interested in, not you, you—'

He stared at her. It was the one appeal which could have touched him. On his face, dark and scarred, she saw a scowling wonder. A slow smile followed. Then:

' "Blithering ass" are the words you want...I'm sorry.' He held out a tentative hand 'If—'

Her fingers touched his. They regarded each other gravely for a moment, laughed together; then Joyce Melfort dismounted, sat down, clasped her hands about her knees, and watched...

You must figure her so, evening after evening. For the meetings went on. Almost every evening she rode across the sands to find Mogara, with some new modification imposed upon his model, waiting for the sunset wind.

And presently, in between times of the test-flying and the calculations abstruse, they would find themselves deep in talk - talk that ranged away from aeronautics and back to it and away again. She found his mind the encyclopaedia of sheer fact, the mind of the scientist, a little warped, almost passionless but for that the desire and pursuit of knowledge; hers was to him revelation of how knowledge may be transmuted to idealism and hope and purpose...

Except a sardonic scepticism for all enthusiasms nationalist and religious he had the no-philosophy of life. She made him see all human existence in the terms of high Adventure - the Adventure scarce begun, the struggle from the slime to the stars. *Per ardua ad astra*. Every scrap of new knowledge was equipment for that Adventure; every man who fought the beast in himself and the anti-christ many-guised, who kept the honest ledgers and the open mind, who knew the ache of wonder and a desire beyond fulfilment - he fought in the spear-head of the Adventure...

And Mogara, his model half-forgotten, would brood and listen till he too glimpsed faith and belief in that Republic in the skies which lies beyond our shadowed uncertainties, which sometimes seems but a generation away.

Sometimes, as they talked, they would lift their heads and see the wheel and glitter of the Squadron Leader Melfort's aeroplanes practising dusk landings at Heliopolis.

VII

'A nigger chappie with a bee in his bonnet and one of those helicopter-thingummys. He's been at it for months, they say, practising out on the sands beyond Helmieh. Saw him myself last night when I went up to do a spot of night-flying'.

Joyce Melfort came riding against the sunset of the tenth day since her first encounter with Mogara. Fragments from the chatter at her brother's table the previous evening rode with her, like buzzing gnats...She had been coldly angry, then wondering and amused. Now, with an amazement, she found herself angry again.

From far across the sands Mogara waved to her, absent-mindedly. As she rode towards him the buzzing of an aeroplane engine grew loud overhead. She glanced upwards, saw one of the machines of her brother's squadron dip towards her and Mogara as though they were the bombing target, and then rise and wheel back towards Heliopolis.

'Now that that anachronism's gone—'

She reined in, dismounted, and stood watching in silence. Mogara clicked out the wings of the much-tried model, set revolving the little dial and pointer in its heart, and then launched the contrivance into the air.

He did not stop to watch its progress, but turned round towards her with the now not-infrequent smile. ' "Hope springs eternal - " ' he patted the neck of her nuzzling mount. '- If you're not bored with the performance by now, I think your horse must be...Eh?'

She had caught his arm in the painful grip. 'Quick! Look!'

Mogara wheeled round and stared skywards, stared at a flapping-winged model which neither failed nor descended, which rose and rose with steady purr of miniature engine and then began to wheel overhead in great circles...

Its inventor gulped, swore inadequately, and then found Joyce Melfort's hands gripping his, shaking them up and down.

'Why, you've won, you've won!' She glanced up for reassurance and then executed a little dance. 'My dear man, can't you realise it? Waken up! Aren't you glad?...'

Her voice died away. There came in her eyes the terror and expectation. Unaccountably in his arms, she saw his scarred face terrifyingly close. So, the moment she would remember forever, and then, kissed by him, there awoke in her something like a dream forgotten... That - then they were apart, and she had slashed him across the face with her riding-whip.

He staggered a little under her blow, and then, in a queer silence, not looking at her, brought out a handkerchief, and dabbed at the blood-pringling weal which flushed angrily on his unscarred cheek. He lowered the scrap of linen, looking at it in a kind of wonder, and at that Joyce Melfort's stricken remorse found voice.

'Oh, I'm sorry...I was a beast. But you shouldn't - '

He smiled at her, without a hint of mockery, with dull eyes. He was very quiet - dazedly quiet.

'I know I shouldn't. That was the only possible reply.' He turned away uncertainly, fumbling with the handkerchief. 'And now you'd better go.'

He expected to hear the sound of her footsteps going towards the horse. Instead, there was complete silence. He glanced round again. She stood where he had kissed her, in her eyes an angry flame of courage and resolution. She began to speak.

'Listen: I'm sorry - because I hit you. Not because you kissed me. Why shouldn't you?' Her voice quivered a little, but her eyes were very unwavering. 'I - I wanted you to.'

They stared at each other. Overhead, absurdly, and in the circles drawing gradually earthwards, wheeled the unheeded ornithopter model. Mogara shook his head...

She found herself listening to an impossible renunciation from an impossible lover, the while the darkness came flowing across the sands.

'...You're splendid to have said that. But to-morrow - and the next day - it'll sound impossible. To you it sounds half-impossible even now...English - and I'm a mongrel. Your people -' He seemed to forget what he had intended to say. His voice trailed off. He shrugged, and held out his hand, and was oddly shy, and stammered for the first time since she had known him.

Thanks for you - for it.' Her limp fingers touched his. They smiled at each other strainedly. 'This isn't anything, you know. We aren't anything. And there's still your Adventure. For both of us. Always there's the Adventure...'

She found herself mounted and riding towards Heliopolis. A hundred yards away she looked back and saw Mogara snatch a magic bird out of the darkness, like a boy playing with a dream.

VIII

And less than a dream was it presently to seem to him. In the Zeitoun hut he sat and stared at the ornithopter model. Successful. He had won. Successful.

He went to a mirror and saw the ghostly reflection of his own face, scarred on both cheeks...So it had actually happened.

He began, mechanically, to prepare a meal. What was it he had said? The Adventure: still the Adventure...Aeronautics not enough now. Something to follow and believe in. *She* believed in it...

He heard the galloping horse stop at his garden-gate; heard hasting footsteps come up to the open door of the hut. For a moment a figure was dim against the night-dimness, and then Joyce Melfort was in the room.

They stood facing each other. He saw her breast rise and fall, breathing as might one who had run a race.

'M. Mogara - did you or did you not kiss me out there?'

He nodded whitely. Thereat she gave a sigh, and suddenly collapsed, limply, happily, into a chair.

'Then that's all right. Because you'll have to marry me now, in spite of my deplorable ancestors. Where can I throw my hat?' She jumped up in expostulation. 'My dear, whoever told you that was the way to cook a sausage?'

She knelt over the sputtering oil-stove, and, so kneeling, wheeled round and laughed up at him. "Poor brother Reginald!...' She stopped to make mirthful appraisement of her finger-nails. She was incoherently light-hearted. 'Knew as soon as I got home that he knew. That was *his* machine that came bombing us this afternoon. He'd heard about us - came down to spy, my dear...Was waiting for me, he and Adrian - they'd been quarrelling- and oh! what does it matter what he said? I felt too sick to notice much till Adrian broke in with a kind of shout. 'Who? *Simon Mogara*'? Stared from one to other of us and then laughed and laughed, and then grew white and furious. '*Nigger*? Why, damn your impudence - !' and it all came out, and so did I, and made for the stables, leaving Reggie like a ghost and Adrian shouting wishes to you...What an evening! Who'd have guessed it? Whoever? And now-'?

His queer, frozen silence made her glance up. In a moment she was beside him. 'Why, why - Simon!...'

IX

It was some time before either of them stirred from that position wherein she had told her eager secret amazing. Smell of burning sausage roused Joyce. She broke away and danced to the oil-stove, and Mogara, released from necessity to hold her in his arms, sank down into the chair she had vacated and stared at his yellow boots as though they were the footwear unbelievable...

An hour later, on parting under the stars at the garden-gate, he heard her gay answer to his question come out of the dimness: 'Why, soon as ever, dear!' Dimly from her saddle she bent towards him to give him the ghostly kiss. Then had the whimsical thought and laughed a grave little laugh.

'But our children - whatever'll they be citizens of?'

Her hand, warm and assured, in his, he stood and looked up at her, and beyond her at the stars, at the years he saw with their difficulties and disillusionments and perhaps the bitter shames for her to face. But in his voice she heard only the tenderness as he answered with the jest that was more than jest, that would surely cry its promise through all their lives.

'Why - the Republic in the skies!'

X

For East is West and West is East and the little fascistic German blesses as the Aryan symbol exclusive the swastika they worshipped in the Temples of Chichen-Stza...Eh? You see, the good Adrian, until provoked beyond endurance, had held it as a dark and mirthful secret that the Melfort grandmother, wealth-bringing, had been a 'white mulatto' of Jamaica.

REPEAT PLEASE

DILYS ROSE

She rings the doorbell. She speaks through the entryphone. It is noon. She is always on time, sometimes a little bit early. She says *Hello it's Jane. Teacher.* Teacher Jane thinks I do not remember her voice from one week to the next. I press the button and the downstairs door opens for her. I wait for her to knock on my door.

When Teacher Jane knocks on my door I open it. This is the arrangement. She comes once a week to teach me English words. She says *Hello how are you.* She smiles a big smile. She wants that I say *I am very well thank you.* I say only *Come* and she follows me inside.

I am not so very well thank you. I am cold. Since I have been here, since I came down the steps of the plane at London three years ago I feel as if the sun has not touched me. It rained the day I arrived, not the rain we have at home, not the big bright drops which crash down and vanish. Here the rain wraps itself around you like a wet sari.

Ali met me at the airport. He was holding an umbrella and a raincoat. He gave me the coat. He told me I would need a coat. He took my suitcase and began walking. I followed him. We travelled by bus, by train. We walked up a windy street and stopped at the downstairs door. He showed me my name next to his on the entryphone. We walked up the stairs. He took me inside. The flat was empty. He told me this would be home. It is not home. It is only a house.

When Teacher Jane comes I am tired. Since Izmir was born I do not sleep. I try to sleep but the baby wakes me, or my dreams do.

I am walking, feeling the hot earth under my feet. I am walking to the river, the wide slow yellow river. Beside me is my sister. She has her small pitcher on her head. A plane crosses the sky and we look up. It is not one of the great white birds which bring wives to husbands across the world. It is small and black, buzzing. My sister does not know the difference. She waves at it and runs down the bank into the water.

When Jane rings my doorbell I do not want to answer it. I do not want this to be my door. I cannot step outside into the yard and throw rice to the chickens. I cannot pick fruit from the tree. Teacher Jane says *Hello how are you*. I say only *Come* because that is all that is necessary. Jane is not doctor. She is teacher of words only. She cannot make baby eat, cannot mend my dreams. She cannot find Ali a better job. He goes out in the morning, early. He comes home in the middle of the night. I get up, prepare some food. He eats, he tells me how many curries were sold at the restaurant. He smokes some cigarettes and goes to sleep. Ali goes to sleep and I lie beside him, waiting for the baby to wake up.

We wade until we are waist deep. We begin to wash, my sister splashing and ducking her head underwater. On the far bank, the ferry is loading up with passengers, the local ferry which has standing room only, in one straight line. I count seven women, one little old man.
On the far bank it is peaceful. There is a temple, a small tea plantation and a forest of tall trees. My grandfather told us that these trees came all the way from Scotland. He would go to the forest often, to walk, he'd say, but with only one leg he did not walk so much. Mostly he would sleep in the shade of the Scottish trees.

Teacher Jane sits on the bed and opens her bag. She takes out a notebook and a pencil. This is the lesson beginning. She empties the contents of her bag on to the floor, piece by piece. She stops at each item and says its name. She says this name two or three times then I must *Repeat please*. When Jane's bag is empty - and my room is untidy again - she asks me the names again and I remember one or two. Paper, pencil, book - always Jane has books and newspapers and magazines. I think in her house she must have only books and magazines because each time she brings different ones. In my house there is only the Asian newspaper. Ali reads it. I use it to wrap up the vegetable peelings.

After I have said paper, pencil, book, diary, hairbrush, cigarettes, matches, keyring, we do her shopping. She holds up a carrot. *Carrot*, she says. She lays it beside the hairbrush and points to the hairbrush. *Carrot* ?'she says. She wants me to say, *No, it's not a carrot, it's a hairbrush*. I say only, *No*. This is not important to me. The baby is important, and Ali. I have no room in my heart for carrots and hairbrushes. I will not make this house into a home because I know the English word for a vegetable I do not very much like.

Ali says I must learn to speak English so that he can go on longer trips to his brother's house in Leeds. There is not enough room for all of us to visit. Anyway, Ali is going on business. I do not know what business. Ali says I do not need to know. We do not agree about this and I worry in case he is maybe doing something dangerous. But money must be sent to our home town somehow and in the restaurant he earns so little.

Baby wakes up. *Baby crying*, says Jane. I too say *Baby crying* and Jane says, *Good*. But now she must sit, not teaching, while I feed Izmir. I do not have enough milk. I am a poor cow. When Izmir has emptied each breast he cries for more. I get the tinned milk. They gave it to me at the clinic. I show it to Jane. *OK?* I say. *Sorry*, says Jane. I point to the writing. I want her to read the instructions on the tin. I want her to teach me the right mixture but she doesn't understand. Why does she teach me the words for carrots and hairbrushes and not *Help me please?* All Jane does is stare at Izmir's tiny crumpled face and be afraid. Afraid that just by looking she will make the crying worse. Afraid that if she held him in her arms he would break.

The ferry is standing at the platform. And then the sudden disturbance at the bank, the ferryman running into the forest, the boat sliding away from the bank without its oars, the boat rocking, the monkeys screeching as the black plane returns, low this time, roaring, trailing a filthy ribbon of smoke. And then the rattle of gunfire and the ferry passengers tossed like logs into the water. The river is streaked with red. This is my sleeping dream. It will not go away. It is the past and the past will not go away. My grandfather was dead by the time he was brought ashore, the river mud streaming over his body.

My waking dream is of the future. It also will not go away. Ali tells me I live too much in my imagination and that I will be happier here, will feel safer here once I have learned more about this country, once I learn English. He says I must put everything from home behind me. He says I must spend more time outside, looking around me, and not so much time inside myself. He says when Izmir is older, he can play in front of the house. There is a small concrete yard. I have planted some flowers out there, by the wall, but I do not sit in the yard and Izmir will not play there when he is older. I will not let him. My waking dream will not let me leave him there. In my mind I see a car stopping, a grey car with dark windows. Two men get out. I cannot tell what they look like, only that they are dressed in suits and wear dark glasses. Everything happens in a flash

When I tell Ali my dream, he asks me if they are Asian men or white men. I do not know but I know there is a reason and it is Izmir they want, not the fair-haired child next door. There is no accident. They pull Izmir off his toy train, bundle him into the car and drive off. Ali says these things happen here only on the television.

The lesson begins again when Izmir has cried himself to sleep. Jane fetches the clock from the window ledge and points to the time. *Half-past twelve*, she says. She makes the hands move round the clock and tells me the time. *One o'clock. What time is it*? and I must *Repeat please.* At one o'clock Jane will pack up her bag and go away. I want her to go because I am tired yet I do not like to be alone, in this house which is not a home.

Jane sees me yawning before she has finished with the time, so she puts back the clock. She smiles and says *Sleepy*? and I say *Sleepy*, then *Tea*? and she says *Thank you very much.* We go into the kitchen, leaving Izmir asleep in his pram. There is now a table and two chairs. While we are drinking our tea I hear a small noise at the door. *Postman?* says Jane. *Postman*, I say. *Letters*, says Jane. I will fetch the letters when Jane goes away.

Jane wants to show me something special. She has a magazine with a shiny cover. She turns the pages. There are pictures of watches and cars and men in English suits and girls in short dresses. Also of perfume bottles and underwear and big country houses. Also of soldiers and operations and mountains. She stops at a photograph of a mountain covered with trees. These are the Scottish trees my grandfather was so fond of. I have been living in this country for three years now. I have not seen any of these trees, except in December little ones which are taken indoors and dressed up.

Look, says Jane. She turns the page and points. It is my own village, my own river. There is no ferryboat at the landing. There are no people laying out laundry on the bank or washing in the river but I know they are all there somewhere, out of sight, watching the pictures being taken, standing maybe right behind the photographer, telling him what to put in his picture. Did my sister too run over and watch or was she still too frightened of that spot?

Your home, says Jane. She is very happy to be showing me the river, but I cannot see that peaceful empty river. The noise is in my ears, the buzzing and the roars, the rattles and the screams. And the smell of burning fills my nostrils. I close my eyes to block out the bloody picture I see taking shape over the peaceful one and I am thinking, yes, Ali is right: I live too much in my imagination, and then Jane is jumping up from the table and shaking my arm and shouting *Look!* *Look*, and I see smoke creeping round the door and I know that the smell of burning is not a phantom from the past but is the present, is here, now, in my house. Jane stands back as I run for Izmir.

The hall is black with smoke. At the door is a burning ball of rags and the carpet and the wallpaper have caught fire and I know now that it was not the postman who came today. I am filling up buckets of water at the sink and Jane is throwing the water at the fire in between shouting through the open window, *Fire! Fire!* and *Help! Help!*, and I am repeating again and again everything she says as loudly and clearly as I can.

ELVIS IS DEAD

CARL MACDOUGALL

I've always liked Elvis; ever since I was fourteen and went up to Tam Broon's after school. His sister had just bought Heartbreak Hotel. Tam played it and I liked it. After I'd heard it a couple of times I went out and bought it. I've still got it, still play it sometimes; just an old 78 but the music's good.

It's hard saying what I like about Elvis. I like his music. His style's changed a lot from things like Hound Dog and Don't Be Cruel and Blue Suede Shoes and all these great numbers. I like his style. I mean, if he was just somebody walking about ordinary you wouldn't think much of him. But Elvis's style is his and I like it. His gear's good. I like his hair and sideburns too; but best I liked everything, especially his style.

I wrote a poem about Elvis when I was at school but the teacher said it was rubbish and tore it up.

When I went to work I got kidded on a lot because I wore his gear: drainpipes, drape jackets and a wee bootlace tie. It never bothered me much. They were just old guys who went on a lot about the war and what it was like when they were young and how they never had anything. I felt sorry for them. It never really bothered me what they said: all my pals wore the same gear and we used to go up to each other's houses and play Elvis records. Sometimes we played Fats Domino and Little Richard but most of the time we played Elvis numbers like Jailhouse Rock and Teddy Bear.

We went to the dancing sometimes and used to jive. Some guys dressed up in Marlon Brando gear and we used to fight them. Nothing like it is now. Just a fight. I feel sorry for these kids. I mean, they've nothing to look up to, no one to respect the way we looked up to Elvis.

The Locarno used to have dancing to records at dinner-time. I worked near there and went nearly every day. It was good. They used to play Elvis records and sometimes Bill Haley and The Platters and other good rock'n' roll stars whose names I've forgotten except Marvin Rainwater who made a record called A Whole Lotta Lovin which I quite liked. He never had another hit after that.

I met Betty at the dancing one dinner-time. She had her hair piled up and I thought it was nice. She must have gone to a lot of bother with it at her work before she came out. I danced her a couple of times and they played Love Me Tender and I got her up for it. We danced close and I asked her for a date and she said okay.

I don't know how long we were going out with each other before we got married. We had to get married. I don't think we were going with each other very long. I can't remember.

When we got married we got a house near her mother in Sword Street. I got a dog and called him Shep but he got run over. He was an Alsatian.

Betty had a wee boy and we got a house off the corporation because the one in Sword Street was too wee. Betty's brother did the flitting to our new house in the Milton. She called the wee boy John, after me. For a while I thought about calling him Elvis, but she said that was daft, that it would be hard on him when he went out to play with other kids and I could see what she meant. Anyway, we settled in and things went fine.

I always had an interest in Elvis's career, even when he was in the army and made records like Wooden Heart. But I stopped seeing all my old pals when I got married and never really bothered. I still bought every new Elvis record when it came out, but that was all. I got the albums as well.

Because I never had a trade it was sometimes hard getting work, but we got by all right. Then I got a start where I am now. I don't mind it. The money could be better but so could a lot of other things. I don't know how I've stuck it so long. Always said I was going to chuck it. Used to look for other jobs then I got fed up. So here I am still working away.

I suppose it's the kids really. You don't like to see them going without. When I was first married I changed my job a lot till I got onto the steel erecting. That was good money and I liked it. It's a good feeling when you've got money in your pocket. You can dress nice and do what you like. Me and Betty used to go out a lot then; sometimes we went to the dancing, sometimes we just went to the pictures, especially if there was an Elvis picture on. Her mother watched wee John and we could do what we liked. Sometimes we went to a big fancy restaurant in the town and had steaks. Funny the way you notice things. One night I looked at the waiter's hands when he was putting out the dinners. They were soft, like a woman's hands. They were nicer than Betty's hands. I looked at mine and they were red and hard with a lot of cuts. After that I felt everybody was looking at them. I didn't like to go out for a meal much after that; kept looking at people's hands. And your house never looks the same after you've been out like that. You get a taxi home and your street doesn't look the same, never mind your house. I'd sometimes wish we were going to a big fancy hotel or someplace nice instead of back to our house. We stopped going for meals. We fought a lot when we got home and she said it wasn't worth it.

Then her brother went to South Africa and wrote back and said it was good; all the sunshine and they'd got a car and bought a new house. When Betty said we should send for the papers, I said, If you like.

And that's how we went to South Africa. I got good references, handwritten ones, not done by a secretary nor nothing like that. We went to Joburg. It took us a while to settle because we didn't take much with us. I got a job and worked away fine. There weren't a lot of people we knew; Betty's brother was okay at first, but they had their own life to lead so we left them to it. I didn't like the way they treated the darkies, but that's their business, and Betty got fed up with nothing to do all day. We got a flat and done it up nice. I took lessons and got a wee car when I passed my test. We started saving up for a new house and had a good bit put by when Betty got pregnant again. The hospital bills and stuff would have been too much, so we sold the car and used the house money to come home.

We got a house in Glenrothes and moved up. Been here a while now. Betty had a wee girl and we called her Priscilla after Elvis's wife and I got a job where I am now. It's nice here, different from Glasgow. I hardly ever think about going back. The houses are good and I live near the work. There's not much to do sometimes, but you get into the way of it. We usually stay in and watch the telly. There's shops handy and they've put a lot of sculptures up, along the roads and places like that. It makes a change. Betty got in with some women here and they had a group for the kids. She went a lot at first but fell away. She started going again when we had our third, Lisa, but stopped when Lisa went to school.

It's funny how things happen. I thought everything was all right. For one thing I never thought about Elvis dying. I never imagined him dead. When I saw it on the news I was shattered, couldn't believe it. They showed a film of him doing a performance in Las Vegas. It was great; he looked so alive. But he must be dead.

A couple of days after that I was watching the funeral and all the people crying; it made me think about what it was like, you know, when I was younger. It was as if I knew it would never happen again. John was home on leave and going back to his unit. He's stationed in Belfast and we worry about him sometimes, especially when you see the news. He came in drunk, had a fight with Betty, then left the next day. She wasn't speaking to me. When I asked what was wrong she said I didn't stick up for her and that he'd no right coming in drunk. I said, You're only young once.

Anyway, I came back tonight and saw the letter. I thought it was funny; she'd put a salad out for my tea:

Dear John,
Theres stuff in the cupboard and as far as I no all the bills are paid. I've taken Priscilla and Lisa and some of our stuff. We have gone to my mothers dont come up. We will be alright. The insurance is due £2.60 on Friday in the envelope at the back of the clock. I want sometime away and no you understand. Its what we spoke about.
your loving wife,
Betty

I don't know what to think. The kids'll miss their school. It's daft. When we did talk she never said anything about going. She just said she was fed up. I never thought she was like that.

MANDELA DAY

It was 25 years they take that man away
Now the freedom moves in closer every day
Wipe the tears down from your saddened eyes
They say Mandela's free so step outside.

Oh Mandela Day
Oh Mandela's Free

It was 25 years ago this very day
Held behind four walls all through night and day
Still the children know the story of that man
And we know what's going on right through your land.

25 years ago
Oh Mandela Day
Oh Mandela's Free

If the tears are flowing, wipe them from your face
I can feel this heart beat moving deep inside
It was 25 years they took that man away
And now the world come down say Nelson Mandela's free

Oh Mandela's Free

The rising sun sets Mandela on his way
It's been 25 years around this very day
From the one outside to the ones inside we say
Oh Mandela's Free
Oh set Mandela Free

Oh Mandela Day
Oh Mandela's Free

25 years ago
What's going on!
And we know what's going on
Because we know what's going on.

                    Jim Kerr, Charles Burchill, Michael MacNeil

POINTS OF CONTACT: ROBERT LOUIS STEVENSON IN THE SOUTH SEAS

JENNI CALDER

> A polite Englishman comes today to the Marquesas and is amazed to find the men tattooed; polite Italians came not so long ago to England and found our fathers stained with woad; and when I paid the return visit as a little boy, I was highly diverted with the backwardness of Italy, so much a matter of the day and hour, is the pre-eminence of race.

Robert Louis Stevenson wrote this after his first encounters with the people of the Marquesas in 1888. It was this ability to take observation and experience outside the perspectives of Victorian convention that makes him a remarkable commentator. He viewed his own and other societies with a curiosity and avid interest which took him way beyond the usual social and moral boundaries.

Stevenson's six years in the Pacific islands began when he and his family left San Francisco in June 1888 in the schooner yacht *Casco*. By that time he was a writer of considerable success and reputation. The breakthrough had come with the publication of *Dr Jekyll and Mr Hyde*, in which he examined some of the darker aspects of Victorian society and its damaging hypocrisy. Stevenson had no patience with hypocrisy, and the lack of it gives his observations of Polynesian life an unusual freshness and frankness. The preconceptions he brought with him to the Pacific were those of a vivid imagination rather than prejudice.

In each island he visited Stevenson looked first for the point of contact. He delighted in the exoticism, the tropical landscapes, the graceful people, the strange artefacts, but he sought out the similarities. In the Marquesas he recognised a parallel with the Scottish Highlands.

> Not much beyond a century has passed since [the Highlanders] were in the same convulsive and transitory state as the Marquesans of today. In both cases an alien authority enforced, the clans disarmed, the chiefs deposed, new customs introduced, and chiefly that fashion of regarding money as the means and object of existence. The commercial age, in each, succeeding at a bound to an age of war abroad and patriarchal communism at home. In one the cherished practice of tattooing, in the other a cherished costume, proscribed.

This ability to make connections proved richly rewarding. The result of sympathy, it was the basis of communication and understanding. Stevenson was eager to learn of the traditional life and culture of the people he encountered. Because he could locate himself in an essentially tribal context and could draw on tribal customs and folklore he was able to 'trade' in a currency that was appreciated and valued.

> ...the black bull's head of Stirling procured me the legend of *Rahero*; and what I knew of the Cluny Macphersons, or of the Appin Stewarts, enable me to learn, and helped me to understand, about the *Tevas* of Tahiti. The native was no longer ashamed, his sense of kinship grew warmer, and his lips were opened. It is this sense of kinship that the traveller must rouse and share...

In Tahiti especially 'kinship' brought Stevenson much more than an exchange of folklore. At Tautira, on the other side of the island from the port of Papeete, Stevenson spent nine weeks as the guest of the local Chief Ori a Ori and his sister Princess Moe, with whom Stevenson and his wife Fanny became firm friends. They spent many hours together, swapping history and story, legend and poetry. Stevenson produced English versions of some of the poetry Ori recited. The gains for Stevenson were prolific - 'collected songs and legends on the spot; songs still sung in chorus by perhaps a hundred persons, not two of whom can agree on their translations; legends, on which I have seen half a dozen seniors in conclave and debating what came next'. But the greatest reward was the friendship of Ori: 'the best fortune of our stay at Tautira was my knowledge of Ori himself, one of the finest creatures extant'.

Stevenson made no assumptions about the superiority of 'civilisation': indeed, back in Honolulu, with its electricity and telephones, he fretted at being 'oppressed by civilisation', and he was only too aware of the artificialities and the pretensions that the civilised world imposed. Unlike most observers and anthropologists of the time he did not assume that the passing of tribal tradition meant progress. He commented with regret on the disappearance of the 'old society', aware of both loss and the erosion of dignity. Of the Gilbert Islands he remarked 'the spear and the shark-tooth sword are sold for curiosities': in other words, what were once significant objects had been reduced to souvenirs.

In a similar way he saw significant lives reduced to a kind of tourist show, and this he found offensive. Equally offensive were the attempts to force the islanders to adopt European conventions, especially European dress. Commenting on a Gilbert Islands woman wearing only a short skirt he wrote 'she moved with incomparable liberty and grace and life', but 'bundle her in a gown and she wriggles like an Englishwoman'. He saw, as most whites in the Pacific failed to see, that to enforce the customs and expectations of an alien culture was to cause cruel and destructive dislocation. He was vituperative at missionaries who sanctimoniously insisted on island women wearing ankle-length dresses. The processes and effects of dislocation angered and saddened him.

Although Stevenson exulted in many of his Pacific experiences - 'life is far better fun than people dream who fall asleep among the chimney stacks and telegraph wires', he wrote to a friend in London - he did not romanticise them. His depiction of the Polynesians was coloured by no 'noble savage' ideal - he admired Ori a Ori as an equal, not as a picturesque relic of an age of innocence. Equally, when he found islanders (or anyone else) who were lazy or unreliable he said so. He was not always able to free himself from his Calvinist upbringing, but whatever that imposed was unselective in its effect. Stevenson had a well-honed sensitivity to double standards.

He showed an extraordinary adaptability, the result of a natural ability to make friends and find common ground as well as of an eager interest in new situations. He had an innate respect for humanity, and at the same time a shrewd understanding of human weakness and vulnerability, and their independence of time and place and culture. During his stay in Honolulu he enjoyed the company of King Kalakaua, who was trying to revive traditional Polynesian culture and bring an untraditional political unity to the islands. There was little hope of success: the Americans, the Germans and the British were too strongly entrenched and had too much to lose. Kalakaua's motives were hardly disinterested, yet Stevenson found him a fascinating character, and learned a great deal about Polynesian politics from him. He was also impressed, and somewhat astonished, by Kalakaua's drinking habits. He commonly downed five or six bottles of champagne at a sitting, after which he was 'quite presentable, though perceptibly more dignified at the end'.

In 1890 Stevenson made his home at Vailima on the Samoan island of Upolu. A large house was built to accommodate his extended family and attempts were made to cultivate the jungle that was the Vailima 'estate'. Stevenson relied on native labour, though both he and Fanny did their share of work, clearing the land, weeding and planting. His attitude to the Samoans was paternalistic, but it was also shaped by integrity. He expected his employees to work honestly: in return he looked after them, a role that he clearly enjoyed.

> I am the head of a household of five whites, and of twelve Samoans,
> to all of whom I am chief and father: my cook comes to me and asks
> leave to marry - and his mother, a fine old chief woman, who has never
> lived here, does the same. You may be sure I grant the petition.

Stevenson took his position as 'chief' seriously, and it led him into involvements that caused consternation in Britain. He was incensed at the political manipulations of the colonalist powers in Samoa, and his support for the Samoan chief Mataafa made him very unpopular with British officialdom, which was anxious to avoid trouble. In 1893 a tense situation erupted into a war between a German-backed puppet chief and the 'rebel' Mataafa. Stevenson continued to support and assist Mataafa, and wrote a series of letters to *The Times* exposing the manoeuvrings and collusions of Britain and Germany. His book *A Footnote to History* gives a detailed account of the background to the conflict, but there were those who tried to discredit Stevenson by branding him a naive meddler.

Stevenson's value as a witness to what survived of traditional Polynesian life and to the operations of late nineteenth-century imperialism are only now being fully recognised. His response to the Polynesians themselves was complex - empathetic, honest, interested, admiring, with a paternalistic sense of responsibility, in some respects shaped by his time and his background, in others extraordinarily independent of both. He was describing, in letters, fiction and non-fiction, a place and a time full of difficulty and contradiction.

The Pacific is a strange place; the nineteeth century only exists there in spots: all around, it is a no man's land of the ages, a stir-about of epochs and races, barbarisms and civilisations, virtues and crimes.

There were no clear-cut divisions or definitions. Much of the fiction Stevenson was writing at this time illustrates this 'stir-about' and focuses particularly on the barbarity of the so-called virtuous, and vice versa. The best example of this is his superb story 'The Beach of Falesa'.

In all his writing on the South Seas he set down with clarity and purpose what he saw and experienced, and he wrote with a stronger sense of what he shared with other members of humanity than of distance. He hated exploitation, he hated the moral hollowness of what he called 'dingy civilisation', but perhaps most of all he was saddened at the diminishing of humanity that was the inevitable consequence of colonialist intrusion, on both victim and perpetrator. He saw what few saw a hundred years ago and what many fail to see now, that moral prerogatives belong to no particular race or group or nationality.

THE EMPIRE THAT NEVER WAS

Norman Easton

> Resolved (God willing) to settle and plant a colony in some place or other not inhabited in America, or in or upon some other place by consent of the natives thereof ...
> Council-General of the 'Company of Scotland Trading to Africa and the Indies' 8 July 1698.

But what if the natives say 'No!'

Earlier in the seventeenth century, the natives of Virginia and New England said 'No' to the ever-growing demand of the English colonists for native American land. The Powhatans in Virginia were almost exterminated, while the surviving women and children of the Wampanoags and Narragansetts were sold by the New England Puritans as slaves for the West Indies plantations. All these Indians had befriended the colonists until the colonists began to dispossess them of their lands.

We Scots harbour a nobler feeling about our own attempt at Empire. When two Scots visited Darien in 1985 and reported that the Cuna Indians remembered us kindly in their folk tradition, the news warmed our hearts not half so much because we were concerned about the Cuna as because we were concerned about ourselves. Our empire would have been a nice empire. We needed to know that the 'the natives thereof liked us.

Our first expedition to Darien in 1698 consisted of five ships and 1200 men. Forty-six years earlier, in 1652, Jan van Riebeeck had landed at the Cape with his three ships and 125 men, among whom were a handful of Scots. Van Riebeeck was not intending to found a colony at all - his mission was to set up a self-supporting refreshment station for Dutch ships rounding the Cape *en route* for the East Indies.

It was five years before the first Dutch farmers broke the soil on Khoi land, and seven years before the first Khoi attacks on the Dutch colony. We Scots were only at Darien for three years and we never did get round to breaking the soil. The Cuna people remained our allies for those three years because they needed our support against a common enemy.

In 1659, when the Khoi attacked the Dutch, an attempted mutiny was uncovered among the whites. Had the Khoi tribes all acted together and the white mutineers succeeded in their plan, the Cape Colony might have vanished as completely in seven years as our quarrelsome colonists in 'Caledonia' did in three years.

To work their new farms the Dutch imported slaves from 1657 onwards. How would the Scots have solved the labour problem on their plantations in Darien?

For almost two hundred years the Dutch (and later British) colony at the Cape depended on a loyal Khoi soldiery for survival; but where are the Khoi today? As a people, as a culture, they have vanished. We Scots were already training a corps of Cuna soldiers in the three years we were at Darien.

In 1698 there were still fewer than a thousand whites at the Cape. In three years some three thousand Scots descended on Darien. Had we gone south to the Cape instead we would have outnumbered the Dutch.

We meant business. If our colony at Darien had succeeded, would there be any Cuna Indians left today to sing our praises, or would they have vanished like the Narragansett or the Khoi?

Dìreach a'dìon an còirichean féin

> ...Dh'fhalbh iad aig earball an luchd-creachaidh a chogadh an aghaidh dhaoine geala, dubha 's ruadha nach d'thug riamh aobhar oilbheum dhaibh, ach a bha dìreach a'dìon an còirichean féin mar bu dual do shluagh gaisgeanta, àrd-inntinneach.
> - Aonghas Mac Eanruig arguing in *Guth na Bliadhna*, Autumn 1912, that since Culloden the Gaels had followed their own destroyers '... to war against white, black and red people who had never given them any cause for offence but were just defending their ain rights as a heroic, high-minded people ought'.

We Scots often seem to suffer collective amnesia about the nature of the Scots at empire. We credit ourselves with a humane, liberal attitude towards native populations, with an understanding that we would not grant to the English, and we have always traced that self-proclaimed insight to our own double status. Last century we were more likely to stress our role as an equal (?) mother country to the British Empire, but now, in the post-colonial period, it is comforting to assume the status of colonised rather than coloniser, sinned against more than sinning, so that we can claim, when things get awkward, that, really, it was nothing to do with us. A variant of this argument focuses on the Gaels and stresses their status as colonial victims, blurring the distinction between Lowland (Scots-speaking) and Highland (Gaelic-speaking) Scotland. Whether the Gaels are an internal colony of a colony, or whether all-Scotland constitutes one unitary colony, we cannot exonerate all ill deeds done in empire by reference to our own, or the Gaels', colonial status.

Aonghas Mac Eanruig does not absolve the Gaels from blame (or by inference any of us Scots) even though he stresses their status as colonial victims:

> *Is i an taing a fhuair iad o Iain Buidhe a' cheart taing a thoill iad. Dh'iomain*
> *e iad féin agus gach neach a bhuineadh dhaibh o dhùthaich an gaoil.*
> (The thanks they got from John Bull was the thanks they deserved. He drove them and everyone that belonged to them out of the land they loved.)

Can we absolve ourselves? What if we revise our position in the world? Was it not just English influence, English orders, economic conscription blameable on the English, leaders who were English-educated or maybe even had English genetic ancestors that were responsible for any ill action committed by us in what was, really, after all, don't you think, an English Empire? And didn't the English always say it was theirs anyway?

If we just run up the St Andrew's Cross and haul doun the Union Jack, surely the redeeming rain of independence will wash away the stain of empire?

If Darien had been successful and we had created an empire of our very own - the empire that never was - would ours not have been a kindly empire, bringing democratic civilisation to the barbarous savage and Presbyterian virtue to the hell-bound heathen?

> To Scotland's just and never-dying fame
> We'll in Asia, Africa and America proclaim
> Liberty! Liberty! - nay to the shame
> Of all who went before us.

The Edinburgh street-balladeer who penned the above, when the Darien scheme was yet being planned, doubtless had the colonies of their Catholic Majesties in mind, and Presbyterian 'liberty' in his heart, for Scotland in 1698 was no egalitarian paradise. If it was our 'liberty' we would transplant to our future colonies in 'Asia, Africa and America' - an oligarchy of merchants and landowners playing leapfrog for each other's favours - then it would be tyranny indeed to the free peoples we planted it on. If it was our Presbyterian tolerance we would visit on our colonies - and the Darien venture was an exclusively Presbyterian affair - woe betide both heathen and heretic. If we were going to compete with our European neighbours in the slave economies of the Caribbean, where would we get our dirt cheap labour force from? Liberty, liberty, *nay* to our shame!

Gar the Blackimores wirk!

> *Bha barrachd thràillean aig na Ceallaich na aig duine sam bith eile an Siorrachd Moore. Luchd-togail a'chotain. Chaill sinn trì cheud dhiubh an dèidh a'Chogaidh Shìobhalta. Bha Gàidhlig aca.*
> (The Kellys had more slaves than anyone else in Moore County. Cotton pickers. We lost three hundred of them after the Civil War. They spoke Gaelic.)
>
> The Reverend Professor Douglas Kelly interviewed by Ronnie Black. *The Scotsman*, 13 February 1988 .

Well before the Darien venture, Scots merchants were active in trade with, and in, the slave economies. Indeed transporting human bodies for profit was nothing new to Scots merchants. In 1684 the Gibson brothers of Glasgow profited greatly from the transportation of defeated covenanters to slavery in the English colonies. James Gibson was a director of the Company of Scotland, and served as its agent in Amsterdam. Was it his experience as a white slaver or only his money that won him the command of the *Rising Sun*, the office of Commodore of the Second Expedition of 1699, and the status of Councillor of our colony of Caledonia?

For a hundred years, starting with the original covenanters defeated at Dunbar in 1650, the trade in human bodies was an established part of Scottish commercial life. It was even possible to sell yourself to the merchants for the price of your passage to the colonies in the hope of surviving your term of enslavement to see a better future. A succession of white 'bonded-servants' - the judicially dispatched, the kidnapped vagrant, the unattended child - were shipped to the plantations by our guid Scots merchants. Aberdeen's white slavers were simply unlucky when in 1740 they sold a kidnapped child to a Scot in America who was himself a former bonded-servant. That child returned to haunt them as 'Indian Peter' Williamson. But merchants in other Scottish cities were at the same game, and so were the Gaels.

In 1739 Norman Macleod, younger of Berneray, acting it appeared as middleman for Macleod of Dunvegan and MacDonald of Sleat, carried out a series of 'slave-raids' on the coasts of these Gaelic chieftains' territories in Skye and Harris. Tradition suggests these raids were not the only slaving ventures in the West Highlands. We should not, however, assume that white Scots so enslaved would necessarily side with the blacks. In 1717 a Gael in bonded-service in Maryland, Donald Macpherson, told of his hopes in a letter home evidently dictated to someone who could write nae bad phonetic Scots:

> My Mestire says til me, Fan I kan speek lyk de Fouk hier I sanna pi pidden di nating pat gar his Plackimores wurk...

A people who can enslave each other thus, is unlikely to stint itself when it comes to another 'race' and the evidence from North Carolina is before us. The Highland tacksmen saw no problem in exchanging the paternal relationship between them and their dependants in Scotland for the paternal relationship between them and their slaves in the Carolinas. And we know which would yield the better quality of life.

There seems little doubt but that our brave new 'Caledonia' would have been a slave economy. How else would we make it pay the hefty returns we were out to get to place our little country on an equal footing with our European neighbours.

The planters in Caledonia were each to get grants of land, although, paralleling the 'liberty' we had at home, the size of the grants would be related differentially to social rank. Mimicking the social order in Scotland, districts in Caledonia were to consist of a mere fifty to sixty 'freemen inhabitants' who would elect one from among their number to represent them in the Parliament of the Colony. What about the unfree inhabitants who would labour on the plantations of the sixty planters? Who would they be? Where would they come from? What about the native Cuna Indians whose land we would be planting - would they not object? Like all the other conflicts in North America and the Caribbean it seems inevitable that we would have had ultimately to fight the Cunas for the land - to drive them out or kill them. Surely they would have chosen to die rather than be our slaves? We would have needed to bring in slaves from Black Africa, and doubtless our own Scots bonded servants to act as overseers and gar the Blackimores wirk.

The Intention of God

> ...surely it could never have been the intention of God to allow Indians to rove and hunt over so fertile a country and hold it forever in

unproductive wildness, while Scotch and Irish and English farmers could put it to so much better use.

- Daniel Muir, Wisconsin 1850s, as recalled by his son John Muir in *The Story of My Boyhood and Youth.*

If we want to know how the Scots would have behaved in 'the empire that never was' we shouldnae just look at the myth, we should look at what Scots did get up to in the empires we were involved in. Daniel Muir, a Scot of pious egalitarian principles, emigrated to the independent empire of the United States in 1849. In 1834 US President Andrew Jackson, himself of Scots-Irish descent, devised an 'apartheid' scheme, more than a century before the Afrikaners, whereby all the Indians in the existing States would be deported beyond a 'permanent Indian frontier' beyond which line no white settlement would be allowed.

The settlement of Wisconsin had already breached the intended 'frontier', before it could be implemented, so that the 'permanent Indian frontier' was moved a great distance westward to engulf the lands of still free Indians.

How Muir justified his occupancy of Indian land can be seen above. In his son's book that statement counters the view of a fellow Scots settler, George Mair, who took the part of the '...unfortunate Indians, children of Nature... now being robbed of their lands and pushed ruthlessly back...' but it was surely too late to argue this way when both he and Muir were settled on some of the stolen territory.

In Cape Colony in 1825, another Scottish settler of liberal principles, Thomas Pringle, active in the liberal cause in the politics of the white colony, faced the same dilemma. Having settled in land which he had no real right to, his Scottish liberalism was hopelessly tainted. While he could champion the cause of natives within the Colony who accepted the rule of the Colony, those natives who rejected the Colony's legitimacy he had no option but to fight, even though he seems to have been aware at some level that the natives were just defending their rights:

> Your damnations against my Bushman Commando do not alarm me. There is no 'damned spot' on my hands... If attacked I will resist even to slaying them, approve who may...I pity them more than blame them...they have scarcely any choice but of predatory warfare and precarious existence, or servitude to the Boers...

But there was a 'damned spot' on the hands of all Scots settlers, that indelible stain which came from settling in, from taking over, someone else's land, whether or not you believed you could make 'better use' of it. In fairness, though, the spots on the hands of most of our settlers were as nothing compared to the blood-spattered limbs of our brave Scots colonists in Gippsland, Australia...

> ...The [Highland] brigade coming up on the blacks camped around the waterhole at Warrigal Creek surrounded them and fired into them, killing a great number, some escaped into the scrub, others jumped into the waterhole, and as fast as they put their heads up for breath, they were shot until the water was red with blood.

Thus 'Gippslander' described the massacre in 1844 of between sixty and one hundred and fifty men, women and children of the Kurnai people at the hands of the self-styled 'Highland Brigade' organised by Aonghas MacMhaolain from among his fellow Gaels in the land he called 'Caledonia Australis'. When MacMhaolain arrived in the land of the Kurnai in 1840 there were between two and three thousand Kurnai in several tribal groups. The Braiakolung tribe drove off MacMhaolain's herdsmen in 1840 since, quite understandably, they objected to him taking their land. MacMhaolain did not seem to care that they were 'díreach a'díon an cóirichean féin' for his response was to organise his men and massacre the Braiakolung at two sites thereafter known as Boney Point and Butcher's Creek. In 1857 there were only ninety-six Kurnai people left alive. A holocaust. But then it could never have been the intention of God...?

Children of Nature

While not every Scots colonist was a genocidal murderer, no-one in Scotland during the period of European overseas imperialism could be unaffected by our basic racist assumptions. Even William Latto (Tammas Bodkin) - a man as anti-imperialist as could be found in the Scotland of his day - was subject to two basic racist flaws in his thinking... as witness these extracts from the *People's Journal* of 27 September 1879:

> The Zulus werena seekin to interfere wi us in any shape or form... Cetewayo, puir fallow... aboot to be sent aff...to St Helena or some either prison home equally loathsome to a child of nature like him... albeit I've nae particular affection for Pagans... yet I like to see abody getting fairplay...

Cetewayo was a 'child of nature' and a 'pagan', a fit subject for pity and condescension but not truly equal unless brought up to the European standards of civilisation and converted to the white man's religion.

The notion that tribal people were children of nature was no innocent idea, for this self-same concept underlay the attitude of white European colonists and missionaries throughout the colonial period. You did not have to be malevolent in intent to subscribe to this racist notion, quite the contrary: it lent itself to benevolence in the grand, paternal, manner. Commenting on the 1915 rebellion in Nyasaland, which he described as 'a native spasm', W T Livingstone, biographer of *Laws of Livingstonia*, says of the Scots missionary that 'Dr Laws had always believed that Ethiopianism had a germ of good in it which should have been recognised and wisely dealt with...There was no need to be afraid of them making mistakes - every race learned through stumbling...' A clearer statement of paternalistic racism would be hard to find. W T Livingstone would seem to think the blacks were toddlers throwing a particularly nasty tantrum, but Robert Laws saw in them the promise of teenagers who had gone astray. It was the high-handed action of a Scots plantation manager called Livingstone towards his labour force that sparked off this inconvenient event. The parental discipline was just a bit too strong for the children to take.

The kind of thinking represented by Robert Laws, while kindly meant no doubt, existed on a continuum with the thinking that gave birth to apartheid. While British colonialists chose to debate how long it would be before Africans reached that age of maturity when they might be able to cope with running their own affairs - and some like Ian Smith, whose father came from Hamilton, believed that that prospect should be delayed indefinitely - the Afrikaners took the clear-cut line that the children would never grow up at all. When it came to the crunch there wasnae much to choose between the Rhodesians and the Afrikaners where their parental rights were concerned.

Red, white and black

So how would we have conducted ourselves in the empire that never was, if 'Caledonia' had flourished and the 'key to the universe' had truly turned for us? Having driven out or reduced the native population and established our slave plantations - as we later did in the Carolinas - we would have looked again at the continent which had early attracted us. An Amerindian and an African, shouldering cornucopias, supported the coat of arms of our 'Company of Scotland Trading to Africa and the Indies'. When would we land in Africa? Already in 1701 on the failure of the Darien venture, the Company of

Scotland had sent two of its surviving ships - the *Speedy Return* and the *Content* - to trade off the African coast. We had nearly two hundred years before the final European 'scramble' for the continent. Who can doubt we would have had our slice? And what would we have done with it? I suspect we would have joined hands with our beleaguered co-religionists and familiar trading partners, the Dutch. How would our African colony have differed from theirs, and would we not have rapidly caught up on a colony whose white population was so tiny? Imagine our African colony justified by the pious logic of a Daniel Muir, pioneered by an Aonghas MacMhaolain, planted by slave-owners like the Kellys, agonised over by a conscience stricken Thomas Pringle, its natives patronised by a Robert Laws, its battles won by regiments of Gaels. And if this horror had been cut off from its Scottish motherland at an early stage, perhaps when slavery was still the norm, would not our Presbyterian elect have twisted itself in inward-looking isolation into something uncannily like the Dutch Reformed Church that justified apartheid?

I do not believe the Scots at empire that I have mentioned above were influenced in any of their actions by English imperialism. I see the logic of their actions as springing from Scottish thinking, from the Scottish variant of European imperialism - from a hidden Scottish colonialism beneath the Union Jack. We would have done exactly the same under our own flag, and we would have manipulated the Gaels to fight for our Empire just as blindly as they did for the British Empire. Toubacanti and Ticonderoga have much in common!

In the end perhaps it is us who are the children. Perhaps there was more truth than we realise in the lordly words of Professor J R Seeley of Cambridge, in his classic lectures of 1883:

> If in these islands we feel ourselves for all purposes one nation though in Wales, in Scotland and in Ireland there is Celtic blood and Celtic languages utterly unintelligible to us are still spoken, so in the Empire a good many French and Dutch and a good many Caffres and Maories may be admitted without marring the ethnological unity of the whole.
> (J R Seeley - *The Expansion of England*)

We lowland Scots, note well, were not even credited with existence by Seeley - so readily did he absorb all English or Scots speaking whites into his global 'Greater' England. At least our Gaelic neighbours had a place, lower down on the ethnic hierarchy, unlike 'the native Australian race' which was too 'low in the ethnological scale' to count. Were us lowland Scots too low on the scale of civilisation to succeed as Imperial masters?

If so, then I firmly believe that the mark of our ascent to civilisation as a people will be our willingness to teach Warrigal Creek, as part of our Scottish history, alongside Glencoe, to teach Darien together with the story of the Scottish-owned slaves of the Carolinas.

When we can do that - and when we can acknowledge that we too could have been the Afrikaners - then perhaps we will have attained a level on the ethnological scale which will allow us to assert our rights as a Sister people to all our kindred, geala, dubha 's ruadha, in this our common world.

WIND OF CHANGE

Harold Macmillan

It is a great privilege to be invited to address the members of both Houses of Parliament in the Union of South Africa. It is a unique privilege to do so in 1960, just half a century after the Parliament of the Union came to birth. I am most grateful to you all for giving me this opportunity, and I am especially grateful to your Prime Minister who invited me to visit this country and arranged for me to address you here today. My tour of Africa - parts of Africa - the first ever made by a British Prime Minister in office, is now, alas, nearing its end, but it is fitting that it should culminate in the Union Parliament here in Cape Town, in this historic city so long Europe's gateway to the Indian Ocean, and to the East.

It is, as I have said, a special privilege for me to be here in 1960 when you are celebrating what I might call the golden wedding of the Union. At such a time it is natural and right that you should pause to take stock of your position, to look back at what you have achieved, to look forward to what lies ahead ...

No one could fail to be impressed with the immense material progress which has been achieved. That all this has been accomplished in so short a time is a striking testimony to the skill, energy and initiative of your people. We in Britain are proud of the contribution we have made to this remarkable achievement. Much of it has been financed by British capital. According to the recent survey made by the Union Government, nearly two-thirds of the overseas investment outstanding in the Union at the end of 1956 was British. That is after two staggering wars which have bled our economy white.

But that is not all. We have developed trade between us to our common advantage, and our economies are now largely interdependent. You export to us raw materials, food and gold. We in return send you consumer goods or capital equipment. We take a third of all your exports and we supply a third of all your imports. This broad traditional pattern of investment and trade has been maintained in spite of the changes brought by the development of our two economies, and it gives me great encouragement to reflect that the economies of both our countries, while expanding rapidly have yet remained

L

interdependent and capable of sustaining one another. If you travel round this country by train you will travel on South African rails made by Iscor. If you prefer to fly you can go in a British Viscount. Here is a true partnership, living proof of the interdependence between nations. Britain has always been your best customer and, as your new industries develop, we believe that we can be your best partners too ...

In the twentieth century, and especially since the end of the war, the processes which gave birth to the nation states of Europe have been repeated all over the world. We have seen the awakening of national consciousness in peoples who have for centuries lived in dependence upon some other power. Fifteen years ago this movement spread through Asia. Many countries there of different races and civilisations pressed their claim to an independent national life. Today the same thing is happening in Africa, and the most striking of all the impressions I have formed since I left London a month ago is of the strength of this African national consciousness. In different places it takes different forms, but it is happening everywhere. The wind of change is blowing through this continent, and whether we like it or not, this growth of national consciousness is a political fact. We must all accept it as a fact, and our national policies must take account of it. ...

Finally in countries inhabited by several different races it has been our aim to find means by which the community can become more of a community, and fellowship can be fostered between its various parts. This problem is by no means confined to Africa. Nor is it always a problem of a European minority. In Malaya, for instance, though there are Indian and European minorities, Malays and Chinese make up the great bulk of the population, and the Chinese are not much fewer in numbers than the Malays. Yet these two peoples must learn to live together in harmony and unity and the strength of Malaya as a nation will depend on the different contributions which the two races can make.

The attitude of the United Kingdom towards this problem was clearly expressed by the Foreign Secretary, Mr Selwyn Lloyd, speaking at the United Nations General Assembly on 17 September 1959. These were his words:

> In those territories where different races or tribes live side by side the task is to ensure that all the people may enjoy security and freedom and the chance to contribute as individuals to the progress and well being of these countries. We reject the idea of any inherent superiority of one race over another. Our policy therefore is non-racial. It offers a future in which Africans, Europeans, Asians, the people of the Pacific

and others with whom we are concerned, will all play their full part as citizens in the countries where they live, and in which feelings of race will be submerged in loyalty to new nations.

I have thought you would wish me to state plainly and with full candour the policy for which we in Britain stand. It may well be that in trying to do our duty as we see it we shall sometimes make difficulties for you. If this proves to be so we shall regret it. But I know that even so you would not ask us to flinch from doing our duty.

You, too, will do your duty as you see it. I am well aware of the peculiar nature of the problems with which you are faced here in the Union of South Africa. I know the differences between your situation and that of most of the other states in Africa. You have here some three million people of European origin. This country is their home. It has been their home for many generations. They have no other. The same is true of Europeans in Central and East Africa. In most other African states those who have come from Europe have come to work, to contribute their skills, perhaps to teach, but not to make a home.

The problems to which you as members of the Union Parliament have to address yourselves are very different from those which face the Parliaments of countries with homogenous populations. These are complicated and baffling problems. It would be surprising if your interpretation of your duty did not sometimes produce very different results from ours in terms of Government policies and actions.

As a fellow member of the Commonwealth it is our earnest desire to give South Africa our support and encouragement, but I hope you won't mind my saying frankly that there are some aspects of your policies which make it impossible for us to do this without being false to our own deep convictions about the political destinies of free men to which in our own territories we are trying to give effect. I think we ought, as friends, to face together, without seeking to apportion credit or blame, the fact that in the world of today this difference of outlook lies between us.

I said that I was speaking as a friend. I can also claim to be speaking as a relation, for we Scots can claim family connections with both the great European sections of your population, not only with the English-speaking people but with the Afrikaans-speaking as well. This is a point which hardly needs emphasis in Cape Town where you can see every day the statue of that great Scotsman, Andrew Murray. His work in the Dutch Reformed Church in the Cape, and the work of his son in the Orange Free State, was among Afrikaans-speaking people. There has always been a very close connection between the Church of Scotland and the Church of the Netherlands.

The Synod of Dort plays the same great part in the history of both. Many aspirants to the Ministry of Scotland, especially in the seventeenth and eighteenth centuries, went to pursue their theological studies in the Netherlands. Scotland can claim to have repaid the debt in South Africa. I am thinking particularly of the Scots in the Orange Free State. Not only the younger Andrew Murray, but also the Robertsons, the Frasers, the McDonalds - families which have been called the Free State clans, who became burghers of the old Free State and whose descendants still play their part there. ...

I certainly do not believe in refusing to trade with people because you may happen to dislike the way they manage their internal affairs at home. Boycotts will never get you anywhere, and may I say in parenthesis that I deprecate the attempts that are being made today in Britain to organise the consumer boycott of South African goods. It has never been the practice, as far as I know, of any Government of the United Kingdom of whatever complexion to undertake or support campaigns of this kind designed to influence the internal politics of another Commonwealth country, and my colleagues in the United Kingdom deplore this proposed boycott and regard it as undesirable from every point of view. It can only have serious effects on Commonwealth relations, on trade, and lead to the ultimate detriment of others than those against whom it is aimed.

I said I was speaking of the interdependence of nations. The members of the Commonwealth feel particularly strongly the value of interdependence. They are as independent as any nation in this shrinking world can be, but they have voluntarily agreed to work together. They recognise that there may be and must be differences in their institutions, in their internal policies and their membership does not imply the will to express a judgement on these matters. or the need to impose a stifling uniformity. It is, I think, a help that there has never been question of any rigid constitution for the Commonwealth. Perhaps this is because we have got on well enough in the United Kingdom without a written constitution and tend to look suspiciously at them. Whether that is so or not, it is quite clear that a rigid constitutional framework for the Commonwealth would not work. At the first of the stresses and strains which are inevitable in this period of history, cracks would appear in the framework and the whole structure would crumble. It is the flexibility of our Commonwealth institutions which gives them their strength.

Mr President, Mr Speaker, Honourable Ministers, Ladies and Gentlemen, I fear I have kept you a long time. I much welcome the opportunity to speak to this great audience. In conclusion may I say this? I have spoken frankly about the differences between our two countries in their approach to one to the great current problems with which each has to deal within its own sphere of responsibility. These differences are well-known. They are matters of public knowledge, indeed of public controversy, and I should have been less than honest if by remaining silent on them I had seemed to imply that they did not exist. But differences on one subject, important though it is, need not and should not impair our capacity to co-operate with one another in furthering the many practical interests which we share in common.

The independent members of the Commonwealth do not always agree on every subject. It is not a condition of their association that they should do so. On the contrary, the strength of our Commonwealth lies largely in the fact that it is a free association of independent sovereign states, each responsible for ordering its own affairs but cooperating in the pursuit of common aims and purposes in world affairs. Moreover these differences may be transitory. In time they may be resolved. Our duty is to see them in perspective against the background of our long association. Of this at any rate I am certain - those of us who by grace of the electorate are temporarily in charge of affairs in your country and in mine, we fleeting transient phantoms on the great stage of history, we have no right to sweep aside on this account the friendship that exists between our countries, for that is the legacy of history. It is not ours alone to deal with as we wish. To adapt a famous phrase, it belongs to those who are living, but it also belongs to those who are dead and to those who are yet unborn. We must face the differences, but let us try to see beyond them down the long vista of the future.

I hope - indeed, I am confident - that in another fifty years we shall look back on the differences that exist between us now as matters of historical interest, for as time passes and one generation yields to another, human problems change and fade. Let us remember these truths. Let us resolve to build, not to destroy, and let us remember always that weakness comes from division, strength from unity.

*From the address * by Harold Macmillan to Members of both Houses of Parliament of the Union of South Africa, Cape Town, 3 February 1960*

* At home right wing Conservatives formed the Monday Club to commemorate as 'Black Monday' the day on which the speech was delivered and to condemn its contents.

oideachadh ceart

do john agard is jack mapanje

nuair a bha mi òg
cha b'eachdraidh ach cuimhne

nuair a thàinig am bàillidh, air each
air na mnathan a tilleadh anuas
as na buailtean len eallaichean frainich
sa gheàrr e na ròpan on guailnean
a sgaoileadh nan eallach gu làr,
a dìteadh nam mnà, gun tug iad gun chead
an luibhe dhan iarradh e sgrios,
ach gum biodh na mnathan
ga ghearradh 's ga ghiùlain gu dachaidh,
connlach stàile, gu tàmh nam bó
(is gun deachdadh e màl as)

cha b'eachdraidh ach cuimhne
long nan daoine
seòladh amach
tromh cheathach sgeòil
mu éiginn morair
mu chruaidhchas morair
mun cùram dhan tuathan,
mu shaibhreas a fheitheamh
ceann thall na slighe,
long nan daoine
seòladh amach
sgioba de chnuimheagan acrach
paisgte na clàir,
cha b'eachdraidh ach fathunn

cha b'eachdraidh ach cuimhne
la na dìle, chaidh loids a chaiptein
a sguabadh dhan tràigh
nuair a phòs sruthan rà is chonain
gun tochar a ghabhail

a proper schooling

for john agard and jack mapanje

when i was young
it wasn't history but memory

when the factor, on horseback, came
on the women's descent from
the moorland grazings laden with bracken
he cut the rope from their shoulders
spreading their loads to the ground,
alleging they took without permit
a weed he'd eliminate
were it not that women
cut it and carried it home
for bedding to ease their cows' hard rest;
and there was rent in that weed

it wasn't history but memory
the emigrant ships
sailing out
through a fog of stories
of landlords' anguish
of landlords' distress
their concern for their tenants,
the riches waiting
beyond the voyage,
the emigrant ships
sailing out
a crew of starved maggots
wrapped in their timbers,
it wasn't history but rumour

it wasn't history but memory
the day of the flood, the captain's lodge
was swept to the shore
when the streams of rha and conon married
taking no dowry
but david the servant

ach dàidh an sgalag
a dh'fhan 'dìleas dha mhaighstir'
agus cuirp nan linn as a chladh

cha b'eachdraidh ach cuimhne
an latha bhaist ciorstaidh am baillidh
le mùn a poit a thug i bhon chùlaist
dhan choinneamh am bràighe nan crait
gun bhraon a dhòrtadh

cha b'eachdraidh ach cuimhne
an latha sheas gaisgich a bhaile
bruach abhainn a ghlinne
an aghaidh feachd ghruamach an t-siorraidh
a thàinig air mhàrsail, sa thill gun òrdag a bhogadh
le sanasan fuadach nan dùirn

cha b'eachdraidh ach gràmar
rob donn
uilleam ros
donnchadh bàn
mac a mhaighstir

cha b'eachdraidh ach cuimhne
màiri mhór, màiri mhór
a dìtidhean ceòlar
cha b'eachdraidh ach cuimhne
na h-òrain a sheinn i
dha muinntir an cruaidhchas
dha muinntir an dùbhlan

agus, nuair a bha mi òg
ged a bha chuimhne fhathast
fo thùghadh snigheach,
bha sgliat nan dearbhadh
fo fhasgadh sgliat
agus amuigh
bha gaoth a glaothaich
eachdraidh nam chuimhne
eachdraidh nam chuimhne

AONGHAS MACNEACAIL

who stayed 'true to his Master'
and the corpses of centuries from the cemetery

it wasn't history but memory
the day kirsty baptised the factor
with piss from a pot she took from the backroom
to the meeting up in the brae of the croft
not spilling a single drop

it wasn't history but memory
the day the township's warriors stood
on the banks of the glen river
confronting the sheriff's surly troops
who marched that far, then returned without dipping a toe,
clutching their wads of eviction orders

it wasn't history but grammar
rob donn
william ross
duncan ban
alexander macdonald

it wasn't history but memory
great mary macpherson
her melodic indictments,
it wasn't history but memory
the anthems she sang
for her people distressed
for her people defiant

and when i was young,
though memory remained
under a leaking thatch,
the schoolroom slate
had slates for shelter
and outside
a wind was crying
history in my memories
history in my memories

AONGHAS MACNEACAIL

notes on *oideachadh ceart* (a proper schooling)

the first five stanzas refer to incidents which occurred in my native north skye community during a period of social upheaval which lasted from the mid-19th century till about 1922. the incidents are not presented chronologically.

rha and *conon* are the rivers which coverge, but do not meet, in the groin of the valley where my birthplace, uig, is situated.

kirsty, the 'baptist', who was active in the early 20th century, is, at the end of 1985, still living, but very old.

rob donn mackay, of sutherland, william ross, of skye, duncan ban macintyre, of glen orchy, and alexander macdonald, of moidart, were major gaelic poets of the 18th century. magnificent, but heavy going for 12 year olds, as poetry, or as grammar.

mary macpherson, *mairi mhor nan oran* (great mary of the songs) was, according to tradition, born in uig, though her name is usually associated with skeabost, also in skye. outstanding among 19th century bards, she is seen as the laureate of the *highland land league,* which campaigned for land law reform.

RIVONIA

Hamish Henderson

How Rivonia developed

It was at a party in the South London flat of my old friends Douggie and Queenie Moncrieff that I first thought of fitting anti-apartheid words to the well-known Spanish Republican tune 'Long live the 15th Brigade' ('Viva la Quince Brigata' alias 'El Ejecito del Ebro' - the Army of the Ebro). The refrain of the Spanish song includes the girl's name Manuela - which suggested Mandela - and the Rumbala chorus suggested African drums. (This was not long after the end of the Rivonia trial). The song was sung by me a little later in Athens at a folktale conference and began to circulate internationally.

In September 1964 I sent a copy of the song to the ANC office in London and received a reply from Raymond Kunene dated 13th October 1964 (see below). I then asked Roy Williamson and Ronnie Brown of the folk duo 'The Corries' to record the song for me; this they did and I sent several copies to Raymond Kunene who sent one on to Dar es Salaam (see letter of 22nd January 1965 below). Some months later I heard from several sources - including (if I remember rightly) Abdul Minty - that the song had been carried across to Robben Island by prisoners who had heard it while awaiting trial. I was naturally very proud to think that it had may have been heard by Nelson himself.

The song has been recorded two or three times. Ewan MacColl included it on his anti-apartheid cassette 'White Wind Black Tide' in 1987. More recently Roy Harper has included it on an LP. Another version as sung by the group Alfé in the mid-1970s is included on the LP 'Freedom Come-All-Ye' produced by Claddagh Records, Dublin in 1977. In this 'Rumbala, rumbala rumba la' is replaced by 'Ubugwala, ubugwala' (in a cowardly way) and the refrain 'Mkhululeni Umandela' (free Mandela) is added to the original text.

RIVONIA
Air: Viva la 15 Brigata

They have sentenced the men of Rivonia
Rumbala rumbala rumba la
The comrades of Nelson Mandela
Rumbala rumbala rumba la
He is buried alive on an island
Free Mandela Free Mandela
He is buried alive on an island
Free Mandela Free Mandela

Verwoerd feared the mind of Mandela
Rumbala rumbala rumba la
He was stopping the voice of Mandela
Rumbala rumbala rumba la
Free Mbeki Goldberg Sisulu
Free Mandela free Mandela
Free Mbeki Goldberg Sisulu
Free Mandela Free Mandela

The crime of the men of Rivonia
Rumbala rumbala rumba la
Was to organise farmer and miner
Rumbala rumbala rumba la
Against baaskap and sjambok and keerie[*]
Free Mandela Free Mandela
Against baaskap and sjambok and keerie
Free Mandela Free Mandela

Set free the men of Rivonia
Rumbala rumbala rumba la
Break down the walls of their prison
Rumbala rumbala rumba la
Freedom and justice Uhuru
Free Mandela Free Mandela
Freedom and justice Uhuru
Free Mandela Free Mandela

Power to the heirs of Luthuli
rumbala rumbala rumba la
The comrades of Nelson Mandela
Rumbala Rumbala Rumba la
Spear of the Nation unbroken
Free Mandela Free Mandela
Amandla Umkhonto we Sizwe[†]
Free Mandela Free Mandela

[*]baaskap: white domination   keerie: club, cudgel
†Amandla Umkhonto we Sizwe: power to the spear of the Nation

AFRICAN NATIONAL CONGRESS
(SOUTH AFRICA)

3 Collingham Gardens,
London SW5
England
Telephone: FRObisher 1914

13th October 1964

Dear Friend

We thank you most heartily for the song you have arranged. It is spirit of this character that will indeed carry us through the immense task of liberation.

Your contribution is greatly appreciated, indeed there are great similarities between the Spanish struggle against fascism and ours.

Anti-Apartheid has generally evoked the same idealism as the Spanish civil war. We however hope that ours will see the end of tyranny soon.

We shall send a copy of your arrangement to Africa and also the Anti-Apartheid groups here. Please keep in touch with us.

Wishing you all the best.

Yours fraternally

RAYMOND KUNENE
British and European Representative
African National Congress

AFRICAN NATIONAL CONGRESS
(SOUTH AFRICA)

3 Collingham Gardens,
London SW5
England

22nd January 1965

The School of Scottish Studies,
27 George Square,
Edinburgh 8

Dear Friend

We are very pleased at the contribution you have made through the Mandela composition. When I forwarded the copy of your song to our main office in Dar es Salaam there were ecstatic comments from all the friends there.

We heartily express our congratulations for this inspiring song. We hope to make a record of freedom songs and we shall be pleased to include this song.

Should you come down to London we would be very pleased to meet you. It is our desire to have more songs of this nature. The song has after all been from time immemorial the most potent form of expressing protest. I shall send you a radio programme on freedom songs that we are now in the process of making. From it you perhaps can make adaptations.

With all our best wishes.

Yours fraternally,

RAYMOND KUNENE
British and European Representative
African National Congress

FROM BOYCOTT TO SANCTIONS

ROBERT HUGHES

In 1959, Chief Albert Luthuli, President of the African National Congress issued a clarion call to the international community calling for individuals to boycott South African produce.

Thus began the international moves which would lead to the adoption of sanctions as the main weapon by which external pressure would be used as part of the liberation struggle in South Africa. Many thousands of people were moved by Chief Luthuli's appeal and the brutal nature of the apartheid state, and more and more people became concerned to end European colonisation in Africa.

There is no clear line through which the advance from boycott to sanctions can be traced. The successful adoption of sanctions and isolation of South Africa owe as much, if not more, to events inside the country as to the passionate rhetoric of the advocates of sanctions and isolation. That may seem a harsh judgement of the advocates of sanctions. The truth is probably that there was an interaction between advocacy and events in South Africa and that one reinforced the other. As the savagery of oppression became more known and understood, people became more receptive to the case for sanctions. Gradually the individual boycott of South African goods, which persists today as the most direct way in which people can demonstrate their solidarity with the people of South Africa, evolved.

In 1960 Liverpool City Council decided to make it a condition of contract that no goods of South African origin should be supplied to any of its purchasing departments. In 1964, Aberdeen Town Council became the first in Scotland to follow suit. This policy, first seen in Aberdeen as a modest, well-meaning, but possibly ineffectual gesture of no historical significance, was soon to be the focus of a sustained attack on the Labour controlled authority.

Unknown at the precise moment when the decision was taken, the local shipyard, Hall, Russell & Co. had obtained an order to build trawlers for the South African Company, Richard Irvine & Sons, (Cape Town) Ltd. The South Africa Foundation, then a fledgling pro South African business organisation, which described itself as 'non-political', thrust its way onto the scene. It suggested that the order worth £1,000,000 for the nine trawlers would be cancelled unless the 'boycott resolution', was rescinded by the City Council. Headlines from Aberdeen's morning daily newspaper give a flavour of the reactions:

> £2,000,000 BOMBSHELL: Anger over Aberdeen Town Council's 'boycott' decision (*The Press and Journal*, 22 February 1964)

> ABERDEEN LABOUR COUNCILLORS ARE IDIOTS, SAYS MP (*The Press and Journal*, 24 February 1964)

> THE SHIPYARD IN PERIL: Boycott could sink us, says boss (*The Press and Journal*, 29 February 1964)

I described the South Africa Foundation as a 'South African government propaganda front organisation'. The South African Foundation retaliated with the threat of legal action unless this 'falsehood' was withdrawn. I responded that the main providers of finance to the Foundation appeared to be the South African Railways and Harbours Board, the Iron and Steel Corporation (ISCOR) and the electricity generating companies, and pointed out that these were all either directly nationalised industries or parastatal companies. I said that I believed my remarks were fair political comment. I sweated for a few weeks but heard no more mention of legal action.

Reporters swarmed all over Aberdeen seeking reactions, especially from the shipyard workers leaving the yard after their shift. Typical comments reported were, 'We don't care who we build ships for, we'll build them'. When I went myself to speak to the men, they expressed sympathy for the case of the people of South Africa but said that they would still build the ships. In the event the order was not withdrawn.

It was a period of intense political and economic pressure, but the Labour Councillors stood firm. Apart from short periods during which Labour lost control of the Council, the policy of boycott has remained until this day.

The record of political support by the Council for the African National Congress has grown since then. In 1984, Aberdeen conferred the Freedom of the City upon both Nelson and Winnie Mandela. Aberdeen is probably unique amongst local authorities in having conferred the Freedom of the City on three South Africans. Field Marshall Jan Smuts, the Prime Minister of South Africa received his honour in 1942.

Thus the old order gives way to the new.

In parallel with the development of personal and local authority action, the international sanctions debate continued. Again it is difficult to present a precise history or to suggest that the structure was even in its evolution. Here too there was the interaction of events and advocacy. Cause and effect were inexorably intertwined.

We can now speak with certainty of the correctness of the case for sanctions. My memory of the times as to how the argument was won is that there was not always such certainty. There were hesitations, there were political discussions and arguments. There were times when particular ideologies came into play, when it was clear that the plight of the South African people seemed to be peripheral to the arguments, and that ideology was more important than the realities of the situation.

Those of us who were concerned with breaking down the apartheid state were always aware that major sanctions activity could cost jobs both in South Africa and in Britain. Our judgement was that mass unemployment and poverty were endemic in South Africa as a result of apartheid economics and could only be altered by the speedy end of apartheid. We judged that the pursuit of that goal was preferable to doing nothing and thus helping to perpetuate and even exacerbating the oppression of the people.

There was another strand of debate, particularily in Labour and socialist circles. The Trotskyist left argued that sanctions would hold back the revolution in South Africa. The argument was that apartheid could not be ended without revolution and that revolution could only come with the creation of an industrial society and an urban proletariat. That mechanistic and single road to socialism or emancipation was rejected by the majority. We believed that the people of South Africa could control their own destiny and should not be compelled to wait until the capitalist industrial revolution fulfilled its destiny either in South Africa or in the capitalist west.

How different it all is now when the only opponents of sanctions are the Tories who always opposed sanctions from the beginning.

Of course no greater claims for sanctions should be made than are justified by events in South Africa. Change is coming in South Africa because of many influences. The armed struggle has had a part to play. The activities of the people of South Africa through the trade union movement and the political struggle of the United Democratic Front have obviously been major factors.

Sanctions HAVE had an important part to play. How important will only be accurately quantified when historians have access to all the accounts and documents currently held in secret. What CAN now be said with certainty is that many thousands of individuals, many hundreds of local councillors took part in a movement unlike any other in history. This surpassed the activities of people in other causes in bringing about real international pressure for change and brought nearer to reality a democratic non-racialist South Africa. So many South Africans suffered for this, they were imprisoned, tortured, killed by the apartheid system. Those who are helping to consign apartheid to the dustbin of history have much to be proud of.

ANTI-APARTHEID GROUPS GIRD FOR ALL-OUT BATTLE TO HALT NEW SHIP

WILLIAM ALLAN   *People's World, 23 December 1984*

SAN FRANCISCO: Anti-apartheid activists here were preparing for civil disobedience actions at midweek as the arrival of another Dutch ship bearing South African cargo was anticipated.

The battle against South African cargo in the San Francisco Bay Area has reached a new stage following the dramatic action by longshore workers who last month refused to unload the cargos.

'With the next ship scheduled to arrive this week, the struggle moves into the public domain,' said Leo Robinson, a rank and file member of the International Longshoremen's and Warehousemen's Union (ILWU), Local 10, a leader in the earlier dockside action. 'The civil disobedience forces will have to take over. Because of the injunction, we have to unload the ships.'

The Pacific Maritime Association went to court on December 4th and obtained an injunction to force the longshore workers to unload cargo at San Francisco Pier 80. After a hectic meeting the Local 10 executive board voted to obey the court order. An arbitrator also ruled for the PMA, ordering financial penalties against workers whose protest had stirred the anti-apartheid movement around the state and nation.

Nearly two hundred anti-apartheid protesters took to Oakland streets on December 22nd to speak out against apartheid and ships from there bringing in cargo made by slave labour. Their principal demand, carried on placards and voiced in shouted slogans as they marched to City Hall, was that no ships be allowed to unload in West Coast ports and that no dock space be rented in ports to ships coming from South Africa.

Robinson told the protestors that the refusal of longshoremen to unload the Nedlloyd ships, before the injunction, was an act of conscience against apartheid, which he termed, 'a crime against humanity'.

ILWU Local 3 in Wilmington, California (near Los Angeles) in a recent resolution urged the ILWU leadership to discuss some type of West Coast action against apartheid.

They said, 'Local 13 is strongly opposed to the imprisonment of eleven trade union leaders in South Africa as well as the hundreds of freedom fighters. The apartheid government is carrying out the most dictatorial oppression and violence against the black majority.'

'We wish to go on record urging the longshore division to discuss some type of action. We must join hands with all democratic minded people in this country to help stop the slaughter and imprisonments in South Africa,' the workers said.

Made available to the *People's World* by ILWU members is a long list of 37 unions, locals and international officers who sent messages and greetings, to ILWU Local 10, its anti-apartheid committee and in some cases to the international union here in San Francisco.

The South African Congress of Trade Unions (SACTU) sent a mailgram greeting the actions of the longshoremen in refusing to unload the cargo, as did William Winpisinger, President of the International Association of Machinists.

Among unions sending congratulations were the Sheetmetal Workers Union, Amalgamated Transit Workers, Food and Allied Workers, Seafarers International Union, and the International Oil, Chemical and Atomic Workers.

Greetings also came from many locals including International Moulders Union Local 164, Bay Area; Shipbuilders Local 61, Pittsburgh, Pennsylvania; United Auto Workers, Wayne, Michigan; Master Mates and Pilots, offshore Local Middleton, Virginia; International Typographical Union Local 21, Bay Area; Hospital workers 1421, Los Angeles; ILWU Local 37, Seattle.

Also on the list are the central labour councils of Alameda, San Francisco, Santa Clara and Contra Costa counties, Oakland Educational Association, American Federation of Government Employees Local 476 in Washington DC, Carpenters Lodge 2435 in Inglewood California, culinary workers in Boston, teachers in New York, and many more.

Speakers at the anti-apartheid rally in front of Oakland City Halls December 22nd were Alameda County Supervisor John George, Oakland City council members Wilson Riles Jumior, and Berkeley Mayor Eugene 'Gus' Newport.

Riles reported that meetings of civil disobedience forces have been held to work out strategy for the 'Boston Tea Party' protest when the Nedlloyd shop arrives.

Newport told the rally that the South African Krugerrand is being sold by Consumer Distributors (a major national catalogue sales store) on University Avenue in Berkeley and that action must be taken to stop these sales. 'We can't allow that,' he said.

In Washington DC US Representative John Conyers, has charged on December 29 that he has evidence that the Reagan Administration permits the export of military and police equipment to South Africa.

Conyers, one of the nineteen US Congress members arrested in the US in anti-apartheid protests over the past month charged, 'The State Department has lifted export restrictions of military and military potential equipment on the munitions list.' The list contains items that require a licence before being sold to a foreign country.

Conyers said that between 1981 and 1983, the Reagan Administration allowed the export of $28.3 million in munitions to South Africa. Preliminary figures for the first quarter of 1984 show the amount of munitions list equipment licensed for export to South Africa amounted to $88 million.

HOW WE GOT RID OF
SOUTH AFRICAN AIRWAYS

WILLIE ANDERSON

In 1985 and early 1986 during a six-month long determined and persistent picket campaign by members of the Anti-Apartheid Movement (Victoria) and its supporters, the office of the South African Airways in downtown Melbourne was closed. The office was situated on prime land adjacent to the Melbourne stock exchange in the heart of the finance district of the city.

Efforts by SAA to relocate in the city were of no avail. The media coverage around the protest campaign had deemed SAA a high risk tenant.

The leafleting accompanying the protest highlighted to the Melbourne public the brutality and repression existing in South Africa. The police presence at our pickets meant that the media were more willing than usual to report the picket to the general public.

During the six month period of the picket there was a steady decline in the Australian share of the South African tourist industry. People seemed to be less interested in travelling to South Africa.

Simultaneously, the Anti-Apartheid Movement (Victoria) were demanding the withdrawal of all landing rights in Australia to SAA, the closing of the South African Embassy in Canberra and for the Australian Government to sever all economic, cultural and sporting ties with South Africa.

In mid-1987 the Australian Government informed South African Airways and the Pretoria régime that, under the international airlines agreement, it was giving official notice of withdrawal of landing rights in Australia to South African Airways.

Under this agreement, SAA ceased to enter Australia in early 1988. This situation still holds.

NELSON MANDELA AND THE FREEDOM OF SCOTLAND'S CITIES

BRIAN FILLING

When Nelson Mandela stepped out of prison at 4.15 pm on Sunday 11 February 1990 after more than 27 years incarceration by the apartheid regime of South Africa the people of the world joyfully celebrated and Mrs Margaret Thatcher cancelled her scheduled press conference. Mandela's powerful speech delivered immediately following his release had silenced the British Prime Minister.

Mrs Thatcher, the leading international opponent of sanctions against South Africa, had hoped to use Mandela's release as a platform on which to rehearse her well-worn argument against sanctions. Nelson Mandela's dignified speech - thanking the South African people and their organisations for their heroic struggle, thanking the international community for its solidarity, renewing the call for sanctions and re-dedicating himself and the African National Congress to the struggle for freedom - made it impossible for Mrs Thatcher to state her case ... that day. Soon she was again calling for the relaxation of sanctions.

Nelson Mandela's release from gaol was the outcome of the South African people's struggle, supported by the international community. The overthrow of Portuguese fascism and colonialism in 1974 had led to the independence of Angola and Mozambique the following year. Heartened by the Angolan/Cuban defeat of the invading South African army in Angola, the young people of South Africa gathered in peaceful protest against the enforced use of Afrikaans in school and were massacred during the Soweto Uprising of 1976.

The Anti-Apartheid Movement, founded by Archbishop Trevor Huddleston and others, had been active in Scotland throughout this period and in 1976 a Scottish Committee was formed with John Nelson as secretary.

When Glasgow's Lord Provost David Hodge hosted a lunch for the South African Ambassador Matthys Botha in September 1978 a thousand strong picket gathered outside the City Chambers in answer to a call from the Scottish Committee of the Anti-Apartheid Movement. The Lord Provost's comment that one couldn't expect people to come out of the jungle and go straight into government outraged many people as it was clearly seen as a reference to Zimbabwe gaining its independence at this time. The Labour Group withdrew the whip from the Lord Provost and he remained outwith the group until he retired from the council at the next election.

It was against this background that a resolution calling for the Freedom of the City to be awarded to Nelson Mandela was passed by a local Labour Party branch. The resolution went through various committees and was eventually proposed by the Labour group to the Council.

The Council agreed to make the award and it was conferred at a ceremony in the City Chambers on 4 August 1981 by the new Lord Provost, Michael Kelly. Ambassadors and High Commissioners from sixteen Commonwealth nations and Ruth Mompati, ANC Chief Representative in the UK, attended the ceremony at which the Vice-President of Nigeria, Alex Ekwueme, accepted the award on behalf of Nelson Mandela. In presenting the award Michael Kelly quoted from Mandela's trial speech:

> During my lifetime I have dedicated myself to this struggle of the African people. I have fought against white domination and I have fought against black domination. I have cherished the ideal of a democratic and free society in which all persons live together in harmony and with equal opportunities. It is an ideal which I hope to live for and to achieve. But if needs be it is an ideal for which I am prepared to die.

Lord Provost Kelly concluded, 'It is for this idealism that Mandela is awarded the Freedom of Glasgow.'

Glasgow continued its campaign for the release of Mandela with Lord Provost Kelly launching a world-wide mayors' petition at the United National Special Committee in New York. The petition was signed by some three thousand mayors throughout the world. Councillor Robert Gray, who succeeded Michael Kelly as Lord Provost, led a large delegation of civic leaders to 10 Downing Street on the twenty-first anniversary of the life-sentencing of Nelson Mandela on 12 June 1985.

On 16 June 1986 Essop Pahad of the African National Congress and Lord Provost Gray renamed a Glasgow city centre street after Nelson Mandela. As a consequence the South African Consulate on the fifth floor of the Stock Exchange building now resides in Nelson Mandela Place!

On Sunday 12 June 1988, the day following the 1988 Wembley concert, which celebrated Nelson Mandela's seventieth birthday,

8 FREEDOM OF THE CITY FOR MANDELA
Ruth Mompati (Chief Representative of the African National Congress in the UK) addressing an Anti-Apartheid Movement meeting in the City Chambers , Glasgow, on 4 August 1981 when Nelson Mandela was awarded the Freedom of the City of Glasgow.

9 GOVAN MBEKI ADDRESSES THE SECHABA CONFERENCE
On 23 September 1990 Govan Mbeki opened the Sechaba International Conference on Cultural Resistance to Apartheid. Alongside Govan Mbeki are Brian Filling and Archbishop Trevor Huddleston.

Lord Provost Susan Baird, together with ANC President Oliver Tambo and Archbishop Trevor Huddleston, launched the 'Nelson Mandela: Freedom at 70' Glasgow-London March from Glasgow Green before a rally of thirty thousand people.

Throughout Scotland there were anti-apartheid campaigns and as in Glasgow there were also friends of the apartheid regime to be found. When the proposal to award the freedom of the City of Aberdeen to Nelson and Winnie Mandela was first made in 1983, opposition to the award was led by Tory Council group leader Gordon Adams. He predicted that if the award was given to the Mandelas there would be 'no end to the ridiculous nonsense', adding:

> The obvious conclusion is that any political rabble-rouser who is sympathetic to the Socialist cause could be in line for becoming a Freeman of Aberdeen. It's all rather distasteful and totally out of line with the philosophy behind the honour in the past.

There was an element of truth in what he said. Jan Christian Smuts, Prime Minister of South Africa, had been awarded the Freedom of Aberdeen in 1942!

The Aberdeen Evening Express commissioned National Opinion Poll (NOP) to carry out a survey on the question. In its leader column of 5 January 1984, headlined 'DON'T give Mr Mandela this honour,' the *Evening Express* reported that 55% of those interviewed were against the award being given. Gordon Adams used this so-called reflection of public opinion (based on 500 interviews) in his campaign to stop the award being made.

The Aberdeen Anti-Apartheid Group ran a campaign of leaflets, petitions and meetings exposing the evil system of apartheid and arguing the case for Aberdeen's highest honour to be given to the Mandelas, two people who had made such sacrifices for freedom and who symbolised the resistance of the people of South Africa to apartheid.

The Council met on 20 February 1984 to decide the issue and by 30 votes to 13 agreed to award the Freedom of the City of Aberdeen to Nelson and Winnie Mandela. The vote which narrowly secured the necessary two-thirds majority had the whole Labour group, nearly all the Liberals and 1 Tory councillor voting for the proposal with the remaining 12 Tories and 1 Liberal voting against.

But the controversy wasn't over. A few days later the President of the Chamber of Commerce, Charles Skene, condemned the move as 'completely irresponsible' and warned that it could embarrass businessmen who export to South Africa. His statement continued:

The Chamber are aware that in 1964 when the former Aberdeen Town
Council decided to ban purchases of South African goods the action
was widely reported and seriously embarrassed North-East exporters
to South Africa. We believe that this action will cause similar embar-
rassment to North-East exporters.

Mr Skene's remarks served merely to further encourage the boycott campaign!

On 29 November 1984 Lord Provost Henry Rae awarded the
freedom of the city of Aberdeen to Nelson and Winnie Mandela. The
honours were accepted by Solly Smith, African National Congress
Chief Representative in the United Kingdom and Adelaide Tambo,
wife of Oliver Tambo, President of the African National Congress.
Accepting on behalf of Winnie Mandela, Mrs Tambo pointed out
that:

> Though this honour is being awarded to Winnie Mandela, we, the
> women of South Africa, accept it as an honour to all those women who
> have borne the struggle over the years and suffered untold miseries.
> The women whose husbands have been hanged and murdered in
> South Africa's racist gaols, the women who have lost their sons and
> daughters in Soweto, Langa, Port Elizabeth, Tembisa, Sharpeville,
> Sebokeng, in the Vaal Triangle, the women whose husbands and sons
> were killed in Matola, Mozambique, Lesotho, Swaziland, the women
> who have been left to support families on meagre salaries or no money
> at all whilst their husbands, sons and daughters have travelled to
> foreign lands to equip themselves educationally and otherwise to
> right the state of affairs in our country.

Annually since the award the Aberdeen Anti-Apartheid Group
has held a demonstration and rally to commemorate the granting of
the Freedom of the City to Nelson and Winnie Mandela.

Every year local authorities throughout Britain hold 'Ten Days of
Action against Apartheid'. During the period, 16-26 June, running
from the anniversary of the Soweto Uprising to South African
Freedom Day, councils fly the ANC flag, mount exhibitions, sponsor
cultural events, re-name streets and bridges and along with the Anti-
Apartheid Movement generally raise the issue of isolating the apartheid regime.

On 23 June 1986, as part of this nationwide activity, Lord Provost
Tom Mitchell conferred the Freedom of the City of Dundee on
Nelson Mandela, and Dundee thereby became the third Scottish city
to make such an award. That same year Edinburgh District Council
unveiled a statue named 'Woman and Child' in Festival Square
commemorating the freedom fighters of the South African Libera-

tion Movement. It had never been possible for the Labour group there to find the necessary two-thirds majority on the Council to award the Freedom of Edinburgh to Mandela. However the commissioning of a portrait of the South African leader and the creation of a Mandela room in the City Chambers did not please supporters of the apartheid regime including Tory group leader, Paul Martin.

Mr Martin, who, in his position as British Youth Council (Scotland) General Secretary, had written a conference paper on South Africa rejected by the BYC International Committee, was instrumental in inviting the South African Consul-General to a BYC conference in Edinburgh on 22 March 1986. The conference was picketed by the Scottish Committee of the Anti-Apartheid Movement and many affiliated organisations withdrew from the British Youth Council. Shortly afterwards the BYC closed its Scottish branch and Mr Martin found other work with the Scottish Confederation of British Industry. Ironically some of the BYC furniture found storage space in the office of the Scottish Committee of the Anti-Apartheid Movement and John MacKinnon, the Scottish Organiser, was to be seen sitting in a rather luxurious chair rumoured to have been Mr Martin's!

In addition to the three Scottish cities which have given 'Freedom' to Nelson Mandela, Midlothian District Council as one of its many anti-apartheid activities over the years has also conferred the award. Four authorities in England (Newcastle, Hull and the London Boroughs of Greenwich and Lambeth) and one in Wales (Islwyn) have done likewise. Another local authority, Sheffield City Council, which has held the chair of the National Steering Committee for Local Authority Action Against Apartheid since its inception, has also taken the decision to grant Mandela Freedom of the city but has still formally to make the award.

Some of the local government councillors in Scotland who have opposed the awards to Mandela have gone to South Africa as guests of the South African government. It was following one of these trips that the Scottish-South Africa Club and then the Scottish-South Africa Society were established with some of these councillors taking office. With the South African Consul-General as Honorary President and the Deputy Consul-General acting initially as secretary it is plain that the Scottish-South African Society was simply a creation of the Consulate designed to further its propaganda work in a battle which it felt it was losing.

It was a great victory for the freedom forces in South Africa and for all those who had supported them internationally when Nelson Mandela, Walter Sisulu, Govan Mbeki and the other Rivonia trialists were released and the African National Congress was unbanned.

These events did not signify the end of apartheid: the main pillars of that 'crime against humanity' remained in place. The need for acts of solidarity was as great as ever. As Nelson Mandela said on 16 April 1990, speaking to 76,000 at Wembley and to millions of people throughout the world watching television:

> The apartheid crime against humanity remains in place. It continues to kill and maim. It continues to oppress and exploit. ...
> Therefore do not listen to anyone who says that you must give up the struggle against apartheid. Dear friends, ... you are allies in the common struggle to bring freedom, democracy and peace to all the people of South Africa. There are some people in the world who wish to support the South African government by giving it rewards and carrots. ... We, representing the overwhelming majority of the people of our country, turn to you for support, which we need much more than ever before ... .

CONTENTS

DATE NIGHT DELIGHT   157

INTRODUCTION

MY NAME IS CHRIS STARK. I'M A BBC RADIO 1 presenter, a huge Watford fan, and I spent twenty-four years sitting at the wrong end of the bath. I went to the University of Southampton, and I left with two things: a 2:2 degree and a massive passion for cooking.

But it wasn't always that way...

I turned up at my uni kitchen on day one of Freshers' Week completely clueless. The journey to Southampton had been long and uncomfortable, with me wedged in between bags of shopping, kitchen equipment and supplies, none of which I knew how to use. I was just unprepared and out of my depth. Seriously. I blew up the kettle attempting to boil pasta inside the first week.

Fast forward to now, and I have developed a passion for cooking good food that I wish I had properly explored at university. I am determined that you can learn from the many mistakes I have made, and I've teamed up with a top chef to produce a guide to food that covers every area of uni life. If I can do this, trust me, so can you!

It's the book I wish I had been given before I headed off to university. THE ultimate student cookbook. I'm prouder of this than my dissertation and it was certainly a lot more fun to create.

This book will take you through recipes and ideas for every bit of your student life. From those long nights in the library to the meal that cheers up your newly single housemate. From the hangover food you need after a big night out to the perfect fuel for your impending sport trial.

Unlike so many other student cookbooks, this one is coming from someone that understands the real uni life: what you do and don't have time for, what you can and can't afford, what is and isn't going to look epic on Instagram. I've learnt from all my mistakes to pass that hard-won wisdom on to you. Nearly everything in this book can be made for under a fiver, assuming you have all the basics stocked, and doesn't matter whether you are a meat eater or a vegetarian – again, most of the recipes are adaptable for both.

A wise man (David Hasselhoff) once said, 'Some people stand in the darkness, afraid to step into the light'.

Don't let that be you. Accept this cookbook as your guide and step forward fearlessly into the light. (Just don't forget to turn it off afterwards – electricity is expensive.)

Good luck, and happy cooking! x

STORE CUPBOARD ESSENTIALS

BEFORE WE DIVE HEADLONG INTO THE VARIOUS exciting recipes in this book, let's take a brief pause to make sure you'll actually have everything you need. I suggest working through the 'kit list' overleaf before you set off for your new accommodation. Arrive with it all in the back of the car and you won't be caught short for kit.

And when you arrive and you're all unpacked, take an hour to locate your nearest supermarket and get stocking up on everything in our 'store cupboard essentials' list. It's a big shop but a lot of it will go a long way, and you'll want it all at one time or another. Make the investment now, thank yourself later.

After all, it won't be a good look if you end up having to beg your new housemates to cadge a spatula, a big chunk of (expensive) cheese, three eggs and someone's best new frying pan, just to make an omelette for lunch on day one.

As the Scouts say, 'Be prepared'!

Kit list

SAUCEPAN

You'll need an all-purpose medium one for cooking and a large one for boiling pasta, rice and potatoes.

FRYING PAN

Get a decent-sized one, preferably non-stick – a good frying pan gets a lot of use!

TEASPOON AND TABLESPOON

For measuring.

BAKING TRAY AND A ROASTING TRAY

A flat baking tray does for most things, but if you want to do a roast, you'll need a deeper roasting tray.

CASSEROLE DISH WITH A LID

Not essential, but very useful if you're going to be cooking stews, curries and pasta sauces for four people or more.

CHOPPING BOARD

Preferably two – then you can do more prep in advance. Cut your veg on one and chicken, meat or fish on the other.

CHEF'S KNIFE (A LARGE, LONG KNIFE)

A sharp one! If you use it a lot, pick up a cheap knife sharpener to keep it that way.

SMALL SERRATED KNIFE

Really useful for cutting up tomatoes and fruit and as a second all-purpose knife. If you like to slice your own bread, a serrated bread knife can do both.

WOODEN SPOON

If you've got a non-stick frying pan, a metal spoon can damage it. Wooden spoons are very cheap – get a few!

CHEESE GRATER

SPATULA AND TONGS

MIXING BOWL

KITCHEN SCALES

Most of these recipes don't require kitchen scales, but they are really useful. If you're planning on doing any baking – they're essential.

CLING FILM

SLOW COOKER

Well worth the investment. You can pick these up pretty cheaply and they are a game changer.

SHIT! YOUR FAMILY HAVE DROPPED YOU OFF, you're faced with a kitchen you have no idea what to do with, and after the eternal sunlight of Freshers' Week is over, the long winter of the Christmas term begins. You need food you can cook once and eat forever. Don't worry, I've got ya.

Step into the kitchen and mark your territory (but not by weeing in the corner – even after a big night, that's not a good look). It's time to step up and dominate this vital step in your Uni life.

The reality is, Freshers' Week is going to be a shock to the system. Between parties every night, and meeting loads of new people, this is the time to establish yourself. If you're a 'Re-Fresher' (back for second or third year), you know the drill.

One of the most nerve-racking parts of this will be moving into accommodation with total strangers. You just don't know who you're going to get landed with! I was mostly lucky, however, I did temporarily have to share a *room* with a guy who, pretty early on, I caught enjoying himself into a sock. It wasn't ideal. So, you can't pick your new flatmates, but it's no bad thing trying to get them on side early-doors. Being able to bang together simple comfort food is an easy way to do this for a bit of Freshers' Week bonding.

This chapter aims to set you up with simple, but hearty, food that can last you a few days. Less time cooking, more time partying. Also, importantly, you can microwave most of this stuff after it's cooked to stop you attempting to cook late at night and with impressive blood-alcohol content. It's *really* dangerous and your housemates will hate you if you set off the fire alarm (yes, like I did).

So, without further ado, read on for recipes to help you win over your new housemates, recipes to help you recover from the dreaded 'Freshers' Flu' and recipes that can be made quickly to set you up for a big night out.

So, first time in the kitchen. Good luck... and sock it to them! (But, please, not in the way my old flatmate did.)

Super-easy beginner Bolognese

Serves ④

Prep time: 20 mins

Cook time: 1 ½ hours (more if you can!)

You CANNOT go wrong with this. If you are brave enough to step up and cook for your new housemates, this is the recipe to do. The key is cooking the sauce very gently, until it's super-rich. I only found this out when I accidentally left it for longer than I should, and I've sworn by it ever since! The best thing about this meal (other than how it tastes) is that this Bolognese sauce can be cooked in advance and frozen. Leave to cool completely, then pop in a freezer-proof container. It will keep in the freezer for up to two months. Sorted.

• •

Ingredients

2 tbsp olive oil

1 onion, diced

1 tsp garlic purée (or 2 chopped garlic cloves)

1 carrot, peeled and finely chopped

2 celery sticks, finely chopped

500g beef mince (or use ½ beef and ½ pack of good-quality sausages)

400g tin chopped tomatoes

1 tsp dried oregano

400ml beef stock (made from a stock cube)

salt and freshly ground black pepper

500g spaghetti, to serve

Vegetarian: use Quorn mince and a vegetable stock cube.

Flavour tip: throw in some chopped mushrooms for the last half hour of cooking and scatter over torn fresh basil leaves to serve.

Method
1. Heat a large saucepan over a medium heat. Pour in the oil and once hot, add the onion and garlic and cook over a low heat until really soft. Add the carrot and celery and carry on cooking until they're softened too.

2. If you are using the sausages, split the skins, take out the meat and roughly chop. Turn up the heat, add the beef and sausage and cook over a high heat until browned.

3. Add the tomatoes and oregano to the pan and stir well. Pour in the stock, bring to a simmer, then reduce the temperature to simmer gently for at least 1 hour, but as long as possible, until the sauce is thick and rich. Taste and season.

4. When you're ready to eat, cook the spaghetti in a large saucepan of boiling water with a pinch of salt, according to the packet instructions. Once the spaghetti is cooked through, drain and eat with the Bolognese sauce.

Chris's 'cheap as chips' chilli con carne

Serves 4

Prep time: less than 30 mins

Cook time: 1 hour

Make friends with anyone by dropping this C-bomb. A student staple, it even comes with a drinking game: say the name of this recipe five times. If you trip up ... you do a shot. Good luck! Another recipe that can keep in the freezer for up to two months.

· ·

Ingredients

1 tbsp vegetable oil

400g–500g beef mince

1 large onion, diced

1 tsp garlic purée (or 2 chopped garlic cloves)

1 tbsp paprika

2 tbsp dried chilli flakes

2 tbsp tomato purée

400g tin chopped tomatoes

500ml beef stock (made from a stock cube – chicken or veg is also fine)

½ tsp dried mixed herbs

400g tin red kidney beans, drained and rinsed well

salt and freshly ground black pepper

300g rice, to serve (see tip)

natural yoghurt, to serve

Vegetarian: use Quorn mince and a vegetable stock cube.

Method

1. Heat a frying pan over a medium heat and add the vegetable oil. Once hot, fry the beef mince to golden brown in two batches. Once fried, add each batch to a colander that is sat over a saucepan to catch any excess fat.

2. Using the same frying pan, add the beef fat, onion and garlic with a pinch of salt. Cook for 5–7 minutes until the onion is soft and translucent. Add the fried mince back to the pan with the paprika and chilli flakes and cook for 2 minutes. Add the tomato purée and cook for another 2 minutes.

3. Transfer all the ingredients to a large saucepan and add the chopped tomatoes, stock, dried herbs and kidney beans. Stir well, bring to the boil and simmer for 45 minutes until the chilli has thickened. Taste and adjust the seasoning if necessary.

4. Meanwhile, cook the rice in a separate saucepan. Serve the chilli with the cooked rice and an ample amount of yoghurt on top.

Foolproof way of cooking rice: 1 part rice, 2 parts water. Add both to a pan, bring to the boil and simmer for 8 minutes. Take off the heat and put a lid on it for a further 4 minutes. Easy!

'Freshers' Flu' spicy tomato soup

Serves 4

Prep time: less than 10 mins

Cook time: 30 mins

I hate to break it to you, but Freshers' Flu *will* get you. No one can explain what it is, or why it's so potent, but when it hits you ... you know. This soup recipe was hard-won wisdom for me, and although soup might not be your first thought (what goes down might come up – I hear ya!), this is the meal to recharge you and give your body the goodness it needs to go again.

. . . .

Ingredients

2 tbsp vegetable oil

1 onion, thinly sliced

1 small carrot, peeled and thinly sliced

2 tsp tomato purée

2 tsp paprika

2 x 400g tins chopped tomatoes

2 tbsp natural yoghurt

salt and freshly ground black pepper

Flavour tip: buying a pot of herbs such as basil (and keeping it alive) is a great way to give dishes, including this soup, a quick chef upgrade. Flavour town.

Method

1. Pour the vegetable oil into a large saucepan and heat for 1 minute. Add the onion and carrot and lightly colour over 5 minutes (the longer, the better, as this will release their natural sugars).

2. Add the tomato purée and paprika and cook for 2 minutes, stirring constantly.

3. Add the chopped tomatoes, bring to the boil and simmer for 20 minutes.

4. Pour in the yoghurt, then blend using a hand whisk or a blender to chunky or smooth, whatever you prefer. Taste and adjust the seasoning with salt and pepper if needed.

Sweet potato and chickpea 'communal' curry

Serves 4

Prep time: 15 mins

Cook time: 30 mins

I've gone with this recipe for a communal curry because at a time where you are eating a lot of beige, this is a tasty way to get some goodness inside of you. You can experiment with this a bit by throwing in other veggies, but the sweet potato in this is a really tasty replacement for any meat that you might usually use (if you're that way inclined). A great one to make for your student flat: easy to make in bulk and anyone can enjoy it. A crowd-pleaser.

● ●

Ingredients

2 tbsp vegetable oil

1 onion, thinly sliced

1 large carrot, peeled and thinly sliced

1 medium-sized sweet potato, peeled and diced into 2cm cubes

1 tbsp ground turmeric

1 tbsp medium curry powder

1 tbsp chilli powder

500g passata

400g tin chickpeas, drained and washed well

100g frozen peas

salt and freshly ground black pepper

rice, to serve (see tip)

natural yoghurt, to serve

Method

1. Begin to prepare the curry by heating the oil in a large saucepan and lightly caramelising the onion, carrot and sweet potato over a medium heat for 8–10 minutes.

2. Add the tumeric, curry powder and chilli powder and cook for 1 minute. Add the passata and chickpeas, bring to the boil, then reduce the heat to simmer for 20 minutes.

3. Meanwhile, cook the rice in a separate saucepan.

4. Once the sauce has thickened, add the peas and yoghurt, stir and bring back to the boil. Taste and season as needed. Serve the curry with the cooked rice.

Stroganoff Before-You-Dancey-Off

Serves ④

Prep time: 20 mins

Cook time: 20 mins

So quick and easy, this is the perfect meal before a big night out! It's made with mushrooms, but I sometimes add beef. The key is the smoked paprika, which brings it to life.

• •

Ingredients

1 tbsp vegetable oil

2 white onions, finely diced

1 tbsp garlic purée (or 4 chopped garlic cloves)

350g beef frying steak, thinly sliced

600g button mushrooms, sliced

1 tbsp smoked paprika

1 tbsp English mustard

200ml vegetable stock (made from a stock cube)

200ml sour cream (save a little back for a cheffy swirl)

a squeeze of lemon juice

salt and freshly ground black pepper

rice, to serve (see tip)

Vegetarian: substitute the beef for 2 sliced aubergines and cook in the same way.

Flavour tip: upgrade this with a huge dollop of wholegrain mustard stirred in just before serving; it's a great texture and gives the dish an unbelievable depth of flavour.

Method

1. Heat a frying pan over a medium heat and add the oil. Once hot, add the onion and garlic and cook gently for 5 minutes.

2. Add the beef to the pan and fry for 2 minutes to brown the edges, then add the mushrooms. Continue to fry over a medium heat for 5 minutes. Add the paprika and mustard and mix well. Stir in the stock, bring to the boil and simmer for 5 minutes.

3. Meanwhile, cook the rice in a separate saucepan.

4. Remove the stroganoff from the heat, stir in the sour cream and squeeze of lemon juice and mix it all together. Taste and add salt and pepper as needed. Serve the stroganoff with the rice.

Pizza Naan

Serves ④

Prep time: less than 30 mins
Cook time: 10 mins

Your new housemates are back from a night out. It's a heavy responsibility, but your people need a hero. They're out of money and hungry – only you can save them. This recipe takes minutes, uses leftovers, and is the perfect end-of-night food. Be that end-of-the-night hero. If you don't have any naan, you could use tortilla wraps.

Is it fried bird? No.
Is it some grains? No!
It's … Pizza naan!

· ·

Ingredients

4 medium-sized plain naan

½ jar of roasted red peppers, drained

12 cherry tomatoes, halved (or a jar of passata)

8 rashers of back bacon (smoked or unsmoked is fine), cut into strips

200g cheddar cheese, grated

4 tsp lime pickle (1 tsp for each naan)

Vegetarian: leave out the bacon!

Flavour tip: we all have some condiments lurking at the back of the fridge. Mango chutney, garlic mayo and sriracha are all great additions.

Method

1. Preheat the grill to high. Line the grill rack with foil (you'll thank me in the morning when cleaning up is minimal!)

2. Spread the naan out on the rack. Spread the tomatoes or a few tablespoons of passata over the top of each one, then sprinkle the peppers, bacon and cheese evenly over them. Grill on high until golden brown.

3. Dollop the lime pickle in and around the hot naan. Serve with some of your favourite condiments.

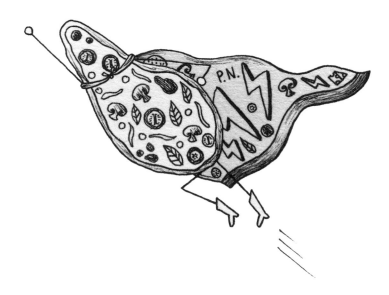

'Starkay Satay' Noodles

Serves ④

🥄 Prep time: less than 20 mins

📅 Cook time: 15 mins

This was one of my finest discoveries. Peanut butter and coconut milk make a great DIY satay sauce. Be in and out of the kitchen quick before someone bothers you for some of your food, and watch out for the lurkers – they will soon get a sniff off this and appear. Pack out this filling noodle dish with plenty of fresh veg and strips of chicken, if you fancy.

• •

Ingredients

300g boneless chicken thigh meat, diced

2 tbsp soy sauce

zest and juice of 1 lime

2 tsp cornflour

400g dried noodles (2 nests per person)

4 tbsp vegetable oil

1 onion, thinly sliced

½ broccoli, cut into florets and stalk thinly sliced

1 carrot, thinly sliced

50g smooth peanut butter

2 tbsp sweet chilli sauce

400ml tin coconut milk

100g mangetout, thinly sliced

50g frozen peas

50g roasted peanuts, lightly crushed

Vegetarian: removing the chicken and adding firm tofu to this dish works just as well.

Flavour tip: adding some sliced spring onions and sesame seeds at the end might make you consider quitting university and becoming a chef!

Method

1. Put the chicken in a bowl, add the soy sauce, lime zest and cornflour and mix together well. Cover and leave to marinate for 5 minutes. If you are using tofu, do the same step.

2. Bring a large pan of water to the boil, add the noodles and cook for 2 minutes. Once cooked, drain with a colander and rinse under running water until cold. Drain again and drizzle with 2 tablespoons of the vegetable oil, coating them well before setting aside.

3. Heat a large frying pan over a high heat until hot, add the remaining oil and fry the onion, broccoli stalk and carrot for 1 minute. Stir in the peanut butter, chilli sauce and coconut milk. Bring the pan to the boil, then turn down the heat to a simmer. Add the marinated chicken or tofu and poach for 5 minutes. Throw in the mangetout, peas and broccoli florets and simmer for another 2 minutes.

4. Return to the boil, stir in the lime juice and cooked noodles and heat until they are piping hot. Serve with the crushed peanuts on top.

'The One-Pan Gnocchi Plan'

Serves 4

Prep time: 10 mins
Cook time: 30 mins

Every student cookery book wangs on about pasta, but an easy way to switch it up is to use gnocchi. It uses a similar method, however these little potato dumplings of joy are a great point of difference. If you don't have a bag of fresh spinach, use any veg you have in the freezer – spinach, peas or broccoli.

. . . .

Ingredients

a knob of butter
1 garlic clove, sliced
250g bag of baby spinach, washed and drained
1 pack of gnocchi

200g creamy blue cheese (like gorgonzola or dolcelatte), cut into cubes
100ml double cream
freshly ground black pepper

Method

1. Preheat the oven to 190°C (170°C fan)/gas 5. Bring a large pan of water to the boil.

2. Add the butter and garlic to a large frying pan. When the butter melts, add the spinach and cook for a few minutes until wilted.

3. Add the gnocchi to the boiling water (you can cook them from frozen) and cook for a few minutes until they rise to the surface. As they come to the top, spoon them out with a slotted spoon into an ovenproof dish. Add the spinach to the dish with the cheese and cream. Season with black pepper.

4. Bake in the oven for 20 minutes or until golden and bubbling.

Chapter Two

FOOD FOR THOUGHT

OIL

BRAIN FOOD

TOMATOES

FRESHERS' FLU MIGHT FEEL LIKE IT LASTS forever, but Freshers' Week only lasts, well, a week. As lectures and seminar schedules kick into gear, your life starts to shape into some kind of routine. Or that's how it's meant to be. In the absence of nagging teachers and parents, a different kind of schedule was becoming prominent in my life. And it was all based around the nightlife of a Southampton student.

I'd also started getting involved with the Uni's student radio station, for which we would streak through lectures, prank other students and generally cause havoc. All was well until I was banned after one particular stunt. I like to imagine, though, that 'Battle-nips' was just ahead of its time. The nadir was missing an exam after a night DJing a boat party on the Solent. (Maybe it was a tad distasteful to bang on the *Titanic* theme song on a real boat, but there was also something oddly moving about it. A bit like watching *Snakes on a Plane* on a plane. Or *Blue Planet* in the bath.) All of this, however, meant the academic side of things had begun to take a real hit.

So, it was retakes for me and, year-on-year, I managed to do enough to get by. But I didn't make it easy for myself. I got through powered by energy drinks and industrial amounts of sugar. I also had a strange routine during exam time to celebrate when an exam was finished. I would always visit the toilets below the Stag's Head student pub and go for a number two. I can't explain why. Maybe it felt like I was flushing away that particular subject, or maybe it was just a result of the many cans of Red Bull I was living on. But it wasn't healthy.

Long story short, I was concerned I was going to get a Third. But on results day, after about three minutes of frantically hitting 'Refresh', there was the good news . I'd got a 2:2! It was right there on the screen. I sat there for a minute, happy, but sad that Uni was now over. Proud, but feeling lucky to have scraped through. Worried about what I was meant to do next. But mostly, just so happy.

I want you to get that feeling, too, and I hope this chapter can provide you with the fuel to do the all-nighters, to power through coursework, and to make it happen for yourself. Above all, to help you truly *enjoy* that celebratory poo. Everyone deserves that particular moment, and that's why arguably this is the most important chapter in the book. Feed your brain the right stuff, be its friend, and don't rely on energy drinks that'll give you the squits in the middle of an exam.

Some of the recipes in this section will push our budget boat out towards our five pound price cap – but, hey, you can't put a price on A-grades!

'Eggy Spice': baked eggs with spinach, tomato and red onion

If you're setting yourself up for a day-long library session, what better to have for breakfast than a plate of eggs? Here comes the nerdy info... They're a fantastic source of vitamins B6 and B12, and contain choline, which creates neurotransmitters that regulate mood and memory. Boiled, fried, poached or scrambled, you can rely on an egg to prepare you for the day ahead! Have a go at these recipes and take pride in becoming an Egg Head.

Serves 4

Prep time: less than 10 minutes

Cook time: 15 minutes

Spinach, bake it, cool it, taste it, who do you think you are? You can be the forgotten Spice Girl here – 'Eggy Spice'. Spice up your life with this easy and nutritious recipe!

Ingredients

2 tbsp vegetable oil

½ red onion, thinly sliced

2 tsp garlic purée (or 4 chopped garlic cloves)

250g bag of baby spinach, washed and drained

400g tin chopped tomatoes

4 large eggs

salt and freshly ground black pepper

crusty bread and sriracha sauce, to serve

Flavour tip: add 1 tsp dried chilli flakes with the garlic

Method
1. Preheat the oven to 200°C (180°C fan)/gas 6.

2. In a medium-sized frying pan, heat the oil and begin to fry the onion for 2 minutes. Add the garlic and cook for 1 minute, then add the spinach and wilt down.

3. Pour in the chopped tomatoes and cook until the sauce has reduced by about half. Season with salt and pepper.

4. Remove the mixture from the heat and put into a ovenproof dish. Make a small well in each of the four corners of the dish and crack an egg into each one. Bake for 8–10 minutes, or more depending if you prefer your eggs cooked for longer.

5. Serve with a bowl of crusty bread and sriracha sauce.

Veggie eggucated-fried rice

Serves ❷

🍳 Prep time: 10 mins

📟 Cook time: 10 mins

Fried rice needs cold rice, so this recipe is *ideal* for using up some of last night's leftovers. If you have rice in the fridge, use that. Or you can use the pouches of rice available now in every supermarket, in all sorts of flavours.

This scavenger-style stir-fry is also packed with plenty of protein from the eggs, and to scale it up with vitamins, just add extra veg. The more greens the better! Give this a try, it tastes amazing – it's an eggucation.

∙∙

Ingredients

3 eggs, lightly beaten

1 tbsp soy sauce

2 tbsp vegetable oil

1 tsp garlic purée (2 finely chopped garlic cloves)

4 spring onions, sliced

250g pouch of ready-cooked rice or leftover cold rice (make sure you refrigerate cooked rice not more than an hour after cooking)

a handful of frozen peas or sweetcorn (or both)

Method

1. Beat the eggs with the soy sauce.

2. Heat a large frying pan (or wok if you've got one) until hot, then add the oil. When it is hot, add the garlic and half the spring onions and stir-fry for 1–2 minutes until just softened.

3. Add the rice and stir-fry for 2–3 minutes, breaking up any lumps with a fork, until heated through. Stir in the peas or sweetcorn and cook for 1 minute until hot.

4. Add the eggs to the rice and stir-fry for 2–3 minutes, or until the eggs have just set. Serve up immediately with the remaining spring onion scattered over the top.

Smashed avo on toast

COME AND AVOCADO IF YOU THINK YOU'RE SMART ENOUGH
Avocado is one of the healthiest fruits you can eat and if you're gonna learn anything today: yes, it's true, avocado is a fruit! Rich in vitamins B, C and K and packed with monounsaturated fats (those are the good ones!), avocados boost both memory and concentration – exactly what you need when you're struggling mid-revision session.

Serves **1**

Prep time: 5 mins
Cook time: 2 mins

So simple and delicious, this is perfect for when you need a quick and nutritious breakfast or snack. This is a rare breakfast that is green, which makes you feel like you are starting the day on a slightly more healthy note. Plus you can bang this out 10 mins before you have to leave for a lecture, and even eat it on the walk there. Ideal.

Ingredients

2 slices of sourdough bread
½ garlic clove
extra-virgin olive oil, for drizzling
1 ripe avocado
½ lime
a few sprigs of fresh coriander, chopped
salt and freshly ground black pepper

Flavour tip: mash in some dried or fresh chilli, top with a fried or poached egg or some crispy chorizo and sliced roasted red peppers.

Method

1. Toast the sourdough slices and rub with the cut side of the garlic, then drizzle over a little of the olive oil

2. Slice the avocado, squeeze over the lime juice and arrange on the toasted bread.

3. Crush the avocado into the toast with a fork or your knife – it can be as chunky or smooth as you like. Season with salt and pepper, then add a drizzle of the olive oil and a squeeze more lime juice. Sprinkle with the coriander leaves.

The 'Don't-Quit' veg fritters with guacamole

Serves 2-3

🖐 Prep time: 15 mins

📅 Cook time: 10 mins

Keep going! You can do this. I hated it when I was deep into a day of work, looking for any distraction and feeling like I wasn't getting anywhere. This recipe is the boost you need to carry on. A quick easy meal to make, that tastes like a treat. Quickly regroup by making these healthy treats, and then go slay!

. . . .

Ingredients

2 corn on the cobs (or 200g frozen sweetcorn) or 2 courgettes

100g self-raising flour (or plain flour and ½ tsp baking powder)

2 eggs

1 lime, halved

1 red onion, finely chopped

2 handfuls of coriander, chopped

1 ripe avocado

2 tomatoes, finely chopped

a couple of jalapeño slices from a jar or ½ fresh chilli, finely chopped

2 tbsp vegetable oil

salt and freshly ground black pepper

Flavour tip: add chilli to the corn fritters or some crumbled feta to the courgette ones.

Method

1. First, make the fritters. Cut the kernels off the corn by standing each one upright on a plate and slicing downwards with a sharp knife. If you're using courgettes, grate onto a paper towel-lined plate, then pat dry with the paper.

2. Mix together the flour, a pinch of salt and a good grinding of black pepper in a bowl. Whisk in the eggs with a fork, then whisk in a good squeeze of lime juice and a couple of tablespoons of water if the batter looks very thick. Stir in your corn or courgette, half the red onion and half the coriander.

3. Now, make the guacamole by mashing the ripe avocado in a bowl with a fork and generously squeezing over more lime juice. Add the tomato, chilli, remaining red onion and coriander. Taste and season with salt and pepper, adding more lime juice if needed.

4. Heat the oil in a frying pan, drop spoonfuls of the fritter mixture into the pan and flatten them a bit. Cook for a few minutes on one side, then turn over and cook the other side until golden brown on both. Serve the fritters with the guacamole.

First-class salmon parcels

Packed full of omega-3, salmon is one of the best brain foods out there. If you're sat in despair, feeling like nothing's going in, take a break from revision and prep yourself some salmon (with some greens on the side, for that extra brain boost!). You might be surprised by how revitalised you feel afterwards.

Serves ❷

🖐 Prep time: 15 mins

🗓 Cook time: 25 mins

Here's a recipe that you can prep up in advance and bung in the oven when hunger strikes. Wrap up these little parcels and post them into the oven to deliver yourself an amazing dinner.

· ·

Ingredients

½ red onion, thinly sliced

12 cherry tomatoes, halved

½ courgette, cut lengthways and into 2cm chunks

¼ aubergine, cut into 2cm chunks

1 tsp garlic purée (or 2 chopped garlic cloves)

2 salmon fillets, skinless and bone free

1 generous tbsp dry white wine

1 generous tbsp olive oil (vegetable or rapeseed oil are also fine)

2 tbsp dried mixed herbs

salt and freshly ground black pepper

Vegetarian: you can replace the salmon with a mix of any baby veg – just cut down the cooking time to 15 minutes.

EAT SLEEP RAVE REHEAT

Method

1. Preheat the oven to 190°C (170°C fan)/gas 5. Make two x 15cm squares using greaseproof paper and two slightly bigger squares with aluminium foil. Put the foil on the bottom, followed by the greaseproof paper, to make two sheets.

2. Divide the vegetables and garlic evenly and pile up in the middle of the two sheets. Put the salmon on top and scrunch the sides of the foil upwards on all sides.

3. Divide the white wine, oil and mixed herbs between the two and season with salt and pepper. Seal the foil together to make two parcels.

4. Bake in the oven for 25 minutes.

Creamy smoked salmon risotto

Serves ②

Prep time: 10 mins
Cook time: 40 mins

With this recipe we are using smoked salmon, which may sound expensive for a midweek meal, but it is no more costly than cooking with red meat! And remember you can't stint on A grades! Treat yourself.

• •

Ingredients

1 litre chicken or vegetable stock (made from 2 stock cubes or pots)

4 tbsp butter or olive oil

1 small onion, finely chopped

1 mugful of risotto rice

1 pack of smoked salmon, chopped

100g cream cheese or mascarpone

2 tbsp chopped herbs, such as parsley, basil or dill (if you have them)

a squeeze of lemon juice

Vegetarian: swap the salmon for asparagus spears that have been chopped into thirds and cooked for 3 minutes until just tender in the simmering stock.

Flavour tip: A very little dash of a smooth white wine will lift the flavour even further.

Method

1. Put your stock into a small pan and heat up until simmering.

2. Heat the butter or oil in another large saucepan or frying pan and fry the onion for about 10 minutes over low heat until softened but not browned. Stir in the rice and cook for 2 minutes, stirring all the time to coat in the oil.

3. Add a ladleful of the hot stock and mix into the rice. Keep the heat low so that the rice is gently simmering and stir continuously. When that stock has been absorbed, add another ladleful and keep doing this until the rice is just soft – this should take about 25 minutes. You may not need all the stock or you might need a bit more – every risotto is different!

4. Take the risotto off the heat and add the salmon, cream cheese, herbs, if using, and a squeeze of lemon juice. Put the lid on the pan if you have one and set aside for a few minutes. Taste and season with freshly ground pepper and add more lemon juice, if you need it.

'Freggie Salad' with kale, spinach and apple

Foods like spinach and kale are really good for you, as they contain so many vitamins and minerals, including antioxidants. You can add them to salads, throw them in a smoothie or bake up some kale chips (put the kale on a tray, drizzle with oil and add salt, then bake in the oven until dried out and crispy). Make these two recipes to become the new Professor Greens.

Serves 2

Prep time: 20 mins
Cook time: 5 mins

This is a salad that utilises God's kitchen, combining fruit and veg ('freggie' as we shall now know it) to make something a bit special. If you're in the mood for brain food, this is like throwing everything at the problem. Trust me, it's an amazing solution. Also, in a slightly trendy twist, this recipe uses raw turnip, which is cheap and tastes great in this. Go for it. It's the smart move.

• •

Ingredients

1 slice of bread
1 tbsp vegetable oil
50g kale, washed, stalks removed and thinly shredded
50g spinach, washed, stalks removed and thinly shredded
½ lemon or 1 tbsp lemon juice

1 eating apple, cored and cut into matchsticks
1 medium-sized turnip, grated
20g cheddar cheese, grated
salt and freshly ground black pepper

Method

1. Preheat the oven to 220°C (200°C fan)/gas 7.

2. Start making the croutons by cutting the slice of bread into 1cm cubes. Drizzle with the oil and bake for 5 minutes until they are golden brown. Remove and drain any excess oil.

3. Add the shredded kale and spinach to a bowl and squeeze over the lemon juice and 1 teaspoon of salt, massaging them into the leaves. Let it sit on the side for 2 minutes.

4. Add the apple, turnip, cheese and croutons and mix carefully before serving.

'Genius Greens' with chilli and bacon

Serves ④

Prep time: 5 mins

Cook time: 10 mins

I always thought spring greens were the epitome of boring, so I added a little life to them by stir-frying them with chilli and bacon. This will work with any cabbage or spinach.

· ·

Ingredients

2 tbsp olive oil

4 rashers of streaky bacon, chopped

1 red chilli, chopped

1 tsp garlic purée (or 2 chopped garlic cloves)

a bunch or bag of spring greens, tough stalks removed, leaves roughly sliced

salt and freshly ground black pepper

Vegetarian: leave out the bacon and add a splash of soy sauce just before serving.

Flavour tip: nuts or seeds toasted in the dry frying pan before you cook the bacon are delicious sprinkled over the top.

Method

1. Heat the oil in a large frying pan over a high heat. Add the bacon and fry for a few minutes until just starting to turn crisp and golden.

2. Add the chilli and garlic to the frying pan and stir for 1 minute. Add the spring greens and stir for about 5 minutes, shaking the pan to get them well mixed in with the bacon, until they are just starting to wilt – don't overcook them! Season with salt and pepper and serve.

Simple vegetable broth

Serves **4**

Prep time: 15 mins

Cook time: 20 mins

Take vegetable stock of this one-pot recipe. It's super-
quick, vegan friendly, and full of veggies to power the brain.
Unleash the inner boffin with this simple vegetable broth.
Deviating from the recipe to incorporate other veg is fine
too: try spinach, spring onions and courgettes.

• •

Ingredients

2 tbsp vegetable oil
½ red onion, thinly sliced
1 tsp garlic purée (or 2 chopped
    garlic cloves)
1 broccoli, cut into florets and the
    stalk thinly sliced
1 carrot, grated
¼ white cabbage, thinly sliced

2 tsp ground ginger
1 tsp dried chilli flakes
1 litre vegetable stock
50g dried spaghetti, broken into
    small pieces
4 tbsp frozen peas
salt and freshly ground black
    pepper

Flavour tip: add fresh or tinned tomatoes to this to turn it into more of a minestrone, plus sprinkle with parmesan to serve.

Method

1. Add the vegetable oil to a large saucepan with a lid and heat over a medium heat for 1 minute. Add the onion, garlic, broccoli stalks and carrot with a pinch of salt and cook for 3–5 minutes with the lid on, shaking the pan every so often, until they start to soften.

2. Add the cabbage along with the ginger and chilli flakes. Stir the mixture, put the lid back on and cook for another 2 minutes.

3. Add the vegetable stock and bring to the boil. Throw in the pasta and continue to cook for 6 minutes.

4. Add the broccoli florets and peas and cook for a further 3 minutes. Taste and adjust the seasoning with salt and pepper before serving.

'Fuse-lighting' fusilli tuna and broccoli pasta

Serves ❷

Prep time: 5 mins

Cook time: 12 mins

This recipe is so wonderfully basic that you can give your well-exercised brain a rest, whilst simultaneously lighting your mental fuse with a pasta recipe full of veggies.

• •

Ingredients

200g fusilli or your favourite pasta shape

½ broccoli, cut into florets

4 tbsp vegetable oil

½ red onion, finely diced

1 tin of tuna, drained

150g frozen peas

a generous glug of sweet chilli sauce

salt and freshly ground black pepper

Vegetarian: leave out the tuna and add sliced courgette to the pan with the onion, cooking until soft.

Method

1. Cook the pasta in a large saucepan of boiling water with a pinch of salt, according to the packet instructions. Five minutes before the pasta is ready, add the broccoli florets.

2. Meanwhile, heat 2 tablespoons of the vegetable oil in a large saucepan over medium heat. Fry the onion for 6 minutes or until translucent. Add the tuna, peas, sweet chilli sauce and 3–4 tablespoons water and bring up to just simmering.

3. Drain the pasta and broccoli in a colander and drizzle the remaining oil over, coating evenly (this will stop the pasta from sticking). Add to the saucepan and taste, then adjust the seasoning with salt and pepper.

The Academic Asparagus Omelette

'ASPARAGUS TIPS' TO IMPROVE YOUR GRADES
Although it makes your wee smell awful (beware), this is another veggie known to have incredible benefits to the brain and also (winner, winner) anti-ageing properties. Now, I'm happy to fully believe this because, trust me, university can age you badly. And if you're not feeling clever enough from all the brainy recipes and even brainier puns we've had so far, this omelette is 'a-spare-I-guess'...

Serves 1

Prep time: 5 mins
Cook time: 10 mins

I know I've made the name of this sound like a Harry Potter spell, however this IS magic. A quick-and-easy asparagus omelette that makes the most of asparagus when it's in season. Serve up this veggie brain buster in super-quick time to give you everything you need for a major library session.

. . . .

Ingredients

a few spears of asparagus
2–3 eggs
a knob of butter

a handful of grated cheddar or parmesan cheese
salt and freshly ground black pepper

Flavour tip: add any fresh herbs you have to the whisked eggs.

Method

1. Hold each asparagus spear at both ends and bend gently until it breaks. It will naturally split where the tough, woody part ends, and you can just throw these ends away.

2. Fill a medium-sized frying pan with water, bring to the boil and cook the asparagus for 4 minutes until just tender. Drain, slice in half lengthways and set aside.

3. Whisk the eggs and some salt and pepper with a fork.

4. Wipe out the frying pan and grab yourself a spatula, then put back on a low to medium heat and add the knob of butter.

5. When melted, pour in the egg and swirl to cover the base of the pan. Cook gently, tilting the pan slightly and pulling the egg as it sets from the edges into the pan's centre. When the omelette is set and browned on the bottom, but still slightly liquid on top, add the asparagus and cheese along the middle of the omelette and fold the two sides over it. Flip over so the seam is on the bottom and slide out of the pan on to your plate.

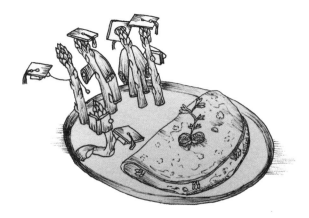

Chapter Three

FOOD FOR SPORT: FROM GIN TO THE GYM

EAT MY GOAL

NOODLES

HORNETS

HARDER
BETTER
PASTA
STRONGER

UNIVERSITY IS A GREAT PLACE TO GET INTO sport, at whatever level, and this chapter is designed to give you that extra boost if you go down that path. Whether that's a sports team or society, yoga classes, a shiny new gym membership or just getting in the odd casual jog.

I tried out at with the football team, but following a particularly heavy night out before our first game, and an 8–1 thumping (I scored, to be fair), I moved away from Sunday morning football. It was a short and not particularly beautiful career.

The nearest thing to sport I did otherwise (apart from Pub Golf) was to start DJing the Wednesday Athletic Union nights at a legendary local club called Jesters, a venue proud to have once been voted one of the worst clubs in the UK. There I saw many things that have scarred me. Every Wednesday night, the sport teams would descend upon this palace of dreams to compete in fast-paced drinking games. As a Fresher, you had to learn it all, fast. This was a night steeped in tradition. One of the oddest being that whenever the Baywatch theme song was played, everyone had to head to the dancefloor, en masse, and take off their clothes. From the DJ booth, this was a strangely magnificent sight to behold. Almost animalistic. I've never been travelling, really, but I imagine it's what it must be like to gaze in wonder at herds of buffalo, gazelles and elephants migrating across the Serengeti.

Wednesday AU nights would always end up with a 3 a.m. korma at local curry house, Manzils (big-up Tariq and everyone at Manzils – the things those poor guys had to deal with on Wednesday nights).

However, this isn't the chapter for 3 a.m. curry recipes. Instead, I've worked out a few meal suggestions that we hope will set you up in the best possible way for any sport trial, your next trip to the gym or, really, anything more athletic than taking your morning poo.

Enjoy – and listen out for the *Baywatch* drums …

Harder, Better, Pasta, Stronger: pasta bake with beetroot, broccoli and mozzarella

Serves

Prep time: less than 10 mins
Cook time: 35 mins

This purple pasta bake looks amazing and my flatmate, who was a rower, swore by this recipe. Everyone sporty I knew at Uni LOVED a blender. Honestly, they would blend all sorts. This recipe is one for you blenders out there… and the only cooking is for the pasta and broccoli. Packed full of healthy goodness.

· ·

Ingredients

300g dried penne pasta
1 broccoli, cut into small florets
300g cooked beetroot
1 tsp garlic purée (or 2 chopped
   garlic cloves)

½ tsp dried chilli flakes
125g mozzarella cheese, shredded
sea salt flakes

Method

1. Preheat the oven to 220°C (200°C fan)/gas 7.

2. Cook the pasta following the instructions on the packet.

3. Meanwhile, cook the broccoli florets in boiling water for 2 minutes.

4. To make the sauce, put the drained beetroot into a blender and add 3 tablespoons water, the garlic, chilli flakes and a good sprinkling of sea salt. Blend to a smooth paste.

5. Once the pasta is cooked, drain and put back into the pan. Pour in the beetroot sauce and cooked broccoli and mix through.

6. Tip out into an ovenproof dish and add shredded pieces of mozzarella on top. Cook in the oven for 20 minutes or until the top is golden brown.

Speedy salmon noodle broth

Serves ❶

Prep time: 5 mins

Cook time: less than 10 mins

This salmon noodle broth takes just minutes to cook in the microwave. But be careful – the microwave can bite back! If the salmon is spitting and you get it in the eye, you will look like a pirate. And that's not a strong look.

• •

Ingredients

500ml vegetable stock

1 nest of noodles

2 tbsp soy sauce

2 tbsp sweet chilli sauce

1 tsp dried chilli flakes

1 skinless and bone-free salmon
  fillet, diced

a handful of frozen peas

1 carrot, peeled and grated

sesame seeds

Vegetarian: swap the salmon for chopped frozen or fresh veg – broccoli, mushrooms, cauliflower and peppers all work well.

Flavour tip: zesting a lime into the broth at the start and finishing with the juice is a perfect way to lift this dish to heaven!

Method

1. Pour the stock into a bowl that can go in the microwave.

2. Add the noodles, soy sauce, sweet chilli sauce and chilli flakes. Cover with cling film, pierce with holes and cook for 3 minutes on full.

3. Add the diced salmon and cook for another 2 minutes. Add the peas and carrot and cook for 1 more minute.

4. Serve with a sprinkling of sesame seeds.

The 'Get Fit-ata Faster' frittata

Serves 4

Prep time: 10 mins
Cook time: 20 mins

Frittatas are the ultimate quick dinner and an excellent way to use up any leftover bits and pieces left lurking in the fridge at the end of the week, which I loved as anything I was thinking of throwing away would get thrown in ... within reason. If you are heavily into the gym, no doubt you enjoy smashing eggs, and this is a tasty way of cooking them up and can be eaten hot or cold (if you're the kind of wrong'un that might take this to the gym). Master this dish and never go hungry again.

. . . .

Ingredients

1 tbsp olive oil
1 onion, thinly sliced
1 red pepper, deseeded and chopped (or any veg you have in your fridge)

200g chorizo, skin removed and roughly chopped
a handful of frozen peas
6 eggs
50g parmesan, grated
sea salt and freshly ground black pepper

Vegetarian: replace the chorizo with leftover new potatoes, chopped and fried in the oil until golden.

Flavour tip: add some torn fresh basil or parsley in with the eggs or sprinkle a handful over the top to serve.

EAT SLEEP RAVE REHEAT

Method

1. Preheat the grill to high.

2. Heat the olive oil in large frying pan and fry the onion until soft. Add the red pepper and fry just until it softens, then turn up the heat a little, add the chorizo, and cook for a few minutes until it releases its red oil and goes slightly crispy. Finally, add the peas and cook until warmed through.

3. Lightly beat together the eggs, Parmesan and a good pinch of salt and pepper.

4. Pour the egg mixture into the frying pan over a low heat and cook just until it starts to set, shaking the pan to stop everything sticking to the bottom.

5. When the frittata is about three-quarters set, pop under the grill to quickly brown the top. Allow to cool a little before cutting into wedges to serve.

Vegan 'clean-and-jerk' baked bean burger

Serves 4

Prep time: 20 mins, plus 1 hour chilling

Cook time: 20 mins

One for you weightlifters out there! As much as I love a dirty burger, my obsession never helped me sculpt my body to its optimum capacity. Since watching *Game Changers* on Netflix, I've realised eating vegan would have helped me on that front. I'm hoping this recipe will enable you to achieve a better sporting legacy than me at uni.

. . . .

Ingredients

2 x 400g tins baked beans
100g breadcrumbs (from a packet or crumble up your own from stale bread)
150g jerk barbecue sauce or marinade
½ white cabbage, shredded

2 red onions, thinly sliced
2 carrots, peeled and grated
vegan mayo
4 burger buns
salt and freshly ground black pepper

Method

1. Preheat the grill to high.

1. Empty the tins of beans into a sieve and rinse under running water for 2 minutes, discarding the sauce. Drain well.

2. Place the beans into a bowl, add the breadcrumbs and jerk seasoning and crush with a fork. Shape into four even burger patties. Put in the fridge for an hour so the burger mix firms up.

3. In the meantime, make the coleslaw by adding the cabbage, red onion and carrot to a bowl. Bind with the vegan mayonnaise, season to your liking and set aside.

4. Once the patties have firmed up, place on a baking tray and grill on each side for 3 minutes until golden brown.

5. Lightly toast the burger buns. Build your burgers, starting with the burger patties and topping with a generous helping of coleslaw between the buns.

'Easy energy' berry and banana smoothie

Serves 1   Prep time: 5 mins

The key here is to use frozen berries, which you can keep in the freezer and use whenever you want! Makes it a ton cheaper too. This is a great healthy smoothie you can whizz up in seconds, full of fruit and fibre, which will give you the boost you need to tackle any sports trial.

Ingredients
150g frozen berries (any kind)
½ banana, roughly chopped
50ml natural yoghurt

100ml milk (any kind)
1 tbsp honey, or to taste

Method
1. Place all the ingredients into a blender and whizz until smooth. Add a little more milk if too thick, and extra honey if you like it sweet. Pour into a tall glass and enjoy.

The chocolate, banana and avocado 'Triathlon Shake'

Serves ❶ (a generous glass)   🖐 Prep time: 5 mins

I promise you that this is less of an ordeal than a triathlon, however, like its namesake, it does include three distinct elements. I've got a confession to make. I was dead against this idea until my friend made me this shake and I didn't even notice it contained avocado. It's a great way of sneaking avocado into what is essentially a delicious milkshake. Another one for the blenders, this will give you a much-needed boost whilst you train. You can swap the cocoa powder, yoghurt, honey and milk for just chocolate milk to make this a three-ingredient recipe – a bit less healthy though!

• •

Ingredients
½ ripe avocado

½ ripe banana, chopped (frozen if you want the shake to be ice cold)

2 tbsp cocoa or cacao powder

4 tbsp natural yoghurt

200ml milk (any kind)

1 tbsp honey, to taste

a tiny pinch of salt

Method
1. Place all the ingredients into a blender and whizz until smooth. Add a little more milk if too thick, and extra honey if you like it sweet. Pour into a tall glass and enjoy.

'Veteran' banana and peanut butter pancakes

Serves ②

Prep time: 10 mins

Cook time: 10–15 mins

Although these pancakes taste awesome, I doubt many people would like me describe the overripe bananas you could use as 'old'. So, rather, I'm going to borrow a sporting reference here and call the bananas 'veterans' – they were world class in their day, but still can produce a magical performance on their night. In this case, mixed up with peanut butter to form a world-beating double act.

• •

Ingredients

2 large eggs
80g smooth peanut butter
200g plain flour
2 tsp baking powder

50ml semi-skimmed milk (milk
    alternatives also work)
3 over-ripe/blackened bananas
a squeeze of honey
vegetable oil, for frying

Method

1. Preheat the oven to 120°C (100°C fan)/gas 1/2.

2. Place all the ingredients, except one banana, the honey and oil, into a blender and blend until smooth.

3. Heat a frying pan over medium to high heat. Add 1 tablespoon of the oil and heat up for 1 minute. Spoon about 3 tablespoons of the mix into the pan to make an American-style pancake, then drop in more of the mix – a normal-sized pan will take about three pancakes at a time. When making pancakes, imagine the frying pan is a clock face: drop the first one at '12:00' and spoon the mix clockwise. This way you always know which one was put in the pan first and which one to turn! Fry the pancakes for 1 minute, then turn over and cook them on the other side.

4. Once cooked, place on an ovenproof dish and put in the oven to keep warm. Repeat the process until you have no mix left.

5. Stack the pancakes high and top with a sliced banana and a squeeze of honey.

Pesto chicken with fridge-raider 'bulging muscles' salad

Serves 4

Prep time: 20 mins, plus 10 minutes chilling

Cook time: 20 mins

I had this packet of something called 'bulgur' in the cupboard for months on end with no idea what the hell it was. I took the plunge and used it. Revelation! Working on the strong assumption that 'bulgur salad' equals 'bulging muscles', this is a healthy recipe that makes you feel great. Top with tender chicken skewers for a high-protein, low-calorie meal. By the way, you do need skewers for this. Soak wooden skewers in water ahead of time to stop them burning.

· ·

Ingredients

200g bulgur wheat
2 tbsp paprika
1 small jar of basil pesto
400g chicken breast, diced into 2cm cubes
1 small tin sweetcorn
1 small tin chickpeas
1 small packet of precooked green lentils
½ red onion, diced

½ cucumber, split in half, deseeded and diced
handful of spinach, shredded
2 tbsp natural yoghurt
5 cherry tomatoes, halved or quartered
salt and freshly ground black pepper

Vegetarian: substitute the chicken for courgette and yellow peppers.

Flavour tip: finish the dish with a scattering of pomegranate seeds and fresh basil.

Method

1. Preheat the oven to 220°C (200°C fan)/gas 7.

2. Begin by preparing the salad. Add the bulgur wheat to a pan, covering it with cold water, then add the paprika. Bring to the boil, reduce the heat and simmer for 8 minutes. Cover with a lid and set aside to cool to room temperature.

3. In a bowl, stir the pesto into the chicken and place in the refrigerator for 10 minutes. Thread onto eight skewers and bake in the oven for 20 minutes, turning halfway through.

4. Meanwhile, rinse the sweetcorn and chickpeas in a colander under running water for 2 minutes. Drain well.

5. Place the cooked bulgur wheat into a serving bowl along with the sweetcorn, chickpeas and lentils and mix well. Add the red onion, cucumber and spinach and season to your liking.

6. Place the skewers on top of the salad and spoon over a dollop of yoghurt and a few cherry tomatoes.

Chapter Four

SLOW COOK AND CHILL

SLOW COOK AND CHILL

BEEF STOCK

CHICKEN STOCK

VEG STOCK

S

P

LAGER

ITS EASY TO GET INTO A LAZY RUT OF EATING the same old junk, which actually just ends up making you feel more sluggish and time-poor. I was living all the stereotypes, buying myself the cheapest chicken nuggets, fish fingers and potato waffles I could find. The priority was saving money for nights out, and food strictly came second.

What I eventually learned, though, is that setting aside time to make proper dinners will make you feel more organised, more lively and more motivated. Plus, if you can get in a few veggies, you always will feel better for it.

But there's a right way and a wrong way to do this. I'll explain...

Two experiments define my life at that moment, and both pissed my poor housemates off mightily. The first arose when I was in a rush to make cheese on toast as a little midnight snack. The big idea I had was to turn the toaster on its side to act like a grill. Never try it. The flames went up, the fire alarm went off, and the entire H Block of Glen Eyre Halls of Residence was completely evacuated.

The next era-defining culinary experiment happened

soon after I began making pasta for the first time. I'd been making it in a pan for a few weeks now and I thought, just this once, it might be a clever idea to try adding it straight to the kettle, and boiling it in there. What a great hack, I thought! What a time-saver! *Never try it.* The kettle made a horrendous squealing noise, which preceded all the electrics in our kitchen cutting out. It goes without saying my housemates weren't the biggest fans of my chef skills at this point.

So, anyway, the moral of the story is: quick hacks aren't always best. Sometimes, it's worth doing it right and taking your time. We are bringing you a chapter here that gives you amazing meals, often with minimal effort, minimal washing-up and generally involving no fire-alarm disasters. This is a chapter where your weapon is a piece of equipment called a slow cooker. You can pick these up pretty cheaply, and they are an absolute game changer. You can make so much more than just stews in a slow cooker, as this chapter will show. You can even do drinks in it for parties, or mulled wine on Bonfire Night. They're also ideal for batch cooking: leave it for hours and just let it do its thing. (N.B. don't worry if you really can't afford a slow cooker: we've also included an oven alternative method!)

So, whether you trying to win over your housemates after a late-night fire alarm, or you've made it to date three and are looking to 'Netflix and Slow Cook', get yourself this bit of kit and watch your life change.

The Lamb and Chickpea Degree Tagine

Serves ④

Prep time: 30 mins

Cook time: 4 hours high/
8 hours low

This recipe is as exotic as it got for me! Chickpeas are healthy, cheap and last forever. But the addition of the more pricey lamb (if desired) takes this tagine to the next level. This is an amazing meal, which comes into its own once Freshers' Week is done and winter starts to roll in. Enjoy!

• •

Ingredients

2 tbsp vegetable oil

8 boneless lamb breast/leg steaks

1 onion, chopped

3 large carrots, cut into big cubes

1 tbsp ras-el-hanout

2 tsp ground cumin

1 tsp mild chilli powder

400g tin chickpeas, rinsed and
drained

1 tbsp tomato purée

750ml lamb or chicken stock (or
veg stock if you're on a veg ting)

1 sweet potato, peeled and cut into
cubes

50g dried apricots, sliced

1 tsp honey

2 tbsp dried mixed herbs

salt and freshly ground black
pepper

couscous or rice, to serve

Vegetarian: remove the lamb steaks and add 200g of courgette, cut into chunky pieces.

No slow cooker, no problem: follow the instructions below, but instead of tipping it into the slow cooker, transfer everything into an ovenproof dish and cook in a preheated oven at 120°C (100°C fan)/gas 1/2 for 3 hours.

EAT SLEEP RAVE REHEAT

Method

1. Heat the oil in a frying pan, add the lamb breast steaks and fry over a high heat until they are seared and golden brown on each side. Remove and set aside on a plate.

2. Fry the onion in the same frying pan (don't wash it, you want all that flavour) for 5 minutes. Add the carrot, spices and chickpeas and fry for another 2 minutes.

3. Stir in the tomato purée and cook for 1 minute. Add the stock and bring to the boil, then tip everything into the slow cooker.

4. Add the sweet potato, dried apricots, honey and mixed herbs. Cook on low for 8 hours or high for 4 hours. Taste and season before serving with couscous or rice.

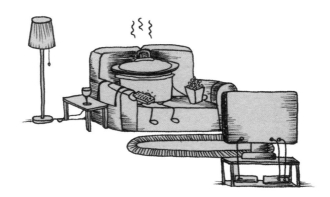

'Out on the pull' pork baps

Serves 4

Prep time: 20 mins

Cook time: 8–10 hours high/
4–5 hours low

Pulled pork made in a slow cooker has to be one of the easiest recipes ever! Bung it all in, sit back, and in a few hours' time you'll be tucking into tender, rich, delicious pork. Pile this slow-cooked, melt-in-the-mouth pork onto bread rolls for the ultimate sandwich.

. . . .

Ingredients

400g tin baked beans
3 tbsp tomato purée
1 tsp hot smoked paprika
1 tsp hot chilli powder
1 tsp dried chilli flakes
5 tbsp orange juice
1 onion, thinly sliced

4 pork shoulder steaks
salt and freshly ground black
    pepper
toasted buns or rolls, to serve
home-made coleslaw (from the
    vegan 'clean-and-jerk' baked
    bean burger recipe on page 74),
    to serve

Vegetarian: substituting the pork for 1 packet of quorn chicken pieces also works an absolute treat…just no need to shred them!

Flavour tip: score some more chef points by showcasing your condiment stash: my go-to would be sriracha sauce! Adding the zest of a lime at the beginning and finishing with the juice will also give you the edge.

No slow cooker, no problem: follow the instructions below, but instead of tipping it into the slow cooker, transfer everything into an ovenproof dish and cook in a preheated oven at 120°C (100°C fan)/gas 1/2 for 3 hours.

Method

1. Put the baked beans, tomato purée, spices, orange juice and onion into a slow cooker with some freshly ground black pepper. Add 5 tablespoons of cold water and stir well.

2. Add the pork steaks to the slow cooker and turn several times in the sauce until well coated. Cover and cook on low for 8–10 hours or high for 4–5 hours until the pork is very tender.

3. Remove the pork, shred with two forks, and put back into the mix, stirring well. Taste and season, then serve the pulled pork mix in toasted buns or rolls with the coleslaw.

'C'est la vie' Irish stew

Serves ④

Prep time: 20 mins

Cook time: 4 hours high/
8 hours low

So authentic you will be singing B*Witched on loop…
(another way to wind up any flatmates that are starting to
get on your nerves a bit). To be sure, to be sure, cuts of lamb
are super flavoursome when slow cooked. Using cheaper
cuts will save money, without scrimping on flavour! This
stew also contains pearl barley, another cheap ingredient
that can be added to any slow-cooked dish to make it more
filling. For housemates that are Irish, or those with tentative
links to Ireland (pretty much everyone on St Patrick's Day),
this will be the ultimate Irish stew.

· ·

Ingredients

2 tbsp vegetable oil

100g smoked streaky bacon, cut
into strips

500g cheap stewing lamb (the
cheapest cuts are found at a
butcher's – just ask!), diced

2 tbsp plain flour

2 onions, thickly sliced

a handful of chantenay carrots (or
2 normal ones, cut into cubes)

2 celery sticks, sliced

4 medium potatoes, peeled and cut
into big cubes

2 tsp dried thyme or 4 sprigs of
fresh thyme

2 bay leaves

2 tbsp tomato purée

1 can of Guinness (or any stout)

500ml lamb or chicken stock (or
veg stock if you're on a veg ting)

100g pearl barley

salt and freshly ground black
pepper

EAT SLEEP RAVE REHEAT

Vegetarian: swapping out the lamb for meaty mushrooms works well.

Flavour tip: for extra greens, add some chunks of leek in with the pearl barley or serve with cabbage cooked in a frying pan with a couple of tablespoons of water and butter.

No slow cooker, no problem: follow the instructions below, but instead of tipping it into the slow cooker, transfer everything (including the pearl barley) into a casserole dish and cook over a low heat for 2 hours until the lamb is tender.

Method

1. Add the bacon to a frying pan with the oil and cook until golden brown, then put into the slow cooker. Keep the fat in the pan and turn the heat up to medium.

2. Once the pan is hot, add the cubes of lamb and colour on all sides to golden brown. Add the flour and continuously stir until the flour turns a brownish colour. Transfer to the slow cooker.

3. Add the onion, carrots, celery, potato, thyme, bay leaves, tomato purée, stout and stock to the slow cooker. Cover and cook on low for 6 hours or high for 3 hours.

4. Stir in the pearl barley and cook on low for 2 hours or high for 1 hour more until the pearl barley is tender. Taste and season before serving.

Veggie lasagne

Serves ④

Prep time: 30 mins,
Cook time: 2.5 hours high /
5 hours low

Okay, I admit this perhaps isn't how mama made it, but it tastes wonderful. Doing this in one pot over a bit of time makes the veggies taste amazing. In truth, lasagne can take up a lot of kitchen space to create, and can be incredibly time consuming, but this recipe solves those issues using your new mate – the slow cooker. This hearty vegetable lasagne will be loved by vegetarians and meat-eaters alike; it's the ultimate comfort food. Serve with a green salad and crusty bread if you have any kicking around.

• •

Ingredients

1 tbsp vegetable oil

2 red onions, sliced

1 tbsp garlic purée (or 2 chopped garlic cloves)

2 peppers (any colour), deseeded and sliced

3 courgettes, sliced

400g tin chopped tomatoes

1 tsp dried thyme or organo

1 vegetable stock cube

1 aubergine, sliced lengthways into 1cm slices

8 dried sheets of lasagne sheets

1 ball of mozzarella, drained and sliced

salt and freshly ground black pepper

fresh basil leaves, to garnish (if you have them)

Flavour tip: fancy a bit of garlic bread with this? Before putting it in the oven, sprinkle a few dashes of hot sauce over the bread!

No slow cooker, no problem: follow the instructions below, but instead of layering it in a slow cooker, just layer it into an ovenproof dish and bake in a preheated oven at 160°C (140°C fan)/gas 2 for 30 to 45 minutes.

Method

1. Heat the oil in a large frying pan. Add the onion and garlic and fry for 6 minutes until they have softened but are not browned. Add the peppers and courgette and cook for 3 minutes more.

2. Add the chopped tomatoes, dried thyme or oregano and crumble in the stock cube. Bring to the boil and simmer for 5 minutes, then taste and season.

3. Place half the aubergine slices on the base of the slow cooker and cover with half the lasagne. Add half the vegetable mix, followed by the remaining aubergine slices, then the remaining lasagne sheets. Top the lasagne sheets with the remaining vegetable mix.

4. Cover and cook on low for 5 hours or high for 2 ½ hours until the pasta is cooked through. Turn off the slow cooker, dot the slices of mozzarella over the top, cover and leave for 10 minutes to allow the cheese to melt. Garnish with some fresh basil leaves (if you have some) and serve.

'Cock in a van'

Serves ④

Prep time: 30 mins,

Cook time: 3 hours high/
6 hours low

Slow-cooked 'coq au vin' or, to us students, 'chicken and wine' – you will hear the same joke from your housemates when you announce that you are making this, so I thought you might just as well make it the name of the recipe. The great thing about this one is that the end result genuinely made me look like I was a top-class chef. Chicken tender and falling off the bone with the crispy bacon and slightly charred shrooms! See what I mean. Serve with good crusty bread or mashed potatoes.

. . . .

Ingredients

2 tbsp vegetable oil

100g smoked streaky bacon, cut into strips

8 chicken thighs and drumsticks

300g whole shallots, peeled

2 carrots, peeled and cut into big cubes

1 tsp garlic purée (2 chopped garlic cloves)

1 celery stick, thickly sliced

1 tbsp tomato purée

2 tbsp plain flour

½ bottle of red wine

150ml chicken stock

1 tsp dried thyme

1 bay leaf

200g button mushroom, halved

salt and freshly ground black pepper

Vegetarian: swapping in soya-based *faux* chicken works just as well.

Flavour tip: whacking a great dollop of wholegrain mustard and a generous sprinkling of parsley in at the end of the cook earn this dish the *ooh la la* from everyone!

No slow cooker, no problem: follow the instructions below, but instead of tipping it into the slow cooker, transfer everything into an ovenproof dish and cook in a preheated oven at 120°C (100°C fan)/gas 1/2 for 1 ½ hours.

Method

1. Add the bacon to a frying pan with 1 tablespoon of the oil and cook until golden brown, then put into the slow cooker. Keep the fat in the pan and turn the heat up.

2. Once the pan is hot, add the chicken thighs and drumsticks and colour on both sides to golden brown. Remove and put into the slow cooker. Using the same pan, cook the shallots, carrots, garlic, celery and tomato purée for 2 minutes over a high heat. Add the flour and continuously stir until the flour turns a brownish colour.

3. Add the red wine and reduce by two-thirds – it will resemble a bit of a gluey mess, but trust me, this is fine! Add the stock and bring to the boil. Place everything into the slow cooker with the dried thyme and bay leaf and stir well.

4. Cover with the lid then cook on high for 3 hours or low for 6 hours, until the chicken is very tender.

5. Just before serving, heat the remaining oil in a frying pan and fry the mushrooms over a high heat. Scatter over the chicken, taste and season, then serve.

'Hide the sausage' casserole

Serves ④

🖐 Prep time: 15 mins

📅 Cook time: 3 hours high/
6 hours low

Fennel and pork are a lovely combination in this slow-cooker stew. I know, I know, do you REALLY need fennel? I've always thought this, but the combo really works. You don't need anything with this, but if you do fancy something on the side, try some crusty bread to mop up the sauce or boiled baby potatoes. Tastes so good you'll have to hide this in the freezer once cooked or people will help themselves. Hence 'hide the sausage casserole' – another perfect recipe to 'slow cook and chill' with ;)

· ·

Ingredients

8 pork sausages,
2 tbsp vegetable oil
1 fennel bulb, sliced
1 red onion, finely chopped
1 carrot, roughly chopped
1 tsp mild chilli powder
1 tsp paprika

1 tsp ground cumin
200ml chicken stock
400g tin of beans (whatever's in
your cupboard – mixed, butter,
borlotti, cannellini – even baked!)
salt and freshly ground black
pepper

Vegetarian: swapping out the sausages for non-meat alternatives will be just as good.

Flavour tip: upgrading to smoked paprika and finishing with toasted fennel seeds is all you need to take this dish to new heights.

No slow cooker, no problem: follow the instructions below, but instead of tipping it into the slow cooker, transfer everything into an ovenproof dish and bake in a preheated oven at 160°C (140°C fan)/gas 2 for 30 minutes.

Method
1. Begin by colouring the sausages in a frying pan with the oil over a high heat until they are browned all over. Once browned, add to the slow cooker.

2. Add the vegetables, spices, stock and baked beans over the top and stir well.

3. Cover with the lid and cook on low for 6 hours or high for 3 hours. Taste and season before serving.

Slow-cooker drunken beef bourguignon

Serves ④

🥄 Prep time: 30 mins

📅 Cook time: 3 hours high/
6 hours low

This recipe is dreamy slow-cooker magic. The slow cooker enables you to easily make more, so you can freeze and do the same for your next serving. And it's perfect for a big gathering, or as a date night dish – I find that conversation flows thanks to the whole bottle of red wine used to cook this deliciously rich beef stew. (A bonus: the longer the wine infuses, the better effect you get!)

....

Ingredients

1 bottle of red wine

1kg braising steak, cut into small pieces

4 tbsp vegetable oil

3 large onions, chopped

2 celery sticks, chopped

2 carrots, peeled and chopped

100g smoked streaky bacon, cut into strips

300g button mushrooms, halved

2 bay leaves

2 tbsp dried thyme

2 tbsp tomato purée

3 tbsp plain flour

1 beef stock cube

salt and freshly ground black pepper

Flavour tip: make the stock super-beefy by adding 1 tbsp marmite.

No slow cooker, no problem: follow the instructions below, but instead of tipping it into the slow cooker, transfer everything into an ovenproof dish and bake in a preheated oven at 160°C (140°C fan)/gas 2 for 2 hours.

Method
1. The day before you wish to make this, place the beef in a large bowl or container and pour over the red wine. Marinate in the fridge for 8 hours.

2. Heat half the oil in a large frying pan. Remove the meat from the wine (saving the wine for later), pat dry and fry the beef chunks for 3 minutes in batches until browned all over. Scoop out each batch with a slotted spoon and transfer to a plate. Continue this process until all the meat has been browned.

3. Heat up the remaining oil in the frying pan and add the onion, celery, carrot and bacon and fry for 7–8 minutes until just starting to brown. Add the mushrooms and cook until browned.

4. Add the herbs, tomato purée and flour and cook for another 2 minutes. Then add the wine (from the marinade) and reduce the sauce by two-thirds. Crumble the stock cube into the stew, bring to the boil, then pour into the slow cooker and cover with a lid.

5. Cook on high for 3 hours or low for 6 hours until the meat is falling apart, but not mushy. Taste and season before serving..

Chapter Five

SKINT AS A FLINT

A S EVERYONE KNOWS, A LARGE PART OF UNI LIFE
is doing the best you can to keep costs down. You're
paying for books, accommodation and a few nights out,
using what's left of your student loan after tuition is paid,
plus the spare change you find down the back of the sofa.
You find everyone is either growing their hair out or
shaving it off, you wear jumpers around the house to keep
the heating bill down, and people become really territorial
about toilet roll.

Generally speaking, our house was quite savvy when
it came to saving money. We got a good deal on moving
into a converted old person's home. As soon as we looked
around, we knew it was perfect. It still had bars on the walls,
which would be ideal for when we were a bit wobbly after
a night out. We economised in other ways, too. We'd make
home-made decorations for birthdays and we always had
inventive ways of doing cheap fancy dress (it's amazing
how many themes can be covered with a check shirt or
some building overalls). For my twenty-first birthday, my
housemates bought an inflatable paddling pool shaped

like a train, which we put in the living room. A genius move, which saved on buying in loads of drinks and, importantly, cups. Everyone could just drink straight from the pool from straws. We emptied everything we had into it and, as people arrived, they would contribute whatever they had. All was fine until someone got a bit carried away and decided to go for a semi-naked swim, which naturally put everyone off what was essentially the world's largest fishbowl. It was a lot like Augustus Gloop spooning the chocolate river into his mouth – and one of my very unhappy housemates went full Willy Wonka on the situation.

Needless to say, this was also a time in my life when I was well-placed for a bit more bargain-basement experimentation in the kitchen. But eating really cheap, although important, taught me some valuable lessons. I used to buy mutton pellets that could be thrown straight into the frying pan. It was about £1 for a kilo of the stuff, but it was nasty.

But there is no good reason for you to live like this when the chips are down and it's 'breadline time' – and in this chapter, I want to give you a load of recipes that you can cook when you're down to your last few quid, and a few simple ingredients in the back of the cupboard.

Good luck – enjoy these simple ideas, none of which involve drinking around a naked third year with a straw or using frozen mutton pellets!

Mac 'n' cheese

Serves ④

🖐 Prep time: 10 mins

🗓 Cook time: 30–40 mins

This is a *grate, easy-cheesy* way to make a mac 'n' cheese. You may find the timings can *Brie* a bit different among ovens, but the most important thing you can *fon-do* is not to let the pasta overcook and turn to mush. TOP TIP: you can use mozzarella instead but it's important to use ready-grated *mozzarella ella ella eh eh eh* for this recipe for a really *Gouda* smooth sauce, otherwise you'll end up with a blobby mess! *Nacho* what you want.

• •

Ingredients

400g macaroni (or you can use any other dried pasta shapes)
60g butter
60g plain flour
850ml cold milk

200g Cheddar cheese, roughly grated (or use up any scraps of cheese you have in the back of your fridge)
salt and freshly ground black pepper

Flavour tip: sprinkling some breadcrumbs over before baking is the one – or scatter with crispy bacon.

Method

1. Preheat the oven 180°C (160°C fan)/gas 4.

2. Cook the macaroni in a large saucepan of boiling water with a pinch of salt, according to the packet instructions.

3. Meanwhile, make the cheese sauce by putting the butter, flour and milk into a large saucepan and setting over a low heat. Bring up to the boil slowly, stirring all the time with a wooden spoon or a whisk. Once it has almost come up to the boil, the sauce will begin to thicken. Turn down the heat to low and let it cook for another 5 minutes, stirring occasionally.

4. Add 150g of the cheese and stir until it melts in, then season well with salt and pepper.

5. Drain the macaroni and add to an ovenproof dish. Pour in the cheese sauce, sprinkle over the remaining cheese and bake in the oven for 20–30 minutes until golden.

Cheesy meatball sub

Serves ④

Prep time: 20 mins
Cook time: 40 mins

Having this recipe in this book is, for me, redemption. I lived off meatball subs for a time (from the obvious chain store) as I lived opposite one of them in my second year. Sometimes I'd eat them twice a day. And at night, the forfeit for losing a game of Beer Pong was to do naked dashes to and from the store. The beauty of this particular sub is you can choose however many inches you'd like. Not just 6 inches, not just a 'foot-long'. If you want 7 or 8 inches, well, you go have 7 or 8 inches! This is how I liked it. And if you're like me, go MASSIVE on the cheese.

Ingredients

3 tbsp olive oil
1 onion, finely diced
1 tsp garlic purée (or 2 chopped garlic cloves)
400g–500g beef mince
½ 400g tin chopped tomatoes

1 tsp dried oregano
a pinch of dried chilli flakes (optional)
4 sub rolls, split
4 handfuls of grated mozzarella or Cheddar cheese

Vegetarian: use Quorn mince instead of the beef.

Flavour tip: add fresh basil or rocket when you sandwich the subs together.

Method

1. Heat a frying pan over a medium heat. Pour in 2 tablespoons of the oil and, once hot, add the onion and garlic and cook for 5–7 minutes until the onion is soft and translucent.

2. Remove from the heat and spoon out the onion mix. Put half into a bowl with the beef mince and some salt and pepper. Mix together well, then divide the mixture into small balls with your hands.

3. Put the pan back on the heat, add another tablespoon of oil and fry the meatballs until well browned. Tip back in the remaining onion mix, the tomatoes, oregano, chilli flakes, if using, and some salt and pepper and cook for about 15 minutes until the sauce has reduced a bit.

4. Preheat the grill to high and line the grill rack with foil. Lightly toast the rolls, then remove the bases and pile up with the meatballs while you scatter the cheese over the tops and toast until hot and bubbling. Put the sandwich together and eat immediately.

Fiery spaghetti alla puttanesca

Serves ❷

Prep time: 5 mins
Cook time: 12 mins

This dish is a stone-cold Italian staple. Supposedly popularised in Naples around the time of the Second World War, the recipe has a 'colourful' history that you can Google for yourselves! Whether or not the stories about this dish are true, it's certainly quick enough to whip up between activities in your busy student life – and, once you have the staple ingredients in your store cupboard, the unit cost per meal is about a pound, if not less. And a bonus point: the salty, robust flavours of this delicious meal will actually bring out the best in that cheap, ragged wine you've not been wanting to drink!

Ingredients

1 tbsp olive oil
enough spaghetti for two
½ tin anchovy fillets, finely diced
1 tsp dried chilli flakes
½ tsp garlic purée (or 1 finely chopped garlic clove)
400g tin chopped tomatoes

1 tbsp sliced black olives from a jar
1 tbsp capers, plus 1 tbsp brine water from the jar
salt and freshly ground black pepper
Parmesan shavings, to serve

Flavour tip: ½ teaspoon dried oregano and a squeeze of lemon would add another layer of flavour to a dish already bursting with character.

Method

1. Simultaneously bring a large saucepan of salted water up to the boil for the spaghetti, whilst warming the olive oil in a second saucepan on a medium to low heat. Once the oil is coating the pan and the water is boiling, throw the diced anchovies and chilli flakes into the oil and the spaghetti into the water to cook according to the packet instructions.

2. Sauté the anchovies and chilli flakes for 1 minute and then add the garlic and sauté together for another 2 minutes, or until the anchovies begin to really soften, which will produce a lovely warm flavour in the final dish.

3. Add the chopped tomatoes to the anchovy mix, stir up, then throw in the black olives and capers, being sure to add a splash of the brine water from the caper jar. Easy and delicious bonus flavouring!

4. Allow the sauce mixture to gently bubble on a low-ish heat, stirring occasionally, until the spaghetti is ready. At this stage, the sauce should be fragrant and piping hot.

5. Drain the spaghetti (keeping just a tiny splash of the water to add back), then throw in the sauce and mix together. Add salt and pepper to taste (you won't need much, if any) and top with Parmesan shavings. Enjoy whilst hot!

'Gourmet Beans à la Toast'

Serves ❷

Prep time: less than 10 mins

Cook time: 15 mins

This is one of my favourite recipes as you take the most stereotypically 'student' meal and turn it into something genuinely a bit gourmet. Seriously, you could serve this up on a date. Here's the thing: everyone loves beans on toast, but it has a rap for being the lazy option. Serve this up with pride, give it the fanciest name you can think of, maybe light a candle or two, and enjoy.

•••

Ingredients

4 tbsp vegetable oil

½ red onion, finely chopped

1 tsp garlic purée (or 2 chopped garlic cloves)

1 tbsp dried chilli flakes

1 tsp paprika

2 tbsp tomato purée

½ 400g tin cannellini beans, rinsed and drained

½ 400g tin blackeye beans, rinsed and drained

½ 400g tin red kidney beans, rinsed and drained

1 tin chopped tomatoes

a good squirt of tomato ketchup

buttered toast and a fried egg or grated cheese on top, to serve

Flavour tip: adding a handful of freshly chopped parsley to the beans and a dash of Tabasco over the fried eggs are well worth it. Sourdough toast is the on-trend option for bread here, too.

Method

1. Heat a saucepan over a medium heat and add half of the oil. Add the onion and cook for 5 minutes. Add the garlic, chilli flakes and paprika and cook for 1 minute until everything has softened.

2. Add the tomato purée and cook, whilst continuously stirring, for 2 minutes. Add all the beans and stir in the chopped tomatoes with 100ml water.

3. Bring to the boil and simmer until the mixture is a rich, paste-like texture. Squirt in a good amount of tomato ketchup for a little acidity.

4. Serve on top of buttered toast, topped with a fried egg or grated cheese.

Easy-cheesy quesadillas

Serves 2

Prep time: 10 mins,

Cook time: 15 mins

Super easy, cheap and quick to make, quesadillas are what you need when you're so hungry you're eyeing up just nailing whatever tinned food you have in the back of the cupboard. You've probably got all the ingredients for these quesadillas in your cupboard and fridge right now. It's a super-simple, back-pocket, 100 per cent customisable easy dinner recipe that was always a winner in our halls. And as a bonus, these quesadillas also freeze really well, something I only learnt a few years later. So if you make a big batch today, you can refrigerate or freeze the leftovers for another easy meal later in the week.

Ingredients

75g chorizo ring, cut into small cubes (skin removed, if you want)

a generous splash of sriracha sauce

4 tbsp sour cream

1 tbsp mayo

4 flour tortillas

4 large handfuls of grated Cheddar cheese

4 spring onions, thinly sliced

Guacamole (see page 48) (optional)

Vegetarian: leave out the chorizo and replace with chopped tomato, chilli and fresh coriander.

Flavour tip: experiment – you need the cheese for gooeyness, but almost anything else goes! Leftover roast chicken, tomato salsa, cooked or refried beans, veg or cooked sweet potato.

Method
1. Heat a large frying pan over a medium heat and cook the chorizo until just starting to crisp. Remove from the pan and wipe the pan clean with a piece of paper towel. Reheat the pan.

1. Make the sriracha dip by mixing together the sriracha, sour cream and mayo.

2. Lay a tortilla on the dry frying pan and sprinkle over half the cheese, spring onions and chorizo. Place another tortilla on top and push down.

3. Cook the quesadilla for 2–3 minutes over a medium heat to allow time for the cheese to melt and the bottom to turn golden. Use a spatula to press the quesadilla down while it cooks to help heat the filling. Flip and cook the other side until that is golden too. Repeat with the remaining ingredients.

4. Use kitchen scissors or a sharp knife to divide the quesadillas into eighths. Serve with the sriracha dip and guacamole.

'Friday night, do it right' chicken curry

Serves 4

Prep time: 15 mins

Cook time: 30 mins

Do me a favour. Scan this one, print it off, fold it up and keep it in your wallet or your purse. It lives there now. You'll thank me next time you reach into it to stump up for that lazy Friday night takeaway that'll set you back £10 or more. For absolutely minimal effort (and for the budget expense of the mini chicken breast fillets we suggest in this recipe) you can instead make yourself a Friday night curry that's twice as nice at a quarter of the price. Result.

Ingredients

4 tbsp vegetable oil

I large onion, finely chopped

1 tsp garlic purée (or 2 chopped garlic cloves)

1 thumb-size piece of fresh ginger, peeled and finely chopped

4–6 tbsp tikka masala paste (use more if you like it hot)

400g pack of chicken breast mini fillets, chopped into chunks

400g tin chopped tomatoes

1 small pot of cream (double or single – whatever you've got)

4 tbsp natural yoghurt (optional)

a handful of fresh coriander

salt

300g rice, to serve (see tip)

mango chutney, naan and/or poppadoms, to serve

Vegetarian: substitute the chicken for small chunks of sweet potato and aubergine.

Flavour tip: whip up a quick cooling raita with the rest of the yoghurt. Spoon some into a small bowl, then break open a garlic clove with the back of a knife, add to the yoghurt with a sprinkle of salt and set aside while you make the curry. Just before serving, remove the garlic and stir in a couple of tablespoons of finely chopped cucumber.

Method

1. Begin to prepare the curry by heating the oil in a large saucepan and frying the onion for 8–9 minutes until it is soft and starting to brown. Add the garlic and ginger and carry on cooking for another few minutes.

2. Stir in the masala paste and fry for 1 minute. Add the chicken, turn up the heat and cook for 8 minutes, stirring continuously in the sauce.

3. Add the tomatoes, then fill the tomato tin half way up with water and add that too. Turn down the heat and simmer for 15 minutes, stirring occasionally.

4. Meanwhile, cook the rice in a separate saucepan.

5. Once the sauce has thickened, stir in the cream and yoghurt and cook just until warmed through. Taste and season as needed and scatter over loads of coriander. Serve the curry with the cooked rice, mango chutney, naan or poppadoms.

Leftover toasties

The humble toastie – anyone can make these. If you're flicking through this book because you're hungry and you've landed on this page, these are the easiest of things to make. I'm listing a few of these as they are the loves of my life. Here are some of my favourites…

The Full English

Makes **1**

🖐 Prep time: 5 mins

📅 Cook time: 15 mins

For when you're feeling fragile.

• •

Ingredients

2 rashers of bacon

1 egg

a few sliced mushrooms

2 slices of bread

soft butter

1 tomato, sliced

Method

1. Fry the bacon, egg and mushrooms in a frying pan until the bacon is crisp, then set aside.

2. Butter the bread slices on one side. Add one slice of bread, butter side down, to the frying pan. Pile up the tomato slices, bacon, egg and mushrooms. Top with the other slice, buttered-side up.

3. Cook the toastie for 2–3 minutes over a medium heat until the bottom turns golden and crispy. Flip and cook the other side until that is toasted too. Eat immediately, straight from the pan.

The Bangin' Bolognese Toastie

Makes **1**

Prep time: 5 mins

Cook time: 10 mins

A textbook hangover throw-together.

• •

Ingredients

2 slices of bread

soft butter

4 tbsp leftover Bolognese sauce
(see page 22)

a handful of grated Cheddar
cheese

Method

1. Butter the bread slices on one side only and heat up a frying pan.

2. Once hot, add one slice of bread, butter side down. Pile up the Bolognese sauce and the cheese. Top with the other slice of bread, buttered-side up.

3. Cook the toastie for about 4–5 minutes over a low heat to allow time for the filling to melt and the bottom to turn golden and crispy. Use a spatula to press the toastie down while it cooks to help heat the filling. Flip and cook the other side until that is toasted too. Eat immediately, straight from the pan.

The Ultimate Tuna Toastie

Makes ❶

🕐 Prep time: 5 mins

📅 Cook time: 10 mins

Embrace being a melt with this tuna toastie.

• •

Ingredients

2 slices of bread

soft butter

1 small tin tuna, drained

2 tbsp mayo

2 spring onions, finely chopped

a handful of grated Cheddar
  cheese

salt and freshly ground black
  pepper

Flavour tip: you can add pretty much anything to tuna, so experiment!
Finely chopped celery or apple both add texture.

Method

1. Butter the bread slices on one side only and heat up a frying pan.

2. Put the tuna in a bowl and stir through the mayo and spring onion.
Season with salt and pepper.

3. Once the pan is hot, add one slice of bread, butter side-down. Pile
up the tuna mix, then sprinkle over the cheese. Top with the other
slice of bread, buttered-side up.

4. Cook the toastie for about 4–5 minutes over a low heat to allow
time for the filling to melt and the bottom to turn golden and crispy.
Use a spatula to press the toastie down while it cooks to help heat
the filling. Flip and cook the other side until that is toasted too. Eat
immediately, straight from the pan.

The Nacho Toastie

Makes **1**

🖐 Prep time: 5 mins

🗓 Cook time: 15 mins

Try this one for a tangy flavour kick!

· ·

Ingredients

2 slices of bread

soft butter

2 tbsp leftover Chilli (see page 24) or Home-made beans (see page 110)

a handful of grated Cheddar cheese

a handful of tortillas (any flavour)

2 tbsp Guacamole (see page 48)

Flavour tip: if you don't have any leftover chilli or baked beans, replace with a couple of rashers of bacon.

Method

1. Butter the bread slices on one side only and heat up a frying pan.

2. Once hot, add one slice of bread, butter side down. Pile up the chilli or beans, then the cheese and tortillas. Spread the guacamole on the non-buttered side of the other bread slice and use to sandwich the toastie.

3. Cook the toastie for about 4–5 minutes over a low heat to allow time for the filling to melt and the bottom to turn golden and crispy. Use a spatula to gently press the toastie down while it cooks to help heat the filling. Flip and cook the other side until that is toasted too. Eat immediately, straight from the pan.

'Whack it on a jacket!'

Makes ④

🖐 Prep time: 5 mins

📅 Cook time: 1 hour –1 ¼ hours

Jacket potatoes are one of the best things to make as, like toasties, they are cheap, filling and you can put pretty much anything on them! Instead of just doing the same old, give some of these a try. Here's a few of my favourites...

Jackets

••

Ingredients

4 baking potatoes or sweet potatoes

salt and freshly ground black pepper

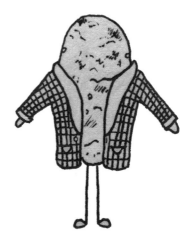

Method

1. Preheat the oven to 200°C (180°C fan)/gas 6.

2. Scrub the potatoes well, then dry with paper towels. Prick a few times with a fork, then bake for 1–1 ¼ hours until soft (45 minutes for the sweet potatoes).

3. Alternatively, pop the potatoes in the microwave on high for 15–20 minutes (a few minutes less for sweet potatoes), depending on if they are medium or large. If you are cooking fewer potatoes, reduce the cooking time (6 minutes for one, 10 for two etc). Test the potatoes by squeezing the sides to see if they're soft. If they're still a bit hard in the middle, keep microwaving in 1-minute slots until they're soft.

4. Cut the potatoes in half, season with salt and pepper and fluff up the soft potato with a fork.

5. Fill with one of the following toppings (all make enough for four potatoes):

Mediterranean sweet potato with whipped feta

Makes ④

Prep time: 20 mins

Cook time: 1 ½ hours

This recipe combines the delicious cheesy tang of feta with oven roasted tomatoes and chorizo to make a topping you might not have tried before. Using sweet potatoes switch up your options here – give the gift of sweet potato to the one you love!

· ·

Ingredients

1 punnet of cherry tomatoes

4 tbsp olive oil

1 tsp dried oregano

100g chorizo ring, cut into small cubes (skin removed, if you want)

200g packet of feta cheese, crumbled

200g Greek yoghurt

a squeeze of lemon juice

salt and freshly ground black pepper

Vegetarian: leave out the chorizo and add a handful of black olives to the tomatoes.

Method

1. While the sweet potatoes are baking, pop the tomatoes into an ovenproof dish, drizzle on 2 tablespoons of the olive oil, sprinkle over the oregano and season well. Add to the oven and bake for 20 minutes or until just beginning to blister and burst.

2. Heat a large frying pan over a medium heat and cook the chorizo until just starting to crisp.

3. Whisk together the crumbled feta, yoghurt, lemon juice, remaining olive oil and some seasoning in a bowl until creamy.

4. Spoon the whipped feta onto the hot potatoes, add the roast tomatoes and their juices and scatter the chorizo on top.

Shepherd's jackets

Makes 4

Prep time: 20 mins
Cook time: 1 ½ hours

Instead of mucking around making mash potato for a shepherd's pie, this recipe deals with the problem by just letting the potato do its thing in the oven. You can whack the filling over it when ready.

● ●

Ingredients

2 tbsp vegetable oil
1 onion, chopped
1 carrot, peeled and finely chopped
1 celery stick, finely chopped
400–500g lamb or beef mince
a good splash of Worcestershire
   sauce
2 tbsp tomato purée

300ml beef stock (made from a
   stock cubes)
a generous splash of milk
3–4 knobs of butter
2 handfuls of grated Cheddar
   cheese
salt and freshly ground black
   pepper

Vegetarian: use Quorn mince and a vegetable stock cube and leave out the Worcestershire sauce.

Method

1. While the potatoes are baking, heat a large saucepan over a medium heat. Pour in the oil and, once hot, add the onion and cook for 5–7 minutes until the onion is soft and translucent. Add the carrot and celery and carry on cooking until they're softened too.

2. Turn up the heat, add the lamb or beef mince and cook over a high heat until browned.

3. Add the Worcestershire sauce and tomato purée to the pan and stir well. Pour in the stock, bring to a simmer, then reduce the temperature to simmer gently for 1 hour until the sauce is thick and rich. Taste and season.

4. Scoop the soft potato out of the inside of the potatoes into a bowl, leaving a thin layer inside the skins. Using a fork, mash the soft potato with the milk and butter and taste for seasoning.

5. Preheat the grill to high.

6. Put the potato skins in a baking tin or ovenproof dish and spoon in the meat mixture. Top with the mash, run your fork over to make lines, and sprinkle with the cheese. Grill until the cheese is golden and melted.

Dhalicious baked potato

Makes 4

Prep time: 20 mins
Cook time: 30 mins

A great way to use some simple spices and cupboard ingredients to make something very different. Go as spicy as you like with this one – especially if you are all trying to save money on heating bills in the cold winter months!

● ●

Ingredients

200g red lentils
1 tomato, chopped
½ x 400g tin coconut milk
1 green chilli, deseeded and thinly sliced
a good pinch of ground cardamom, turmeric and coriander (if you have them)

2 tbsp vegetable oil
1 tsp cumin seeds
1 tsp black mustard seeds
1 onion, finely chopped
3 garlic cloves, sliced
salt and freshly ground black pepper
yoghurt and mango chutney, to serve

Method

1. While the potatoes are baking, put the red lentils in a large saucepan with 500ml water. Bring to the boil, then add the tomato, coconut milk, green chilli and a good pinch each of cardamom, turmeric and coriander, if you have them.

2. Bring to the boil and simmer for about 20 minutes, stirring occasionally, until the lentils are soft and quite mushy.

3. Meanwhile, heat the oil in a frying pan and fry the cumin and mustard seeds. As soon as the mustard seeds start to pop, add the

onion and garlic and cook for 7–10 minutes until the onion is soft and golden.

4. After the 20 minutes, add the onion mix into the lentils and stir through. Cook for 5 minutes more, then season to taste.

5. Spoon the dhal onto the hot potatoes and drizzle over yoghurt and mango chutney to serve.

Hot-dog jackets

Makes 4

Prep time: 5 mins

Cook time: 10 mins

When done right this looks awesome. I definitely wouldn't recommend eating with your hands like a normal hotdog, though!

• •

Ingredients
4 rashers of bacon, finely chopped
4 hot dogs
4 knobs of butter

2 handfuls of grated Cheddar cheese
½ small pot of sour cream
4 spring onions, finely chopped

Vegetarian: use vegetarian hot dogs and leave out the bacon.

Method
1. While the potatoes are baking, fry the bacon in a frying pan until crisp.

2. Cook your hot dogs according to the packet instructions.

3. Cut a wedge out of each hot potato along its length, big enough to fit a hot dog. Fluff up the soft potato with a fork, season and add a knob of butter to each.

4. Slot a hot dog into each baked potato, scatter over the cheese and allow to melt a little. Add a spoonful of sour cream, sprinkle over the spring onions and bacon bits and serve immediately.

Creamy sausage spaghetti
(à la Mug)

Makes ❶ large mug or
❷ small ones

Prep time: 5 mins
Cook time: 10 mins

A quick comfort-food hack that is NOT how mama used to make it. This is pioneering new frontiers in microwave usage – just make sure everything is fully cooked.

• •

Ingredients

60g dried spaghetti, broken in half
300ml boiled water
4 tbsp whole milk
a handful of grated Cheddar
2 tsp Dijon or wholegrain mustard

2 sausages, skins removed,
   chopped
a knob of butter
a handful of chopped basil or
   parsley (if you have)

Method

1. Put the spaghetti into a microwave-safe bowl. Pour in the boiled water to cover, then stir to submerge pasta. Microwave, uncovered, on high for 7 minutes until the pasta is al dente and there is just a bit of starchy water left. Drain.

2. Add the milk, cheese, mustard and some salt and pepper and mix through. Then put the sausage meat into your mug with the butter and microwave on high for 1 minute. Break up a bit more with your fork and microwave for another 1 ½ minutes or until cooked.

3. Stir the spaghetti and cheese mix into the sausage, then top with a bit more grated cheese. Microwave for another 30 seconds or until bubbling, then stir through the herbs, if using.

Chapter six

PARTY FOOD

AT UNIVERSITY, THERE CAN BE A PARTY FOR everything. The end of exams. The end of *Game of Thrones*. The *Love Island* final. The Super Bowl. Groups of mates, banded together, looking for literally any excuse to celebrate – and I mean any. We even had a massive one for the General Election night. Yes, the degree is always meant to be the main focus, but these are the things that really matter.

One of the biggest parties during my time at uni was the night of my Graduation Ball, which happened to coincide with the night of the US elections. As Obama was graduating to presidency, I was going through important changes of my own. I'd battled through three years at Southampton Uni and, much like Obama's, it had been a campaign of ups and downs. The Grad Ball was a formal event, with everyone in suits and ball gowns, and was held at the very posh Southampton Guildhall in the centre of town. As with all major nights, the evening began with games of FIFA, snacks and a few drinking games at the house (I'm not certain if this was the same as Obama's evening, but I assume it was broadly similar). Then, after a journey into town, we continued long into the night at the Guildhall, ending the party with my arms around my friends, proud of all we'd gone through. Emotional to think it was coming to an end. Excited about the future. I always remember the last song of the night: Take That's 'Never Forget'.

I like to imagine, at the same time, across the Atlantic, Obama had his arms around his squad, joyful and emotional, as he threw his hands into the air and belted out the chorus …

Never forget where you've come here from.
Never pretend that it's all real.
Someday soon this will all be someone else's dream.
This will be someone else's dream.

It had been an incredible night. I woke up the next day wearing my suit, my face covered in a sticky brown substance. Nothing to worry about here – it was only the BBQ sauce from the chicken wings we had made before we had gone out.

These are the kind of nights this chapter is all about. You and your friends, sharing good food and great times. These recipes still mostly meet the five pound brief, but are designed to feed lots of people. Be the ultimate host and step up to serve these simple but memory-making meals.

Beer-can chicken

Serves 4

Prep time: 10 mins

Cook time: 1 hour–
1 hour 15 mins

This way of cooking chicken changed my life. Absolute game changer. The sight of a chicken sat on a beer can may look a little undignified to say the least, but it is guaranteed to keep the meat really tender and juicy and it always gets everyone talking. This is delicious done in the oven, but is also great on the BBQ for your summer parties.

· ·

Ingredients

2 tbsp dark brown sugar

4 tbsp cayenne pepper

4 tbsp sweet/smoked paprika

1 tsp dried mixed herbs

2 tbsp vegetable oil

1 medium-sized chicken

1 can of beer

salt and freshly ground black
   pepper

Flavour tip: brushing the bird with sesame oil every 10 minutes throughout the cook will give this the Michelin-star treatment! Also, use the fat that drops into the dish to make some delicious gravy/ sauce. Strain it and just add a chicken stock cube with a splashing of Worcestershire sauce, soy sauce a grind of black pepper, then thicken as normal. Delicious!

Method

1. Preheat the oven to 160°C (140°C fan)/gas 2.

2. Mix the sugar, cayenne pepper, paprika, dried mixed herbs and some salt and pepper together with the oil. Rub the mix all over the chicken.

3. Open the can of beer. You only need half, so best to pour the rest into a glass and enjoy whilst preparing this! Stand the beer can (with the remaining beer in it) upright and wedge the chicken cavity (between the chickens legs) over it. Make sure the can is inserted at least two-thirds of the way up.

4. Place the chicken in an ovenproof dish and roast in the oven for 1½ hours. A good tip to check if the chicken is cooked is to hold the chicken leg bone and try and twist it all the way round. If it does, it is ready; if not, pop it back in the oven until you can!

The Pastry Saint of England: a St George's Day special

Serves 6

Prep time: 30 mins

Cook time: 4 hours

We had this mash-up of steak, red wine, onions and golden pastry after deciding to celebrate St George's Day with the same passion we give St Patrick, and we put a Cross of Saint George on the pie's pastry lid. However, it just looked like a massive 'X' and, when I hit the top of it like a Britain's Got Talent buzzer, my housemates lost it with me. For what it's worth, I would have put the pie through to the next round.

• •

Ingredients

1kg beef frying steaks
3 tbsp vegetable oil
1 large onion, roughly chopped
3 carrots, peeled and chopped
2 tbsp plain flour
200ml red wine

600ml beef stock (made from 2 stock cubes)
2 packs of ready-rolled shortcrust pastry
1 egg, beaten

Vegetarian: replace the beef frying steaks with 6 grilled and chopped portobello mushrooms.

Flavour tip: marinating the beef in the red wine the night before makes the meat super tender! Drain the beef well before frying, holding onto the red wine to add later.

Method

1. Preheat the oven to 160°C (140°C fan)/gas 2.

2. Heat a hob-proof casserole dish and brown the steaks, one by one, in the vegetable oil for 2 minutes on each side, then remove and set aside. You need to do this one by one so you can get a good caramelized colour.

3. Add the onion and carrot to the casserole dish and cook for 7–9 minutes until the onion is soft and starting to colour. Add the flour and stir until the flour turns brown.

4. Put the steaks back into the dish, pour in the wine and cook over a medium heat until the liquid reduces by about two-thirds. Add the stock, bring to the boil, then put the lid on the dish and cook in the oven for 2 ½ hours. Remove and leave to cool to room temperature.

5. Meanwhile, take a sheet of the ready-rolled pastry and use to line a deep 25–30cm pie dish or pastry tin, making sure the pastry just overhangs the edge. You may need a strip from the second sheet too – it is easy to merge the sheets together with your fingers (make sure you leave enough pastry for the top). Once the mixture has cooled, spoon the mixture into the pastry, two-thirds of the way up.

6. Brush the edges of the pastry with the egg and place the remaining sheet of pastry on the top. Press a fork around the edges to seal, then trim any excess pastry with scissors. Egg wash the top of the pastry and make a small hole in the middle – this allows the steam from the pie to get out and stops you having a soggy bottom. No one likes a soggy bottom!

7. Bake in the oven for 45 minutes. When it comes out, cut a cross in the pie. Serve with some mash potatoes, carrots and peas.

One-pan Sunday roast

Serves 4-5

Prep time: 20 mins

Cook time: 1 hour 30 mins

One thing about being away from home is missing the family Sunday roast. So, here's a way of making a one-pan Sunday roast. Minimal cleaning, everyone happy, easy as Sunday morning. This one-pan recipe couldn't be simpler.

• •

Ingredients

1 medium-sized chicken

2 lemons

2 garlic cloves, unpeeled

100g soft butter

500g Maris Piper potatoes, peeled and chopped into roastie-size chunks

5 carrots or parsnips (or a mix), peeled and halved lengthways

3 tbsp vegetable oil

a mug of thin gravy, made from gravy granules

2 handfuls of frozen peas

salt and freshly ground black pepper

Method

1. Preheat the oven to 200°C (180°C fan)/gas 6.

2. Place the chicken in a big roasting tray. Cut one of the lemons in half and stuff into the cavity with the garlic cloves and the other lemon into quarters and scatter around the chicken.

3. Rub the chicken with the butter and sprinkle over some salt and pepper.

4. Arrange the potatoes and carrots or parsnips around the chicken and drizzle with the oil. Roast for 1 hour, basting the chicken with the buttery juices and turning the potatoes a couple of times.

5. After 1 hour, pour in the gravy and add the peas. Return the tray to the oven for 20–30 minutes more or until the chicken is golden and cooked through and the potatoes crispy.

Ultimate wings roulette

Makes 4-5

Prep time: 20 mins,
plus 3 hours marinating

Cook time: 35 mins

Ideal for Superbowl nights, this is also loads of fun and ideal for parties! Watch your poor housemate pick the spiciest one and almost be brought to tears. The best thing about wings is that you can make an absolute bucket load of them and they are still way cheaper than going out for a standard meal, yet taste so much better! Ideally these would all be done on a BBQ, but they can be done in a frying pan too and finished in an oven. Here are my two favourite wing marinades, plus a classic buffalo wings fix. Serve with some sour cream or the blue cheese sauce to calm down the palate.

Wings

• •

Ingredients
1kg chicken wings

Method

1. You can keep the wings whole or divide them in half at the joint.

1. Place the wings in a large resealable plastic bag (you can also use a large bowl and cover with cling film) and pour in your choice of marinade. Squeeze out any air, seal and give the bag a good shake to make sure the chicken is well coated.

2. Leave in the fridge for about 3 hours to marinate, giving the bag an occasional shake when you go past. Remove before cooking to return to room temperature.

3. Start up your BBQ or preheat the oven to 180°C (160°C fan)/gas 4 and grab a large frying pan or griddle pan if you've got one.

4. Drain the chicken and pat dry with paper towels. Cook on the BBQ or in the pan for 15–20 minutes until the chicken wings are dark. If you're cooking in a pan, once they look cooked on the outside, pop them in the oven for another 15 minutes to make sure the chicken is really cooked through, with no pink meat and clear juices if you pierce a wing with a sharp knife.

Hot sriracha wings

∙∙

Ingredients

4 tbsp sriracha sauce

6 tbsp honey

4 tbsp soy sauce

2 tsp garlic purée (or 4 chopped garlic cloves)

juice of 1 lime

salt and freshly ground black pepper

Method

1. Whisk together the sriracha, honey, soy sauce, garlic, lime juice and some salt and pepper with a fork in a bowl and use as a marinade.

Home-made peri-peri wings

∙∙

Ingredients

20 bird's eye chillies – a mix of red and green

5 tsp garlic purée (or 10 chopped garlic cloves)

2 tsp smoked paprika

1 tsp dried oregano

125ml olive oil

juice of 1 lemon

salt and freshly ground black pepper

Method

1. Preheat the oven to 180°C (160°C fan)/gas 4.

2. Roast the chillies for 10 minutes, turning halfway through, then remove and finely chop. Put all the ingredients in a saucepan, bring up to the boil and simmer for 5 minutes.

3. If you have a food processor, add the sauce and blend to a paste. If not, don't worry, just mash up a bit with a fork in the pan.

4. Before marinating the chicken, keep a little bit of the sauce back to serve on the side with the cooked wings.

Buffalo wings with a blue cheese sauce

Makes 4-6

Prep time: 10 mins

Cook time: 25–50 mins

. . . .

Ingredients

1kg chicken wings
100g blue cheese, crumbled
4 tbsp sour cream
4 tbsp mayo
a squeeze of lemon juice

80g butter
125ml hot pepper sauce (Frank's
    RedHot Original if you can get it)
salt and freshly ground black
    pepper

Method

1. Start up your BBQ or preheat the oven to 220°C (200°C fan)/gas 7.

2. Pat the chicken wings dry with paper towels and season well. BBQ or bake the wings for 40–50 minutes (less time on the BBQ), turning halfway through, until crispy and cooked through.

3. Whisk together the blue cheese, sour cream, mayo, lemon juice and some salt and pepper with a fork in a bowl.

4. Melt the butter in a small saucepan, stir in the hot pepper sauce and pour over the hot chicken wings. Toss until they are well coated and serve with the blue cheese sauce.

Spicy mussels with cider and dunking fries

Serves ❷

Prep time: 20 mins

Cook time: 30 mins

Flex your culinary muscles with a variation on the classic 'mussels in wine' recipe that is actually easier than you'd think, and will be unlike anything else served at any other house party. You have to go buy fresh mussels for this (surprisingly cheap), and **make sure you throw away any broken ones** as you do not want to make all of your housemates ill – if you take everyone down, the shopping bill for all the toilet roll will be devastating. However, when you nail this, it's a brilliant sharer with all the dunking fries. It's got loads of cider in too, so treat yourself to a bit of that when you're cooking.

Ingredients

1kg mussels (try and buy really fresh from a fish counter)

1 tbsp butter

1 onion, thinly sliced

1 tsp garlic purée (or 2 thinly sliced garlic cloves)

1 tbsp dried chilli flakes

200ml dry cider (chef's perk is you can have the rest whilst cooking!)

100ml double cream

a handful of roughly chopped flat-leaf parsley or 2 tbsp dried parsley

salt and freshly ground black pepper

oven-bake French fries and mayo, to serve

Method

1. Begin by preparing the mussels. Roughly scrub the outside of the shells and take their little beards off by pulling them in a downward motion whilst holding the mussel between your finger and thumb. Rinse under cold running water for 10 minutes while you get on with making the sauce and cooking the French fries.

2. Before cooking, check the mussels to make sure they are uncracked and closed, or close when tapped firmly on the worktop. If they remain open, they are dead and should be discarded.

3. Place a large saucepan over a medium heat and add the butter, onion, garlic and chilli and fry for 6 minutes until the onion is softened.

5. Stir the mussels into the pan. Add the cider, cover with a lid and cook for 2 minutes; this will steam the mussels. Add the double cream and parsley and continue to cook for 3 minutes more.

5. If any mussels remain closed, remove them and throw them away! Season with salt and pepper and serve alongside a large bowl to put the shells into.

6. Serve with lots of French fries to dunk into the mussels sauce and mayo.

Narcos Nachos

Serves ⑥

🖐 Prep time: 25 mins
📅 Cook time: 30 mins

No illegal toppings in this recipe, however you really can put
what you like on nachos. And a big plate of these, hot from
the oven when you and your housemates are catching up on
Narcos, is the one! We've got a decent number of toppings
here, but you could also throw on some shredded lettuce,
toasted corn on the cob kernels or some pickled red onions.
Remember, any ingredients that you want to be fresh and
crunchy should be added after the nachos go into the oven.
We're talking herbs, greens, tomatoes, fresh salsas, avocado
and guacamole—none of these things are good warm.

• •

Ingredients

1 tbsp vegetable oil

250g beef mince

½ pack of taco seasoning

½ tin or pouch of black beans,
   rinsed and drained

1 large bag of tortillas

250g Cheddar cheese, grated

2 tomatoes, diced

1 avocado, diced, or Guacamole
   (see page 48)

2–3 spring onions, thinly sliced

a few spoonfuls of sour cream

a handful of fresh coriander leaves

sliced black olives or jalapeño
   slices from a jar

Method

1. Preheat the oven to 190°C (170°C fan)/gas 5.

2. Heat a frying pan over a medium heat and add the vegetable oil. Once hot, fry the beef mince until golden brown. Add the taco seasoning, 5 tablespoons water and the black beans and simmer for 10 minutes.

3. Line a large baking tray or ovenproof dish with baking paper. Add the tortilla chips and pop into the oven to bake for 3 minutes or until you can smell them starting to cook but before they go brown (this will help stop the tortillas from going soggy when you load them up).

4. Bring the tortillas out of the oven and top with half the cheese. Let it melt slightly, then add the beef-bean mixture and a final layer of cheese. Put back into the oven and cook just until the cheese has melted.

5. Bring out of the oven and scatter with the tomato, avocado and spring onions. Spoon over some sour cream and scatter with coriander and the olive or chilli slices.

Get Your Chips-and-Dips Out

Serves 4

🖐 Prep time: 30 mins,
plus 20–30 mins marinating

📅 Cook time: 10–15 mins

Lazy days with your housemates watching a film or making an event of the *Love Island* final, there is nothing better and more fuss-free than a load of chips and dips. To keep even your fussiest housemate happy, you need a range of dips varying in flavour and texture. Salsa and a guacamole (see page 48) are always a good idea, as is a sour cream and chives dip. I like adding a chunky dip like this Mexican street corn. Similarly, you want a variety of chips: corn chips, tortillas, crinkle-cut chips, kettle-fried chips and thin potato chips in different flavours will add interest to your platter.

Mexican street corn

••

Ingredients

2 corn on the cobs

1 tbsp vegetable oil

2 ripe tomatoes, finely chopped

½ red onion, finely chopped

a small handful of chopped fresh coriander leaves

a couple of jalapeño slices from

a jar or ½ fresh chilli, finely chopped

a few good squeezes of lime juice

a drizzle of olive oil

½ tsp ground cumin

salt and freshly ground black pepper

EAT SLEEP RAVE REHEAT

Flavour tip: add a couple of handfuls of cooked black beans, drained and rinsed, from a tin or pouch to this.

Method

1. Heat a large frying pan or preferably a griddle, if you have one. Add the oil (if you are using a frying pan – the griddle doesn't need it) and the corn and toast, turning all the time with a pair of tongs, for 10–15 minutes until the corn is toasted and golden brown.

2. Meanwhile, mix together all the other ingredients in a big bowl.

3. Take the corn off the heat and once it is cool enough to handle, cut the kernels off the corn by standing each one upright on a plate and slicing downwards with a sharp knife.

4. Add the warm corn to the rest of the salsa and serve with tortillas.

(more overleaf…)

Fresh tomato salsa

Ingredients

6 ripe tomatoes, finely chopped
½ white or red onion, finely
  chopped
a small handful of chopped fresh
  coriander leaves

a couple of jalapeño slices from
  a jar or ½ fresh chilli, finely
  chopped
a few good squeezes of lime juice
a drizzle of olive oil
salt and freshly ground black
  pepper

Method

1. Mix all the ingredients together and leave to marinate at room temperature for 20–30 minutes before serving. Taste and adjust the seasoning and lime juice as needed. If it's a bit too tart, stir in a small teaspoon of brown sugar. Serve with tortillas.

Sour cream and chives dip

Ingredients

½ small pot of sour cream
1 tsp onion powder
1 tsp garlic powder

a handful of finely sliced fresh
  chives
a squeeze of lemon juice
salt and freshly ground black
  pepper

Method

1. Mix all the ingredients together and serve well chilled with any kind of chips.

The two-hour Christmas miracle

Makes **6-8**

Prep time: 1 ½ hours

Cook time: 2 hours

The most stressful day of the year made easy (easier!). This whole delicious Christmas dinner is also done in less than 2 hours! The great thing is that if you follow the steps properly (which is absolutely key!) and make sure the prep is on point, this is not only the quickest Christmas dinner that will ever be made, but it tastes bloody good! There is a big shopping list as well as methods to follow, but this is the recipe you've been waiting to make all year – so, good luck!

....

Ingredients

TURKEY AND STUFFING

1 onion, thickly sliced

2.5kg turkey crown, at room
   temperature

2 tbsp vegetable oil

12 rashers of smoked streaky bacon

50g butter

4 slices of stale bread, crusts
   removed, roughly chopped

20g pecan nuts, roughly chopped

20g walnuts, roughly chopped

40g dried cranberries (preferably
   unsweetened)

20g sultanas

4 sausages, skins removed, roughly
   chopped

zest of 1 lemon

salt and freshly ground black
   pepper

Ingredients

PIGS IN BLANKETS
12 chipolatas
6 rashers of smoked streaky
    bacon

ROAST POTATOES
1kg Maris Piper potatoes, peeled
    and chopped into roastie-size
    chunks
100ml vegetable oil

BREAD SAUCE
200ml milk
1 rasher of smoked streaky bacon
1 whole garlic clove
1 tsp dried thyme
2 slices of stale bread, crusts
    removed, roughly chopped

GRAVY
2 tbsp plain flour
a good splash of red wine
1 litre chicken stock (made from 2
    stock cubes)
1 tbsp cranberry and redcurrant
    jelly

BUTTERED CARROTS
1kg Chantenay carrots
50g butter
1 whole garlic clove
1 sprig of fresh rosemary

BRUSSELS SPROUTS AND
    BACON
200g Brussels sprouts
3 rashers of smoked streaky
    bacon, chopped
25g butter

Vegetarian: bacon can be removed from the all dishes and substituting a
Tofurky for the turkey works just as well.

Method

1. Preheat the oven to 220°C (200°C fan)/gas 7.

1. Place the onion slices in a large roasting tray, sit the turkey on top and season with pepper. Drizzle over the oil and lay the rashers of bacon across the crown. Cover with foil and roast for 1 hour.

2. Meanwhile, make the stuffing. Melt the butter in a saucepan. Add the bread, nuts, cranberries, sultanas, sausage meat, lemon zest and some salt and pepper to a bowl, pour in the butter and mix well. Divide the mixture into small balls with your hands.

3. Prepare the pigs in blankets by halving the rashers of bacon and wrapping each sausage in a half rasher.

4. Now start the roast potatoes. Put the potatoes in a large pan of boiling salted water and boil for 20 minutes until you can easily pierce them with a sharp knife. Drain in a colander, then put the colander over the saucepan you used for the spuds and shake the colander to scruff them up. This will steam the potatoes dry and rough the surfaces for epic crispy roasties. Add to a roasting tray, pour the oil over and coat well.

5. Remove the turkey from the oven, dot the stuffing balls and pigs in blankets around the bird and put back in the oven, uncovered, for a further 25 minutes. Add the tray of potatoes to the oven at the same time.

6. Make the bread sauce by adding the milk, bacon, garlic and thyme to a saucepan and bringing to the boil. Once boiled, take off the heat and allow to sit for 10 minutes. Remove the bacon and garlic. Add the bread to the milk and whisk over a low heat until it forms a thick paste. Set aside and keep warm.

7. Remove the turkey from the oven and check it is cooked by piercing with a sharp knife – there should be no pink meat and the juices should run clear. Remove to a large platter with the stuffing balls and pigs in blankets, cover with foil and allow to rest for 20 minutes in a warm place (next to the stove is fine). This is critical as it will stop the turkey from drying out and it will remain juicy for carving. Give the pan of roasties a shake, then leave in the oven until crispy and golden.

8. While the turkey is resting, make the gravy and veg. Put the roasting tray on the hob and stir the flour into the turkey juices and onion, scraping up any tasty bits from the bottom of the tray. Add the wine and stir for a few minutes, then add half the chicken stock and the cranberry jelly and leave to gently simmer, stirring occasionally, until thickened, adding more stock as needed.

9. For the carrots, place the carrots in a pan along with the butter, garlic, rosemary and a generous helping of salt and just cover with water. Bring to the boil and simmer for about 5–7 minutes until the carrots are tender enough to take a knife.

10. For the sprouts, cook the Brussels sprouts in a pan of boiling water for 3 minutes, then halve and tip into a bowl to cool a little. In a frying pan, fry off the bacon in the butter until crisp and golden brown. Spoon the bacon out of the pan, leaving the bacon fat, and fry the sprouts hearts-side down until golden brown. Return the bacon to the pan and heat back up.

11. To serve, arrange the roasties around the turkey, pigs in blankets and stuffing balls. Put the sprouts and carrots into sharing bowls. By now you are probably struggling to find anything to put the bread sauce in – IMPROVISE! I served mine in reused yoghurt pots! When everything is completely ready, taste and season the gravy and carefully strain through a sieve into a jug (the gravy needs to be really hot). Carve the turkey at the table with you wearing a chef's apron and a tall chef's hat – you'll look like an absolute Don and have memories for life!

The best mulled wine

Serves 4

Prep time: 5 mins

Cook time: 25 mins

At this time of the year, hot wine seems to be a thing. Apart from anything else, it disguises any suspect smells that have started to emerge in your student house. It arguably smells better than it tastes and that is honestly no bad thing. Get your housemates in the kitchen, sing a few carols, and enjoy a toasty mug of mulled wine. Lightly sweet, spiced and fruity – Christmas in a drink. Just avoid using it for drinking games – it would be a huge error of judgement to attempt to down this.

Ingredients
2 cinnamon sticks
90g brown sugar
2 oranges

10 cloves
1 bottle of red wine

Method
1. Pour 500ml water into a large saucepan and add the cinnamon sticks and sugar.

2. Stud the oranges with the cloves and add too. Bring up to the boil, then lower the heat and simmer for 20 minutes until reduced.

3. Strain into a clean saucepan and pour in a bottle of red wine. Heat until almost boiling, but don't actually boil or the alcohol will evaporate! Serve hot in heatproof glasses or mugs.

Classic summery Pimm's jug

Serves 6   Prep time: 5 mins

If mulled wine is the drink of Christmas, Pimm's is the drink of summer. Get your mush around this classic fruity fix-up to add that extra feel-good touch to your summer street party/quad party/garden party – or literally any other occasion where the sun's out and the fun's loud. Bottoms up!

• •

Ingredients
1 punnet of strawberries
1 orange
¼ cucumber
lots of ice

a handful of fresh mint sprigs
1 bottle of Pimm's No.1
1 litre bottle of lemonade

Method
1. Thinly slice the strawberries, orange and cucumber.

2. Fill up six tall glasses or a large glass jug with ice and add a small handful of the fruit and cucumber to each one with a couple of sprigs of the mint.

3. Fill each glass a quarter full with Pimm's, then top up with lemonade. Finish with another sprig of mint.

Chapter Seven

DATE NIGHT DELIGHT

ROMANCE WAS A BIT OF A ROLLERCOASTER FOR me at Uni. I turned up there already in a relationship, like many others, but it didn't last very long. It's a sad reality that many couples break up in the first few weeks of university (and fair play to those that don't). However, it does mean that university has an incredibly high density of single people all crammed into one place. Not long into my first year, I found myself newly single and, much like my trials in the kitchen, I was not performing well. I don't know if there has ever been a proven link between skills in the kitchen and skills in the bedroom, but towards the end of my first year, as the cooking got better, I found that my romantic outlook had improved, too. Slightly.

Having managed to get a job DJing at a couple of nightclubs, I was often in prime position to see romance blossoming in new and unusual ways. On most nights, there were huge numbers of people in fancy dress, and I've seen some incredible things. On one occasion, I saw Harry Potter being dominated by a Roman centurion. On another, I saw a pirate attempt to land a giant squid. I once witnessed a particularly tender moment between Willy Wonka and one of his Oompa Loompas.

I occasionally embraced the fancy dress myself, once dressing as a Smurf. I wasn't sure how much of my body I should paint to commit to the fancy dress. Was it weirder if I did get lucky for *everything* to be blue, or just everything but that? A true dilemma. The weirdest part of all of this was waking up in the morning with blue sheets and not understanding why for a couple of seconds.

But if you are looking to stoke up the fires of love, then this is the chapter for you. There's no denying that a good dessert is the way to many people's hearts. I've made a bunch of puddings that will be great for any date night you may be so lucky to have. They are easy to make, but taste incredible. One of them you can even make in a mug in the microwave. Easiest afters ever!

And if you're lucky… you may end up with blue sheets yourself!

Heart-shaped chocolate brownies

Makes more than
enough for ❷

👆 Prep time: 10 mins
📅 Cook time: 30–40 mins

An easy chocolate brownie recipe that's simple to make
and tastes fantastic. It's everything you want in a brownie
– fudgy, dark and chocolaty. This is so good as there's not
many ingredients, it's super easy to make and, because it's
a cocoa powder recipe, it's as cheap as (chocolate) chips.
To make the heart shapes – invest in a heart-shaped cutter
or cut by hand!

. . . .

Ingredients
200g butter
75g cocoa powder
4 eggs
450g caster sugar

100g self-raising flour
icing sugar, for decorating
 (if you have)

Method
1. Preheat the oven to 180°C (160°C fan)/gas 4. Line a baking tin or
any ovenproof dish with baking paper. Meanwhile, gently melt the
butter and the cocoa together in a saucepan, stirring, then take off
the heat to cool a little.

2. Beat the eggs and sugar together using an electric whisk or by
hand, putting in a bit of effort. Pour in the cooled butter and cocoa
and stir everything together.

3. Add the flour and fold it in to the chocolate mix, just turning over your spoon or spatula as gently as possible until it is mixed in, but you haven't over-stirred.

4. Pour into the tin or dish and bake for 30–40 minutes, or until the top of the brownie is just firm but the inside still feels really soft. It's important not to overcook if you want your brownies fudgy! Take out after 30 minutes and test by inserting a sharp knife. If the middle is still liquid, put it back in the oven for a little longer, but if it's just set, take out NOW.

5. Use the baking paper to lift the brownies out of the dish and put on a wire or grill rack to cool. Use a heart-shaped cutter to cut out the hearts or shape by hand with a sharp knife, saving the leftover pieces for snacking on. Serve when slightly cooled, with the icing sugar sprinkled over.

Choco 'Lovin' Pots'

Serves ❷

🖐 Prep time: less than 10 mins, plus at least 4 hours setting

📅 Cook time: 10 mins

This pudding recipe is the one for getting you and your date in the mood. The recipe uses dark chocolate, which is a super-libido food: boosting energy whilst (and you're going to have to trust me on the science here) increasing blood flow to, ahem, lower regions. Don't do what I did once, accidentally smashing the bulb of my bedroom light with an exploding cork. The prosecco went everywhere and I had to pay for the fitting out of my deposit. These chocolate pots would have been the wise move.

••

Ingredients

90ml semi-skimmed milk
90ml double cream
1 egg yolk

10g sugar
80g dark chocolate (over 70% cocoa)

Flavour tip: enhance the experience by serving with a few strawberries and some shortbread biccies.

Method

1. Add the milk and cream to a medium-sized saucepan and bring to the boil over a medium heat.

2. Whisk the egg yolk and sugar until the mixture is thick, pale and creamy. This will take roughly 2 minutes of hardcore whisking! Meanwhile, break up the chocolate into a microwaveable container and melt on low in 10 second blasts. Stir each time the bowl comes out of the microwave.

3. When the milk-cream mixture has come to the boil, add a third to the egg yolk mix and whisk until smooth. Pour the mix back into the pan and put it back on the hob over a low heat. You must stir continuously to stop the mix from scrambling. This will take about 4–5 minutes. To test, dip a spoon into the pan and run your finger across the back of the spoon. If the mixture doesn't run back on itself, the mixture is ready. Oh, and by the way, this is the exact same way to make your own custard!

4. Once ready, pour the mixture steadily into the chocolate, whisking continuously.

5. Pour into two moulds, cups or glasses, giving your date a bit more (you'll thank me later). Set in the fridge for at least 4 hours until firm.

6. To serve, allow to get to room temperature for at least 20 minutes, then garnish with the strawberries and serve with the shortbread biscuits.

'Easy-but-deadly' banoffee pie

Serves 2

Prep time: 15 mins, plus
45 mins chilling
Cook time: 5 mins

Try this super-easy banoffee pie recipe when you need a last-minute dessert. It takes just 15 minutes of effort and 45 mins in the fridge. With its awesome combination of banana and toffee, banoffee pie is hard to beat. This one has a biscuit base and is made on the hob, so you're just four simple steps away from dessert heaven.

. . . .

Ingredients

100g digestive biscuits
20g butter
1 tin Carnation caramel

1 large ripe banana, sliced
squirty cream
a few squares of chocolate

Method

1. Place the biscuits in a plastic freezer bag and bash with a rolling pin (or other heavy implement!) until cruhod.

2. Melt the butter in a saucepan over a low heat. Mix in the crushed biscuits. Spoon the mixture into the bottom of two wine glasses and press down to form an even layer. Be super careful not to break the glasses.

3. Spoon the caramel evenly over the biscuit base. Place the sliced banana on top in a rustic manner.

4. Chill the glasses in the fridge for about 45 minutes. When you are ready to serve, squirt out the cream in a cheffy swirl over the top. Take the squares of chocolate, grate over the top and serve.

SOS chocolate pud

Serves ❷

Prep time: 5 mins

Cook time: 2 mins

You've forgotten to buy dessert – no stress! This is the SOS pud to bring out of your locker. You can bake this in a mug, in a microwave. It doesn't get any easier than this for a rescue pudding. It would be a cruel heart that mugged you off after these…

••

Ingredients

90g self-raising flour

30g sugar

1 egg

60ml vegetable oil

40g cocoa powder

50ml semi-skimmed milk

1 tsp chocolate hazelnut spread

ice cream, to serve

Method

1. Place all ingredients except the hazelnut spread into a bowl and whisk vigorously. The mix should resemble a thick batter.

2. Divide evenly between two large microwavable mugs.

3. Cook on full power, uncovered, for about 90 seconds.

4. Once cooked, make a small hole in the middle and spoon in the hazelnut spread. Serve with vanilla ice cream.

Flirty Fruity Eton Mess

Serves ❷   👆 Prep time: 10 mins,

Enjoy a night of passion for less than a fiver… This tastes great and you can make it with your eyes closed! If you're looking to be a Heston in the making, then for other fruity twists try the variations below. If you are making this in advance, keep the cream mix in the fridge and only combine with the fruits just before serving.

• •

Ingredients

125ml double cream
50g Greek-style yoghurt
1 tbsp honey

2 shop-bought meringue nests
100g mango chunks (fresh or frozen)
2 passion fruit

Frozen berry variation: replace the mango and passion fruit with 100g frozen fruits of the forest or any berries mix.

Strawberries and Pimm's variation: replace the mango and passion fruit with 100g strawberries (fresh or frozen), marinated in a splash of Pimm's and lightly crushed.

Method

1. Whip the cream until it has formed soft peaks. If you're whipping by hand, make sure the cream is chilled and pop the bowl in the fridge or freezer to get it cold before you start.

2. Crush the meringue nests and add to the cream. Using a spatula, gently fold in the yoghurt with the honey and meringue pieces.

3. In a separate bowl, crush the mango up a little with a fork and split the passion fruit in two.

4. Spoon a layer of the cream mix into two glasses, filling the glasses one-third of the way. Add a handful of the mango into the mix and scoop out some of the passion fruit seeds with a teaspoon, repeating the process until the meringue mix and fruits are used up. Serve immediately.

Sexy chocolate fondue

Serves ❷

Prep time: 20 mins

Cook time: 5 mins

This is an easy winner. Don't however do what my housemate did, which was to cover a certain area of himself in chocolate. Let's just say, he burnt his puddings. Hardly any prep is needed and it's mere minutes of cooking time to melt the chocolate, which makes this an extremely appealing option to get the food out of the way and get straight to the nitty gritty!

• •

Ingredients

fresh fruit, such as bananas,
    strawberries, pineapple and
    grapes

100g milk chocolate
100g dark chocolate
50ml semi-skimmed milk
15g butter

Method

1. Cut all the fruit into bite-sized pieces and arrange on a large plate/platter. You'll need something to skewer them with to dip into the chocolate – wooden skewers are best, but you can just use forks.

2. Add the chocolate, milk and butter to a microwaveable bowl and microwave on low in 30 second bursts until the chocolate has melted. Stir each time the bowl comes out of the microwave and whisk when the chocolate has melted.

3. Pour into a nice small bowl, set in the middle of the plate of fruit and serve immediately while the chocolate is hot.

Kitchen tips

Storing food

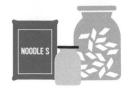

CHICKEN AND MEAT
Pop on the bottom shelf of your fridge so no blood can drip onto cooked food.

FISH
Fish doesn't keep for long, so store in the fridge and use as soon as you can.

HERBS
Buy pots if you can, then you can just pick off the leaves you need and use again. Put a plate underneath and don't forget to water every couple of days.

POTATOES AND ONIONS
Store them in a cupboard not the fridge.

TOMATOES, BANANAS AND AVOCADOES
Keep them out of the fridge and check your avocadoes – when they're lightly soft to the touch, they're ripe and need to be eaten.

OTHER FRUIT AND VEGETABLES
Store in the salad compartment of the fridge if you have one.

EGGS
Keep them in their box in the fridge.

COOKED RICE
If you have leftover rice, you can store in the fridge to use for making fried rice, but refrigerate not more than an hour after cooking and use within a day.

BREAD
Store sliced bread in the freezer. Just pull out a slice when you need.

LEFTOVERS
Grab your cling film – you need to cover any leftovers in the fridge. Eat the next day.

The **use-by date** on food is about safety and shows when you must eat food by, while the **best-before date** shows when a food may start to deteriorate in quality, but is still safe to eat. You can often pick up bargains in the shops on the use-by date, but make sure you eat them that day or freeze straight away if they have a 'suitable for freezing' mark on the packaging.

Using your freezer

If you've got a freezer – use it. It's not just for ice and vodka!

> *If you have leftovers from a dish you've made, cover well or put in a plastic bag before freezing. Any uncovered food that comes into contact with freezing air can get 'freezer burn'.*

> *Freezing meat or leftovers in batches makes them much quicker to defrost and you can just take out what you need.*

> *Curries, chillies, soups and stews all tend to freeze really well and they often taste even better when reheated. Make double of a recipe and you'll have another meal ready-to-go.*

DEFROSTING
Take out any food that needs defrosting the night before and defrost in the fridge. If you forget, you can defrost a freezer bag in a bowl of cold water to speed things up.

REHEATING
To be safe, make sure you heat until piping hot.

ACKNOWLEDGEMENTS

Firstly, I'd like to give huge thanks to James Hodgkinson, and everyone at Bonnier Books for working so hard to get this together. To the brilliant Nathan Eades and Kay Halsey for working so hard to develop recipes with me that will hopefully be a gamechanger to students everywhere. James, in particular: one thing that hasn't changed since my uni days is my complete inability to make deadlines and I'm sorry you've had to experience this. Ha ha, sorry bud.

I had the time of my life at Southampton Uni, although I've got no doubt that a younger me would never have believed that this book would one day be A Thing. I want to thank my gran and my aunties for buying me that first colander and student cookbook. I wish you could have seen this one in the shops, Gran.

My brilliant family, for always supporting my mad ideas. From going to university, to getting into radio, to writing this

book. You always support me. Mum, Dad, Laura and Dom –
I hope this makes you smile.

To my brilliant wife Ria, my gorgeous little Erin and baby
boy, when you're born. You are my world. I hope all these silly
things I do make you smile, and sorry for the embarrassing
stories.

A huge thank you to everyone at Radio 1 for always
encouraging ideas of mine and allowing me to be me.
To Scott Mills, Sam Gregory and Louisa Booth: thank you
for always pushing me forward.

To everyone I had the pleasure of being at Uni with, this
book is for you. For those that I still speak to, and those
I haven't spoken to in a while. We all had the best time,
and it will forever be in my heart. A huge shout-out to my
Brookvale road family, my housemates: you inspire most
of the stories in here. I should also now apologise to my
housemates for my lack of cleaning skills. Especially Liz.
I hope you've just about calmed down.

Thank you to everyone that worked at Glen Bar, you're all
legends and I think about you all so often.

I'm so proud of you all.

Glen Eyre 'til I die.

Starkie x